Mometrix
TEST PREPARATION

STAAR

Test Prep Guide
Grade 5
Math

I0878443

DEAR FUTURE EXAM SUCCESS STORY

First of all, **THANK YOU** for purchasing Mometrix study materials!

Second, congratulations! You are one of the few determined test-takers who are committed to doing whatever it takes to excel on your exam. **You have come to the right place.** We developed these study materials with one goal in mind: to deliver you the information you need in a format that's concise and easy to use.

In addition to optimizing your guide for the content of the test, we've outlined our recommended steps for breaking down the preparation process into small, attainable goals so you can make sure you stay on track.

We've also analyzed the entire test-taking process, identifying the most common pitfalls and showing how you can overcome them and be ready for any curveball the test throws you.

Standardized testing is one of the biggest obstacles on your road to success, which only increases the importance of doing well in the high-pressure, high-stakes environment of test day. Your results on this test could have a significant impact on your future, and this guide provides the information and practical advice to help you achieve your full potential on test day.

Your success is our success

We would love to hear from you! If you would like to share the story of your exam success or if you have any questions or comments in regard to our products, please contact us at **800-673-8175** or **support@mometrix.com**.

Thanks again for your business and we wish you continued success!

Sincerely,
The Mometrix Test Preparation Team

Written and edited by the Mometrix Exam Secrets Test Prep Team
Printed in the United States of America

TABLE OF CONTENTS

Introduction

Thank you for purchasing this resource! You have made the choice to prepare yourself for a test that could have a huge impact on your future, and this guide is designed to help you be fully ready for test day. Obviously, it's important to have a solid understanding of the test material, but you also need to be prepared for the unique environment and stressors of the test, so that you can perform to the best of your abilities.

For this purpose, the first section that appears in this guide is the **Success Strategies**. We've devoted countless hours to meticulously researching what works and what doesn't, and we've boiled down our findings to the four most impactful steps you can take to improve your performance on the test. We start at the beginning with study planning and move through the preparation process, all the way to the testing strategies that will help you get the most out of what you know when you're finally sitting in front of the test.

We recommend that you start preparing for your test as far in advance as possible. However, if you've bought this guide as a last-minute study resource and only have a few days before your test, we recommend that you skip over the first two Success Strategies since they address a long-term study plan.

If you struggle with **test anxiety**, we strongly encourage you to check out our recommendations for how you can overcome it. Test anxiety is a formidable foe, but it can be beaten, and we want to make sure you have the tools you need to defeat it.

Strategy #1 – Plan Big, Study Small

There's a lot riding on your performance. If you want to ace this test, you're going to need to keep your skills sharp and the material fresh in your mind. You need a plan that lets you review everything you need to know while still fitting in your schedule. We'll break this strategy down into three categories.

Information Organization

Start with the information you already have: the official test outline. From this, you can make a complete list of all the concepts you need to cover before the test. Organize these concepts into groups that can be studied together, and create a list of any related vocabulary you need to learn so you can brush up on any difficult terms. You'll want to keep this vocabulary list handy once you actually start studying since you may need to add to it along the way.

Time Management

Once you have your set of study concepts, decide how to spread them out over the time you have left before the test. Break your study plan into small, clear goals so you have a manageable task for each day and know exactly what you're doing. Then just focus on one small step at a time. When you manage your time this way, you don't need to spend hours at a time studying. Studying a small block of content for a short period each day helps you retain information better and avoid stressing over how much you have left to do. You can relax knowing that you have a plan to cover everything in time. In order for this strategy to be effective though, you have to start studying early and stick to your schedule. Avoid the exhaustion and futility that comes from last-minute cramming!

Study Environment

The environment you study in has a big impact on your learning. Studying in a coffee shop, while probably more enjoyable, is not likely to be as fruitful as studying in a quiet room. It's important to keep distractions to a minimum. You're only planning to study for a short block of time, so make the most of it. Don't pause to check your phone or get up to find a snack. It's also important to **avoid multitasking**. Research has consistently shown that multitasking will make your studying dramatically less effective. Your study area should also be comfortable and well-lit so you don't have the distraction of straining your eyes or sitting on an uncomfortable chair.

The time of day you study is also important. You want to be rested and alert. Don't wait until just before bedtime. Study when you'll be most likely to comprehend and remember. Even better, if you know what time of day your test will be, set that time aside for study. That way your brain will be used to working on that subject at that specific time and you'll have a better chance of recalling information.

Finally, it can be helpful to team up with others who are studying for the same test. Your actual studying should be done in as isolated an environment as possible, but the work of organizing the information and setting up the study plan can be divided up. In between study sessions, you can discuss with your teammates the concepts that you're all studying and quiz each other on the details. Just be sure that your teammates are as serious about the test as you are. If you find that your study time is being replaced with social time, you might need to find a new team.

Strategy #2 – Make Your Studying Count

You're devoting a lot of time and effort to preparing for this test, so you want to be absolutely certain it will pay off. This means doing more than just reading the content and hoping you can remember it on test day. It's important to make every minute of study count. There are two main areas you can focus on to make your studying count.

Retention

It doesn't matter how much time you study if you can't remember the material. You need to make sure you are retaining the concepts. To check your retention of the information you're learning, try recalling it at later times with minimal prompting. Try carrying around flashcards and glance at one or two from time to time or ask a friend who's also studying for the test to quiz you.

To enhance your retention, look for ways to put the information into practice so that you can apply it rather than simply recalling it. If you're using the information in practical ways, it will be much easier to remember. Similarly, it helps to solidify a concept in your mind if you're not only reading it to yourself but also explaining it to someone else. Ask a friend to let you teach them about a concept you're a little shaky on (or speak aloud to an imaginary audience if necessary). As you try to summarize, define, give examples, and answer your friend's questions, you'll understand the concepts better and they will stay with you longer. Finally, step back for a big picture view and ask yourself how each piece of information fits with the whole subject. When you link the different concepts together and see them working together as a whole, it's easier to remember the individual components.

Finally, practice showing your work on any multi-step problems, even if you're just studying. Writing out each step you take to solve a problem will help solidify the process in your mind, and you'll be more likely to remember it during the test.

Modality

Modality simply refers to the means or method by which you study. Choosing a study modality that fits your own individual learning style is crucial. No two people learn best in exactly the same way, so it's important to know your strengths and use them to your advantage.

For example, if you learn best by visualization, focus on visualizing a concept in your mind and draw an image or a diagram. Try color-coding your notes, illustrating them, or creating symbols that will trigger your mind to recall a learned concept. If you learn best by hearing or discussing information, find a study partner who learns the same way or read aloud to yourself. Think about how to put the information in your own words. Imagine that you are giving a lecture on the topic and record yourself so you can listen to it later.

For any learning style, flashcards can be helpful. Organize the information so you can take advantage of spare moments to review. Underline key words or phrases. Use different colors for different categories. Mnemonic devices (such as creating a short list in which every item starts with the same letter) can also help with retention. Find what works best for you and use it to store the information in your mind most effectively and easily.

Strategy #3 – Practice the Right Way

Your success on test day depends not only on how many hours you put into preparing, but also on whether you prepared the right way. It's good to check along the way to see if your studying is paying off. One of the most effective ways to do this is by taking practice tests to evaluate your progress. Practice tests are useful because they show exactly where you need to improve. Every time you take a practice test, pay special attention to these three groups of questions:

- The questions you got wrong
- The questions you had to guess on, even if you guessed right
- The questions you found difficult or slow to work through

This will show you exactly what your weak areas are, and where you need to devote more study time. Ask yourself why each of these questions gave you trouble. Was it because you didn't understand the material? Was it because you didn't remember the vocabulary? Do you need more repetitions on this type of question to build speed and confidence? Dig into those questions and figure out how you can strengthen your weak areas as you go back to review the material.

Additionally, many practice tests have a section explaining the answer choices. It can be tempting to read the explanation and think that you now have a good understanding of the concept. However, an explanation likely only covers part of the question's broader context. Even if the explanation makes perfect sense, **go back and investigate** every concept related to the question until you're positive you have a thorough understanding.

As you go along, keep in mind that the practice test is just that: practice. Memorizing these questions and answers will not be very helpful on the actual test because it is unlikely to have any of the same exact questions. If you only know the right answers to the sample questions, you won't be prepared for the real thing. **Study the concepts** until you understand them fully, and then you'll be able to answer any question that shows up on the test.

It's important to wait on the practice tests until you're ready. If you take a test on your first day of study, you may be overwhelmed by the amount of material covered and how much you need to learn. Work up to it gradually.

On test day, you'll need to be prepared for answering questions, managing your time, and using the test-taking strategies you've learned. It's a lot to balance, like a mental marathon that will have a big impact on your future. Like training for a marathon, you'll need to start slowly and work your way up. When test day arrives, you'll be ready.

Start with the strategies you've read in the first two Success Strategies—plan your course and study in the way that works best for you. If you have time, consider using multiple study resources to get different approaches to the same concepts. It can be helpful to see difficult concepts from more than one angle. Then find a good source for practice tests. Many times, the test website will suggest potential study resources or provide sample tests.

Test-Taking Strategies

This section contains a list of test-taking strategies that you may find helpful as you work through the test. By taking what you know and applying logical thought, you can maximize your chances of answering any question correctly!

It is very important to realize that every question is different and every person is different: no single strategy will work on every question, and no single strategy will work for every person. That's why we've included all of them here, so you can try them out and determine which ones work best for different types of questions and which ones work best for you.

Question Strategies

✓ Read Carefully

Read the question and the answer choices carefully. Don't miss the question because you misread the terms. You have plenty of time to read each question thoroughly and make sure you understand what is being asked. Yet a happy medium must be attained, so don't waste too much time. You must read carefully and efficiently.

✓ Contextual Clues

Look for contextual clues. If the question includes a word you are not familiar with, look at the immediate context for some indication of what the word might mean. Contextual clues can often give you all the information you need to decipher the meaning of an unfamiliar word. Even if you can't determine the meaning, you may be able to narrow down the possibilities enough to make a solid guess at the answer to the question.

✓ Prefixes

If you're having trouble with a word in the question or answer choices, try dissecting it. Take advantage of every clue that the word might include. Prefixes can be a huge help. Usually, they allow you to determine a basic meaning. *Pre-* means before, *post-* means after, *pro-* is positive, *de-* is negative. From prefixes, you can get an idea of the general meaning of the word and try to put it into context.

✓ Hedge Words

Watch out for critical hedge words, such as *likely, may, can, often, almost, mostly, usually, generally, rarely*, and *sometimes*. Question writers insert these hedge phrases to cover every possibility. Often an answer choice will be wrong simply because it leaves no room for exception. Be on guard for answer choices that have definitive words such as *exactly* and *always*.

✓ Switchback Words

Stay alert for *switchbacks*. These are the words and phrases frequently used to alert you to shifts in thought. The most common switchback words are *but, although*, and *however*. Others include *nevertheless, on the other hand, even though, while, in spite of, despite*, and *regardless of*. Switchback words are important to catch because they can change the direction of the question or an answer choice.

✓ Face Value

When in doubt, use common sense. Accept the situation in the problem at face value. Don't read too much into it. These problems will not require you to make wild assumptions. If you have to go beyond creativity and warp time or space in order to have an answer choice fit the question, then you should move on and consider the other answer choices. These are normal problems rooted in reality. The applicable relationship or explanation may not be readily apparent, but it is there for you to figure out. Use your common sense to interpret anything that isn't clear.

Answer Choice Strategies

✓ Answer Selection

The most thorough way to pick an answer choice is to identify and eliminate wrong answers until only one is left, then confirm it is the correct answer. Sometimes an answer choice may immediately seem right, but be careful. The test writers will usually put more than one reasonable answer choice on each question, so take a second to read all of them and make sure that the other choices are not equally obvious. As long as you have time left, it is better to read every answer choice than to pick the first one that looks right without checking the others.

✓ Answer Choice Families

An answer choice family consists of two (in rare cases, three) answer choices that are very similar in construction and cannot all be true at the same time. If you see two answer choices that are direct opposites or parallels, one of them is usually the correct answer. For instance, if one answer choice says that quantity x increases and another either says that quantity x decreases (opposite) or says that quantity y increases (parallel), then those answer choices would fall into the same family. An answer choice that doesn't match the construction of the answer choice family is more likely to be incorrect. Most questions will not have answer choice families, but when they do appear, you should be prepared to recognize them.

✓ Eliminate Answers

Eliminate answer choices as soon as you realize they are wrong, but make sure you consider all possibilities. If you are eliminating answer choices and realize that the last one you are left with is also wrong, don't panic. Start over and consider each choice again. There may be something you missed the first time that you will realize on the second pass.

✓ Avoid Fact Traps

Don't be distracted by an answer choice that is factually true but doesn't answer the question. You are looking for the choice that answers the question. Stay focused on what the question is asking for so you don't accidentally pick an answer that is true but incorrect. Always go back to the question and make sure the answer choice you've selected actually answers the question and is not merely a true statement.

✓ Extreme Statements

In general, you should avoid answers that put forth extreme actions as standard practice or proclaim controversial ideas as established fact. An answer choice that states the "process should be used in certain situations, if..." is much more likely to be correct than one that states the "process should be discontinued completely." The first is a calm rational statement and doesn't even make a definitive, uncompromising stance, using a hedge word *if* to provide wiggle room, whereas the second choice is far more extreme.

✓ Benchmark

As you read through the answer choices and you come across one that seems to answer the question well, mentally select that answer choice. This is not your final answer, but it's the one that will help you evaluate the other answer choices. The one that you selected is your benchmark or standard for judging each of the other answer choices. Every other answer choice must be compared to your benchmark. That choice is correct until proven otherwise by another answer choice beating it. If you find a better answer, then that one becomes your new benchmark. Once you've decided that no other choice answers the question as well as your benchmark, you have your final answer.

✓ Predict the Answer

Before you even start looking at the answer choices, it is often best to try to predict the answer. When you come up with the answer on your own, it is easier to avoid distractions and traps because you will know exactly what to look for. The right answer choice is unlikely to be word-for-word what you came up with, but it should be a close match. Even if you are confident that you have the right answer, you should still take the time to read each option before moving on.

General Strategies

✓ Tough Questions

If you are stumped on a problem or it appears too hard or too difficult, don't waste time. Move on! Remember though, if you can quickly check for obviously incorrect answer choices, your chances of guessing correctly are greatly improved. Before you completely give up, at least try to knock out a couple of possible answers. Eliminate what you can and then guess at the remaining answer choices before moving on.

✓ Check Your Work

Since you will probably not know every term listed and the answer to every question, it is important that you get credit for the ones that you do know. Don't miss any questions through careless mistakes. If at all possible, try to take a second to look back over your answer selection and make sure you've selected the correct answer choice and haven't made a costly careless mistake (such as marking an answer choice that you didn't mean to mark). This quick double check should more than pay for itself in caught mistakes for the time it costs.

✓ Don't Rush

It is very easy to make errors when you are in a hurry. Maintaining a fast pace in answering questions is pointless if it makes you miss questions that you would have gotten right otherwise. Test writers like to include distracting information and wrong answers that seem right. Taking a little extra time to avoid careless mistakes can make all the difference in your test score. Find a pace that allows you to be confident in the answers that you select.

✓ Keep Moving

Panicking will not help you pass the test, so do your best to stay calm and keep moving. Taking deep breaths and going through the answer elimination steps you practiced can help to break through a stress barrier and keep your pace.

Final Notes

The combination of a solid foundation of content knowledge and the confidence that comes from practicing your plan for applying that knowledge is the key to maximizing your performance on test day. As your foundation of content knowledge is built up and strengthened, you'll find that the strategies included in this chapter become more and more effective in helping you quickly sift through the distractions and traps of the test to isolate the correct answer.

Now that you're preparing to move forward into the test content chapters of this book, be sure to keep your goal in mind. As you read, think about how you will be able to apply this information on the test. If you've already seen sample questions for the test and you have an idea of the question format and style, try to come up with questions of your own that you can answer based on what you're reading. This will give you valuable practice applying your knowledge in the same ways you can expect to on test day.

Good luck and good studying!

Number and Operations

Decimal Values and Expanded Notation

Decimal values can be split apart based on their place value in **expanded notation**. For example, the value 593.217 can be expanded by writing the value as the sum of its place values.

Consider the number 593.217:

5 represents 5 groups of 100.
9 represents 9 groups of 10
3 represents 3 groups of 1.
2 represents 2 groups of $\frac{1}{10}$.
1 represents 1 group of $\frac{1}{100}$.
7 represents 7 groups of $\frac{1}{1,000}$.

$$593.217 = 500 + 90 + 3 + 0.2 + 0.01 + 0.007$$

$500 + 90 + 3 + 0.2 + 0.01 + 0.007$ is considered expanded form.

Comparing Decimal Values

When comparing decimal values, it is important to remember that digits are compared from left to right according to **place value**. For example, when comparing the values 146.079 and 146.792, start at the left and move to the right one digit at a time, until the digits differ.

146.079 and 146.792 both have 1 in the hundreds place.

146.079 and 146.792 both have 4 in the tens place.

146.079 and 146.792 both have 6 in the ones place.

146.079 and 146.792 do not have the same value in the tenths place. The first number has 0 tenths, and the second number has 7 tenths. The number with 7 tenths is greater.

146.079 is less than 146.792. Using inequality symbols, this becomes $146.079 < 146.792$.

Example

Compare the decimals 274.061 and 274.601 using the symbols >, <, or =.

$274.061 < 274.601$

When comparing decimal values, compare each digit from left to right. When comparing 274.061 and 274.601, start by comparing the value in the hundreds place. Both values have a 2. Move one place value to the right. Both values have a 7. Move one place value to the right. Both values have a 4. Move one place value to the right. 274.061 has a 0 in the tenths place, and 274.601 has a 6 in the tenths place. Since $0 < 6$, 274.601 is the larger number.

Example

Compare the decimals 57.1 and 57.09 using the symbols >, <, or =.

Answer: 57.1 > 57.09

Decimals can be compared using place value. Start by comparing the farthest left digit. Both values have a 5 in the tens place. Move one place value to the right. Both digits have a 7 in the ones place. Move one place value to the right. 57.1 has a 1 in the tenths place, and 57.09 has a 0 in the tenths place. Since 1 > 0, 57.1 is larger than 57.09.

Rounding Decimals

Decimal values fall **between two whole numbers** on a **number line**. For example, 5.7 falls between 5 and 6 on a number line. When rounding a decimal to a whole number, look for the whole number it is closest to on the number line. 5.7 is closer to 6 than 5, so 5.7 rounds to 6. Decimals will not always need to be rounded to the nearest whole number. Decimals can also be rounded to the nearest tenth or hundredth.

For example, round 47.28 to the nearest tenth.

First locate the digit that is in the tenths place. This is 2. Now look to the digit to the right. In this case, the number is 8. If this digit is 5 or more, then the tenths digit will round up. If this digit is 4 or less, the tenths digit will remain the same.

2 is in the tenths place, and 8 is to the right. This means the 2 will round up to 3, so 47.28 rounds to 47.3. This also means that 47.28 is closer to 47.3 than 47.2 on a number line.

The same process applies when rounding numbers to the hundredths place.

For example, round 309.274 to the nearest hundredth.

First locate the digit in the hundredths place. This is 7. Now look to the digit to the right. In this case, the number is 4. Since this digit is 4 or less, the digit in the hundredths place will remain the same. 309.274 rounds to 309.27. This also means that 309.274 is closer to 309.27 than 309.28 on a number line.

Review Video: Rounding and Estimation
Visit mometrix.com/academy and enter code: 126243

Estimating

Many addition, subtraction, multiplication, and division word problems can be solved using estimation. **Estimation** means calculating an **approximate** answer. Estimation can also be used as a strategy for checking the accuracy or reasonableness of an answer. For example, if the estimated amount of time it took you to run 3 miles was 30 minutes, but your calculation showed 300 minutes, you would know that there was an error in your math. Fluency, mental math, and strategies such as compatible numbers can make estimation a quick process. The goal is to use estimation as a quick reference point for the accuracy of an answer. For example, consider the following example:

Hank pays $231 for groceries. Betty pays $198 for groceries. About how much more did Hank pay than Betty?

Use estimation to solve. The question asks "about" how much more, which indicates that estimation will be sufficient. Consider rounding each number to the nearest ten. $231 becomes $230, and $198 becomes \$200. The difference between \$230 and \$200 can be calculated mentally, $\$230 - \$200 = \$30$. Hank spent about \$30 more than Betty.

Estimation strategies can also be used for multiplication and division scenarios:

Paul bought one large bag of dog food. The bag weighs 48 pounds. If Paul feeds his dog 5 cups of food each day, about how many days will the dog food last?

Use estimation to solve. The problem asks "about" how many days, which indicates that estimation is sufficient. The 48-pound bag needs to be divided into groups of 5 to calculate the number of days. However, 48 is not divisible by 5. 48 is close to 50, and 50 is divisible by 5, $50 \div 5 = 10$. So, the bag of dog food will last about 10 days.

Multiplying Multi-Digit Numbers

There are many ways to multiply multi-digit numbers. Some strategies include partial products, the distributive property, the lattice method, and the standard algorithm. The **standard algorithm** is a popular strategy because it is time effective. This process multiplies each digit in one number by each digit in the other number, based on place value. Start by lining up the ones digit for both numbers and stack the two numbers vertically with the larger number on top. For example, when multiplying 526×31, line up the ones digits, and stack the numbers with 526 on top.

$$\begin{array}{r} 526 \\ \times\ 31 \\ \hline \end{array}$$

Step 1: Multiply the 1 by all digits in 526. This is similar to the distributive property. The result is 526.

$$\begin{array}{r} 526 \\ \times\ \ 31 \\ \hline 526 \end{array}$$

Step 2: Write a "place holder zero" under the 6, and cross out the 1. The ones digit has been distributed, and the tens digit is next. The place holder zero will keep the columns aligned during the next round of multiplication.

$$\begin{array}{r} 526 \\ \times\ \ 3\not{1} \\ \hline 526 \\ 0 \end{array}$$

Step 3: Multiply the 3 by all digits in 526. Consider drawing loops over each digit to stay organized. $3 \times 6 = 18$. Notice how 18 is split up into ones and tens. The 1 is placed over tens column, and the 8 is placed under the answer line in the tens column.

$$\begin{array}{r} 1 \\ 526 \\ \times\ 31 \\ \hline 526 \\ 80 \end{array}$$

Step 4: Move to the next digit: $3 \times 2 = 6$. Add the 1 (above). $6 + 1 = 7$, so write 7 under the answer line in the next spot (hundreds place).

$$\begin{array}{r} 1 \\ 526 \\ \times\ 31 \\ \hline 526 \\ 80 \end{array}$$

Step 5: Move to the last digit: $3 \times 5 = 15$. Write 15 under the answer line in the ten thousands and thousands place.

$$\begin{array}{r} 1 \\ 526 \\ \times\ 31 \\ \hline 526 \\ +\ 15780 \\ \hline \end{array}$$

Step 6: Use the standard algorithm to find the sum of the two rows of numbers under the answer line. The sum of 526 and 15,780 is 16,306. This means that the product of 526 and 31 is 16,306.

$$\begin{array}{r} 1 \\ 526 \\ \times\ 31 \\ \hline {}^{1}_{1}526 \\ +\ 15780 \\ \hline 16{,}306 \end{array}$$

Dividing Multi-Digit Numbers

The standard algorithm for multi-digit division is commonly referred to as **long division**. In this strategy, the **dividend** is placed under the division symbol, and the **divisor** is placed to the left of the division symbol. The answer will be placed above the symbol, and the work will occur under the symbol. For example, when dividing 3,190 by 58, place 3,190 under the symbol and 58 to the left of the symbol.

3,190 ÷ 58 becomes:

$$58\overline{)\,3190}$$

The standard algorithm follows a 4-step process.

Step 1: Divide
Step 2: Multiply
Step 3: Subtract
Step 4: Bring Down

Step 1: Figure out how many times the divisor can fit into the first digit of the dividend without going over it. In this case, 58 cannot go into 3 because 3 is too small. Include the next digit. Again, 58 cannot go into 31 because 31 is too small. Include the next digit. 58 can go into 319 because 319 is larger than 58. Use estimation to determine how many times 58 goes into 319. Round 58 to 60. Round 319 to 300. 60 goes into 300 5 times. This estimation can be used to determine how many times 58 goes into 319. Write 5 above the 9. Make sure the 5 is above the hundreds digit because this is the farthest place value considered in the estimation.

$$\begin{array}{r} 5 \\ 58\overline{)\,3190} \end{array}$$

Step 2: Multiply 5 × 58. The product of 5 × 58 is 290. Write 290 below the dividend.

$$\begin{array}{r} 5 \\ 58\overline{)\,3190} \\ 290 \end{array}$$

Step 3: Subtract 319 − 290 = 29.

$$\begin{array}{r} 5 \\ 58\overline{)\,3190} \\ \underline{-290} \\ 29 \end{array}$$

Step 4: Bring down the next digit and repeat the process.

$$\begin{array}{r} 55 \\ 58\overline{)\,3190} \\ \underline{-290} \\ 290 \\ \underline{-290} \\ 0 \end{array}$$

The last value is 0. This indicates that there is no remainder and that 3,190 ÷ 58 = 55.

Representing the Multiplication of Decimals

When multiplying decimals, consider using modeling strategies such as an **area model**. For example, when multiplying 0.6×0.7, use a hundreds grid. Start by shading in 6 tenths vertically.

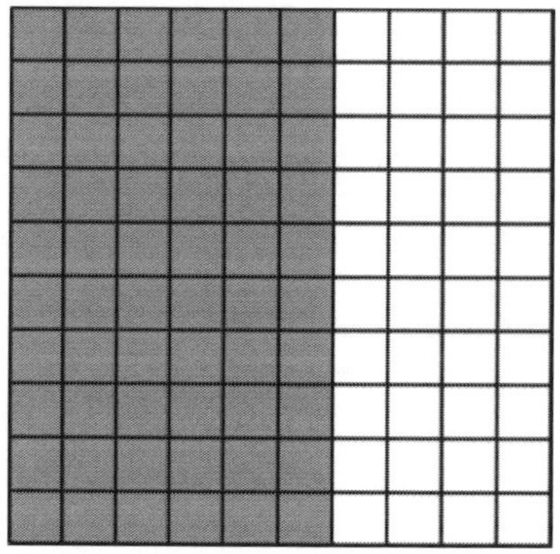

Now shade in 7 tenths horizontally. Notice how one region of the hundreds grid has shading that is now overlapping.

There are 42 hundredths that are shaded and overlapping. This means that the product of 0.6 and 0.7 is 0.42.

When multiplying a decimal by a decimal, consider setting up a slightly different area model. For example, when multiplying 2.3×1.4, start by setting up a square with 4 equal sections. Now write 2.3 as 2 and 0.3, and 1.4 as 1 and 0.4. Fill in the 4 empty squares with the products of each pair. For example, $1 \times 2 = 2$, $1 \times 0.3 = 0.3$, $0.4 \times 2 = 0.8$, and $0.4 \times 0.3 = 0.12$. Now find the sum of all four values: $2 + 0.3 + 0.8 + 0.12 = 3.22$. This means that the product of 2.3 and 1.4 is 3.22.

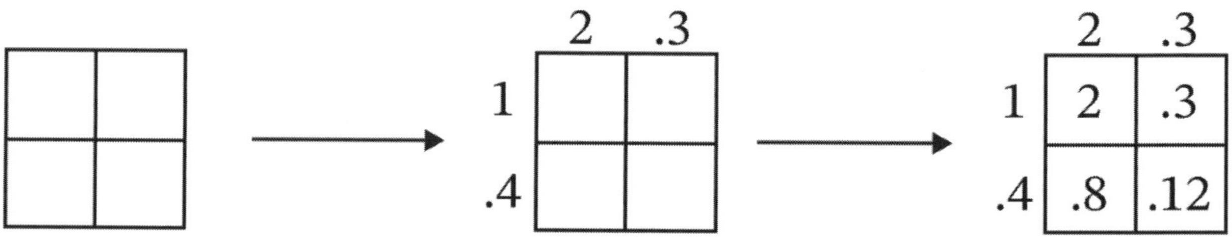

Strategies for Multiplying Decimals

Decimals can be multiplied using strategies involving **place value** or the **standard algorithm**. For example, when a decimal is multiplied by a power of 10, the decimal moves one place to the right. When a decimal is divided by a power of 10, the decimal moves one place to the left. This can be applied to situations involving money.

For example:

$\$4.55 \times 10 = \$45.50$
$\$4.55 \times 100 = \$455.00$
$\$45.50 \div 10 = \$4.55$
$\$455.00 \div 100 = \$4.55$

When decimals are multiplied by whole numbers that are not powers of 10, the standard algorithm can be used. Start by stacking the longer number on top of the smaller number. Shift the numbers to the right. There is no need to line up the decimals. For example, 2.74 × 6.1 becomes:

$$\begin{array}{r} 2.74 \\ \underline{\times\ 6.1} \end{array}$$

Multiply the 1 by each digit in 2.74.
Add a place holder 0.
Multiply the 6 by each digit in 2.74
Find the sum.

Place the decimal. Count the total number of digits to the right of the decimal in 2.74 and 6.1 In this case, there is a total of 3 digits to the right of the decimal. Move the decimal 3 places to the left so that 16714 becomes 16.714. The product of 2.74 and 6.1 is 16.714.

$$\begin{array}{r} {}^{4}\ {}^{2}\quad \\ 2.7\,4 \\ \times\quad 6.1 \\ \hline 2\,{}^{1}7\,4 \\ +\ 16\,4\,4\,0 \\ \hline \boxed{16.7\,1\,4} \end{array}$$

Example

A shop owner chargers $8.50 for homemade candles. What is the cost a customer pays for purchasing 10 candles?

$85.00

When a number is multiplied by 10, the decimal point moves one place to the right. This is true when multiplying decimal dollar amounts such as $8.50 × 10. The decimal in $8.50 moves one place to the right, and the product becomes $85.00.

Example

A baker needs apples for an apple strudel recipe. The baker uses 4 apples that each weigh 3.5 ounces. How many ounces of apples were used?

14 ounces

The baker uses 4 apples that each weigh 3.5 ounces. This means there are 4 groups of 3.5. Multiplication can be used to determine the total number of ounces. Consider using partial products. 4×3.5 can be thought of as $(4 \times 3) + (4 \times 0.5)$. 4 groups of 3 is 12, and 4 groups of 0.5 is 2. Then, $12 + 2 = 14$. So, the baker used 14 ounces of apples for the strudel.

Representing the Division of Decimals

Long division is not the only way to divide numbers with decimals. Decimals can be divided using objects, pictorial models, and area models. For example, consider the following scenario: 1.92 pounds of lemon juice are poured into 12 small containers. How many pounds of lemon juice will be in each container? This scenario represents a division problem: $1.92 \div 12$. 1.92 is the same thing as 192 hundredths. Draw a box to represent 192 hundredths divided by 12.

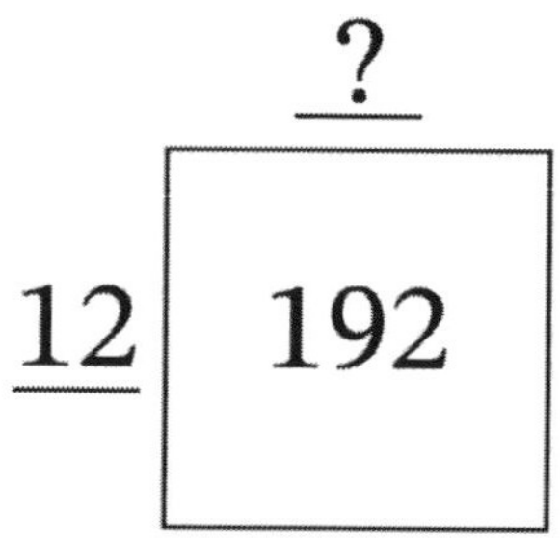

About how many times does 12 fit into 192, without going over? Select a number that is easy to work with without a calculator. For example, choose 10. Write 10 on the answer line, and write the product of 12×10 in the box. Subtract to calculate the leftover amount.

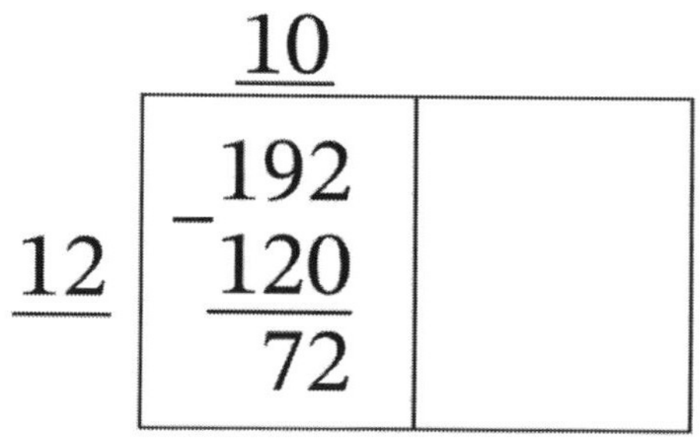

The leftover amount is 72. Set up another box and another answer line. Repeat the process. How many times does 12 fit into 72, without going over? The answer is 6. Write 6 on the answer line. Subtract to find the leftover amount.

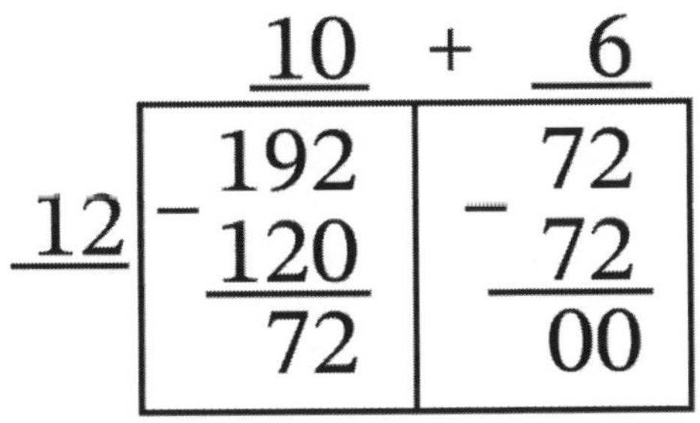

Find the sum: $10 + 6 = 16$. Remember, 16 represents 16 hundredths. This means that the quotient of 1.92 and 12 is 0.16.

Strategies for Dividing Decimals

The standard algorithm, commonly known as long division, can be used to divide decimals. For example, consider the division problem $65.35 \div 2.5$. The first thing to notice is that there is a decimal in the divisor. This needs to be adjusted. The divisor cannot contain a decimal. Get rid of this by multiplying both values by 10. 2.5 becomes 25, and 65.35 becomes 653.5. Now the problem can continue. Remember the 4-step process for long division.

Step 1: Divide
Step 2: Multiply
Step 3: Subtract
Step 4: Bring Down

Bring the decimal straight up into the answer line. The result is 26.14.

```
      26.14
25) 653.50
   -50
    153
   -150
      35
     -25
      100
     -100
        0
```

Example

Jon spent $362.50 on 10 sweaters. Each sweater was the same price. What was the cost of each sweater?

$36.25

When a decimal value is divided by 10, the decimal point moves one place to the left. This process applies to decimal dollar amounts. $362.50 divided by 10 becomes $36.25.

Example

A coach pours 28.4 gallons of sports drink into 8 containers. How many gallons of sports drink will be in each container?

3.55 gallons

Since we are dividing a whole into different parts, we will use division. Consider using the standard algorithm for long division. Follow the four-step process for long division: Divide, Multiply, Subtract, Bring Down. Then repeat. The result is 3.55 gallons.

```
    3.55
8) 28.40
  -24
    44
   -40
     40
    -40
      0
```

Solving Problems Involving Fractions

Fractions can be added or subtracted using objects or models. For example, to solve the problem $\frac{1}{2}+\frac{2}{10}$, draw a rectangle with 10 equal parts. Shade $\frac{1}{2}$ of the rectangle, then shade $\frac{2}{10}$ of the rectangle. The sum is the total amount of the rectangle that has been shaded. In this case, $\frac{7}{10}$. The sum of $\frac{1}{2}$ and $\frac{2}{10}$ is $\frac{7}{10}$.

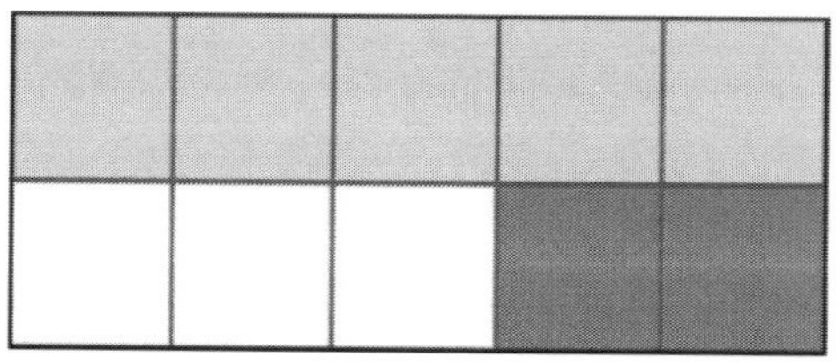

A similar modeling concept can be used when subtracting fractions. Consider the problem $\frac{1}{2}-\frac{3}{8}$. The fractions have different denominators, but a model can still be helpful. Shade half of the rectangle, this shaded region represents $\frac{1}{2}$. To subtract $\frac{3}{8}$ from this, start by dividing the whole into eighths. Now cross off 3 of those eighths. Now there is only one shaded eighth remaining. This means $\frac{1}{2}-\frac{3}{8}-\frac{1}{8}$.

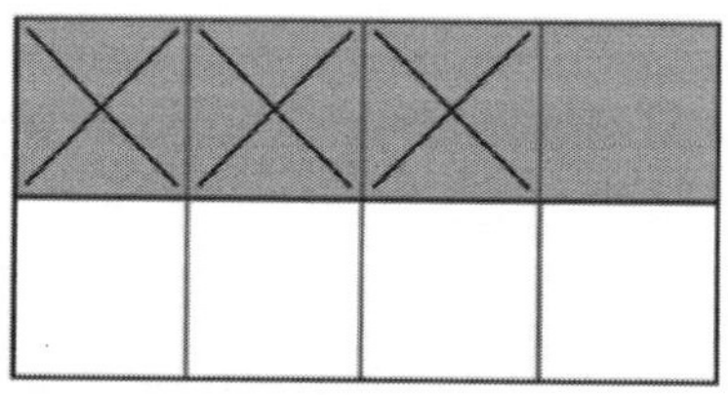

Review Video: Adding and Subtracting Fractions
Visit mometrix.com/academy and enter code: 378080

Multiplying Fractions and Whole Numbers

Modeling strategies can be helpful when multiplying a whole number by a fraction. For example, $4 \times \frac{2}{3}$ can be thought of as 4 groups of $\frac{2}{3}$. There are 8 thirds altogether, so $4 \times \frac{2}{3} = \frac{8}{3}$, or as a mixed number, $2\frac{2}{3}$.

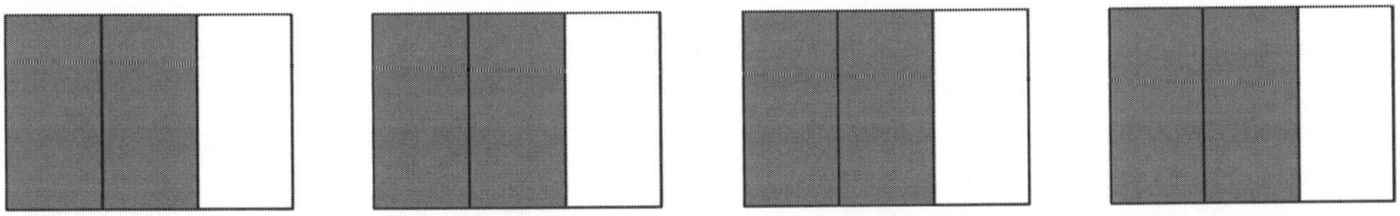

Multiplication is commutative, meaning the order does not matter. This same modeling strategy applies in situations where the fraction is listed first and the whole number is listed second.

Dividing Fractions and Whole Numbers

One way to visualize the concept of fraction division is to use a model. For example, when dividing a unit fraction by a whole number, start by drawing a model of the fraction. For example, for the problem $\frac{1}{8} \div 3$, start by modeling eighths, and then shade one share.

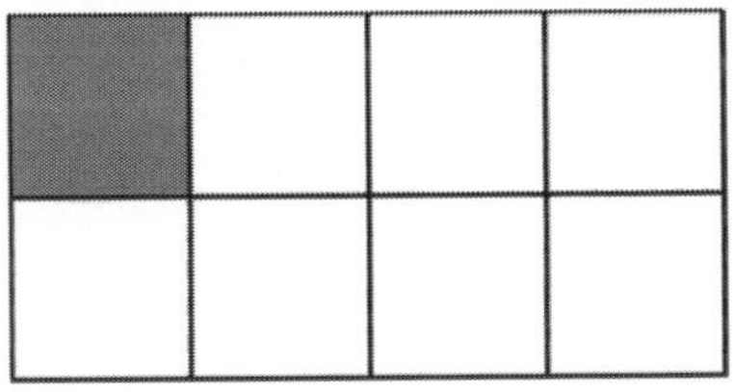

Now divide this shaded eighth into 3 equal shares. The size of one of these shares is now $\frac{1}{24}$ because dividing each eighth into 3 gives 24 total shares. This means that $\frac{1}{8} \div 3 = \frac{1}{24}$.

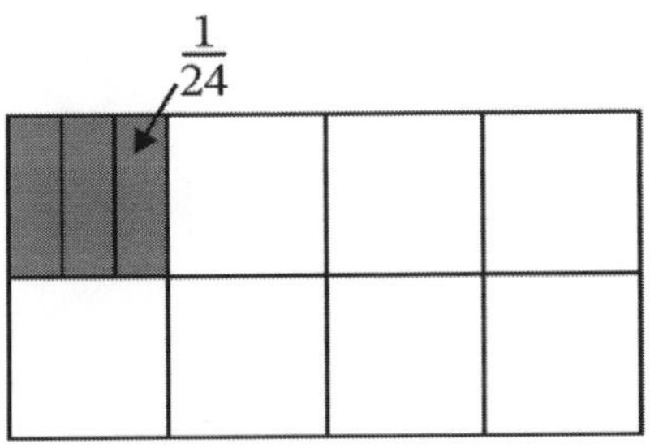

A similar process works when dividing a whole number by a unit fraction. For example,

Consider $4 \div \frac{1}{5}$. Start by drawing a model for 4. Then divide each whole into fifths. How many fifths are there altogether? In this case, there are 20. This means that $4 \div \frac{1}{5}$ is equal to 20.

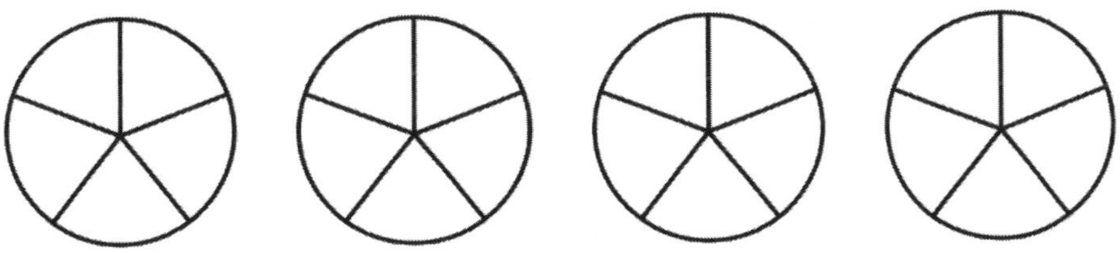

Using Models when Dividing Fractions and Whole Numbers

Consider using a model when dividing fractions by whole numbers or whole numbers by fractions. For example, when calculating $\frac{1}{4} \div 3$, start by modeling $\frac{1}{4}$.

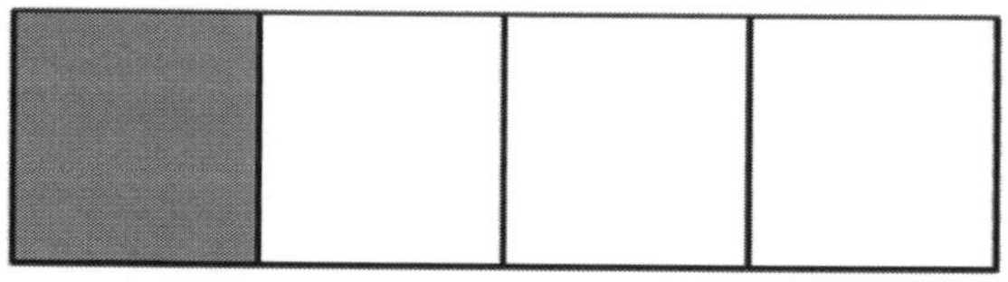

Now divide $\frac{1}{4}$ into 3 equal shares.

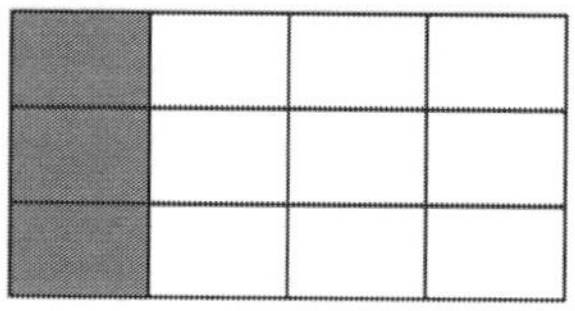

The size of one share is $\frac{1}{12}$. This means that $\frac{1}{4} \div 3$ is $\frac{1}{12}$.

When dividing a whole number by a fraction, use a similar approach. For example, to divide 5 by $\frac{1}{2}$, start by modeling 5 wholes.

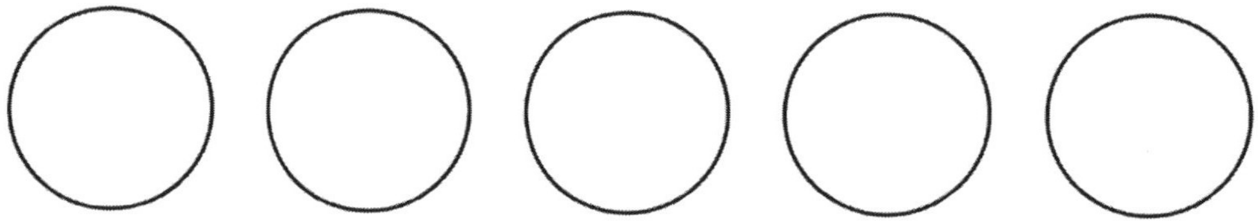

Now divide each whole into halves.

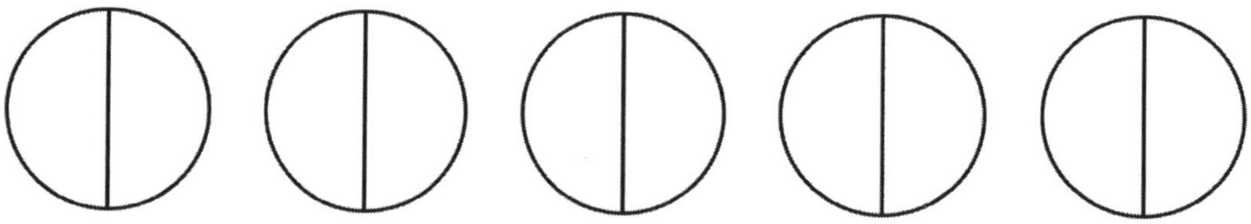

There are 10 halves. This means that $5 \div \frac{1}{2} = 10$.

Another strategy used for dividing whole numbers and fractions involves two steps:
The steps can be referred to as "Multiply and Flip."

For example, to calculate $6 \div \frac{1}{5}$, use the Multiply and Flip technique.

Change the division symbol to a multiplication symbol and flip the second fraction.

6 can be written as $\frac{6}{1}$. $\frac{6}{1} \div \frac{1}{5}$ becomes $\frac{6}{1} \times \frac{5}{1}$. Now multiply the numerators and multiply the denominators. $\frac{6}{1} \times \frac{5}{1}$ becomes $\frac{30}{1}$, or 30.

EXAMPLE

A chef is making pizzas. The chef has 12 pounds of dough, and each crust requires $\frac{1}{7}$ pound of dough. How many pizza crusts can the chef make?

84 pizza crusts

There are 12 pounds of dough, and it needs to be divided into groups of $\frac{1}{7}$. To divide 12 by $\frac{1}{7}$, start by writing both values in fraction form. $12 \div \frac{1}{7}$ becomes $\frac{12}{1} \div \frac{1}{7}$. Now, follow the "flip and multiply" strategy. Change the division symbol to multiplication, and then flip the second fraction. $\frac{12}{1} \div \frac{1}{7}$ becomes $\frac{12}{1} \times \frac{7}{1}$. Now, multiply across and simplify if possible. $\frac{12}{1} \times \frac{7}{1}$ becomes $\frac{84}{1}$, or 84. The chef can make 84 pizza crusts.

EXAMPLE

Matt has $\frac{1}{4}$ of his birthday cake left over. Matt and two of his friends want to share the leftover cake. If he divides the leftover cake into 3 equal shares, what fraction of a whole cake will each person receive?

$\frac{1}{12}$

The scenario can be represented as a division problem. $\frac{1}{4}$ of the cake is being divided into 3 shares is $\frac{1}{4} \div 3$. To divide fractions and whole numbers, set up both values as a fraction. $\frac{1}{4} \div 3$ becomes $\frac{1}{4} \div \frac{3}{1}$. Follow the "flip and multiply" technique. Change the division symbol to multiplication and flip the second fraction. $\frac{1}{4} \div \frac{3}{1}$ becomes $\frac{1}{4} \times \frac{1}{3}$. Now, multiply straight across and simplify if possible, $\frac{1}{4} \times \frac{1}{3} = \frac{1}{12}$. So, each person will receive $\frac{1}{12}$ of the original whole cake.

Adding and Subtracting Rational Numbers

It is important to feel comfortable adding and subtracting numbers fluently. Consider using strategies involving place value or estimation when adding and subtracting. For example, if a savings account contains $4,680 and a checking account contains $2,315 and you need to calculate the total of both accounts combined, place value can be helpful. Add the digits in the corresponding place values to calculate the sum mentally. There are $4 + 2$ thousands, $6 + 3$ hundreds, $8 + 1$ tens, and $0 + 5$ ones. This means there is a total of $6,995 in both accounts.

Consider **estimation strategies** to calculate the difference between dollar amounts in each account. The savings account contains $4,680 which rounds to $4,700 when rounded to the nearest hundred. The checking account contains $2,300 when rounded to the nearest hundred. Subtract these values mentally to get an approximate answer: $\$4{,}700 - \$2{,}300 = \$2{,}400$. This means that the savings account has approximately $2,400 more than the checking account.

EXAMPLE

Julia purchases a backpack for $31, a notebook for $5.50, and a pack of pencils for $9.50. Julia has $55 in cash. Does she have enough money to buy all three items?

Yes, she has enough money to buy all three items.

Start by finding the total cost of the 3 items. Consider using compatible numbers. \$31 and \$9 combine to \$40. Now add \$5 for the notebook. The total is now \$45. Now add the cents. \$45 + \$0.50 + \$0.50 = \$46. The total is \$46. Julia has \$55 in cash, so she has enough money to purchase all three items.

EXAMPLE

A small backyard swimming pool contains 3,398 gallons of water. A pool cleaning company is draining the pool to clean the interior of the pool. At noon the pool contains 2,129 gallons of water. How many gallons of water has been drained from the pool so far?

1,269 gallons

The pool started with 3,398 gallons of water and at noon contains 2,129 gallons. Subtract to determine the number of gallons that have been drained. Use the standard algorithm, and stack 3,398 over 2,129 so that the place value is lined up. Subtract columns from right to left. Regroup if necessary: 3,398 − 2,129 = 1,269.

```
     1
    88
  33~~98~~
 -2129
  1269
```

The pool has drained 1,269 gallons of water by noon.

Algebraic Reasoning

Prime and Composite Numbers

A **prime number** is a number that has exactly **2 factors**, meaning it is only divisible by 1 and itself. For example, the number 7 is prime because 7 can only be divided by 1 and 7. The first ten prime numbers are 2, 3, 5, 7, 11, 13, 17, 19, 23, and 29.

The opposite of a prime number is a composite number. **Composite numbers** have more than 2 factors, meaning they are divisible by more than 2 numbers. For example, 24 is composite because it has more than just 1 and 24 as factors. 24 consists of 1 group of 24, 2 groups of 12, 3 groups of 8, or 4 groups of 6. The factors of 24 are 1, 2, 3, 4, 6, 8, 12, and 24.

Review Video: Prime and Composite Numbers
Visit mometrix.com/academy and enter code: 565581

Multi-Step Problems with Variables

Multi-step word problems can be solved algebraically. In general, equations will consist of variables, coefficients, and constants. **Variables** are letters that represent unknown values. **Coefficients** are located in front of variables and signal multiplication. For example, $2x$ means 2 multiplied by the variable x. **Constants** are numbers that are not attached to variables. This means that constants are fixed values that do not change, regardless of the value of the variable.

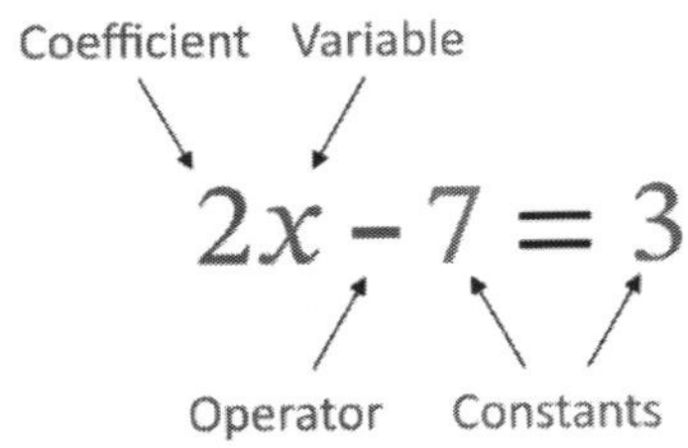

An equation is solved when the value of the variable is calculated. For example, if the equation states that $45 = 9 \times T$, the value of T is 5. This is considered a **one-step equation** because it is solved by dividing both sides of the equation by 9, which requires only one step. However, many equations require more than one step to solve. Consider the following scenario.

The temperature of water in a pool starts at 82°. The temperature rises 0.6 degrees every hour. Right now, the water temperature is 85°. How many hours have passed?

The word problem can be solved using an algebraic equation. Start by stating what is known.

- The water temperature is initially 82°.
- The temperature rises 0.6° each hour.
- Now the water temperature is 85°.

Then identify the unknown. Here, the unknown is the number of hours that have passed. Since the number of hours is unknown, use h as the unknown variable. The goal is to set up a multi-step equation that can be solved for h.

The problem states that the water temperature will eventually be 85°, so start the equation with $85 =$.

$$85 =$$

The problem also states that the temperature will rise 0.6 degrees each hour. This can be represented as $(0.6) \times (h)$.

$$85 = (0.6) \times (h)$$

Since the water temperature starts at 82°, $(0.6) \times (h)$ should be added to 82°.

The result is the following equation.

$$85 = (0.6) \times (h) + 82$$

Solve for the variable h by subtracting 82 from both sides, and then use long division to divide by 0.6.

$$82 + (0.6) \times (h) = 85$$

$$(0.6) \times (h) = 3$$

$$h = 5$$

This means that 5 hours have passed.

Example

Write and solve an equation to solve the following problem.

A school is taking a field trip. There are 331 students attending the field trip. 6 school busses are filled with an equal number of students, and 7 students will ride their bike to the field trip. How many students will be in each school bus?

54 students. $331 = 6b + 7$

Start by listing all the relevant facts.

- The total number of students is 331.
- 6 busses will be full, with an equal number of students on each bus.
- 7 students will ride their bikes

The equation will follow the format of Total Students = Bus Riders + Bikers. Fill in what is provided.

The total number of students is 331, so start the equation with $331 =$.

$$331 =$$

An equal number of bus riders will be placed on 6 buses. It is unknown how many riders will be on each bus. A variable can be substituted in for this unknown value. Use the variable b to represent the unknown number of riders on each bus. There are 6 buses, and b number of students on each bus. The expression $6 \times b$ or $6b$ can be used to describe "six buses with an equal number of students."

$$331 = 6(b)$$

The number of bikers is 7, so add a +7 to the end of the equation.

$$331 = 6(b)\ + 7$$

Now use the equation to solve for the unknown variable, b. The equation is solved in two steps. Subtract 7 from both sides, and then divide both sides by 6. These two steps are considered "inverse operations." Subtracting 7 is the inverse of adding 7, and dividing by 6 is the inverse of multiplying by 6.

$$331 = 6b\ + 7$$

$$324 = 6b$$

$$54 = b$$

This means that there will be 54 students on each bus.

Example

Write and solve an equation order to solve the following problem.

You purchased 4 cups of coffee and left a \$5 bill as a tip. You spent \$25 altogether. How much did each cup of coffee cost?

\$5 per cup of coffee. $25 = 4c + 5$

Generate a list of all relevant information within the problem.

- You spent \$25 altogether.
- You purchased 4 cups of coffee.
- You left a tip of \$5.

Set up an equation that represents the scenario. The equation will follow the format of

\$25 = Cost of Coffee + \$5 tip. Now, substitute the values that are provided. The total cost is \$25, so start the equation with 25 =.

$$25 =$$

4 cups of coffee were purchased, but the cost of each cup is unknown. Substitute a variable in for the unknown cost. Consider the variable c to represent cost. 4 cups of coffee were purchased, at a cost of c, so the expression $4 \times c$, or $4c$ can be used in the equation.

$$25 = 4(c)$$

The tip was \$5, so add a +5 to the end of the equation.

$$25 = 4c + 5$$

Now use "inverse operations" to isolate the variable, c. The inverse of adding 5 is subtracting 5, so subtract 5 from both sides. The inverse of multiplying by 4 is dividing by 4.

$$25 = 4c + 5$$

$$20 = 4c$$

$$5 = c$$

This means that each cup of coffee cost $5.

Numerical Patterns Based on Equations

Equations in the form $y = ax$ or $y = x + a$ can be useful when looking for **patterns** or solving for **unknown values**. For example, consider the following scenario.

A cherry tree grows 7 inches each year. If the tree was planted as a seed, how tall will the tree be after 5 years?

This represents a $y = ax$ scenario because the height of the tree is calculated by multiplying the number of years by 7. In this case, $y = ax$ is represented as

height $=$ 7 $\times$ years. The equation $y = 7 \times 5$ can be solved to calculate the height after 5 years. $y = 7 \times 5 = 35$, so the tree will be 35 inches after 5 years.

This equation, or rule, can be used to create a pattern. For example, plot the tree's height each year in a table. Notice how the height increases by 7 inches each year. The yearly height pattern can be described as $0, 7, 14, 21, 28, 35$ and so on.

Year	0	1	2	3	4	5
Height (in.)	0	7	14	21	28	35

These data points can also be displayed in a graph. For example, plot the years on the x-axis, and the heights on the y-axis. Each data point will form an ordered pair. Notice how the pattern forms a line that increases at a steady rate. This is known as a linear graph.

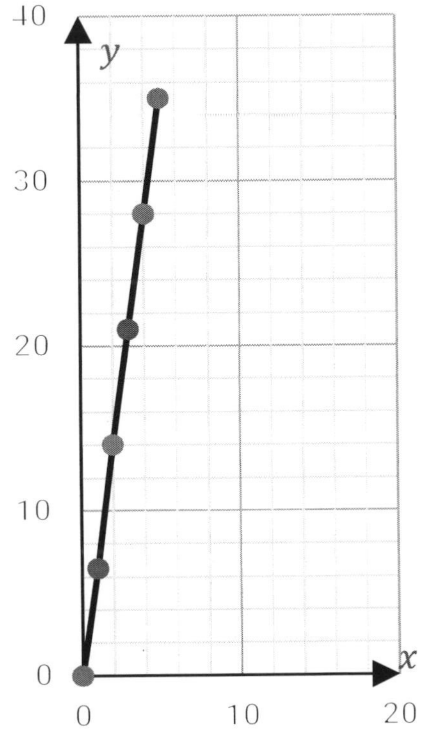

Similarly, $y = x + a$ equations can be used to generate numerical patterns. Consider the following scenario.

Craig is 2 years older than his younger brother Sam. How old will Sam be when Craig is 20?

This represents a $y = x + a$ scenario because Craig's age can be calculated by adding 2 to Sam's age. In other words, $C = 2 + S$. When Sam is 18, Craig will be 2 more than 18, or 20. This equation, or rule, can be represented graphically. Each pair of data points will form an ordered pair on the graph. For example, when Sam is 16, Craig is 18. When Sam is 17, Craig is 19. When Sam is 18, Craig is 20. The pattern forms a line that rises at a steady rate. This is known as a linear equation.

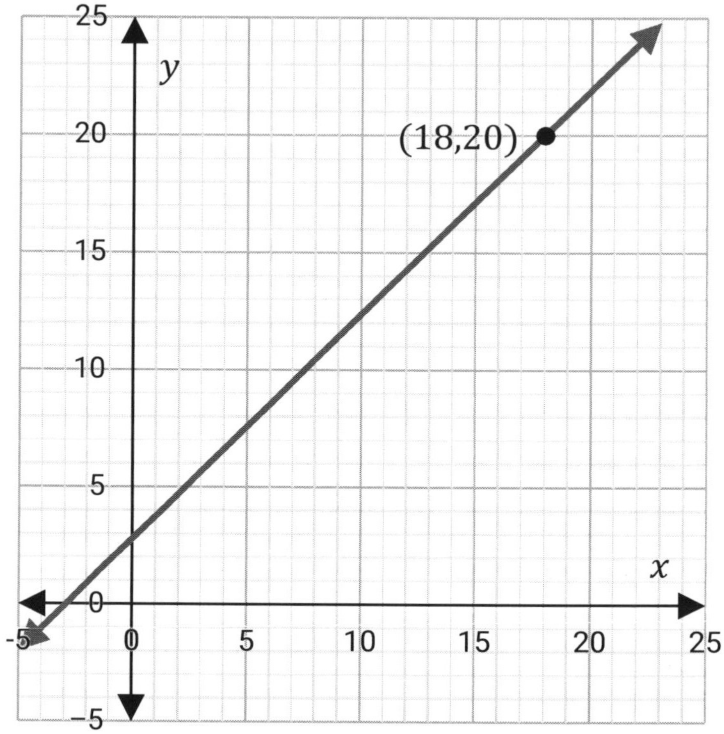

Additive and Multiplicative Relationships

Pattens can be additive or multiplicative. **Additive relationships** add the same number to the x-value to calculate the corresponding y-value. These equations take the form $y = x + a$. For example, $y = x + 8$ is additive. **Multiplicative relationships** multiply the x-value by the same number to calculate the corresponding y-value. For example, $y = 4x$ is multiplicative. It is important to be able to determine if a relationship is additive or multiplicative based on a table or a graph.

For example, the table below shows x- and y-values. Notice how each y-value is 1 more than its corresponding x-value. In other words, $y = x + 1$. This table represents an additive relationship.

x	y
4	5
6	7
8	9
12	13

The table below shows x- and y-values where each y-value is twice the value of x. This can be expressed as $y = 2x$. This represents a multiplicative relationship.

x	6	7	8	9
y	12	14	16	18

When determining if a graph is additive or multiplicative, look at the relationship between the x- and y-variables. For example, in the graph below, there are two ordered pairs plotted: (1,3) and (4,12). Notice how each y-value is 3 times as large as its corresponding x-value.

- (1,3): 3 is 3 times larger than 1.
- (4,12): 12 is 3 times larger than 4.

This means the graph is multiplicative.

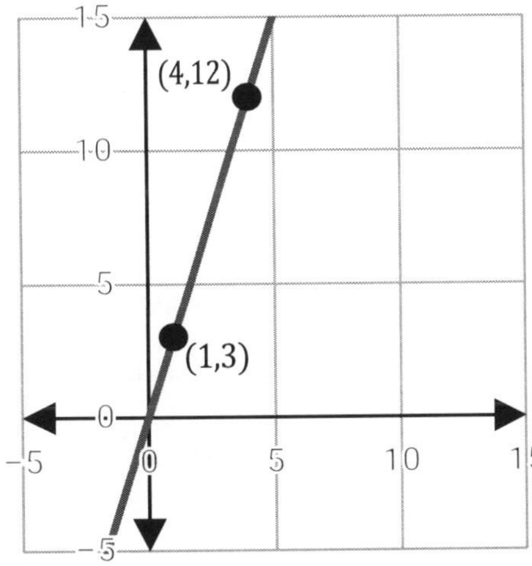

Parentheses and Brackets in Numerical Expressions

Parentheses and brackets are considered **grouping symbols**. These symbols indicate which sections of a numerical expression should be simplified first. Think of parentheses and brackets as layers of an onion. Parentheses are inner layers and brackets are outer layers. When solving expressions, find the middle of the onion and simplify that first. Then gradually work your way to the outermost layer using the order of operations.

Parentheses: ( )

Brackets: [ ]

Parentheses and brackets are used to separate expressions from other terms. For example, consider the expression $[3(2 \times 2 + 8 \times 2)] \div [5 \times 2 + 10]$. Look for the "center of the onion." Look for the math inside the parentheses and simplify this first. $(2 \times 2 + 8 \times 2)$ becomes $4 + 16$ and then 20. The expression is now $[3(20)] \div [5 \times 2 + 10]$. Now move to the math inside of the brackets. Look at the bracket on the left. $[3(20)]$ indicates 3×20, which simplifies to 60. The expression is now $60 \div [5 \times 2 + 10]$. Move to the brackets on the right. $[5 \times 2 + 10]$ becomes $[10 + 10]$ and then 20. Now the expression is $60 \div 30$, which simplifies to 2. By solving the parentheses and brackets first, and following the order of operations, the numerical expression $[3(2 \times 2 + 8 \times 2)] \div [5 \times 2 + 10]$ simplifies to 2.

Review Video: Mathematical Parentheses
Visit mometrix.com/academy and enter code: 978600

Order of Operations

Follow the order of operations (PEMDAS) when simplifying numerical expressions.

P- parentheses and grouping symbols
E- exponents
M- multiplication
D- division
addition
S- subtraction

For example, consider the numerical expression $2[(9 + 21) \div 6]$. Start by simplifying the math inside the parentheses. $(9 + 21)$ simplifies to 30.

$$2[30 \div 6]$$

Now simplify the math inside the brackets. $[30 \div 6]$ simplifies to 5.

$$2[5]$$

Multiply 2 by 5. The result is 10, so $2[(9 + 21) \div 6]$ simplifies to 10.

Review Video: Order of Operations
Visit mometrix.com/academy and enter code: 259675

Example

Simplify the expression: $(4 \times 5 + 100 \div 4) - 15$

30

Use the order of operations when simplifying numerical expressions. This is often referred to as PEMDAS. In the expression $(4 \times 5 + 100 \div 4) - 15$, start by simplifying the math within the parentheses. Remember to follow the order of operations inside parentheses, so complete multiplication and division in order from left to right before adding. $4 \times 5 = 20$ and $100 \div 4 = 25$.

$$(20 + 25) - 15$$

Now, add.

$$45 - 15$$

Finally, subtract.

$$45 - 15 = 30$$

EXAMPLE

$$[(0.75 + 10) - 2 \times 5] + 8.25$$

9

When simplifying expressions, solve the math within grouping elements first. Remember to follow the order of operations within grouping elements, so first simplify the parentheses inside the brackets.

$$[10.75 - 2 \times 5] + 8.25$$

Then, simplify the multiplication inside the brackets.

$$[10.75 - 10] + 8.25$$

Now simplify the subtraction within the brackets.

$$0.75 + 8.25$$

Finally, add.

$$0.75 + 8.25 = 9$$

Solving Problems Related to Perimeter, Area, and Volume

Many word problems will involve perimeter, area, or volume. **Perimeter** is the distance around a two-dimensional shape. **Area** is the space within a two-dimensional shape. **Volume** is the amount of space within a three-dimensional figure.

For example, consider the following scenario.

A school is installing a new rectangular play field. The field is 200 feet wide and 575 feet long. What is the area of the play field? If a student runs around the perimeter of the play field, how far will he or she run?

Different polygons will have different area formulas. The **area formula for a rectangle** is Area = Length × Width. Area = Length × Width becomes $A = 575 \times 200$, which simplifies to 115,000. This means that the total area within the play field is 115,000 square feet.

The perimeter around the play field can be calculated by finding the sum of all four side lengths. In this case, $P = 200 + 200 + 575 + 575$ simplifies to $P = 1{,}550$ feet. If a student runs around the perimeter of the play field, he or she will run 1,550 feet.

Consider another question.

Some of the play field equipment is arriving in large boxes. One piece of equipment arrives in a box that is 14 feet long, 6 feet wide, and 4 feet deep. What is the volume of the equipment box?

Volume formulas will vary depending on the specific three-dimensional figure. In this case, the figure is a rectangular prism. The volume, V, can be calculated as

$V = l \times w \times h$, where l is length, w is width, and h is height or depth. This simplifies to $V = 14 \times 6 \times 4 = 336$, so the volume of the box is 336 cubic feet.

Review Video: Volume and Surface Area of a Cube
Visit mometrix.com/academy and enter code: 664455

Review Video: Volume and Surface Area of a Rectangular Prism
Visit mometrix.com/academy and enter code: 282814

EXAMPLE

A rectangular wooden tabletop is twice as long as it is wide. If the tabletop is 3 feet wide, what is the area of the tabletop?

18 square feet

The area of a rectangle can be calculated using the formula $A = l \times w$, where l and w represent length and width. In this case, the width is 3 feet, and the length is twice this amount, so it is 6 feet.

$$A = l \times w$$

$$A = 6 \text{ ft} \times 3 \text{ ft}$$

$$A = 18 \text{ ft}^2$$

Therefore, the area of the tabletop is 18 square feet.

EXAMPLE

The volume of a cube is 64 cubic inches. What is the perimeter of one face of the cube?

16 inches

The volume, V, of a cube is calculated using the formula $V = l \times w \times h$, where l, w, and h represent the length, width, and height of the cube, respectively. Since the solid is a cube, then the length, width, and height are the same value. Test a few values to determine what the side length is: $2 \times 2 \times 2 = 8$, $3 \times 3 \times 3 = 27$, and $4 \times 4 \times 4 = 64$. This means that each edge of the cube is 4 inches. The perimeter of one face of the cube is the sum of 4 edges.

$$4 + 4 + 4 + 4 = 16$$

The perimeter of one face of the cube is 16 inches.

Geometry and Measurement

Classifying Two-Dimensional Figures

Two-dimensional shapes can be classified and sorted based on properties such as number of angles, edges, and vertices. **Polygons** are two-dimensional figures that are formed by straight lines on a flat surface. One way to sort polygons is based on the number of sides they have.

Graphic organizers can be helpful for sorting polygons into categories. Polygons can be split into three categories. One category contains three-sided polygons called **triangles**, one category contains four-sided polygons called **quadrilaterals**, and one category contains polygons with more than four sides. Notice how the number of sides is always the same as the number of angles and vertices.

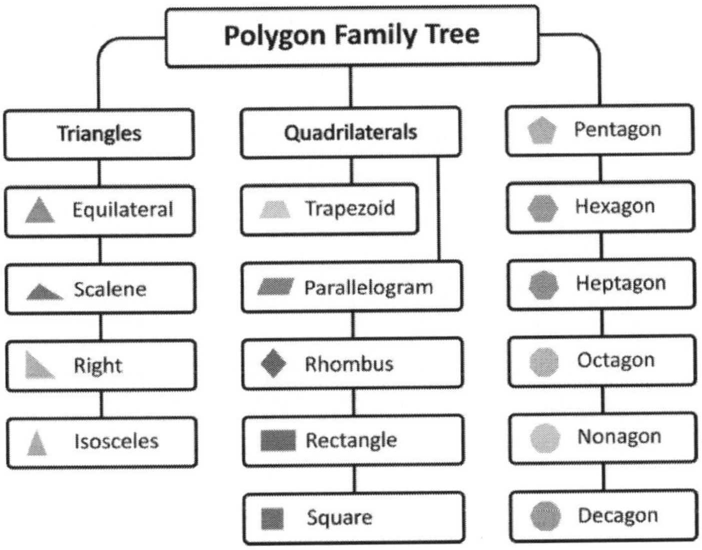

EXAMPLE

Franklin is sorting two-dimensional shapes. He places a rectangle, square, and rhombus into a group, and labels the group "parallelograms." Franklin's friend Henry says that this is incorrect because the group should also contain trapezoids. Is Henry correct?

Henry is not correct. Franklin has labeled the shapes correctly.

Rectangles, squares, and rhombi fall under the umbrella of parallelograms. Parallelograms are defined as four-sided figures with two pairs of opposite sides that are parallel. Trapezoids do not fall into this category because trapezoids only have one set of parallel sides. A trapezoid is shown below.

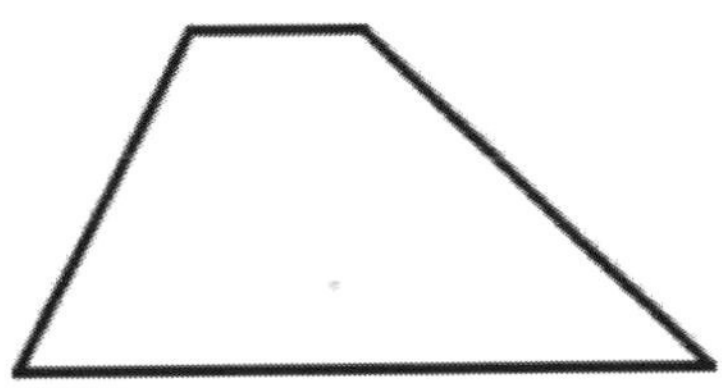

EXAMPLE

Elizabeth states that all squares can be classified as a rhombus, but not all rhombi are classified as squares. Ryan states that all rhombi can be classified as squares, but not all squares can be classified as rhombi. Who is correct?

Elizabeth is correct.

All squares can be classified as a rhombus, but not all rhombi are classified as squares. A square has four congruent sides and four right angles. This qualifies as a rhombus because a rhombus is a four-sided figure with four congruent sides. However, in a rhombus, the angles do not have to be 90 degrees. For example, both figures below can be classified as a rhombus, but only the figure on the left can be classified as a square.

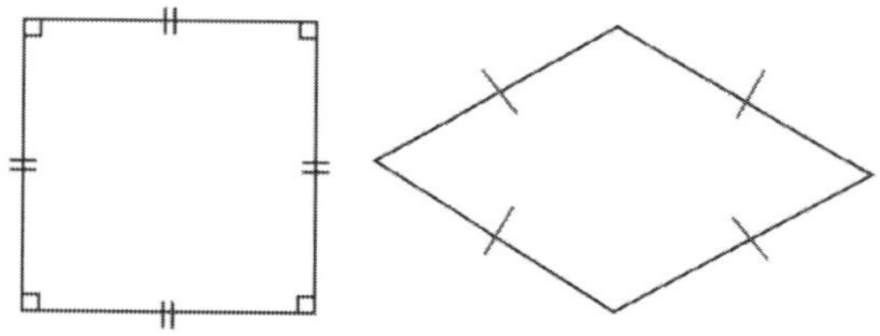

Volume and Cubic Units

All three-dimensional figures occupy space. This space is defined as **volume**. Volume is also known as capacity. Spheres, prisms, pyramids, cylinders, cones, and cubes are common three-dimensional figures that have volume. The volume of a three-dimensional solid is measured in cubic units. For example, a cube has a length, width, and height. A cube that is 1 unit tall, 1 unit wide, and 1 unit deep is called a **unit cube**. The number of unit cubes that fills a solid determines its volume. The formula $V = l \times w \times h$, where l is length, w is width, and h is height, can be used to calculate the volume of a cube or rectangular prism.

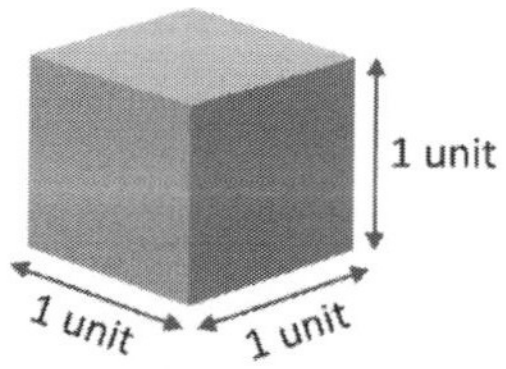

For example, a rectangular prism that is has a height of 4 units, a width of 3 units, and a depth of 6 units has a volume of 4 units × 3 units × 6 units, which is 72 units^3. Remember, this is *not* the volume formula for all three-dimensional solids. Each solid has its own volume formula.

Many solids will have dimensions that give specific units. For example, a cube might have side lengths measured in centimeters, which means the volume would be described as "cubic centimeters," not "cubic units."

Consider the cube below. The side lengths are all 4 centimeters. The volume formula can be applied. $V = l \times w \times h$ becomes $V = 4 \times 4 \times 4$. This simplifies to 64, so the volume of the cube is 64 cm^3.

There are 64 total squares in the cube, so the volume is 64 cm^3. Notice how the volume formula takes less time than counting up each individual square.

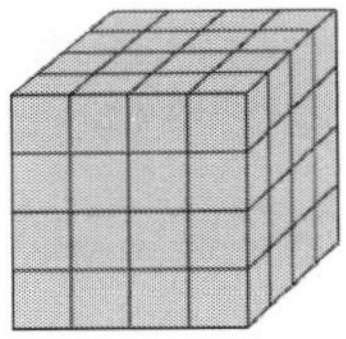

VOLUME OF A RECTANGULAR PRISM

The volume of a rectangular prism can be found in a variety of ways. One option is to simply count every single cube within the prism. This is generally unrealistic because of the amount of time it takes. Another option is to calculate volume based on the number of **layers** within a cube. For example, consider the $5 \times 5 \times 5$ cube below. Notice how there are 5 horizontal layers, and each layer contains 25 unit cubes. There are 5 of these layers, so the total volume can be calculated as 5×25, or 5 groups of 25, which is 125. Therefore, the volume of the cube is 125 cubic units.

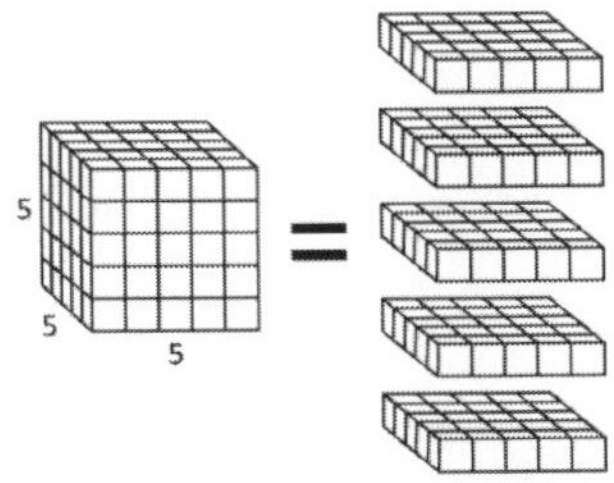

This layering strategy can be applied to cubes and rectangular prisms. For example, the prism below is constructed from 5 horizontal layers. Each layer contains 4 columns and 8 rows. This means that each layer contains 4×8, or 32 unit cubes. Each layer contains 32 unit cubes, and there are 5 layers. Therefore, the total number of unit cubes can be calculated as $5 \times 32 = 160$, or 160 cubic units.

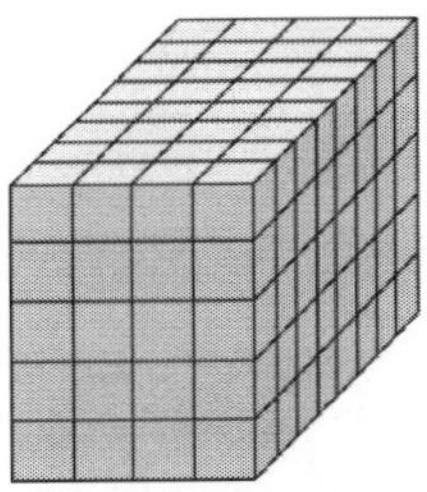

Calculating Conversions

Volume, distance, and mass can be measured using the metric system or the customary system. The **metric system** is generally preferred in math and science because values can be easily multiplied or divided by powers of 10. The metric system is convenient when working with very large or very small values. For example, there are 1,000 meters in one kilometer, so the number of meters can easily be determined if the number of kilometers are provided. For example, there are 5,000 meters in 5 kilometers. 3,000 meters in 3 kilometers. 8,000 meters in 8 kilometers. Metric conversion tables can be helpful for seeing the patterns within the metric system. The table below focuses on the base unit of meters. Notice how 1 meter is equivalent to 1,000 mm, 100 cm, and 0.001 km.

Millimeters	Centimeters	Meters	Kilometers
mm	cm	m	km
1	0.1	0.001	0.000001
10	1	0.01	0.00001
1,000	**100**	**1**	**0.001**
1,000,000	10,000	1,000	1

Review Video: Metric System Conversions
Visit mometrix.com/academy and enter code: 163709

The **customary system** is commonly used in the United States but very rarely in other regions of the world. The units of the customary system are not based on powers of ten. The conversion factors do not follow a pattern, which makes them a bit more challenging to remember. For example, study the table below. Notice how there is not one single pattern or relationship used consistently throughout the table. Each conversion factor is unique to each specific unit. This lack of a consistency is the most significant difference between the metric system and the customary system.

Common Customary Measurements

Length	Weight	Time	Capacity
1 foot = 12 inches 1 yard = 36 inches 1 yard = 3 feet 1 mile = 5,280 feet 1 mile = 1,760 yards	1 pound = 16 ounces 1 ton = 2,000 pounds	1 minute = 60 seconds 1 hour = 60 minutes 1 day = 24 hours 1 week = 7 days 1 year = 12 months 1 year = 365 days 1 leap year = 366 days	1 cup = 8 fluid ounces 1 pint = 2 cups 1 quart = 2 pints 1 quart = 4 cups 1 gallon = 4 quarts 1 gallon = 16 cups

Consider this real-world scenario for a metric conversion. Kristen walks 500 meters to work each morning, and then takes the bus home each evening. If she does this 5 days a week, for 4 weeks, how many kilometers has she walked?

Kristen walks 500 meters, 5 times a week. This means that in one week, she walks 2,500 meters. In 2 weeks she walks 5,000 meters. In 3 weeks she walks 7,500 meters. In 4 weeks she walks 10,000 meters. There are 1,000 meters in each kilometer. This means that the number of kilometers will always be 1,000 times less than the number of meters. Therefore, 10,000 meters is 10 kilometers. 10,000 divided by 1,000 is 10. Kristen has walked 10 kilometers in 4 weeks.

Consider a real-world scenario for where a customary conversion is needed. A long jump runway is 147 feet. How many yards is this?

There are 3 feet in 1 yard. This means that the number of feet will always be 3 times larger than the number of yards. Or, in this case, the number of yards will be 3 times smaller than the number of feet. Divide the number of feet by 3 to calculate the number of yards, $147 \div 3 = 49$. So, the runway is 49 yards long.

Review Video: Measurement Conversion
Visit mometrix.com/academy and enter code: 316703

Coordinate Planes

The **coordinate plane** is a two-dimensional plane formed from the intersection of a vertical and horizontal line. The horizontal line is referred to as the ***x*-axis**, and the vertical line is referred to as the ***y*-axis**. The x-axis and y-axis are perpendicular to each other. The x-axis and y-axis extend out from the **origin**, which is located at the point (0,0). The coordinate plane is sometimes referred to as a **coordinate plane**, and can be used to describe points, or **ordered pairs**. Ordered pairs consist of an x-coordinate and a y-coordinate. The x-coordinate indicates horizontal movement from the origin, to the right or left. The y-coordinate indicates vertical movement from the origin, up or down. In other words, the x- and y-coordinates reflect how far over and how far up an ordered pair is on the coordinate plane. For example, the point (3,2) has an x-coordinate of 3 and a y-coordinate of 2. The point (3,2) is plotted by moving 3 units to the right and 2 units up from the origin (0,0).

Graphing Ordered Pairs

All ordered pairs take the form (x, y), where x describes the horizontal movement, and y describes the vertical movement. For example, consider the graph below. Start at the origin (0,0). The point (3,5) indicates a movement of 3 units horizontally to the right, and 5 units vertically up. The point (3,5) can be plotted on the coordinate plane.

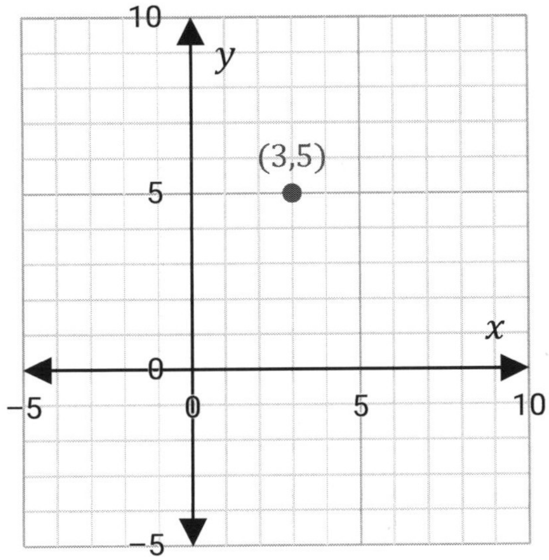

It is important not to swap the x and y locations within an ordered pair. For example, the location of (3,5) is not the same as the location of (5,3).

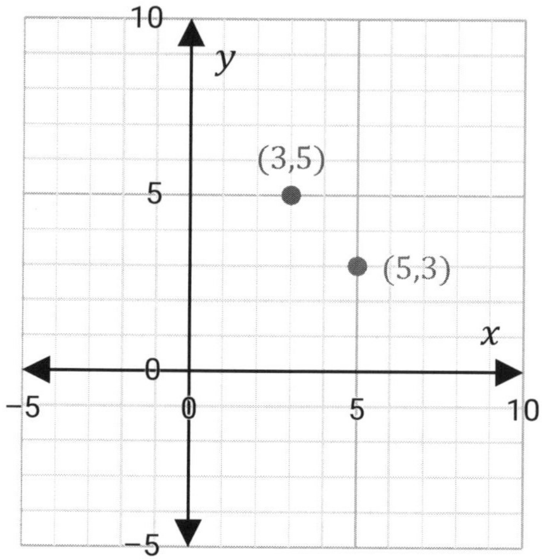

Review Video: Cartesian Coordinate Plane and Graphing
Visit mometrix.com/academy and enter code: 115173

GRAPHING ORDERED PAIRS BASED ON MATH AND REAL-WORLD PROBLEMS

Ordered pairs can be generated from real-world problems or problems involving input-output tables. Any problem that includes an independent variable (x-variable) and a dependent variable (y-variable) can be graphed on a coordinate plane.

For example, the input-output table below shows the relationship between glasses of juice and total cost. Each glass of juice costs $3. The cost depends on the number of glasses; therefore, the cost is the dependent variable. This means that the number of glasses will be the x-variable, and the total cost will be the y-variable.

Cups of Juice (x)	0	1	2	3	4
Total Cost (y)	0	3	6	9	12

Each pair of x- and y-values represents an ordered pair that can be plotted on a coordinate plane. Remember, ordered pairs follow the form (x, y). The ordered pairs for this scenario include (0,0), (1,3), (2,6), (3,9), and (4,12).

Remember, the x-value indicates horizontal movement to the right, and the y-value indicates vertical movement up. Start at the origin (0,0), and then plot each ordered pair. The result is shown below.

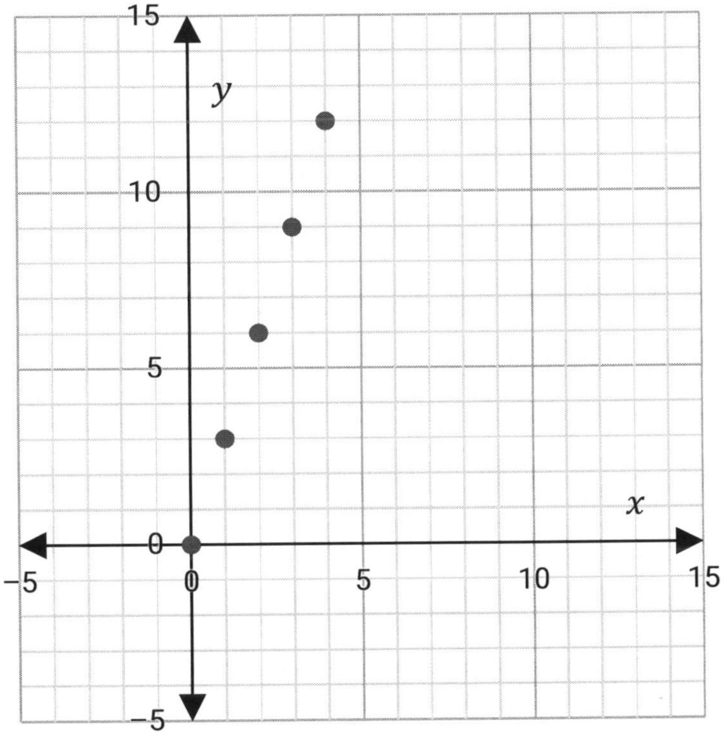

EXAMPLE

John works at an animal shelter. Each day John feeds all the cats. Each cat needs 2 cups of food daily. Find the number of cups of food John will serve if there are 5 cats at the shelter by using a graph.

10 cups

The scenario can be described as a pattern within an input-output table or a graph. Each data point represents a pair of numbers in the table or a point on the graph. The number of cups of food is 2 times the number of cats.

Number of Cats	1	2	3	4	5
Cups of Cat Food	2	4	6	8	10

To set up a graph, remember that the independent variable is located on the x-axis, and the dependent variable is located on the y-axis. In this case, the amount of food depends on the number of cats, so the amount of food is the dependent variable. Label the number of cats on the x-axis and the number of cups of food on the y-axis. Graph each point by moving horizontally for the x-value and vertically for the y-value. For example, if there is 1 cat, move right 1. One cat needs 2 cups of food, so move up 2. The location of "over 1 and up 2" is the point (1,2). Continue plotting points until the number of cups of food is determined for 5 cats. Notice how 5 cats require 10 cups of food. This is data point is located at (5,10).

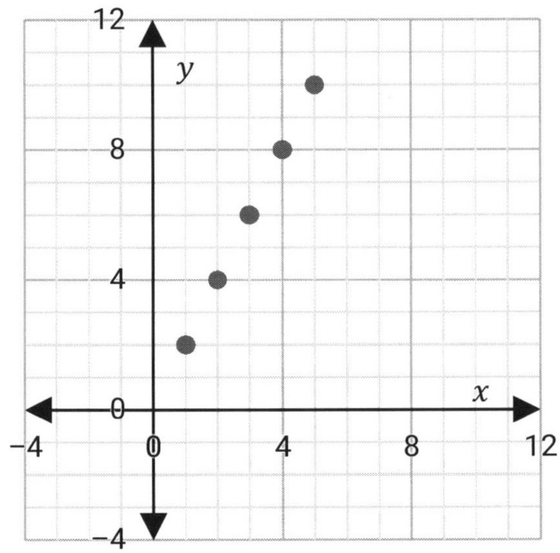

EXAMPLE

The 1st Street Ice Bakery is having its grade opening. The table shows how many cakes the shop sold in the first 7 days. Use the table to create a graph. What day were the most cakes sold?

Day	1	2	3	4	5	6	7
Number of Cakes	4	4	6	3	2	7	6

Day 6

The data points from the input-output table can be used to set up a graph. Each data point represents an ordered pair. For example, on day 1, 4 cakes were sold. This represents the ordered pair (1,4). Each ordered pair can be plotted on the coordinate plane. The point (1,4) is plotted by starting at the origin (0,0) and then moving 1 unit to the right and 4 units up. Plot each ordered pair. The point that is highest is (6,7). This means that the most cakes were sold on day 6.

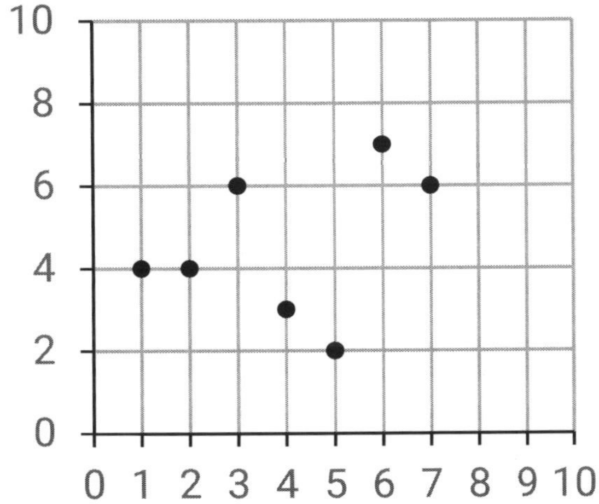

Data Analysis

Representing Data

There is a wide variety of graphing styles to choose from when displaying data. In general, **categorical data**, or data that is organized into categories, is best displayed using bar graphs or frequency tables. However, **numerical data**, or data that consists of numbers, is best displayed using dot plots or stem-and-leaf plots.

Review Video: Data Interpretation of Graphs
Visit mometrix.com/academy and enter code: 200439

Bar Graphs

Bar graphs display data in the form of vertical or horizontal rectangular bars, where the length of the bars indicates the measure of the data. For example, the bar graph below shows the number of pets a group of people own. Notice how the tallest bar is "Cat." The bar extends vertically up to 11 people. This means 11 people own cats.

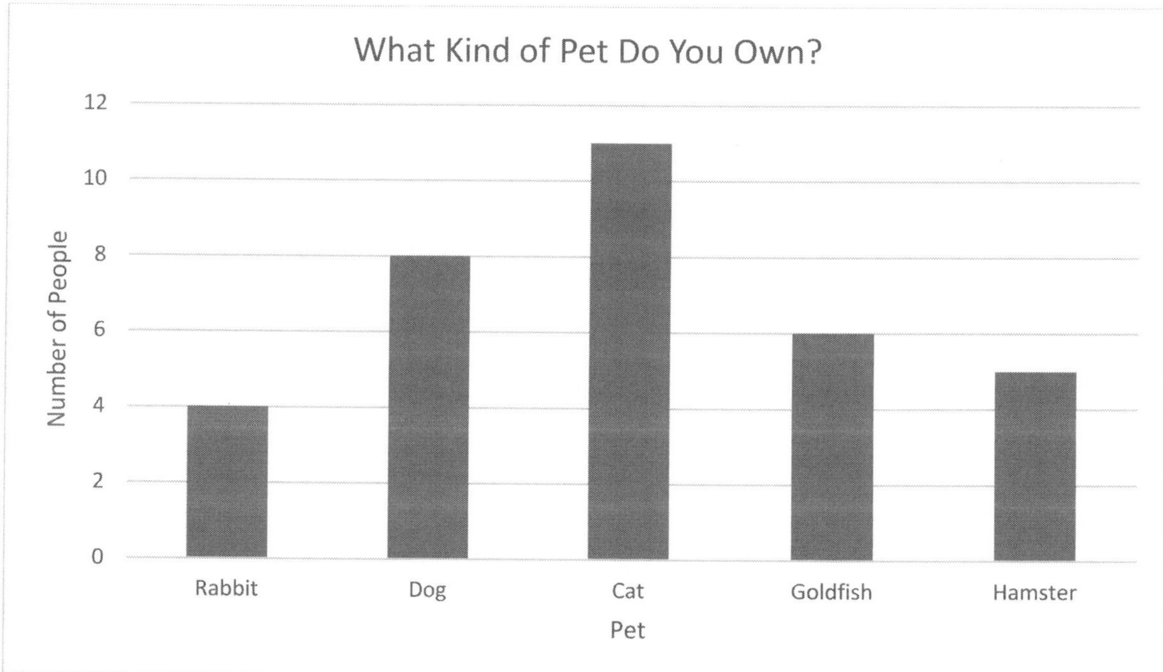

Frequency Tables

Frequency tables use numbers or tally marks to indicate the frequency of each value within a data set. For example, the frequency table below represents shoe color within a 5th grade classroom. Frequency tables are used to emphasize the frequency of one outcome compared to another outcome. Usually, a frequency table is set up as a T-chart. The left column of the T-chart lists all the possible outcomes, and the right column lists the frequency of each outcome. A frequency table provides an organized display of data in a condensed and visual format.

Shoe Color	
Color	**Frequency**
Blue	III
Black	~~IIII~~ I
Red	I
Brown	IIII
Tan	II
White	~~IIII~~ II

Dot Plots

Dot plots are graphs used to show trends, clusters, or groupings within data. Dot plots show individual data points as dots on a graph. The data points are not connected to form a line. If the data points were connected, this would be considered a line graph. Dot plots are very similar to frequency tables, except each data point is plotted individually so that the frequency is displayed as a "stack of dots" rather than a number or tally mark. For example, the dot plot below shows 5 dots over the 2 mile category, meaning 5 separate bike riders rode 2 miles.

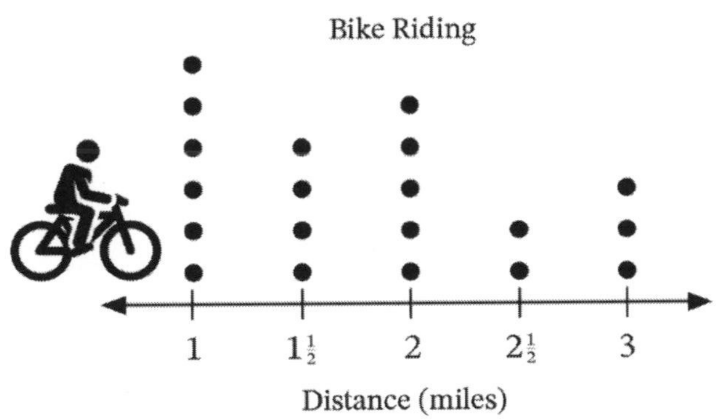

Stem-and-Leaf Plots

Stem-and-leaf plots are graphical displays used to emphasize the shape or distribution of data. Stem-and-leaf plots are similar to a T-chart, where the stem and leaf sections represent a specific place value. For example, the stem-and-leaf plot below shows the ages of people inside a movie theater. The stem represents the tens-place value, and the leaf represents the ones-place value. Notice how the youngest viewers are 1 year old and the oldest viewer is 66 years old.

Stem	Leaf
0	1, 1, 2, 2, 3, 4, 4, 4, 4, 5, 8
1	0, 0, 0, 1, 1, 3, 7, 9

Stem	Leaf
2	5, 5, 7, 7, 8, 8, 9, 9
3	0, 1, 1, 1, 2, 2, 2, 4, 5
4	0, 4, 8, 9
5	2, 6, 7, 7, 8
6	3, 6
Key: 3|1 = 31	

Review Video: Stem-and-Leaf Plots
Visit mometrix.com/academy and enter code: 302339

Representing Data Points

Data points in the form (x, y) can be plotted on a scatter plot to help identify trends or clusters. For example, consider the following table comparing arm span in centimeters to height in centimeters. Each pair of data points, arm span and height, can be plotted on a scatter plot. Arm span and height are not exclusive to the x or y variable, so apply either variable to x and either variable to y. It could be argued that arm span depends on height, or height depends on arm span. In this case, either arrangement will work.

Person	Arm Span (cm)	Height (cm)
1	156	162
2	157	162
3	159	164
4	160	165
5	161	168
6	161	167
7	160	166

To graph the data on a scatter plot, treat each pair of values as an (x, y) coordinate pair. For example, use the arm span values for x and the corresponding height values for y. There will be 7 ordered pairs on the scatter plot: (156,162), (157,162), (159,164), (160,165), (161,168), (161,167), and (160,166).

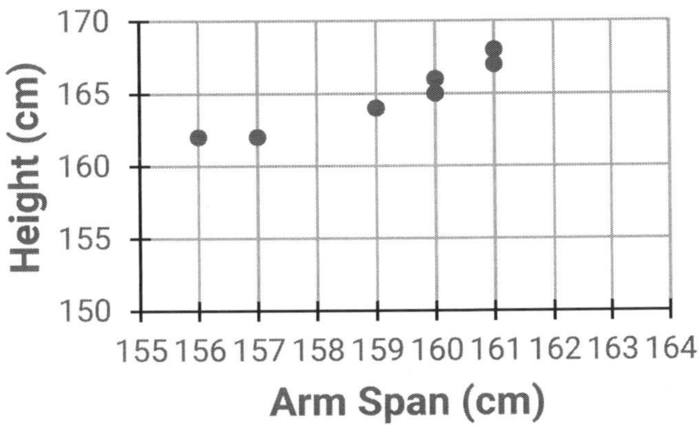

Notice how there is a general pattern or direction to the plotted points. Overall, as the arm span values increase, so do the height values. Scatter plots are effective for spotting trends such as this because the shape or form of the data becomes visual.

Review Video: Scatter Plot
Visit mometrix.com/academy and enter code: 596526

Solving Problems Involving Data

Graphical displays are often used to solve real-world problems. Use the displays below to solve one and two-step problems.

Bar Graphs

The display below is a bar graph that illustrates the relationship between ticket sales and days of the week. Use the bar graph to answer the following one- and two-step problems.

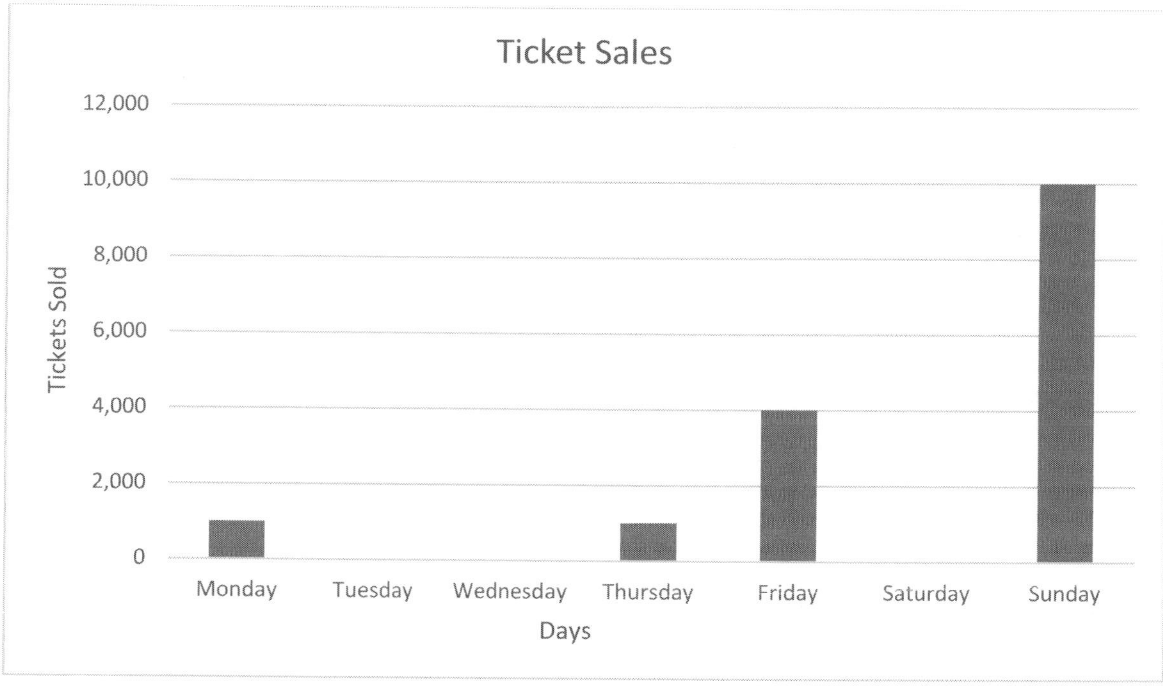

Start by studying the features of the graph.

Notice the labels for the x- and y-axis: Days and Tickets Sold.

Notice the interval for the y-axis: intervals of 1,000.

One-Step Problem: How many tickets were sold on Friday?

- Locate Friday on the x-axis. The bar above Friday extends vertically up to the 4,000 ticket mark. This means that on Friday, 4,000 tickets were sold.

Two-Step Problem: How many more tickets were sold on Sunday than Friday?

- Solve two-step problems one piece at a time. Start by determining how many tickets were sold on Sunday and Friday. The vertical bar over Friday extends to 4,000 tickets, and the vertical bar over Sunday extends to 10,000 tickets. Subtract the two values to calculate the difference: $10{,}000 - 4{,}000 = 6{,}000$. This means 6,000 more tickets were sold on Sunday than Friday.

FREQUENCY TABLES

The display below is a frequency table that illustrates movie genre preferences for a group of 25 people. Each tally mark represents one person. Use the frequency table to answer the following one- and two-step problems.

Movie Choices	Tallies
Scary Movies	𝍸 𝍸 ||
Funny Movies	𝍸 |||
Action Movies	𝍸

One-Step Problem: How many people chose "Funny Movies" as their movie genre preference?

- Each tally mark represents one person. The "Funny Movie" category contains 8 tally marks. This means 8 people chose the "Funny Movie" category as their movie genre preference.

Two-Step Problem: A couple people in the survey changed their mind. Two people switched their vote from the "Scary Movie" category to the "Action Movie" category. How many tally marks are in the "Action Movie" category after the switch?

- Solve two-step problems one piece at a time. Two people are removing their votes from the "Scary Movie" category. This means that the "Scary Movie" category goes from 12 tally marks to 10 tally marks because $12 - 2 = 10$. These two votes are being relocated to the "Action Movie" category. This means the "Action Movie" category goes from 5 tally marks to 7 tally marks because $5 + 2 = 7$. After the switch, the "Action Movie" category contains 7 tally marks.

SCATTER PLOTS

The display below is a scatter plot that illustrates the relationship between dog height and dog weight. A trend line is drawn through the data spread. A **trend line** is used to illustrate the general shape or direction of the data. Use the scatter plot to answer the following one- and two-step problems.

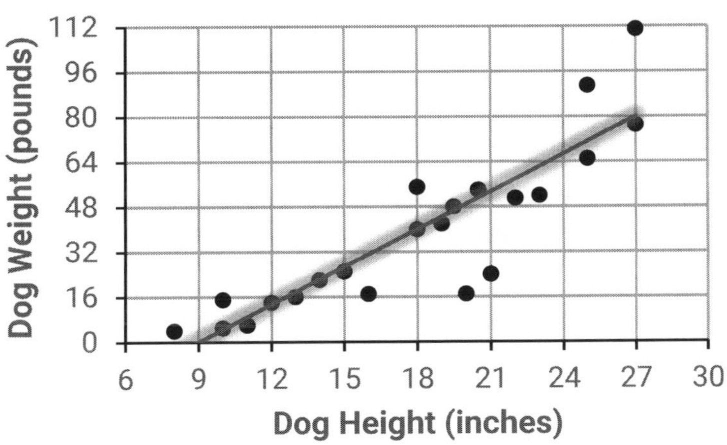

One-Step Problem: Use the scatter plot to estimate the weight of a dog that has a height of 30 inches.

- The weight of a dog that has a height of 30 inches can be estimated by extending the trend line. Notice how the height of 30 inches intersects the trend line at approximately the 96-pound mark. This means a dog that has a height of 30 inches will have a weight of approximately 96 pounds.

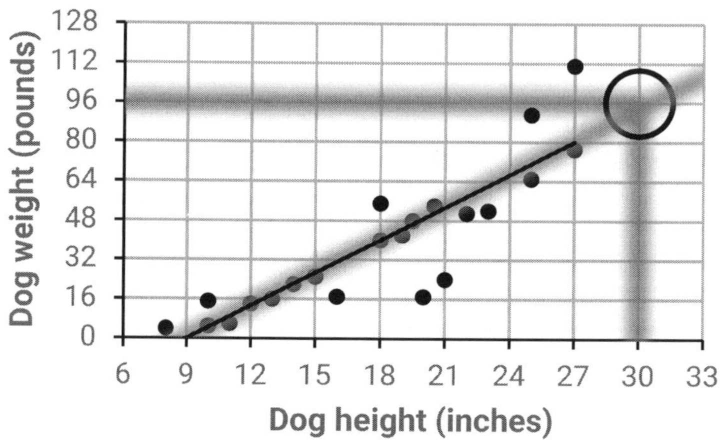

Two-Step Problem: Approximately how much taller is a 48-pound dog than a 16-pound dog?

- Determine the approximate height of a 16-pound dog and a 48-pound dog. Locate the 16-pound mark on the y-axis. Slide right and locate the intersection point of the trend line. Slide down to determine the corresponding height on the x-axis. A 16-pound dog has a height of approximately 12 inches. Locate the 48-pound mark on the y-axis. Slide right and locate the intersection point of the trend line. Slide down to determine the corresponding height on the x-axis. A 48-pound dog has a height of approximately 20 inches. Subtract the heights to calculate the difference, $20 - 12 = 8$. So, a 48-pound dog is approximately 8 inches taller than a 16-pound dog.

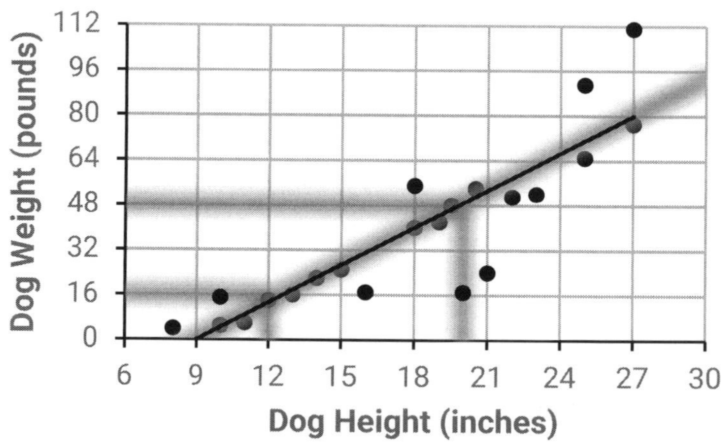

EXAMPLE

The scatter plot shows the population of the United States. In what year was the US population approximately 300 million?

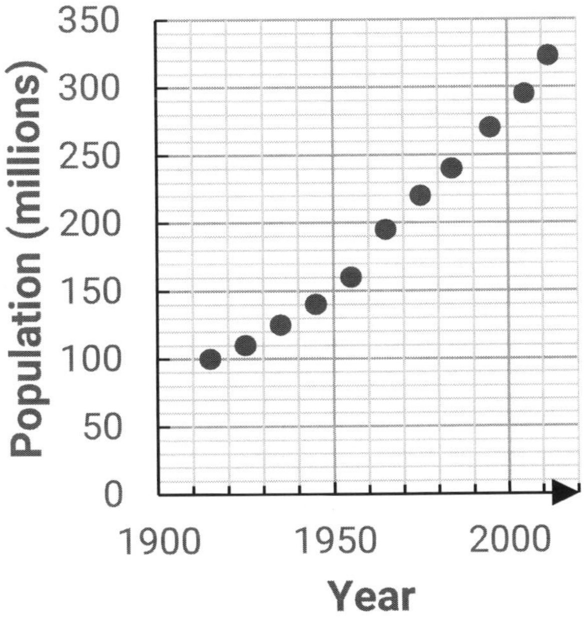

2005

The y-axis displays the population. Find the 300-million mark for population, then slide to the right until a data point is reached. In this case, the closest data point is above the year 2005. Notice how the x-axis increases by 20 years, or 10 years for each hash mark. The data point lays between the marks for the year 2000 and 2010, which means the population was 300 million around the year 2005.

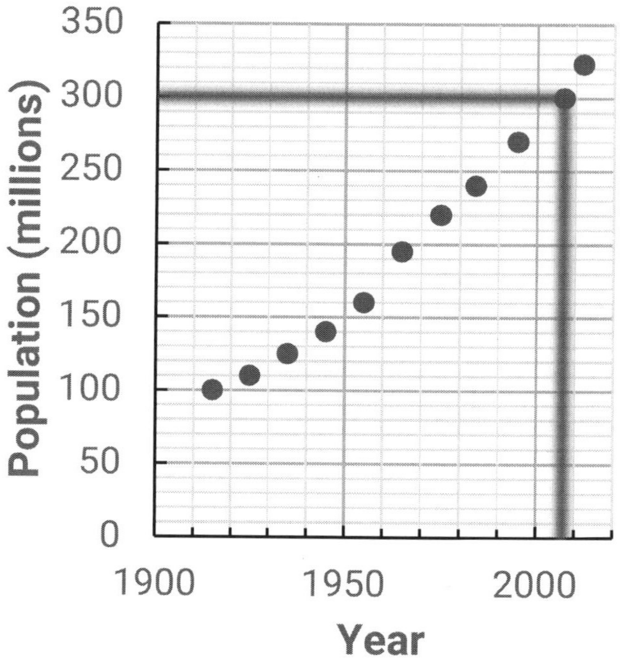

DOT PLOTS

The display below is a dot plot that represents the weight of backpacks for a group of students. Each dot represents one student. Use the dot plot to answer the following one- and two-step problems.

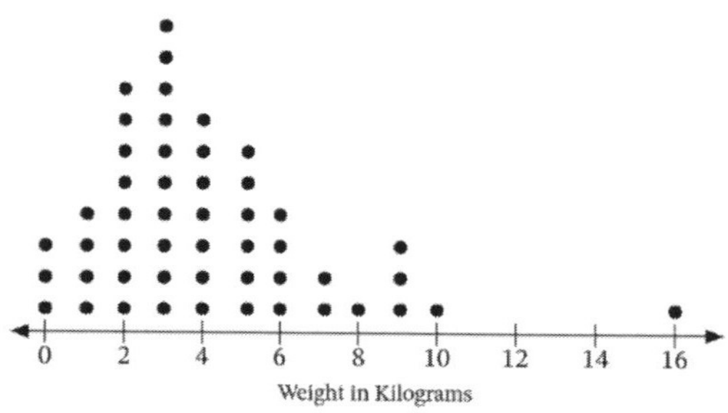

One-Step Problem: How many students are represented on the dot plot?

- Each dot represents 1 student, and there are 50 dots on the dot plot. This means that 50 students are represented on the dot plot.

Two-Step Problem: How many students have a backpack that weighs 6 kilograms or more?

- Identify the weights along the x-axis that are 6 kilograms or more. Weights that are greater than or equal to 6 kilograms include 6 through 16. Count the number of dots located from 6 kilograms to 16 kilograms. In this case, there are 12 dots. Each dot represents 1 student, so 12 students have backpacks that weigh 6 kilograms or more.

Stem-and-Leaf Plots

The display below is a stem-and-leaf plot representing the number of minutes a group of students play outside each day. Use the stem-and-leaf plot to answer the following one- and two-step problems.

Number of Minutes Spent Playing Outside	
2	0 5 5
3	0 5 7 9
4	0 5 5 5 6
5	
6	0 5 6 8
7	0 5
Key: 7|5 = 75	

One-Step Problem: What is the lowest number of minutes listed in the stem-and-leaf plot?

- The stem-and-leaf plot lists the ones digit in the leaf, and the tens digit in the stem. For example, a stem of 2 and a leaf of 0 represents 2 tens and 0 ones. In this case, 20 is the lowest number listed in the stem-and-leaf plot.

Two-Step Problem: One student listed in the stem-and-leaf plot reported playing outside for 30 minutes. How many students reported playing twice this amount?

- 60 minutes is twice as much as 30 minutes because $30 \times 2 = 60$. 60 is listed in the stem-and-leaf plot once, which means 1 student reported playing for 60 minutes.

Number of Minutes Spent Playing Outside	
2	0 5 5
3	0 5 7 9
4	0 5 5 5 6
5	
6	0 5 6 8
7	0 5
Key: 7|5 = 75	

EXAMPLE

The stem-and-leaf plot shows the price of each menu item at Pauli's Italian Restaurant. Amy purchases the most expensive menu item and leaves a tip of $14. What was the price of her meal?

Stem	Leaf
3	6 7 9 9
4	1 2 3 6
5	6 7 8
6	0 5 6
Key: 3|6 = 36	

$80

The stem-and-leaf plot lists the prices for each menu item according to place value. The ones-place value is listed in the leaf, and the tens-place value is listed in the stem. For example, the first row represents 36, 37, 39, and 39. The most expensive menu item listed in the stem-and-leaf plot is $66. $66 + $14 = $80, so Amy spent $80 on her meal.

Personal Financial Literacy

Income Tax, Payroll Tax, Sales Tax, and Property Tax

A **tax** is money that the government collects from its citizens. The government collects taxes to pay for things that the general population needs. For example, tax dollars are used to build things like roads and schools. Taxes are collected in a few ways. Some of the most common are income tax, payroll tax, sales tax, and property tax. Tax on the money that a person earns is called **income tax**. In general, the more money a person earns, the more he or she pays in income tax. **Payroll tax** is a tax that employers must pay. Usually this is calculated as a percentage of the salaries that employers pay for their workers. **Sales tax** is a tax on goods and services. These taxes are collected by the retailer during the sale. **Property tax** is a tax that property owners must pay. Property tax can be applied to homes, vehicles, and even vacant land. Overall, the concept of taxing is a process used by the government to collect money so that large and expensive projects can be built for the betterment of society as a whole.

Gross Income and Net Income

Gross income and net income are slightly different. **Gross income** is all a person's income before any deductions or taxes are taken out. **Net income** is a person's income after deductions, like taxes, are taken out. A person's paystub will indicate what deductions have been taken out and the amount of each deduction. Net income will always be less than gross income. When planning a budget, it is a good idea to build the budget off net income rather than gross income. This is because a person's net income is considered their actual "take home" pay, after taxes.

Unbalanced Budgets

Financial challenges can arise if a budget becomes unbalanced. In other words, if a person is spending more than he or she is earning, the result can be debt. **Debt** is a situation where expenditures, money being spent, exceed revenue, money being earned. Creating and using a budget is a great way to avoid this dilemma. Start by listing out all weekly, monthly, or yearly expenses. This includes variable expenses and fixed expenses. **Variable expenses** will vary over time. For example, grocery bills or restaurant bills can vary month to month. **Fixed expenses** are the same each month. For example, rent payments, phone bills, and car payments generally stay the same each month. It is important to include *all* expenses in a budget. This includes money spent on entertainment, shopping, dining out, buying gifts, taking vacations, and so on. If a budget is not balanced, it becomes necessary to eliminate expenses. It is often unrealistic to drop fixed expenses. However, dropping variable expenses that can be considered "entertainment" is one way to break even or get closer to the goal of a balanced budget.

Loans

In some cases, a person can take out a loan to cover expenses that exceed income. However, if bank loans are not repaid on time, it becomes less likely that a bank will loan a person money in the future. Remember, banks want to ensure that they are repaid the money they loan out to people. When people pay back their loans on time, they build what is called **credit**. When people pay back their loans on time, their credit score will increase. Similarly, when a loan is not paid back on time, a person's credit score will decrease. It is important to maintain a good credit score because banks consider this score when determining whether to lend a person money.

BALANCING BUDGETS

Balancing a budget requires a person to list all his or her expenses and compare this to all of his or her revenue. This is considered a form of financial planning that can prevent people from spending more money than they earn. A budget is a helpful way to track the money that is being earned and the money that is being spent. A budget is a great tool to predict how much money can be saved each month. Budgeting is a way to practice critical saving and spending skills that can be used into adulthood. A budget is said to be "balanced" if the revenue is equal to or greater than the expenditures. In other words, if a person earns more than he or she spends, he or she has a **balanced budget**. To create a budget, list all expenditures within a set time. For example, consider the budget below. All expenses for the month are listed in the table.

Rent	$2,000
Car Payment	$250
Groceries	$580
Phone Bill	$75
Electricity Bill	$140

The budget lists all expenses for the month. The total for all the expenses is $3,045. If the income earner in this scenario earns more than $3,045 in the month, his or her budget will be balanced. Ideally, a person will earn more than he or she spends each month to save money. Saving money is important because life is unpredictable, and large expenses can pop up unexpectedly. For example, large unplanned medical bills can occur, requiring immediate attention. Having a savings account is one way to plan ahead for unexpected expenses.

Practice Test #1

1. Choose from the options below the blank and write in the option that best completes the statement.

The value of the digit 5 in the decimal 674.215 is 5 ___________.

tenths
thousandths
hundredths
thousands

2. Amy is on a summer road trip with her family. Her family needs to travel 432.5 miles over the next 5 days. Her family wants to travel the same distance each day. How many miles should Amy's family drive each day?

a. 76.5 miles
b. 80.5 miles
c. 84.5 miles
d. 86.5 miles

3. Sean and his 4 siblings decide to pool their money together to purchase a Mother's Day necklace. The necklace costs $629.95, and all five of the siblings will contribute the same amount of money. How much money will each sibling contribute?

a. $124.49
b. $125.99
c. $149.99
d. $157.49

4. Elliot asked a group of his friends their ages and how many times they had been on an airplane. The results are displayed in the table below.

Age	9	12	13	13	14	11	12	15
Flights	4	6	6	7	10	4	8	12

Which scatter plot best represents the data from the table?

a.

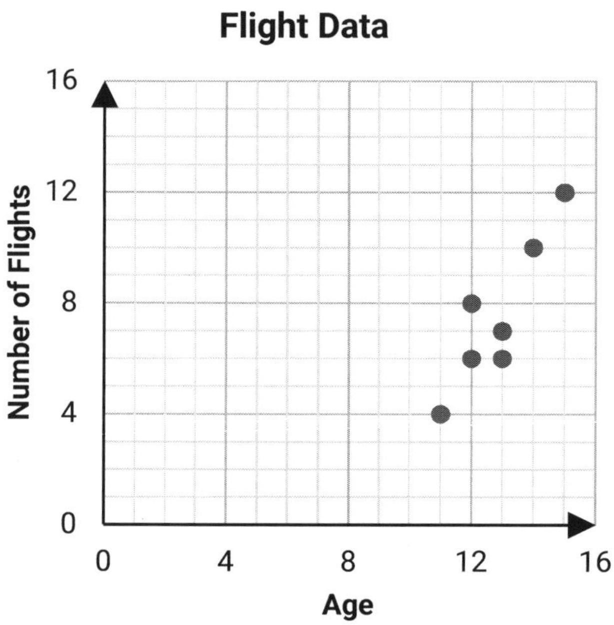

b.

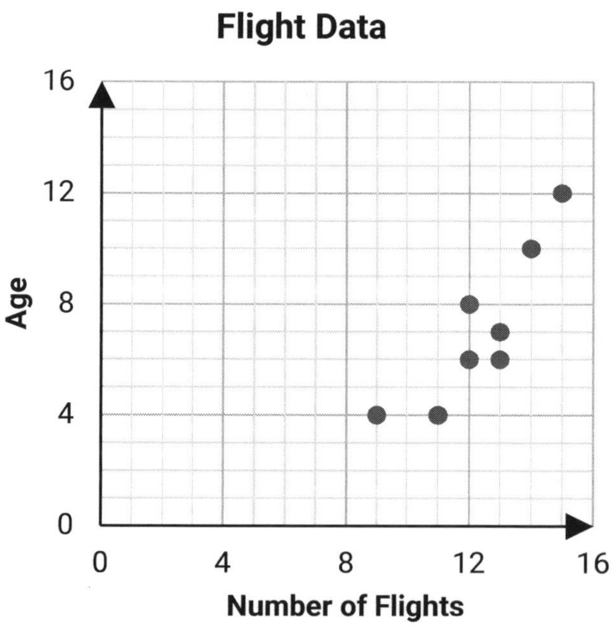

c. 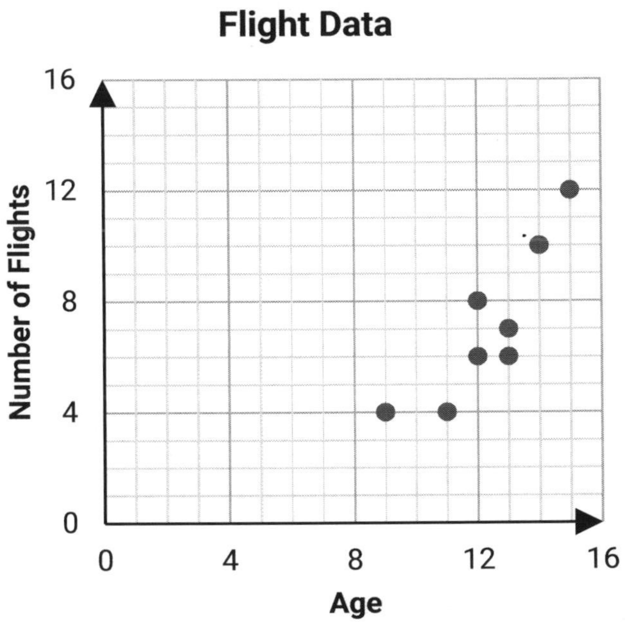
Flight Data
Number of Flights
Age
0
4
8
12
16

d. 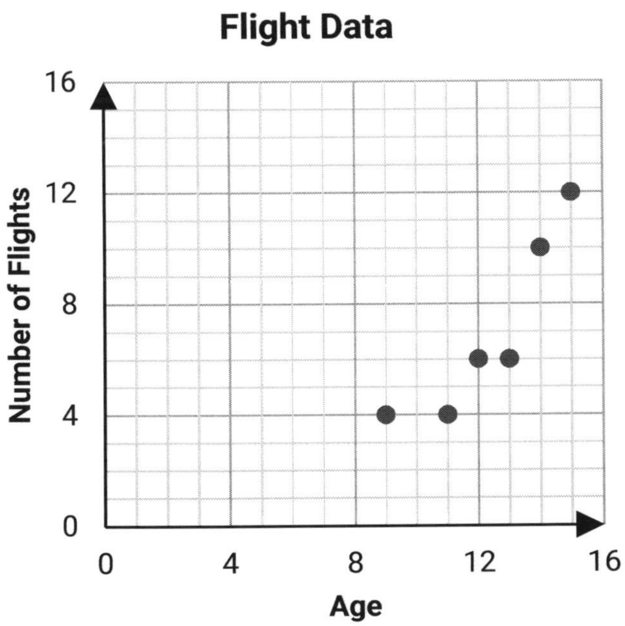
Flight Data
Number of Flights
Age
0
4
8
12
16

5. James has a freezer with a volume of 36 ft^3. Which item shows the possible dimensions of James' freezer?

a. 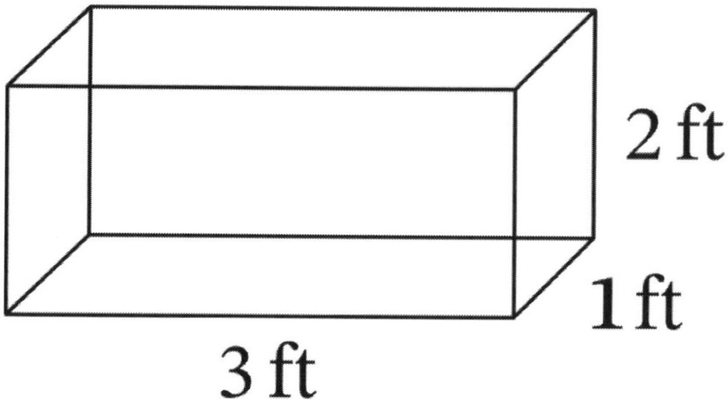

b. 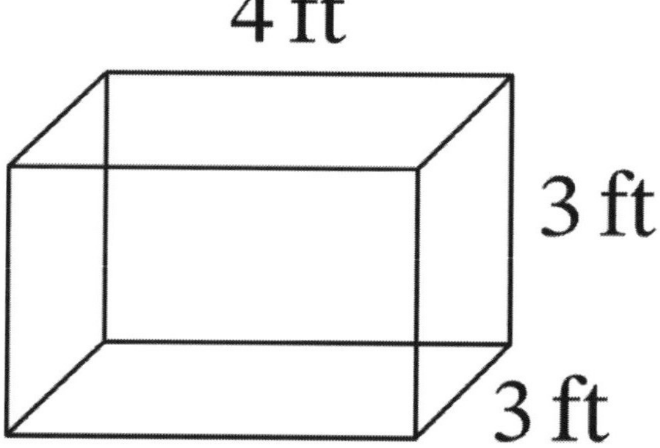

d. 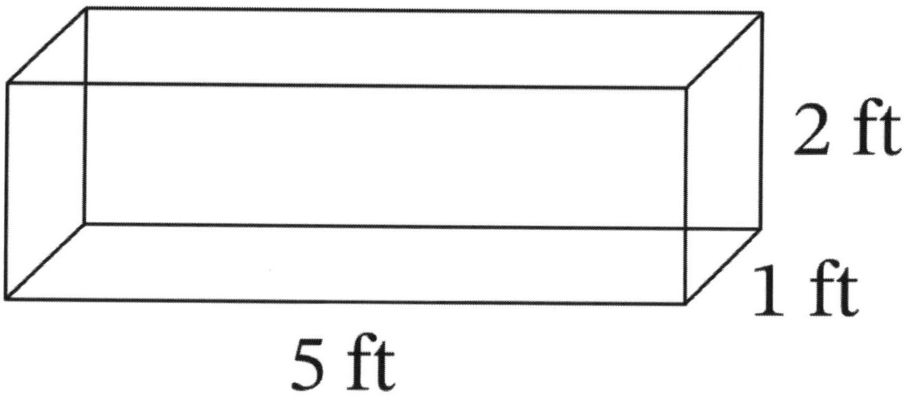

d. 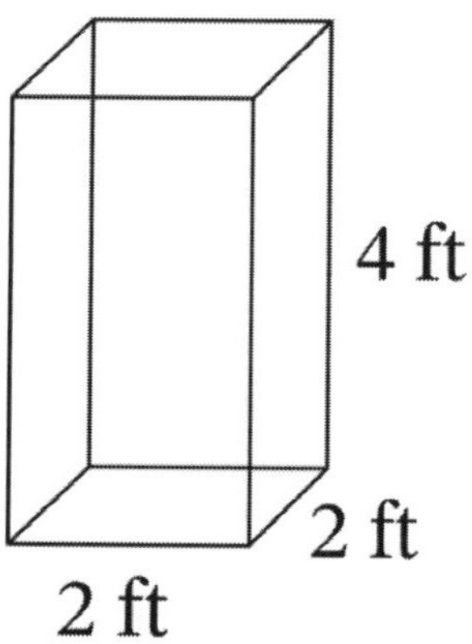

6. The shaded grid represents one whole.

Which shaded grid represents the expression 0.7×0.3?

a.

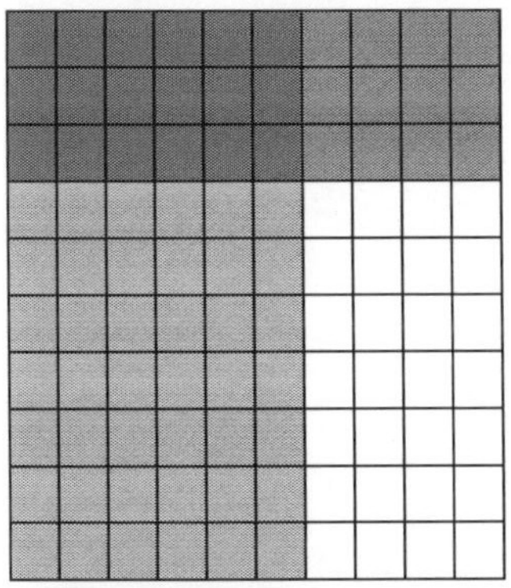

c.

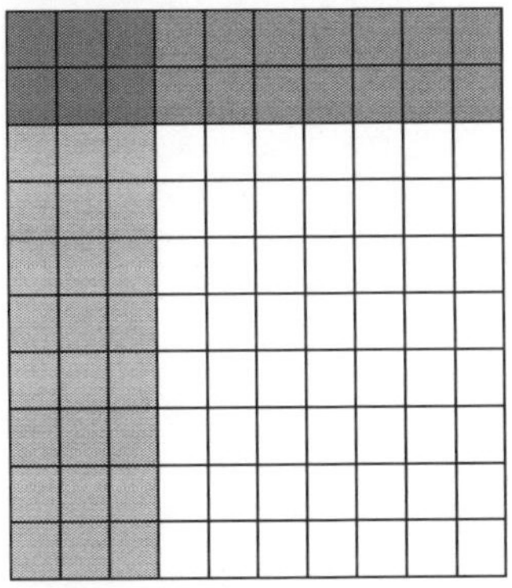

b.

d.

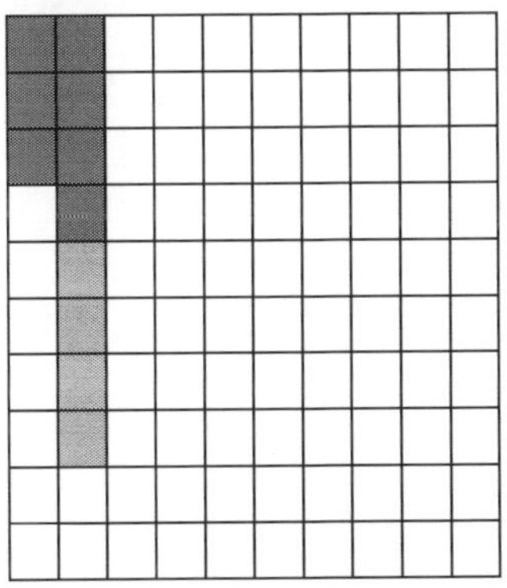

7. A large pitcher contains $\frac{1}{3}$ gallon of apple juice. If the same amount of juice is poured into 5 glasses, how many gallons of juice will each glass contain?

a. $\frac{1}{15}$ gallons

b. 15 gallons

c. $\frac{1}{3}$ gallons

d. $\frac{1}{5}$ gallons

8. Two-dimensional polygons are sorted within the Venn diagram below. Based on the diagram, what could the section on the left be labeled?

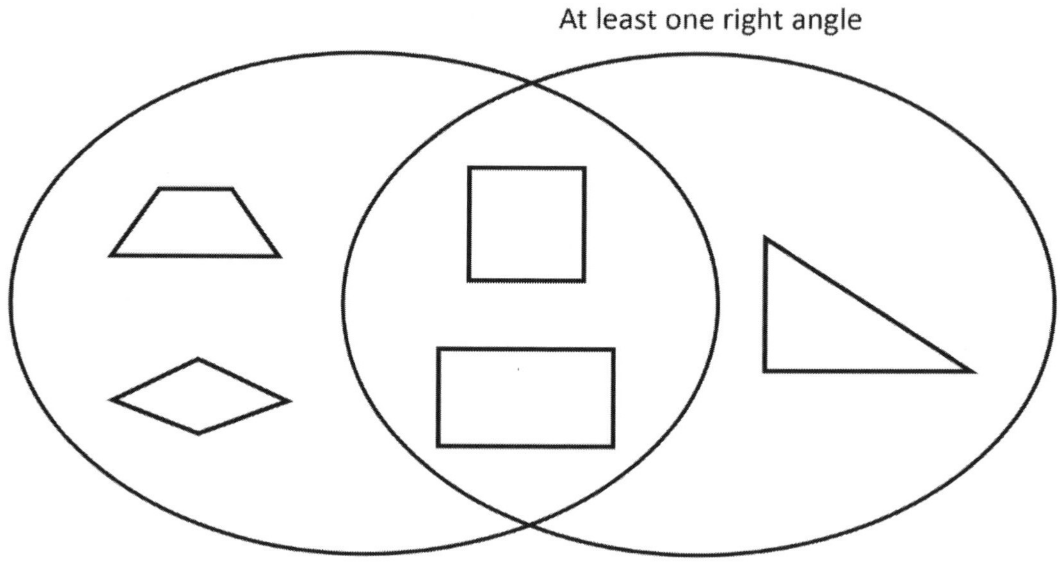

a. At least one right angle

b. Two sets of parallel sides

c. At least one set of parallel sides

d. At least three acute angles

9. Use the graph to correctly plot the data shown in the input-output table.

x	y
10	6
11	12
12	18
13	24

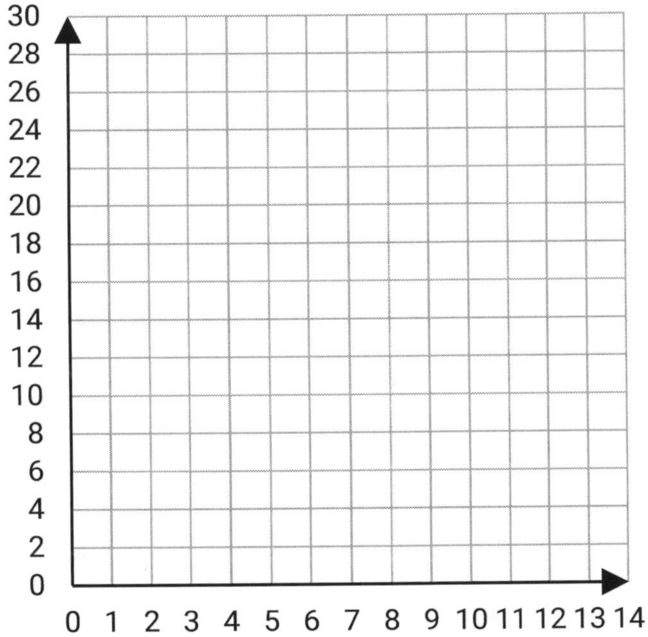

10. Jane practices the piano for $\frac{1}{4}$ of an hour, Monday through Friday. Shade in the model to show the number of hours Jane practices piano each day.

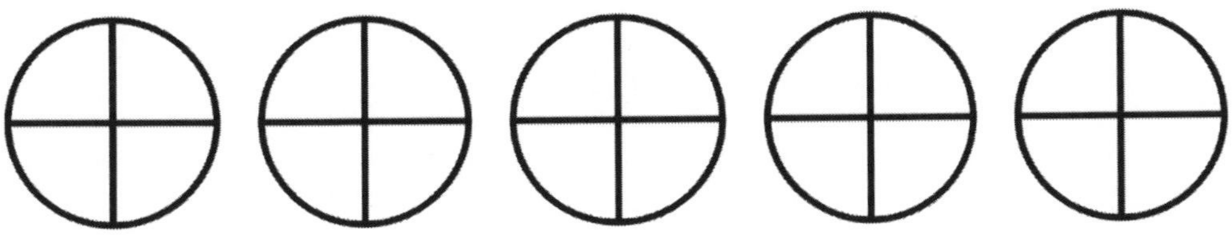

11. Robin earned $2,520 from babysitting this month. If she earned $28 per hour, how many hours did she work this month?

a. 28 hours
b. 84 hours
c. 90 hours
d. 100 hours

12. Jane is a member of a book club. The club is required to read 30 pages each day. Plot the ordered pairs on the graph that show Jane's required total reading over the first 4 days.

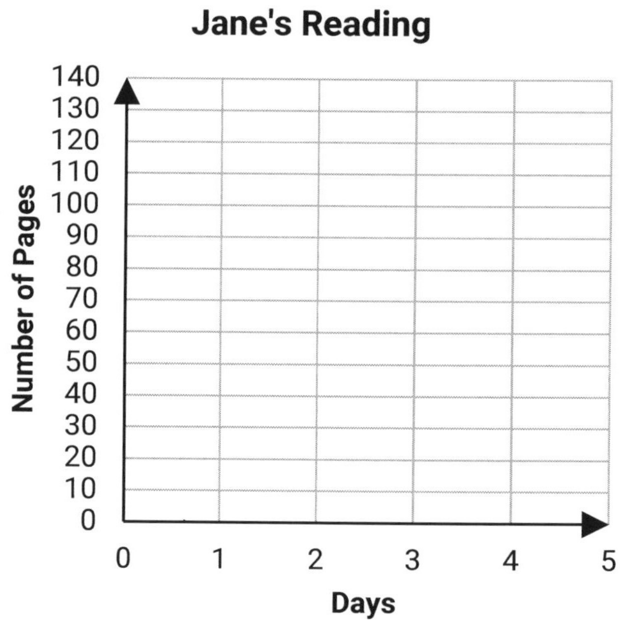

13. Marco's family has 4 dogs. The weight of each dog is listed below. Which two of the following comparisons of dog weight are NOT correct? Select all that apply.

Dog Name	Dog Weight (in pounds)
Franklin	60.34
Willow	55.8
Georgia	60.038
Baxter	56.08

a. Franklin > Georgia
b. Willow > Baxter
c. Baxter < Georgia
d. Georgia < Willow

14. Madison writes the numerical expression $[60(20-3)]+1$. Based on the grouping symbols, what is the correct order in which to solve the expression?

a. Subtract 3 from 20, then divide the result by 60. Then add 1.
b. Subtract 3 from 20, then add 1. Then multiply the result by 60.
c. Subtract 3 from 20, then multiply the result by 60. Then add 1.
d. Subtract 3 from 20, then multiply the result by 60.

15. Coach Ryan is purchasing basketball jerseys for his players. He purchases 3 large jerseys, 6 medium jerseys, and 2 small jerseys. What is the total cost of the jerseys?

Jersey Size	Jersey Price
Small	$18.99
Medium	$22.50
Large	$23.95

a. $244.83
b. $249.83
c. $254.83
d. $344.83

16. Craig lives in Portland and needs to attend a business meeting in Seattle. The train from Portland to Seattle covers a distance of 145.8 miles. If Craig rides the train from Portland to Seattle, and then back to Portland after the meeting, how many miles has he traveled?

a. 145.8
b. 218.7
c. 291.6
d. 437.6

17. Sarah earns $3,000 each month working at a daycare. She created a spreadsheet to track her spending for the month.

Expense	Amount
Health Insurance	$300
Energy Bill	$170
Contribution to Savings Account	$350
Eating out at Restaurants	$280
Rent	$2,100

What adjustment could be made in to help Sarah avoid her expenses exceeding her income next month?

a. Increase the budgeted amount for rent by $200.
b. Reduce the amount of money spent at restaurants by $20.
c. Reduce the amount of money spent at restaurants by $200.
d. Increase the budgeted amount for eating out at restaurants by $200.

18. Mr. Ray conducted a survey with his class of 5th graders. The survey asked students to list the career that is most interesting to them. The results of the survey are provided in the table below.

Career	Number of Students
Chef	1
Teacher	3
Athlete	5
Musician	4
Scientist	4

Fill in the bars on the bar graph to correctly represent the data in the table.

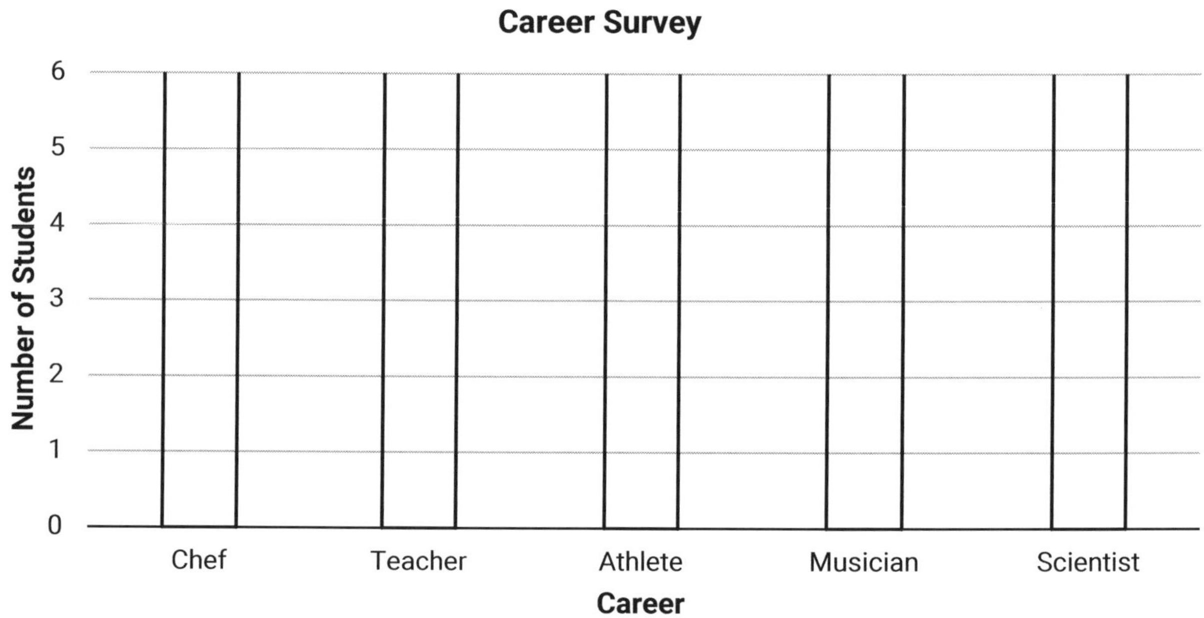

19. Cooper built a tower out of unit cubes. Which choice shows a correct way to calculate the volume of the tower?

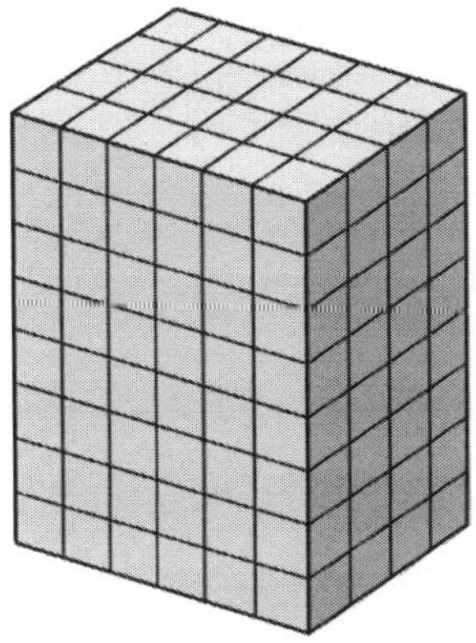

a. $(6 \times 8) + 4 = 52$ cubic units
b. $(6 + 4) \times 8 = 80$ cubic units
c. $(6 \times 4) \times 8 = 192$ cubic units
d. $(6 \times 4) + 8 = 32$ cubic units

20. Jeremy is purchasing canned cherries to make the filling for cherry pies. Jeremy buys 4 cans of cherries, and each can costs $1.56. How much does Jeremey spend on cherries?

a. $6.36
b. $6.24
c. $6.14
d. $5.46

21. Choose from the options below the blank and write in the options that best complete the statement.

Julie is checking out books from the library. She has a few books in her backpack she has renewed for the week, but she wants to check out more books. The table below shows the relationship between the number of books Julie checks out from the library and Julie's total number of books.

Number of Books Julie Checks Out	Julie's Total Number of Books
6	10
7	11
8	12
9	13

The relationship between the number of books Julie checks out and Julie's total number of books is ______________.

additive
multiplicative

This is because Julie's total number of books is always ______________ the number of books Julie checks out.

4 less than
4 more than
4 times more than

22. The Eiffel Tower stands 1,083.2 feet tall. From the very top of the tower down to the visitor's platform is 177 feet. How many feet high is the visitor's platform? Write your answer in the box.

23. Antonio is making homemade pasta. He rolls out a large rectangle of pasta dough and slices it into 4 equal strips. Antonio divides one of the strips into 8 equal pieces to make small shells.

Choose values from the options below and write them in the blanks to create an expression that represents one small shell piece as a fraction of the whole.

$\frac{1}{4}$	$\frac{1}{8}$	4	8

______÷______

24. Fill in the point that can be graphed using the following procedures.

1. Start at the origin.
2. Move 6 units to the right.
3. From this location, move 2 units up.

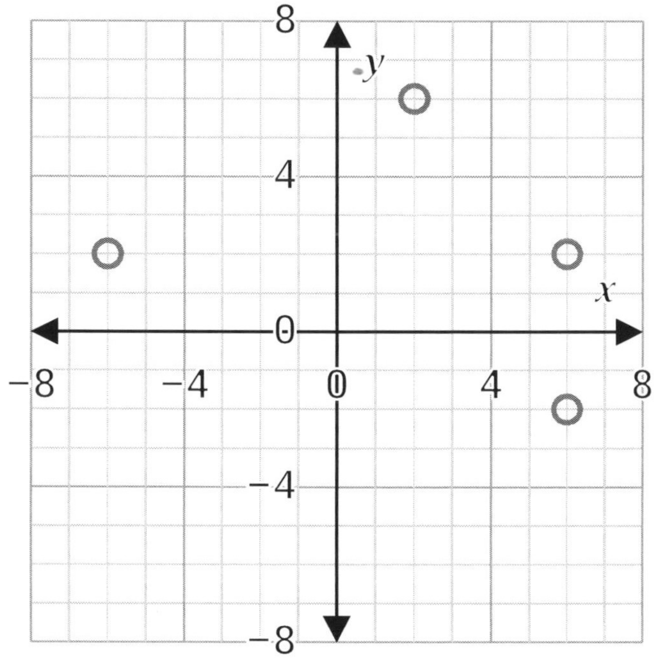

25. Daniel is simplifying the expression $3(60 + 4) - 11$. Which choice describes the role of the parentheses within the expression?

a. Add 60 and 4 before multiplying by 3.

b. Subtract 11 before adding 60 and 4.

c. Multiply 3 by 11 before adding 60 and 4.

d. Add 4 after multiplying 3 by 60.

26. Mr. Lawson planted 15 rows of blueberry bushes. Each row contained 8 bushes. He planted 3 times as many rhubarb plants. How many rhubarb plants did Mr. Lawson plant? Write your answer in the blank.

27. John wants to rent an e-bike to tour the city of Austin. E-bikes can be rented for $40 per hour. John expects to rent a bike for 3 hours. John can calculate the total cost using the equation $y = 40x$, where y represents the price in dollars, and x represents the number of hours. Which graph represents the relationship between time and cost for this scenario?

a.

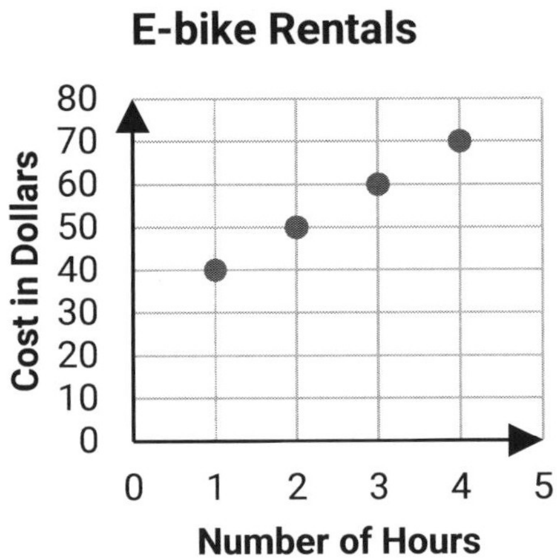

c.

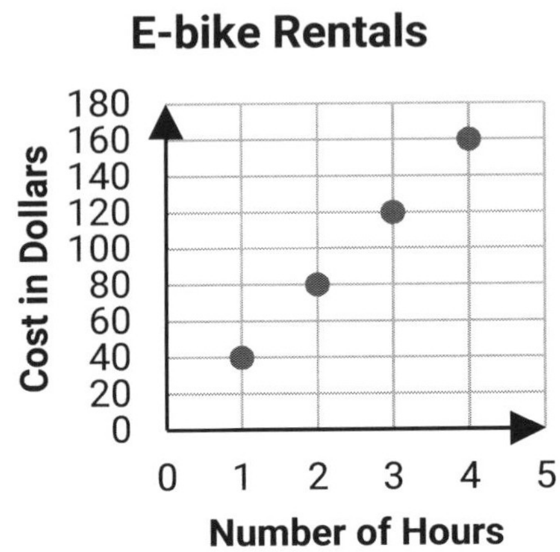

b.

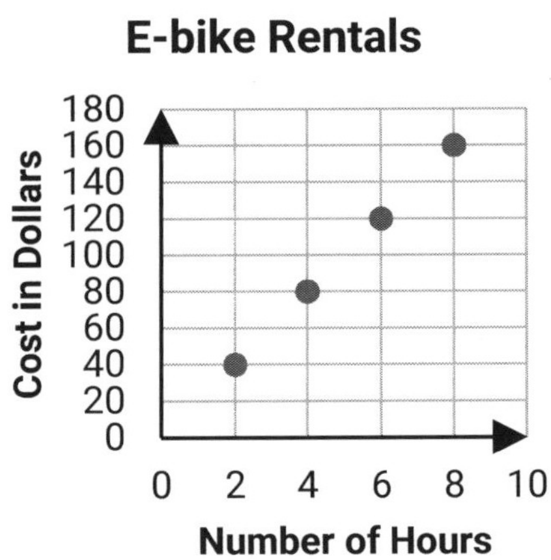

d.

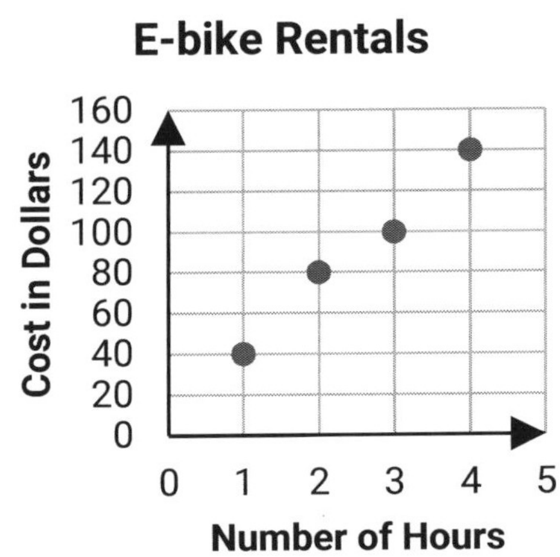

28. Frank is selling snacks at a basketball game. A customer purchases 3 bags of popcorn and 2 hotdogs. If the customer pays for the snacks using four 5-dollar bills, how much is the customer owed in change?

Item	Price
Hotdog	$2.50
Chips	$1.50
Popcorn bag	$3.90

a. $2.30
b. $3.35
c. $3.30
d. $3.70

29. A candy company created a survey to determine which of their new candy flavors is most popular. The results are displayed in the frequency table.

Favorite Flavor	Frequency
Watermelon	2
Grape	16
Cherry	4
Apple	8
Strawberry	11

The results of the survey reveal that about twice as many customers prefer which flavor when compared to the apple flavor?

a. Watermelon
b. Grape
c. Cherry
d. Strawberry

30. What is the value of $6 \div \frac{1}{4}$?

a. 22
b. $\frac{4}{6}$
c. 24
d. $\frac{6}{4}$

31. Lucy is selling lemonade to earn some cash. She uses a lemonade pitcher that holds 2 pints of liquid. On the first day she had to refill her pitcher 6 times to keep up with the lemonade sales. How many ounces of lemonade did Lucy serve on the first day?

a. 12
b. 24
c. 64
d. 192

32. Ms. Erikson is estimating driving distances for possible summer road trips. If she continues to estimate in the same manner, what would Ms. Erikson's estimate be for a road trip that is 359.9 miles?

Distance (in miles)	Estimation (in miles)
194.8	200
145.9	100
308.33	300
356.2	400

a. 300
b. 350
c. 400
d. 450

33. Bryce is walking laps with his dog around a rectangular park. The width of the park is 0.25 miles and the length of the park is 0.65 miles. How far will Bryce walk if he completes 3 laps around the park?

a. 2.7 miles
b. 3.45 miles
c. 4.65 miles
d. 5.4 miles

34. Choose from the options below the blank and write in the options that best complete the statement.

Sam sells pottery from his art studio. He sells large bowls for $45 and small bowls for $28. Claire purchased 8 large bowls and 10 small bowls. David purchased 6 large bowls and 12 small bowls.

______ spent	____ more than	______.
David	$34	David
Claire	$43	Claire

Answer Key and Explanations for Test #1

1. thousandths: TEKS Standard (5.2)(A)

The decimal point separates the ones place from the tenths place. Each digit to the left of the decimal point increases by a factor of 10. Each digit to the right of the decimal point decreases by a factor of 10. In this case, the 5 is located 3 places to the right of the decimal point. In the value 674.215, the 2 is in the tenths place, the 1 is in the hundredths place, and the 5 is in the thousandths place. A 5 in the thousandths place is equivalent to $\frac{5}{1,000}$, or 5 thousandths.

2. D: TEKS Standard (5.3)(G)

432.5 can be separated equally into 5 days of driving. Long division can be applied. Follow the four-step process: Divide, Multiply, Subtract, Bring Down.

5 fits into 4 zero times. However, 5 fits into 43 eight times. Write 8 above the 3.

8 times 5 is 40. 43 minus 40 is 3.

Bring down the next digit. 3 becomes 32.

5 fits into 32 six times. Write 6 above the 2.

6 times 5 is 30. 32 minus 30 is 2.

Bring down the next digit. 2 becomes 25.

5 fits into 25 five times. Write 5 above the 5.

5 times 5 is 25. 25 minus 25 is 0.
Bring the decimal straight up into the answer.

865 becomes 86.5.

$$
\begin{array}{r}
86.5 \\
5\overline{)\,432.5} \\
\underline{-40} \\
32 \\
\underline{-30} \\
25 \\
\underline{-25} \\
0
\end{array}
$$

Amy's family should drive 86.5 miles each day.

3. B: TEKS Standard (5.3)(G)

5 siblings are sharing the cost of a \$629.95 necklace. This represents a division scenario. The amount of money each sibling will contribute can be calculated as \$629.95 ÷ 5. In this scenario, \$629.95 is the dividend, and 5 is the divisor.

The long division algorithm can be applied. Follow the 4-step process: Divide, Multiply, Subtract, Bring Down.

5 fits into 6 one time.

1 multiplied by 5 is 5.

6 minus 5 is 1.

Bring down the next digit, 2. So, 1 becomes 12.

Repeat the process four more times.

Bring the decimal point straight up into the answer line.

```
   125.99
5) 629.95
  -5
   12
  -10
    29
   -25
     49
    -45
      45
     -45
       0
```

The result is 125.99 which represents \$125.99. Therefore, each sibling will contribute \$125.99.

4. C: TEKS Standard (5.9)(B)

Graph C is the only graph that shows all data points graphed correctly. To graph a point that represents the friend who is 9 years old and has gone on 4 flights, start at the origin, then move 9 units to the right and 4 units up. Graph the rest of the points in a similar way.

Graph A is missing the data point for (9,4). This represents a person that is 9 years old and has flown 4 times.

Graph B has incorrect labels for the x- and y-axis.

Graph D is missing the points (12,8) and (13,7). (12,8) represents a person that is 12 years old and has flown 8 times. (13,7) represents a person that is 13 years old and has flown 7 times.

5. B: TEKS Standard (5.4)(H)

The volume of the freezer can be determined using the volume formula for a rectangular prism: $V = l \times w \times h$. The only freezer with a volume of 36 ft^3 is choice B. This freezer has a length of 4 feet, a width of 3 feet, and a height of 3 feet.

$$V = 4 \times 3 \times 3$$

$$V = 36$$

Freezer A has a volume of $V = 3 \times 1 \times 2$ which simplifies to 6 ft^3. Freezer C has a volume of $V = 5 \times 1 \times 2$ which simplifies to $V = 10$ ft^3. Freezer D has a volume of $V = 2 \times 2 \times 4$ which simplifies to $V = 16$ ft^3. Only freezer B meets the volume requirements of James' freezer.

6. B: TEKS Standard (5.3)(D)

Choice B shows 3 horizontal shaded bars and 7 vertical shaded bars. Each bar represents $\frac{1}{10}$, so 3 bars represents 0.3 and 7 bars represents 0.7. The overlapping shaded region of 0.3 and 0.7 is the dark shaded region. There are 21 dark shaded squares. Each square represents $\frac{1}{100}$. There are 21 shaded hundredths, so the answer is $\frac{21}{100}$ or 0.21. The product of 0.3 and 0.7 is modeled correctly in choice B.

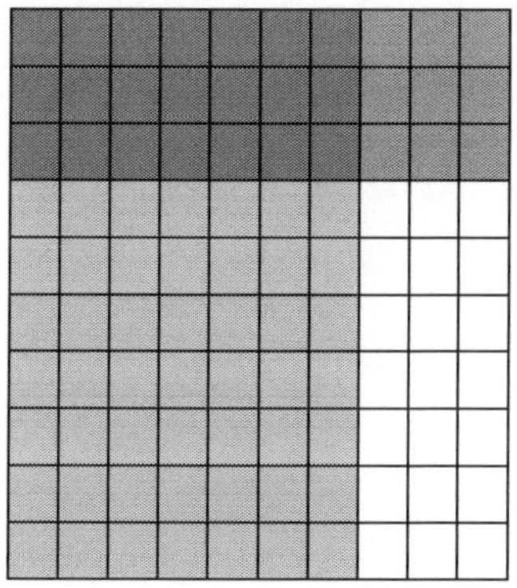

7. A: TEKS Standard (5.3)(L)

$\frac{1}{3}$ gallon of apple juice is poured into 5 glasses. This represents a division scenario, $\frac{1}{3}$ is divided into 5 equal groups. Use the strategy of "Keep, Change, Flip" to calculate $\frac{1}{3} \div 5$. Keep the first value the same. Keep $\frac{1}{3}$ as $\frac{1}{3}$. Change the $\div$ symbol to a $\times$ symbol. Flip the second value. 5 becomes $\frac{1}{5}$. $\frac{1}{3} \div 5$ becomes $\frac{1}{3} \times \frac{1}{5}$. To multiply fractions, multiply the numerators together and the denominators together, resulting in $\frac{1}{15}$. Each glass will contain $\frac{1}{15}$ gallons of juice.

8. C: TEKS Standard (5.5)(A)

The right section of the Venn diagram contains a shape with at least one right angle. The left section of the Venn diagram contains quadrilaterals that all have at least one set of parallel sides. The middle section of the Venn diagram contains polygons that have at least one right angle and have at least one set of parallel sides. Choice C is the only correct label for the section on the left.

Choice A is incorrect because none of the polygons on the left have right angles.

Choice B is incorrect because one of the polygons on the left does not have two sets of parallel sides.

Choice D is incorrect because none of the polygons on the left have at least three acute angles.

9. TEKS Standard (5.8)(C)

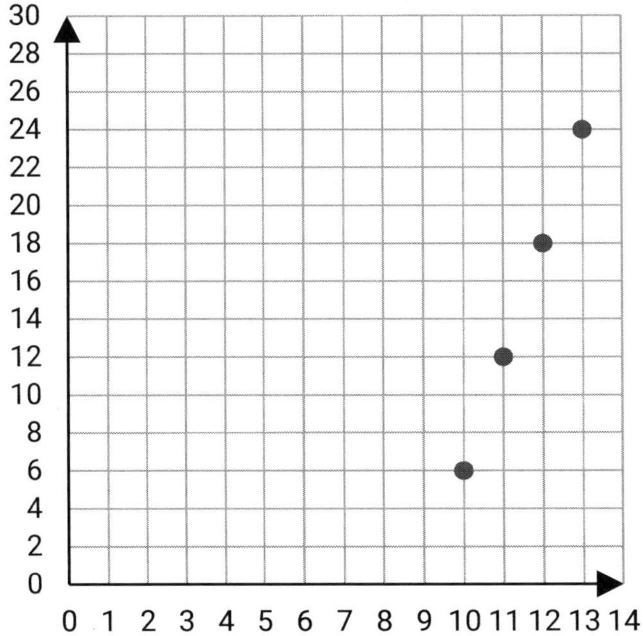

The input-output table displays x-values and y-values that form ordered pairs. The ordered pairs listed in the input-output table are (10,6), (11,12), (12,18), and (13, 24). x-values are listed first, and y-values are listed second: (x, y). x-values are located along the horizontal axis, and y-values are located along the vertical axis. To plot the point (10,6), start at the origin and move 10 places to the right and then 6 places up. Use the same process for the other three points.

10. TEKS Standard (5.3)(I)

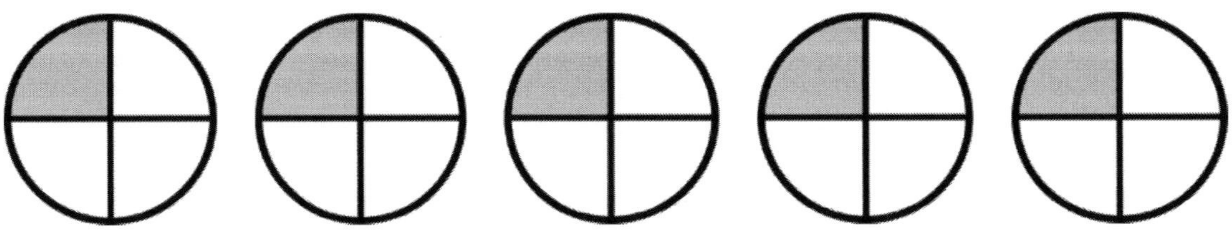

Jane practices $\frac{1}{4}$ of an hour Monday through Friday. This means that Jane practices $\frac{1}{4}$ of an hour 5 days a week. When one wedge on each of the five circles is filled in, the model correctly illustrates 5 groups of $\frac{1}{4}$ as a model.

11. C: TEKS Standard (5.3)(C)

Robin earned $2,520 total and earned $28 per hour. This represents a division scenario. The total number of hours can be calculated by dividing the total amount of money earned by the amount of money earned per hour. 2,520 ÷ 28 can be solved using the long division algorithm.

$$\begin{array}{r} 90 \\ 28\overline{)\,2520} \\ \underline{-252} \\ 00 \\ \underline{-0} \\ 0 \end{array}$$

28 is too large to fit into 2. 28 is too large to fit into 25. 28 fits into 252 nine times. Write 9 above the farthest place value to the right within the number 252.

$9 \times 28 = 252$. Subtract and bring down the next digit, which is 0.

28 goes into 0 zero times. Write 0 below 0. $0 \times 28 = 0$. Subtract. There are no remainders.

The quotient of 2,520 and 28 is 90, so Robin worked 90 hours this month.

12. TEKS Standard (5.8)(C)

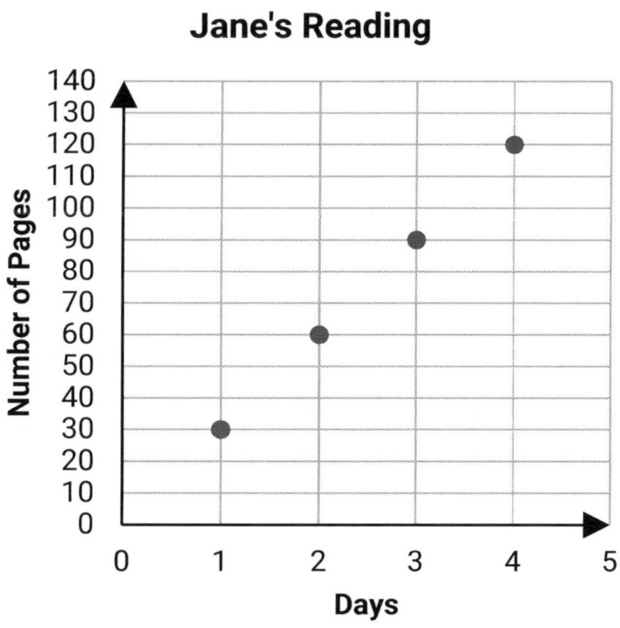

Jane is required to read 30 pages each day. This means that on day 1, Jane will read a total of 30 pages. On day 2, Jane will have read 60 total pages. On day 3, Jane will have read a total of 90 pages. On day 4, Jane will have read a total of 120 pages.

This pattern can be expressed using the ordered pairs (1,30), (2,60), (3,90), and (4,120). The first number in each ordered pair represents the x-value. The second value in each ordered pair represents the y-value.

13. B, D: TEKS Standard (5.2)(B)

When comparing decimal values, compare each place value one at a time from left to right.

6	0.	3	4		Franklin
6	0.	0	3	4	Georgia
5	6.	0	8		Baxter
5	5.	8			Willow

Franklin and Georgia have the same digits in the tens and ones places. However, Franklin has a larger digit in the tenths place. This means that Franklin is the heaviest dog. Georgia is the second heaviest dog.

Baxter and Willow have the same digit in the tens place, but Baxter has a larger digit in the ones place. This means that Baxter is heavier than Willow. Baxter is the third heaviest dog, and Willow is the fourth heaviest dog.

6	0.	3	4		Franklin
6	0.	0	3	4	Georgia
5	6.	0	8		Baxter
5	5.	8			Willow

$$60.34 > 60.034 > 56.08 > 55.8$$

Franklin > Georgia > Baxter > Willow

Recall, the symbol > means, "greater than," and the symbol < means, "less than." The comparisons Franklin > Georgia and Baxter < Georgia are true. Willow is the least heavy dog and Baxter is the second least heavy dog, so Baxter is heavier than Willow. Willow > Baxter is not true because 55.8 is not greater than 56.08. Georgia is the second heaviest dog and Willow is the least heavy dog. This means that Georgia is heavier than Willow. Georgia < Willow is not true because 60.034 is not less than 55.8.

14. C: TEKS Standard (5.4)(F)

The order of operations, or PEMDAS, is a reference to the correct order in which to simplify a numerical expression. PEMDAS refers to parentheses, exponents, multiplication & division, and addition & subtraction. In the expression $[60(20-3)]+1$, the math within the parentheses should be simplified first. In this case, 3 is subtracted from 20. The next step is to multiply the result by 60. The last step is to add 1.

15. A: TEKS Standard (5.3)(E)

Coach Ryan purchased 3 large jerseys that cost \$23.95 each. The cost of the large jerseys can be determined by multiplying 3 × 23.95.

$$\begin{array}{r} {}^{1\,2\ \ 1} \\ 23.95 \\ \times \quad 3 \\ \hline 71.85 \end{array}$$

Coach Ryan purchased 6 medium jerseys that cost \$22.50 each. The cost of the of the medium jerseys can be determined by multiplying 6 × 22.50.

$$\begin{array}{r} {}^{1\,3\quad} \\ 22.50 \\ \times \quad 6 \\ \hline 135.00 \end{array}$$

Coach Ryan purchased 2 small jerseys that cost \$18.99 each. The cost of the medium jerseys can be determined by multiplying 2 × 18.99.

$$\begin{array}{r} {}^{1\,1\quad} \\ 18.99 \\ \times \quad 2 \\ \hline 37.98 \end{array}$$

Coach Ryan's total payment will be the sum of the price of all small, medium, and large jerseys purchased.

71.85 + 135.00 + 37.98 = 244.83. Coach Ryan spent \$244.83 on the basketball jerseys.

16. C: TEKS Standard (5.3)(K)

The train from Portland to Seattle is 145.8 miles. Craig needs to take the train from Portland to Seattle, and then from Seattle to Portland. This means that Craig will travel 145.8 + 145.8 miles. To add the decimal values, stack both numbers and line up the decimal points. Add each column from right to left. Regroup when necessary. The sum of 145.8 + 145.8 is 291.6. Therefore, Craig traveled 291.6 miles.

$$\begin{array}{r} {}^{1\,1\quad} \\ 145.8 \\ +145.8 \\ \hline 291.6 \end{array}$$

17. C: TEKS Standard (5.10)(E)

Sarah earns \$3,000 each month. When added together, her expenses are \$3,200. This means that Sarah's spending has exceeded her income by \$200. The only expense that can realistically be reduced or eliminated is the category for eating out at restaurants. If this expense is reduced by \$200, Sarah will break even. Sarah's income will be \$3,000 and her expenses will be \$3,000. Choice C is the best option for Sarah.

18. TEKS Standard (5.9)(A)

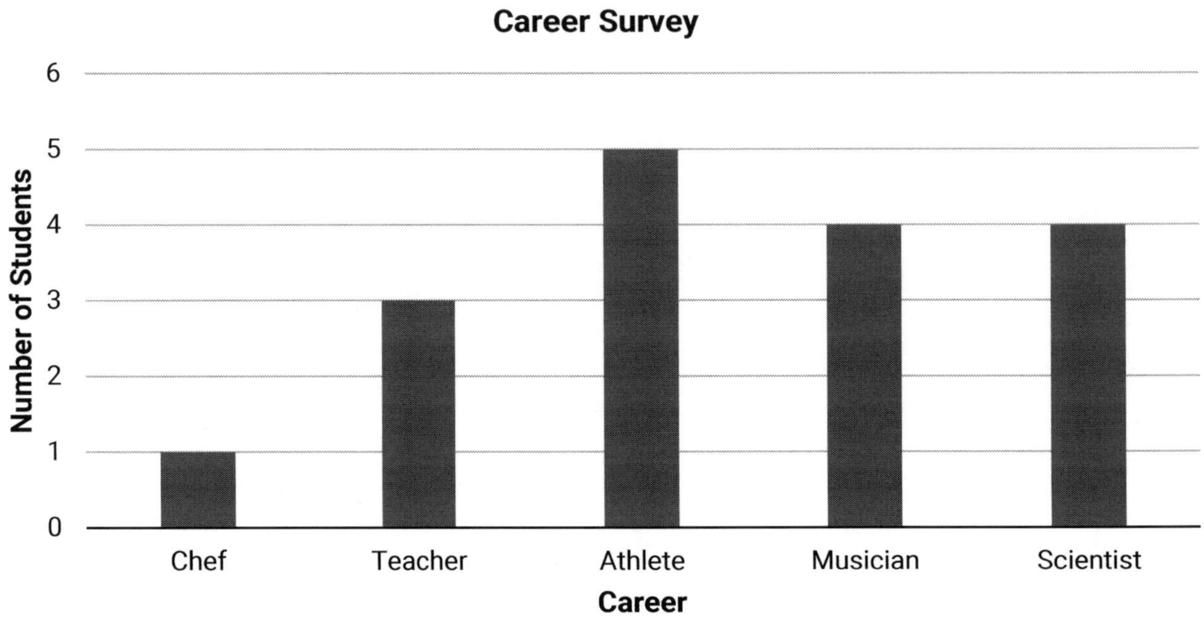

The bar for each career should extend until it reaches the number on the graph that matches the value for that career on the table. The bar for "Scientist" reaches 4, the bar for "Musician" reaches 4, the bar for "Athlete" reaches 5, the bar for "Teacher" reaches 3, and the bar for "Chef" reaches 1.

19. C: TEKS Standard (5.6)(B)

One way to calculate the total number of unit cubes in Cooper's tower is to determine the number of cubes in one layer, and then multiply this value by the number of layers. In this case, there are 6×4 unit cubes in one layer. There are 8 layers in the tower, so $(6 \times 4) \times 8$ will result in the total number of unit cubes.

The total number of unit cubes in the tower represents the volume of the tower. In this case, $(6 \times 4) \times 8$ simplifies to 192, so the volume of the tower is 192 cubic units.

20. B: TEKS Standard (5.3)(E)

Jeremy buys 4 cans of cherries, and each can costs $1.56. 4 groups of $1.56 represents a multiplication scenario. The product of 4 and 1.56 can be calculated using the standard algorithm. Start by stacking 1.56 on top of 4. When multiplying decimals, the place value does not need to be lined up. Line up the farthest digits to the right. In this case, 6 and 4 will be in the same column. Now that the values are oriented, begin distributing the 4 to each digit of 1.56.

$$\begin{array}{r} 1.56 \\ \times \quad 4 \\ \hline \end{array}$$

Multiply the 4 by each digit in 1.56.

$4 \times 6 = 24$. Write 2 above the 5 and 4 under the answer line.

$4 \times 5 = 20$. Add the 2 from above. The result is 22. Write 2 above the 1 and the other 2 under the answer line.

$4 \times 1 = 1$. Add the 2 from above. The result is 6. Write 6 under the answer line.

The result is 624.

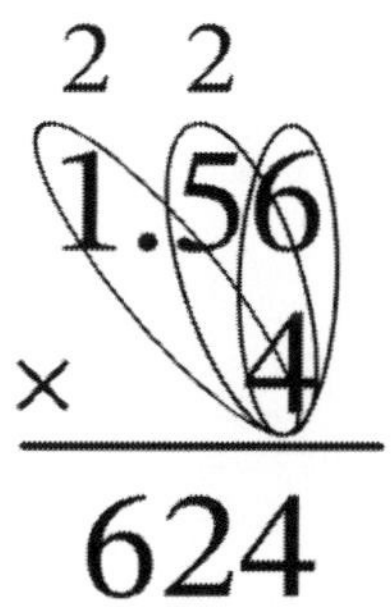

Now, place the decimal point in 624. Count the decimal movements for both 1.56 and 4. Notice there are two decimal movements in the number 1.56. 4 does not have any decimal movements. 2 decimal movements plus 0 decimal movements is a total of 2 decimal movements. This means that the decimal point within 624 needs to also have 2 decimal movements.

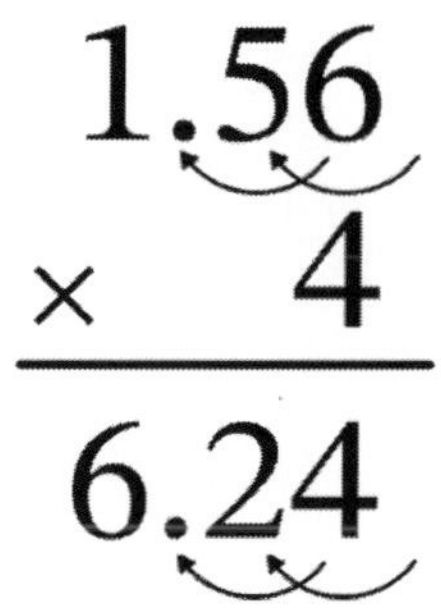

The final answer is 6.24. Jeremy spent $6.24 on canned cherries.

21. additive, 4 more than: TEKS Standard (5.4)(D)

This relationship represents an additive numerical pattern. The total number of books is always 4 more than the number of books Julie checks out. In other words, the total number of books is equal to the number of books Julie checks out plus 4. The equation $y = x + 4$ is an additive relationship. Each value of y is the result of adding 4 to the corresponding x-value. For example, if Julie checks out 10 books, 10 can be added to 4 to calculate the total number of books she has in her possession.

22. 906.2: TEKS Standard (5.3)(K)

The top of the tower has a height of 1,083.2 feet. The visitor's platform is 177 feet lower than the top of the tower. Subtract 177 from 1,083.2 to determine the height of the visitor's platform. 177 is equivalent to 177.0. Stack 1,083.2 and 177.0 and line up the decimal points. Subtract each place value from right to left. Regroup when necessary. The result is 906.2. The visitor's platform has a height of 906.2 feet.

$$\begin{array}{r} {\scriptstyle 0\;10\;7\;13} \\ \not{1}\not{0}\not{8}\not{3}.\,2 \\ -177.\,0 \\ \hline 906.\,2 \end{array}$$

23.$\frac{1}{4} \div 8$: TEKS Standard (5.3)(J)

The whole is divided into 4 strips. Each strip represents $\frac{1}{4}$ of the whole. Dividing one strip into 8 pieces is expressed as $\frac{1}{4}$ divided by 8. In other words, $\frac{1}{4} \div 8$.

24. TEKS Standard (5.8)(B)

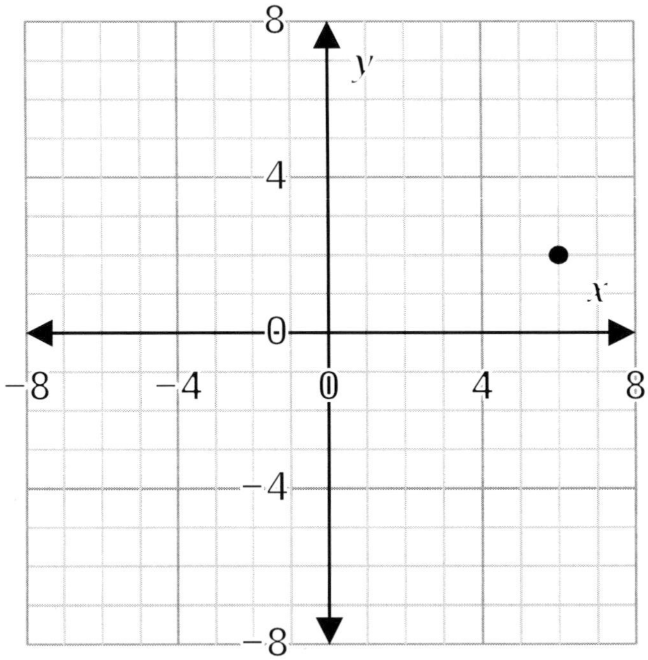

Because we are starting at the origin and moving 6 places to the right and 2 places up, this represents the ordered pair (6,2). The first number listed in an ordered pair represents the x-value, or the horizontal movement from the origin. The second number listed in an ordered pair represents the y-value, or the vertical movement from the origin. The ordered pair (6,2) indicates a horizontal movement of 6 and a vertical movement of 2. This matches the given procedures. $(-6,2)$ and $(6,-2)$ are incorrect due to the negative values. Negative values are not graphed in the first quadrant. (2,6)is incorrect because the x- and y-values are switched.

25. A: TEKS Standard (5.4)(E)

Parentheses and brackets act as grouping symbols within expressions. These grouping symbols are used to represent which section of an expression to simplify first. In this case, the parentheses around $60 + 4$ indicates that 60 needs to be added to 4 before multiplying the sum by 3, and then subtracting 11.

26. 360: TEKS Standard (5.4)(F)

15 rows of blueberries were planted and there are 8 bushes in each row. The expression (8×15) represents the number of blueberry bushes planted. It is given that 3 times as many rhubarb plants were planted, which means (8×15) should be multiplied by 3.

$$3(8 \times 15) = 3(120) = 360$$

Mr. Lawson planted 360 rhubarb plants.

27. C: TEKS Standard (5.4)(C)

It costs John \$40 per hour to rent an E-bike. This rule describes a pattern where 1 hour costs \$40, 2 hours costs \$80, 3 hours costs \$120, and 4 hours costs \$160. The price of each hour increases by \$40. The equation $y = 40x$ is correctly represented in graph C. Graph C displays time on the x-axis, cost on the y-axis, and correct data points. Graphs A, B, and D have the correct axis labels but incorrect data points.

28. C: TEKS Standard (5.4)(B)

Each bag of popcorn costs \$3.90, and Frank sells 3 bags. This simplifies to 3×3.9. Each hotdog costs \$2.50, and Frank sells 2. This simplifies to 2×2.5. The total cost is calculated by finding the sum of 3×3.9 and 2×2.5. The equation $c = 3(3.9) + 2(2.5)$ represents the scenario. To solve for the variable c, multiply 3 by 3.9, and 2 by 2.5.

$$3 \times 3.9 = 11.7$$

$$2 \times 2.5 = 5$$

The sum of 11.7 and 5 is 16.7. This represents \$16.70. The customer spent \$16.70 and paid with four 5-dollar bills. This means that the customer paid \$20 for a purchase of \$16.70. Subtract to calculate the customer's change, $20.00 - 16.70 = 3.30$. The customer will receive \$3.30 in change.

29. B: TEKS Standard (5.9)(C)

The frequency table shows that 2 customers prefer watermelon, 16 customers prefer grape, 4 customers prefer cherry, 8 customers prefer apple, and 11 customers prefer strawberry. Grape (16) had twice as many votes as apple (8). This means that twice as many customers prefer the grape flavor compared to the apple flavor.

30. C: TEKS Standard (5.3)(L)

$6 \div \frac{1}{4}$ can be visualized as 6 wholes being divided into groups of $\frac{1}{4}$. In other words, each whole will be divided into 4 pieces. This results in 24 equal shares of $\frac{1}{4}$. So, $6 \div \frac{1}{4} = 24$.

Another way to solve $6 \div \frac{1}{4}$ is to use the strategy of "Keep, Change, Flip." Keep the first value the same. Keep the 6 as a 6. Change the $\div$ symbol to a $\times$ symbol. Flip the second value so that $\frac{1}{4}$ becomes $\frac{4}{1}$. This results in $\frac{6}{1} \times \frac{4}{1}$. To multiply fractions, multiply the numerators together and the denominators together, resulting in $\frac{24}{1}$, or 24.

31. D: TEKS Standard (5.7)(A)

Lucy's pitcher holds 2 pints of liquid. Since there are 8 ounces in 1 cup and there are 2 cups in 1 pint, there must be 16 ounces in a pint. This means that Lucy's pitcher holds $2 \times 16 = 32$ ounces. Lucy refills her pitcher 6 times. This means that Lucy serves $32 \times 6 = 192$ ounces of lemonade.

32. C: TEKS Standard (5.3)(A)

Ms. Erikson has rounded each driving distance in the table to the nearest hundred. When Ms. Erikson rounds 359.9 miles to the nearest hundred, the result is 400 miles. Answer A is incorrect because 359.9 is nearer to 400 than it is to 300 since 359.9 is greater than 350. Answers B and D are incorrect because Ms. Erikson is rounding to the nearest hundred.

33. D: TEKS Standard (5.4)(H)

The perimeter of the park can be calculated using the formula $P = 2l + 2w$. In this case, the length of the park is 0.65 miles and the width of the park is 0.25 miles.

$$P = 2(0.65) + 2(0.25)$$

$$P = 1.3 + 0.5$$

$$P = 1.8$$

The perimeter is 1.8 miles, which is also the distance walked in one lap. Bryce walks three laps, so his mileage can be determined by multiplying 1.8 by 3.

$$1.8 \times 3 = 5.4$$

Bryce walks 5.4 miles.

34. Claire, $34, David: TEKS Standard (5.4)(B)

Claire purchased 8 large bowls that cost $45 each. This is expressed as 8×45. Claire also purchased 10 small bowls that cost $28 each. This is expressed as 10×28. The sum of these two values determines Claire's total purchase price, c. So, $c = 8 \times 45 + 10 \times 28$. This simplifies to $c = 360 + 280$ and then $c = 640$. Claire spent $640 at the art studio.

David purchased 6 large bowls that each cost $45. This is expressed as 6×45. David also purchased 12 small bowls that cost $28 each. This is expressed as 12×28. The sum of these two values determines David's total purchase price, d. So, $d = 6 \times 45 + 12 \times 28$. This simplifies to $d = 270 + 336$ and then $d = 606$. David spent $606 at the art studio.

Claire spent $640 and David spent $606. The difference is calculated by subtracting 606 from 640: $640 - 606 = 34$. This means that Claire spent $34 more than David.

Practice Test #2

1. Peter is a chicken farmer. He sells eggs each week in town at the farmer's market. Today Peter is packing up eggs into flat cartons of 30 eggs. Peter then stacks up 5 cartons and takes them to the market. How many eggs does Peter take to the market?

a. 90 eggs
b. 120 eggs
c. 150 eggs
d. 180 eggs

2. 360 children have signed up to play in the youth soccer league. The league wants to create teams with 15 players each. How many teams will the league create?

a. 24
b. 36
c. 48
d. 60

3. Anna is a jewelry designer. She can assemble 12 earrings per hour. The equation $y = 12x$ can be used to represent this relationship. Which table represents the rule $y = 12x$?

a.

x	y
1	12
2	13
3	14
4	15

b.

x	y
1	12
2	24
3	30
4	48

c.

x	y
1	12
2	24
3	36
4	48

d.

x	y
0	12
2	24
4	36
6	48

4. Jamie is paid \$22 per hour and received a one-time tip of \$50. The variable x represents the number of hours that Jamie worked. The variable y represents the one-time tip of \$50. Which table represents this scenario?

a.

x	y
1	70
2	80
3	90

b.

x	y
1	72
2	94
3	116

c.

x	y
1	72
2	100
3	133

d.

x	y
1	22
2	44
3	66

5. Ryan travels 15 miles every hour on his bike. Which display shows the correct coordinates for Ryan's bike milage? Plot at least three points on the graph that display the relationship between the number of hours that Ryan bikes and the number of miles that Ryan travels.

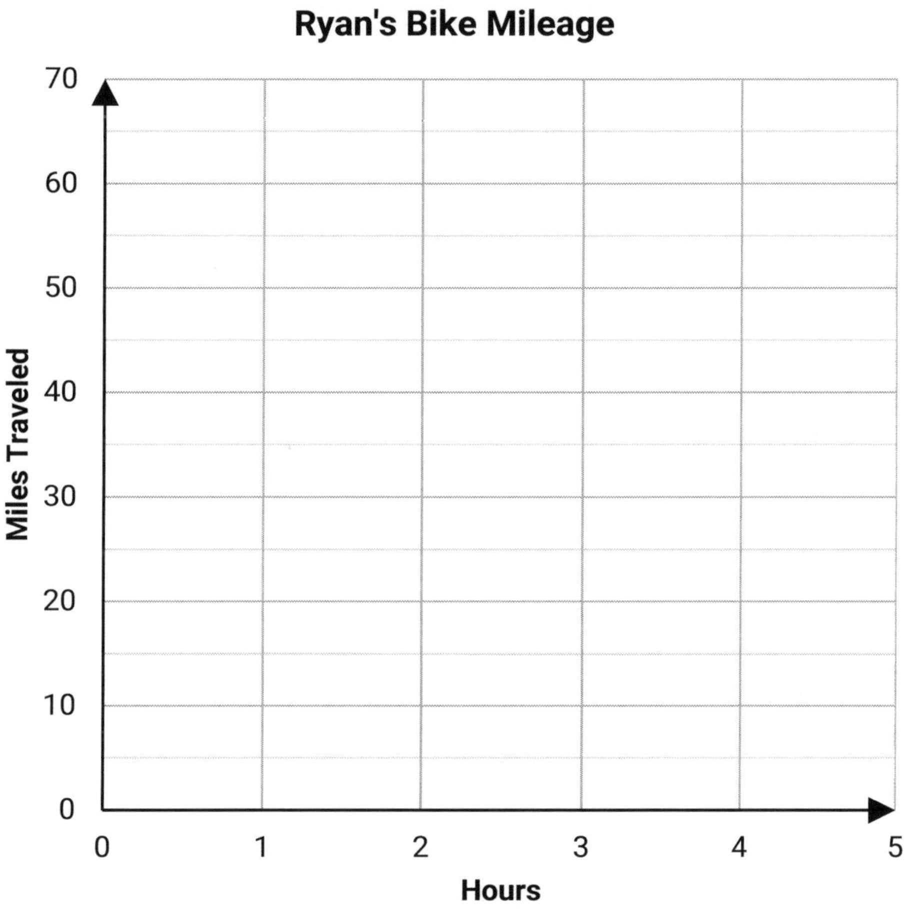

6. Jill is selling strawberry smoothies for $3.50. Plot at least four points on the graph that show the relationship between the number of smoothies that are sold and the amount of money Jill earns.

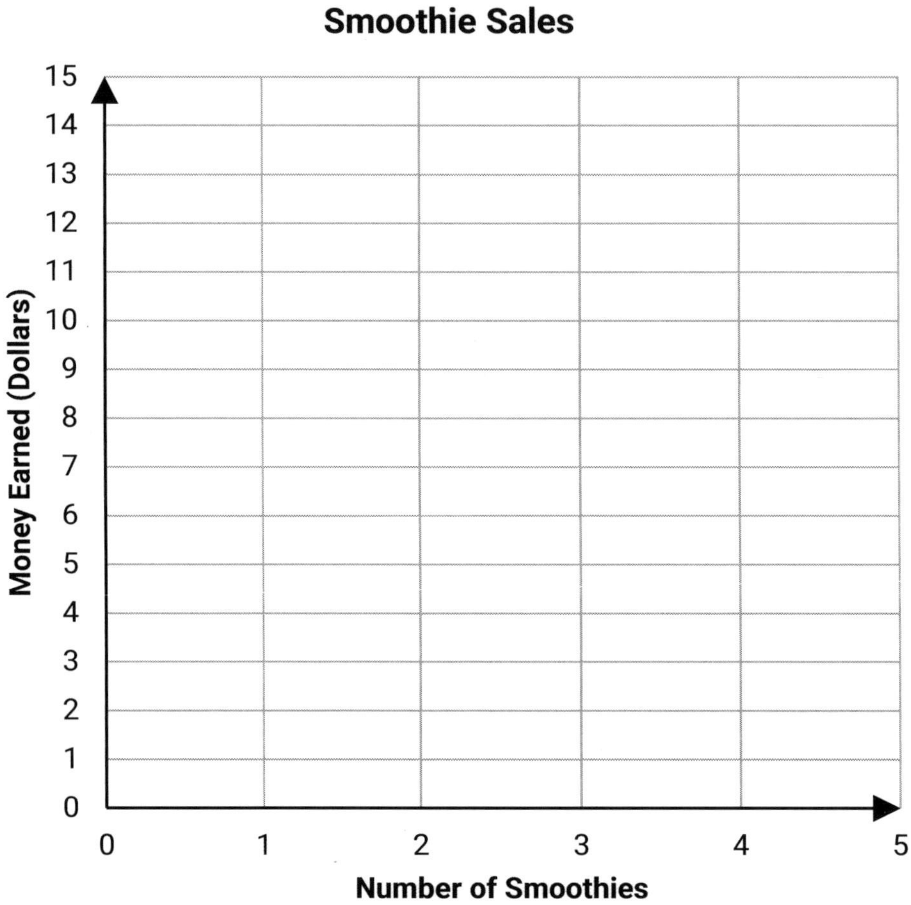

7. Mrs. May has 7 chocolate bars. She gives each student in her class $\frac{1}{3}$ of a chocolate bar. How many students are in Mrs. May's class?

a. 21 students

b. $\frac{7}{3}$ students

c. 28 students

d. 24 students

8. Rylie baked cakes for a fundraiser. Baking all of the cakes required 3 cups of brown sugar. Each cake required $\frac{1}{4}$ cup of brown sugar. How many cakes did Rylie bake for the fundraiser?

a. 10 cakes
b. 11 cakes
c. 12 cakes
d. 13 cakes

9. Jill rides her bike 19 miles every Saturday and 28 miles every Sunday. There are 52 weeks in one year. About how many miles will Jill ride in one year?

a. 1,500 miles
b. 2,500 miles
c. 3,500 miles
d. 4,500 miles

10. Evan keeps track of his monthly expenses in a table. He earns $2,300 each month. Select the best category for Evan to adjust his spending in to ensure his monthly expenses will not exceed his monthly income.

Expenses	Amount
Health Insurance	$310
Cell Phone Bill	$90
Rent	$1,800
Concert Tickets	$200

11. James created a budget based on his monthly expenses. James plans on contributing any extra money he earns each month to his savings account.

Expense	Amount
Energy Bill	$85
Groceries	$450
Car Payment	$280
Rent	$2,000
Entertainment	$425
Savings Account	

James earns $4,350 each month. How much money will James contribute to his savings account each month?

a. $1,250
b. $800
c. $1,500
d. $1,110

12. Tiger Middle School has 455 students ranging from 6th through 8th grade. 108 of these students are in 6th grade. 211 of these students are in 7th grade. How many students at Tiger Middle School are in 8th grade? Write your answer in the blank.

13. Ms. Kay is making cookies for a school bake sale. Ms. Kay fits 6 cookies on each baking pan, and she bakes multiple pans of cookies for the sale. Plot points on the graph that correctly display the data from the input-output table.

Number of pans of cookies	Number of cookies
1	6
2	12
3	18
4	24

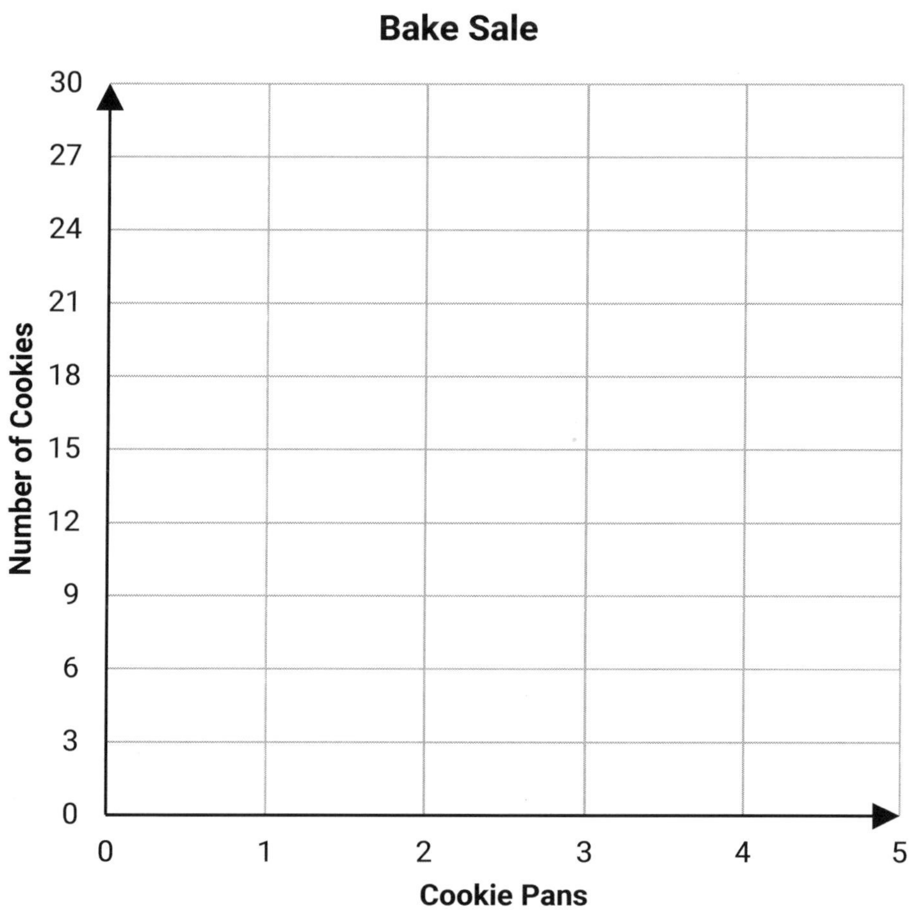

14. The Venn diagram below is set up to sort the polygons A, B, C, and D. Write the letter of each shape where that shape should be placed in the diagram.

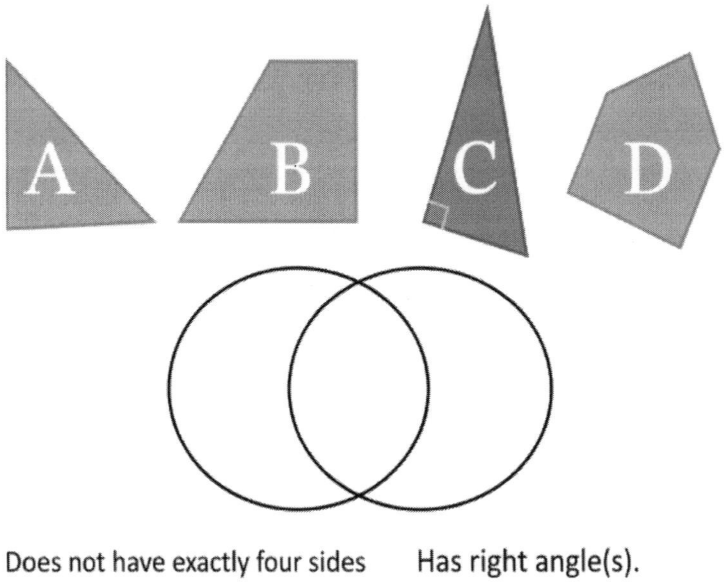

15. An art supply company is shipping out boxes loaded with small tubes of paint. Each box contains 145 tubes of paint. If the art supply company ships 25 boxes, how many tubes of paint are shipped?

a. 3,500 tubes
b. 3,602 tubes
c. 3,622 tubes
d. 3,625 tubes

16. Choose from the values below and write them in the table to create a table that illustrates a multiplicative numerical pattern.

4	6	22	23	24	28	35	42

x	*y*
3	21
5	

17. Gloria is drawing shapes with chalk. What is the perimeter of the shape below?

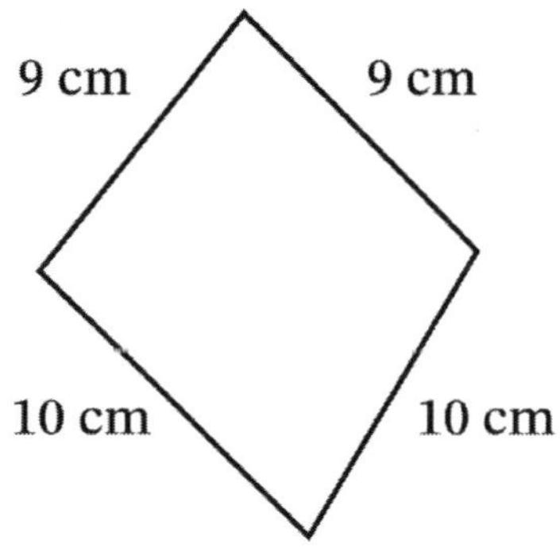

a. 19 cm
b. 29 cm
c. 38 cm
d. 90 cm

18. Mr. Morgan created a bar graph displaying the birthday season of all his 5th grade students.

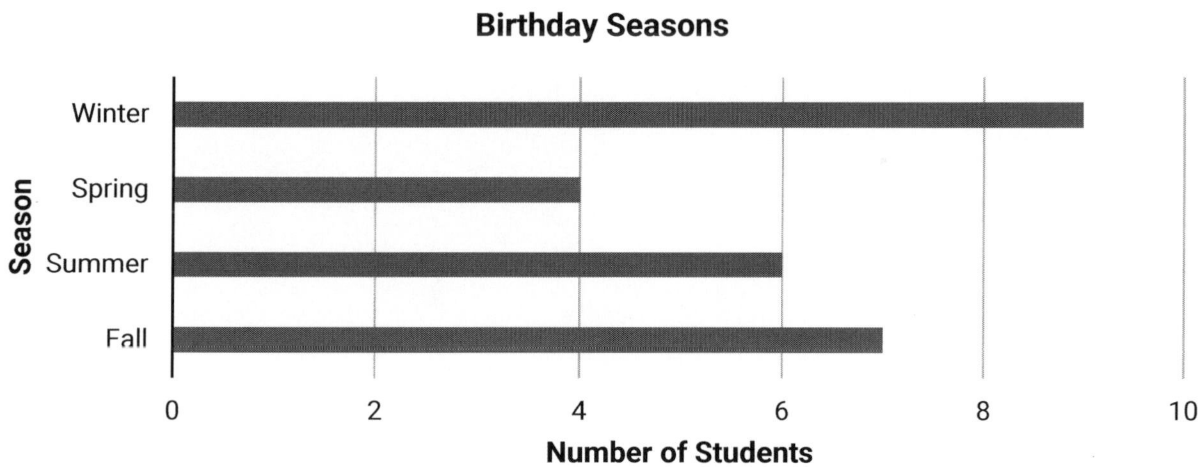

How many students are in Mr. Morgan's class?

a. 26
b. 24
c. 27
d. 25

19. Frances collects coins in her piggy bank. She sorts the coins into separate piles. Her pile of nickels combines to a total of $3.35. How many nickels does Frances have?

a. 67
b. 60
c. 57
d. 50

20. Chef Xi and Chef Shi are baking pies for a large New Year's Eve celebration. Chef Xi bakes 6 pies every hour for 4 hours. Chef Shi bakes twice as many pies as Chef Xi. When Chef Xi and Chef Shi arrive at the New Year's Eve event with their pies, the host has an additional 7 pies. Which expression represents the total number of pies at the event?

a. $2(6 \times 4)$

b. $2(6 \times 4) + (6 \times 4) + 7$

c. $2(6 \times 4) - 7$

d. $2 \times 6 \times 4 + 7$

21. Baily is buying candies at a local candy shop. She buys 3 candies that cost 40 cents each. The decimal area model below represents $1.00.

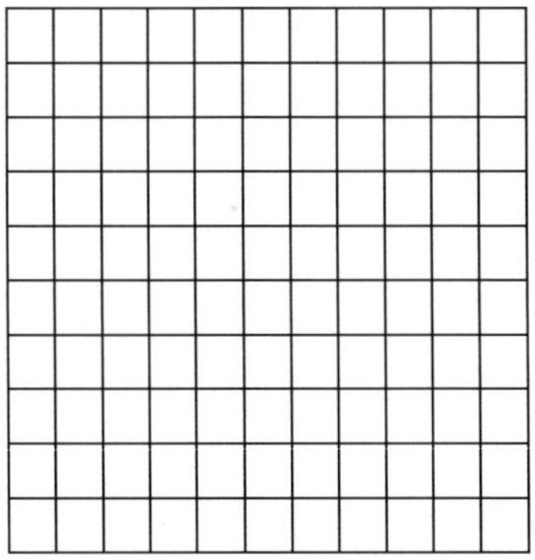

Which decimal area model correctly represents the scenario?

a. 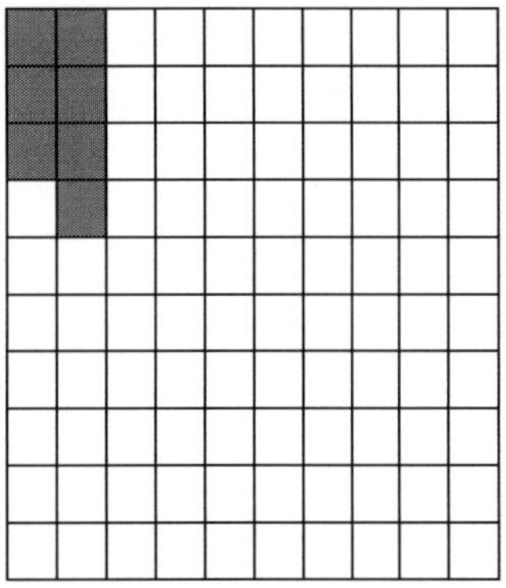

b. 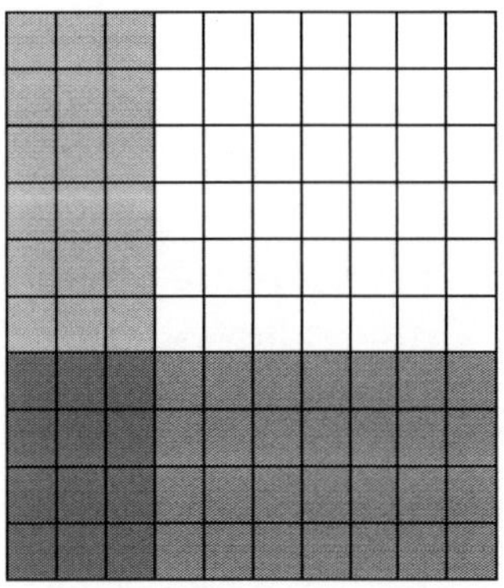

c. 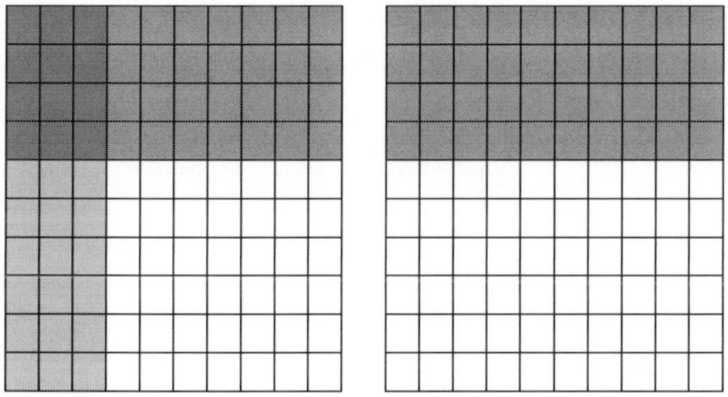

d. 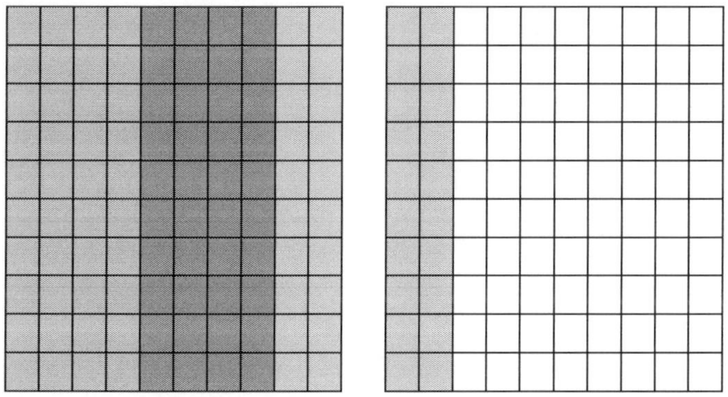

22. Ralph is hiking along a trail that extends 12 miles. So far, Ralph has hiked $\frac{6}{8}$ of the trail. Which expression can be used to determine the portion of the trail that Ralph has completed?

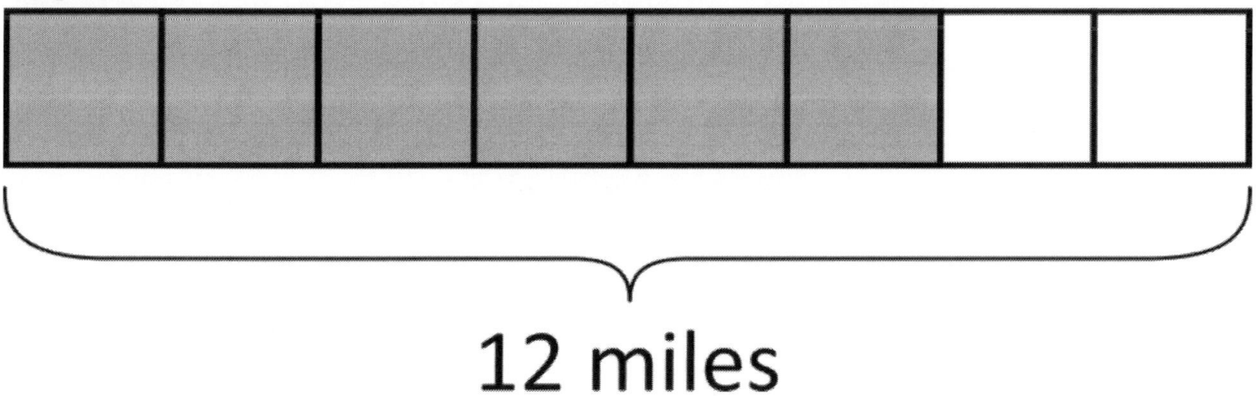

a. $\frac{6}{8} \times 12$

b. $\frac{6}{8} \div 12$

c. $\frac{6}{8} + 12$

d. $\frac{8}{6} \times 12$

23. The table shows the amount of sugar in a serving of three cereals. Wheat Crunch cereal has more sugar than Berry Blast, and less sugar than Frosty Loops. Which choice shows a possible amount of sugar that the Wheat Crunch cereal could contain?

Cereal	Grams of Sugar
Berry Blast	17.09
Granola Grams	17.91
Frosty Loops	17.1
Wheat Crunch	

a. 17.09 grams
b. 17.90 grams
c. 17.091 grams
d. 17 grams

24. Which two choices describe the origin of a coordinate plane? Select all that apply.

a. The starting point for graphing any line.
b. The point (0,0).
c. The location on a coordinate plane where the x- and y-axis intersect.
d. The upper right region of the coordinate plane where x- and y-values are both positive.
e. The point where two lines intersect.

25. An artist is using ribbon to create bows for holiday boxes. Each red bow requires 32.5 inches of ribbon. Each green bow requires 34.5 inches of ribbon. If the artist needs to create 100 bows of each color, how many total inches of ribbon needed?

a. 67 inches
b. 670 inches
c. 6,700 inches
d. 67,000 inches

26. John's paragliding gear consists of a large isosceles triangular wing. The short sides of the wing measure 18 feet each. The perimeter of the triangular wing is 66 feet. What is the length, in feet, of the longest side of the triangle?

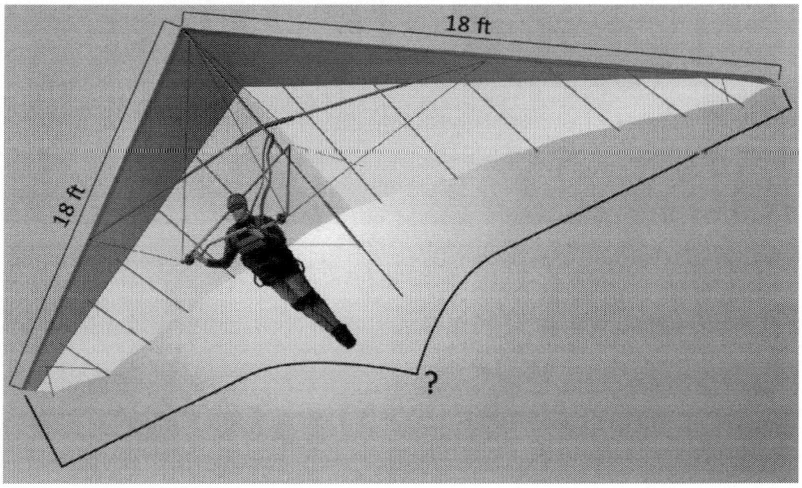

a. 26
b. 30
c. 32
d. 48

27. Sandy is mixing fresh fruit juice for a smoothie recipe. Sandy has $\frac{5}{12}$ cups of lemon juice and $\frac{1}{4}$ cups of lime juice. Sandy mixes the lime juice with the lemon juice. Shade in the fraction strips to illustrate the simplified fraction that equals the total amount of juice Sandy mixed together.

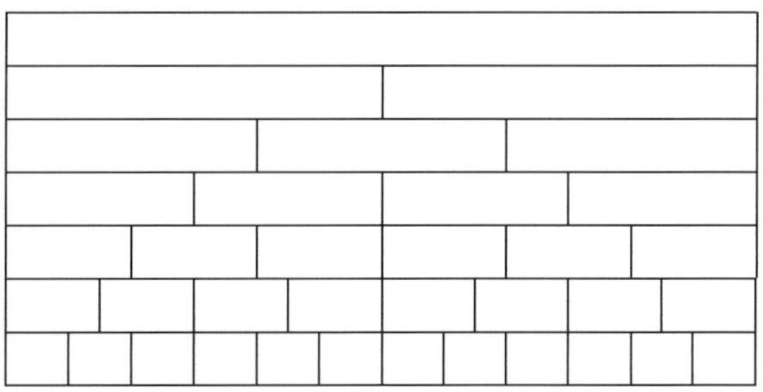

28. An artist sells clay bowls at a local market. This week the artist is selling a set of 6 identical bowls that have a combined weight of 6.54 pounds. What is the weight of each bowl?

a. 1.04 pounds
b. 1.09 pounds
c. 1.15 pounds
d. 1.90 pounds

29. Choose from the options below the blank and write in the option that best completes the statement.

This week Alice, Alyssa, Aaron, and Alex tracked their running milage. Alice ran 36.1 miles, Alyssa ran 36.091 miles, Aaron ran 36.901 miles, and Alex ran 36.6 miles.

_______ ran the highest number of miles this week.
Alice
Alyssa
Aaron
Alex

30. Round 12.65 to the nearest tenth. Write your answer in the blank.

31. Round 4.624 to the nearest hundredth.

a. 4.6
b. 4.62
c. 4.63
d. 462.4

32. Which choice is an example of sales tax?

a. Joshua owns 30 acres of farmland in Kentucky. Each year he pays taxes related to the ownership of this land.
b. Craig owns a company that provides health care for all employees. Craig pays taxes based on the number of employees he hires each year.
c. Susan reports her total income at the end of each year. She pays taxes based on the amount of money she earns each year.
d. Julie owns a shop that sells t-shirts. When a customer purchases a t-shirt from her shop, a small percentage-based tax is added on to the sale price.

33. The 3rd Street Grocery Store is having a sale on produce. Oranges are on sale for $1.14 per pound and apples are on sale for $1.75 per pound. Susan has $10, and she purchases 3 pounds of apples and 4 pounds of oranges. The store clerk charges Susan for the produce, and hands her the change. Susan can receive her change in any of the ways listed below, except one. Which two choices show an INCORRECT amount of change for Susan? Select all that apply.

a. 1 dime and 9 nickels
b. 1 dime, 1 nickel, and 4 pennies
c. 2 nickels and 9 pennies
d. 2 dimes and 9 pennies
e. 3 nickels and 4 pennies

34. Joey does yard work in his neighborhood to earn money in the summer. He charges $25 to mow a lawn and $15 to rake a lawn. This month Joey mowed 8 lawns, raked 6 lawns, and one of his clients gave him a generous $50 tip. Calculate Joey's earnings this month and write your answer in the blank.

$$(8 \times 25) + (6 \times 15) + 50$$

Answer Key and Explanations for Test #2

1. C: TEKS Standard (5.6)(B)

Each carton contains 30 eggs. Peter stacks 5 cartons of eggs. This means that Peter has 5 groups of 30 eggs. In other words, Peter has $5 \times 30 = 150$ eggs.

2. A: TEKS Standard (5.3)(C)

There are 360 children and each team will have 15 players. This represents a division scenario. $360 \div 15$ can be calculated using long division.

$$\begin{array}{r} 2 \\ 15\overline{)\,360} \\ -30 \\ \hline 6 \end{array}$$

15 does not fit into 3. However, 15 fits into 36 two times. Write 2 above the 6 in 36.

$2 \times 15 = 30$. Write 30 below 36. Subtract. The result is 6.

Bring down the next digit in 360, which is 0. 6 becomes 60.

$$\begin{array}{r} 24 \\ 15\overline{)\,360} \\ -30 \\ \hline 60 \\ -60 \\ \hline 0 \end{array}$$

Repeat the process. 15 goes into 60 four times. Write 4 above the 0 in 360.

$4 \times 15 = 60$. Write 60 below 60. Subtract. The result is 0, which indicates no remainders.

Since $360 \div 15 = 24$, the league will create 24 soccer teams.

3. C: TEKS Standard (5.4)(C)

Anna can assemble 12 earrings in 1 hour.

$$y = 12(1) = 12$$

This means that in 2 hours Anna can assemble 24 earrings, and in 3 hours Anna can assemble 36 earrings.

$$y = 12(2) = 24$$

$$y = 12(3) = 36$$

The pattern continues. The number of earrings assembled is determined by multiplying the number of hours worked by 12. The equation $y = 12x$ represents this rule, and choice C is the only table correctly displaying this relationship.

4. B: TEKS Standard (5.4)(B)

Jamie earns \$22 per hour, and a \$50 tip. In order to determine the amount of money Jamie earns, the number of hours should be multiplied by 22 and then added to 50. The only table that matches this pattern is table B.

$$(1 \times 22) + 50 = 72$$

$$(2 \times 22) + 50 = 94$$

$$(3 \times 22) + 50 = 116$$

5. TEKS Standard (5.8)(C)

Correct points may be any three of the following:

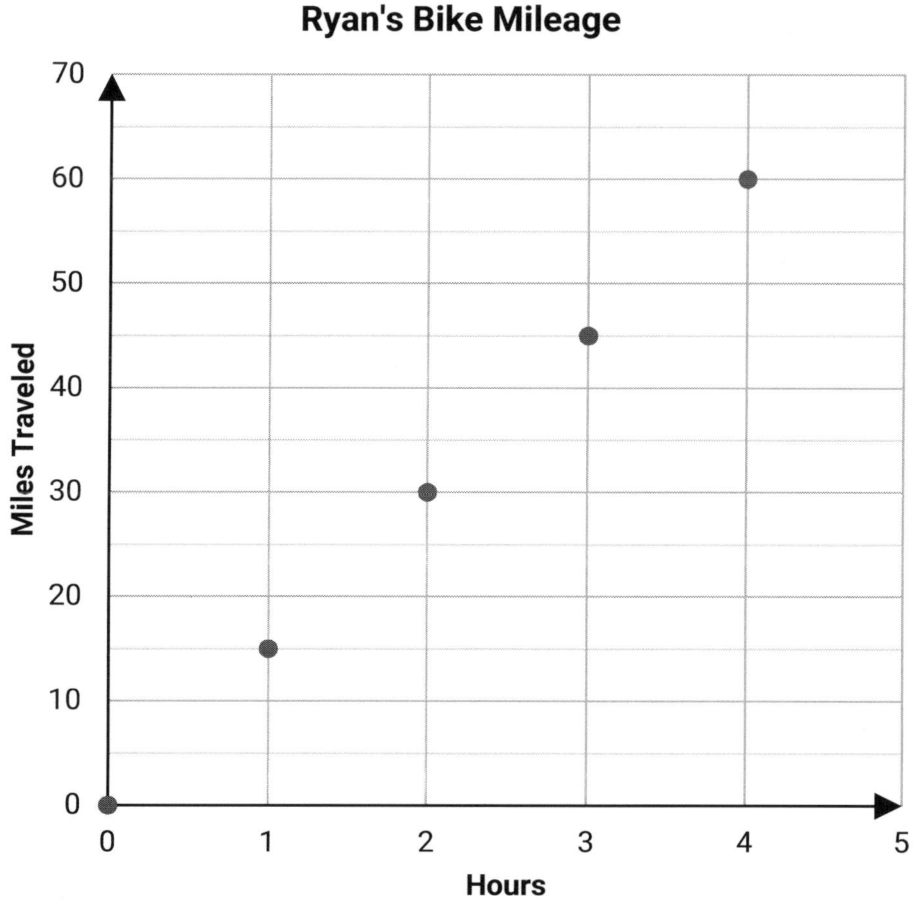

Ryan rides his bike 15 miles each hour. The number of miles he bikes depends on the number of hours he rides his bike. This means that the dependent variable, or y-variable, is the number of miles. The independent variable, or x-variable, is the number of hours. After 1 hour Ryan has traveled 15 miles. This is represented by the ordered pair (1,15). To graph this point, start at the origin and move 1 unit to the right and 15 units up. After 2 hours Ryan has traveled 30 miles. This is represented by the ordered pair (2,30). The pattern continues. As the x-value increases by 1, the y-value increases by 15. The next two points are (3,45) and (4,60).

6. TEKS Standard (5.4)(C)

Correct points may be any four of the following:

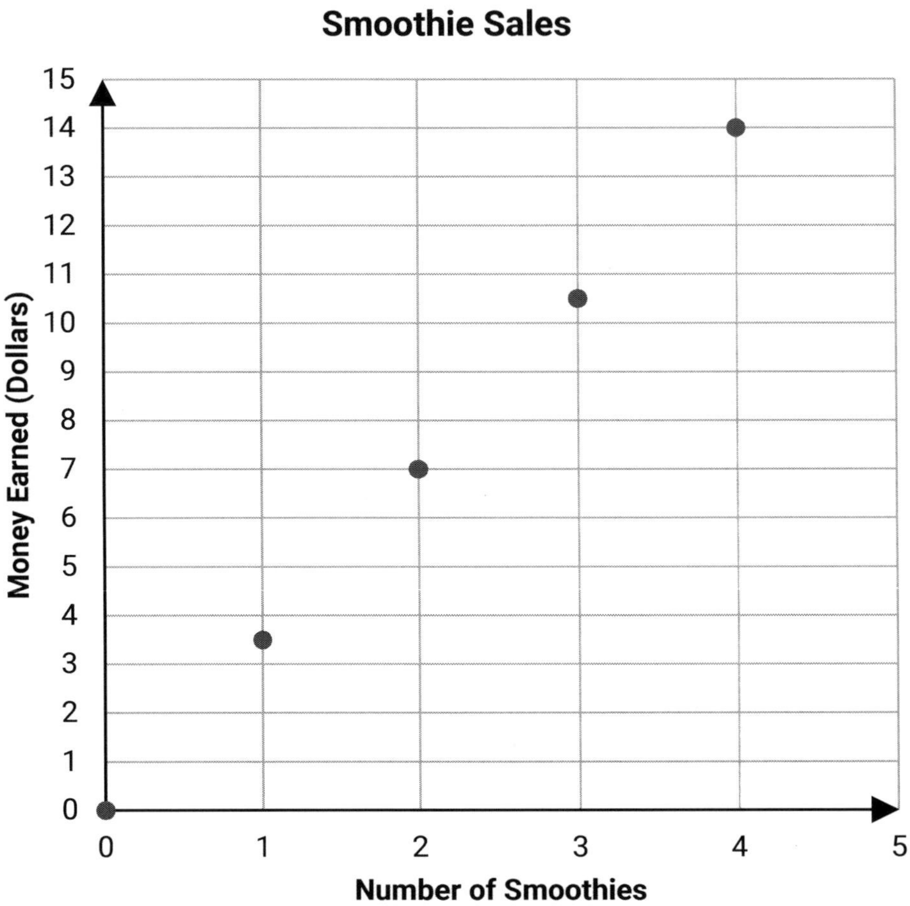

Each smoothie costs \$3.50. This means that the amount of money earned can be calculated by multiplying the number of smoothies by 3.5.

0 smoothies: $0 \times 3.5 = 0$	Money earned: \$0
1 smoothie: $1 \times 3.5 = 3.5$	Money earned: \$3.50
2 smoothies: $2 \times 3.5 = 7$	Money earned: \$7
3 smoothies: $3 \times 3.5 = 10.5$	Money earned: \$10.50
4 smoothies: $4 \times 3.5 = 14$	Money earned: \$14

The amount of money earned depends on the number smoothies that are sold. This means that the amount of money is the dependent variable, y, and the number of smoothies that are sold is the independent variable, x.

The coordinate point that represents the amount of money earned for 1 smoothie is (1,3.50). To plot this point, move over to the value 1 on the x-axis and then move up to the value 3.5 on the y-axis. The other points can be plotted in the same way.

7. A: TEKS Standard (5.3)(L)

Mrs. May is dividing 7 chocolate bars into groups of $\frac{1}{3}$. In other words, Mrs. May is dividing 7 by $\frac{1}{3}$. This can be visualized as 7 wholes that are each divided into 3 equal shares. When 7 bars are sliced into 3 pieces each, the result is 21 small pieces. This means that $7 \div \frac{1}{3} = 21$.

Another way to calculate $7 \div \frac{1}{3}$ is to use the process of "Keep, Change, Flip." Keep 7 as 7. Change $\div$ to $\times$. Flip $\frac{1}{3}$ to $\frac{3}{1}$. So, $7 \div \frac{1}{3}$ becomes $7 \times \frac{3}{1}$. The result is $\frac{21}{1}$, or 21. This means that Mrs. May will have 21 pieces of chocolate. 21 pieces of chocolate indicates that there are 21 students in the class.

8. C: TEKS Standard (5.3)(J)

The total amount of brown sugar used for the cakes is 3 cups. Each cake required $\frac{1}{4}$ cup of brown sugar. To determine the number of cakes, divide each cup of brown sugar into groups of $\frac{1}{4}$. 3 cups divided into groups of $\frac{1}{4}$ results in 12 groups. Rylie baked 12 cakes for the fundraiser.

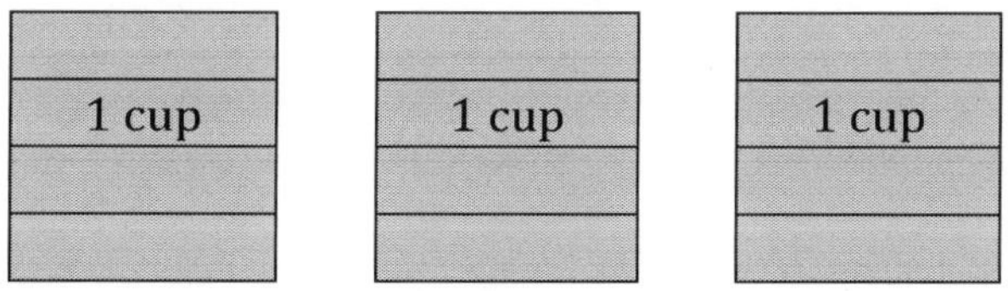

9. B: TEKS Standard (5.3)(A)

Since there are 52 weeks in a year, this means that Jill will ride her bike 19 miles 52 times, and 28 miles 52 times. 19 groups of 52 can be rounded to 20 groups of 50. This can be expressed as $20 \times 50 = 1{,}000$. 28 groups of 52 can be rounded to 30 groups of 50. This can be expressed as $30 \times 50 = 1{,}500$. Now, add $1{,}000 + 1{,}500 = 2{,}500$. So, in one year Jill will ride approximately 2,500 miles.

10. Concert Tickets: TEKS Standard (5.10)(E)

Evan earns \$2,300 each month, and he spends \$2,400 each month. This means that Evan does not have a balanced budget. The expenses for health insurance, cell phone bill, and rent are generally necessary and fixed expenses. However, the expenses in the concert ticket category could realistically be reduced. If Evan reduced spending in this category by \$100, he would have a balanced budget.

11. D: TEKS Standard (5.10)(F)

James earns \$4,350 each month. The sum of his expenses each month is \$3,240.

$$\$85 + \$450 + \$280 + \$2{,}000 + \$425 = \$3{,}240$$

The difference between his income and his expenses is $\$4{,}350 - \$3{,}240 = \$1{,}110$. James can contribute \$1,110 to his savings account each month.

12. 136: TEKS Standard (5.3)(K)

108 students are in 6th grade. 211 students are in 7th grade. Add each place value: $108 + 211 = 319$. There are 319 6th and 7th graders. Subtract this from the total number of students at Tiger Middle School. $455 - 319 = 136$. There are 136 8th graders at the middle school.

13. TEKS Standard (5.8)(C)

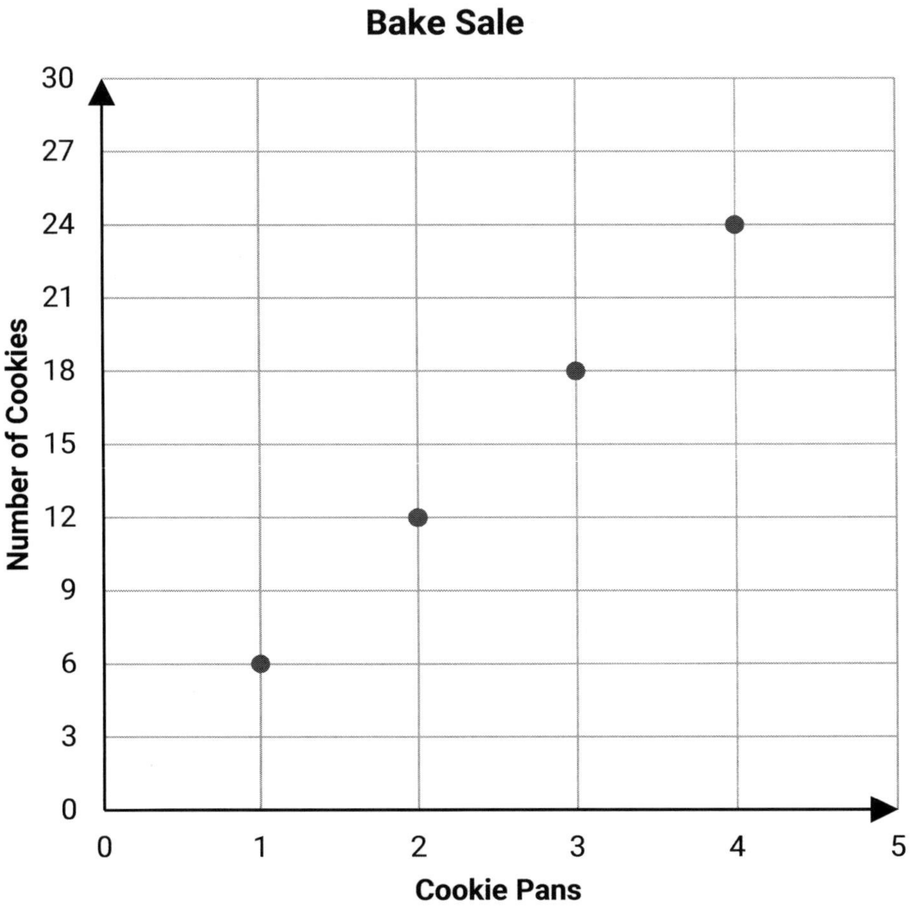

Mrs. Kay fits 6 cookies on each pan. This means that 1 pan will result in 6 total cookies. 2 pans will result in 12 total cookies. 3 pans will result in 18 total cookies. 4 pans will result in 24 total cookies, and so on. This data can be expressed as the ordered pairs (1,6), (2,12), (3,18), and (4,24). To graph the point (1,6), start at the origin and move 1 unit to the right and 6 units up. Plot the rest of the points in a similar way.

14. TEKS Standard (5.5)(A)

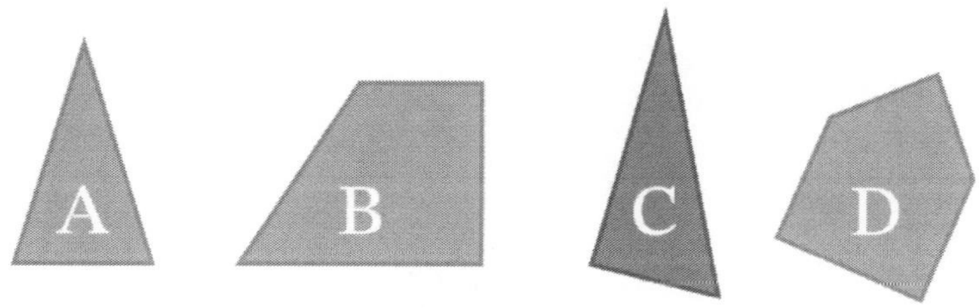

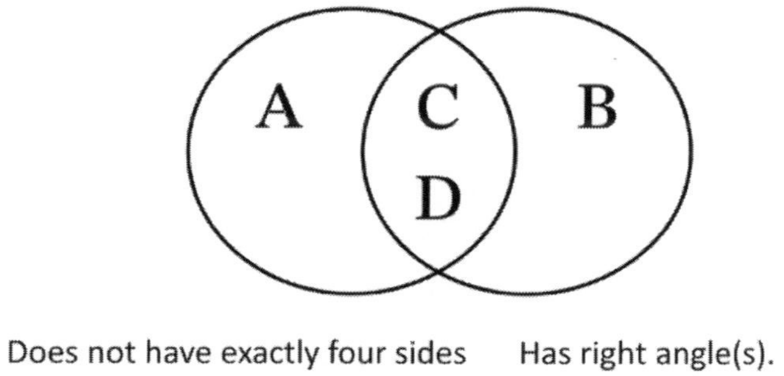

Shapes placed in the overlapping middle section of the Venn diagram need to apply to both rules: does not have four sides, and has right angle(s). The only shapes that do not have four sides and have right angle(s), are shapes C and D. Shape A cannot be placed in the middle section because it does not contain right angles, but it does go in the left section because it does not have exactly four sides. Shape B cannot be placed in the middle section because it has four sides, but can be placed in the right section because it does have two right angles.

15. D: TEKS Standard (5.3)(B)

There are 25 boxes, and each box contains 145 tubes of paint. 25 groups of 145 represents a multiplication scenario. The standard algorithm for multiplication can be applied to find the product of 145 and 25.

Multiply the 5 in 25 by each digit in 145.

5×5 is 25. Write the 2 above the 4 in 145. Write the 5 on the answer line.

5×4 is 20. Add the 2 from above. The result is 22. Write the 2 above the 1 in 145. Write the other 2 on the answer line.

5×1 is 5. Add the 2 from above. The result is 7. Write 7 on the answer line.

$$\begin{array}{r} 2\,2 \\ 145 \\ \times\ 25 \\ \hline 725 \end{array}$$

Repeat the same process for the digit 2 in 25. Don't forget to include a "place holder zero" in the ones place. This ensures that the place values are lined up correctly.

$$\begin{array}{r} 1 \\ 145 \\ \times\ 25 \\ \hline 725 \\ 2900 \end{array}$$

Add both products. In this case, 725 and 2,900. The sum is 3,625. This means that the product of 145 and 24 is 3,625, so 3,625 tubes of paint are shipped.

$$\begin{array}{r} 145 \\ \rightarrow \times\ 25 \\ \hline 725 \\ +\ 2900 \\ \hline 3{,}625 \end{array}$$

16. x-values: 4, 6; y-values: 28, 35, 42: TEKS Standard (5.4)(D)

The y-values are calculated by multiplying the corresponding x-value by 7. For example, $3 \times 7 = 21$, $4 \times 7 = 28$, and so on. x-values are continually multiplied by the same amount, in this case 7. This means the relationship is multiplicative.

17. C: TEKS Standard (5.4)(H)

The quadrilateral has side lengths of 9 cm, 9 cm, 10 cm, and 10 cm. The perimeter is calculated by finding the sum of all side lengths. $9 + 9 + 10 + 10 = 38$. The perimeter of the shape drawn in chalk is 38 cm.

18. A: TEKS Standard (5.9)(C)

The bar graphs displays 7 students with fall birthdays, 6 students with summer birthdays, 4 students with spring birthdays, and 9 students with winter birthdays. This means that there is a total of $7 + 6 + 4 + 9 = 26$ students in Mr. Morgan's class.

19. A: TEKS Standard (5.3)(G)

67 nickels have a total value of \$3.35. This can be demonstrated by dividing \$3.35 into groups of 5 cents. 5 cents in decimal form is 0.05. 3.35 divided by 0.05 can be expressed using long division.

3.35 is the dividend and 0.05 is the divisor. The divisor cannot contain a decimal when using long division. The decimal in 0.05 can be eliminated by multiplying by 100. 0.05 becomes 5. If the divisor is multiplied by 100, the dividend also needs to be multiplied by 100. 3.35 becomes 335. Now the division problem is set up as 335 divided by 5.

$$5\overline{)\,335}$$

Follow the 4-step process for long division: Divide, Multiply, Subtract, Bring Down.

Divide: 5 does not fit into 3. However, 5 fits into 33 six times. Write 6 above the second 3.

Multiply: 6 times 5 is 30. Write 30 below 33.

Subtract: 33 minus 30 is 3.

Bring Down: Bring down the next digit. 3 becomes 35.

Repeat the process.

Divide: 5 fits into 35 seven times. Write 7 above the 5.

Multiply: 7 times 5 is 35. Write 35 below 35.

Subtract: 35 minus 35 is 0.

Bring Down: There are no more digits to bring down. The process is complete.

$$\begin{array}{r} 67 \\ 5\overline{)\,335} \\ \underline{-30} \\ 35 \\ \underline{-35} \\ 0 \end{array}$$

335 divided by 5 is 67. This means that \$3.35 divided by 0.05 is 67. Frances has 67 nickels.

20. B: TEKS Standard (5.4)(F)

Chef Xi bakes 6 pies every hour, for 4 hours. This can be expresses as (6×4).

Chef Shi bakes twice as many pies as Chef Xi. This can be expressed as $2(6 \times 4)$.

The host of the celebration has 7 pies, in addition to the pies that Chef Xi and Chef Shi contribute. This is expressed as $2(6 \times 4) + (6 \times 4) + 7$.

21. D: TEKS Standard (5.3)(D)

Baily buys 3 candies that cost 40 cents each. There are 100 cents in a dollar, so 40 cents represents $\frac{40}{100}$, or 0.4 as a decimal. 3 candies that cost 0.4 each can be represented as three groups of 0.4. Choice D correctly shows 3 groups of 4 tenths, or $3 \times 0.4 = 1.2$. Alternatively, Choice D shows 12 bars of $\frac{1}{10}$, which is equivalent to $1\frac{2}{10}$ or the decimal 1.2. So, choice D represents the amount of money Baily spent on candy, which is \$1.20.

22. A: TEKS Standard (5.3)(I)

Ralph has hiked $\frac{6}{8}$ of the trail, and the trail extends 12 miles. Another way to phrase this is $\frac{6}{8}$ of 12. The statement $\frac{6}{8}$ of 12 represents the multiplication expression $\frac{6}{8} \times 12$.

23. C: TEKS Standard (5.2)(B)

Wheat Crunch has more sugar than Berry Blast, which has 17.09 grams, and less sugar than Frosty Loops, which has 17.1 grams. This means that the amount of sugar in Wheat Crunch is between 17.09 and 17.1. Write equivalent decimal values for 17.09 and 17.1 that extend to the thousandths place.

17.09 and 17.1 becomes 17.090 and 17.100. In this form it becomes easier to recognize the values that fall between the two numbers. For example, 17.091, 17.092, 17.093, and so on, are all greater than 17.090 and less than 17.100. Choice C, 17.091 is one correct possible amount of sugar for the Wheat Crunch cereal because it is greater than 17.090 and less than 17.100.

24. B, C: TEKS Standard (5.8)(A)

Choices B and C correctly describe the origin of a coordinate plane. Choice A is not correct because not all lines pass through the origin. Choice D describes the first quadrant of a graph. The first quadrant of a graph is not the same thing as the origin of a graph. Choice E is incorrect because two lines may intersect at any point, not just the origin.

25. C: TEKS Standard (5.3)(E)

The artist needs 100 red bows that require 32.5 inches of ribbon each. The total amount of red ribbon can be calculated as 100×32.5. When multiplying a decimal value by 100, move the decimal point two places to the right. 100×32.5 becomes 3,250. So, 3,250 inches of ribbon are needed to create the red bows.

The artist needs 100 green bows that require 34.5 inches of ribbon each. The total amount of green ribbon can be calculated as 100×34.5. When multiplying a decimal value by 100, move the decimal point two places to the right. 100×34.5 becomes 3,450. So, 3,450 inches of ribbon are needed to create the green bows.

The total amount of ribbon needed to create all of the bows is $3{,}250 + 3{,}450 = 6{,}700$ inches of ribbon.

26. B: TEKS Standard (5.4)(H)

The wing is an isosceles triangle with two congruent side lengths of 18 feet. The perimeter of the wing is 66 feet, which is the sum of all three side lengths. So, $18 + 18 + x$ is equal 66 feet.

$$18 + 18 + x = 66$$

$$36 + x = 66$$

To solve for x, subtract 36 from both sides.

$$x = 30$$

This means that the longest side of the triangular wing is 30 feet.

27. TEKS Standard (5.3)(H)

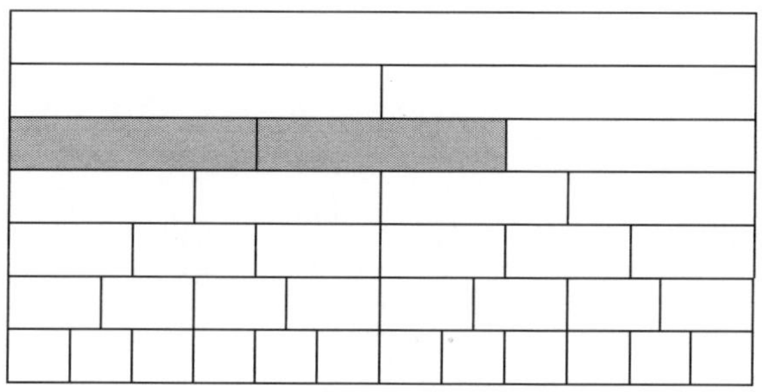

The scenario given in the equation describes $\frac{5}{12} + \frac{1}{4}$ and asks for the sum. One way to solve this problem is to find the two measurements on the fraction strips. Begin with $\frac{1}{4}$ and see that it is equal to $\frac{3}{12}$.Now, add $\frac{3}{12} + \frac{5}{12} = \frac{8}{12}$. Use the fraction strips to see that $\frac{8}{12}$ is equal to $\frac{2}{3}$.

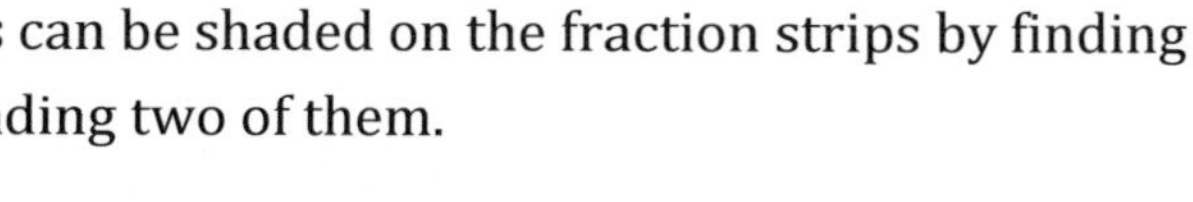

Alternatively, find the least common denominator of the two fractions. The least common denominator is 12. The denominator of $\frac{5}{12}$ is already 12. To change $\frac{1}{4}$ to have a denominator of 12, multiply the numerator and the denominator by 3: $\frac{1}{4} \times \frac{3}{3} = \frac{3}{12}$. Now add the fractions and simplify. $\frac{3}{12} + \frac{5}{12} = \frac{8}{12}$. $\frac{8 \div 4}{12 \div 4} = \frac{2}{3}$. This can be shaded on the fraction strips by finding the horizontal strip with three equal pieces and shading two of them.

28. B: TEKS Standard (5.3)(G)

The total weight of all 6 bowls is 6.54 pounds. Each bowl weighs the same amount, so 6.54 can be divided by 6 in order to determine the weight of one bowl. The long division algorithm can be applied. Follow the 4-step process: Divide, Multiply, Subtract, Bring Down.

Divide: 6 fits into 6 one time. Write 1 above the 6 in the dividend.

Multiply: 1 times 6 is 6. Write 6 below the 6.

Subtract: 6 minus 6 is 0.

Bring Down: Bring down the next digit, which is 5.

Repeat the process.

Divide: 6 fits into 5 zero times. Write 0 above the 5 in the dividend.

Multiply: 0 times 6 is 0. Write 0 below the 5.

Subtract: 5 minus 0 is 5.

Bring Down: Bring down the next digit, which is 4.

Repeat the process.

Divide: 6 fits into 54 nine times. Write 9 above the 4 in the dividend.

Multiply: 9 times 6 is 54. Write 54 below the 54.

Subtract: 54 minus 54 is 0.

Bring Down: There are no more digits to bring down. The problem is completely solved.

Bring the decimal point straight up into the answer. 109 becomes 1.09.

$$\begin{array}{r} 1.0\,9 \\ 6\overline{)\,6.5\,4} \\ \underline{-6} \\ 0\,5 \\ \underline{-\;0} \\ 5\,4 \\ \underline{-\;5\,4} \\ 0 \end{array}$$

Each bowl weighs 1.09 pounds.

29. Aaron: TEKS Standard (5.2)(B)

When arranging decimal values, compare each digit one at a time, from left to right. Start by comparing the farthest digit to the left. All of the values have a 3 in the tens place. Move one digit to the right. All of the values have a 6 in the ones place. Move one digit to the right. All of the values have different digits in the tenths place. The digits in the tenths place include 1, 0, 9, and 6. Rank these from least to greatest, $0 < 1 < 6 < 9$. Therefore, $36.091 < 36.1 < 36.6 < 36.901$. 36.901 is the largest value, which means that Aaron ran the most this week.

30. 12.7: TEKS Standard (5.2)(C)

When rounding 12.65 to the nearest tenth, start by locating the digit in the tenths place. 6 is in the tenths place. Now, look at the digit to the right. If this digit is 5 or more, the tenths digit will round up. If this digit is 4 or less, the tenths digit will stay the same. In this case, the digit to the right of the tenths place is a 5. This means the 6 rounds up to a 7. The number 12.65 rounds to 12.7.

31. B: TEKS Standard (5.2)(C)

The given number 4.624 has a 2 in the hundredths place. The digit to the right of the hundredths place will indicate whether the 2 rounds up to a 3 or remains the same. If the digit to the right of the 2 is 5 or more, the 2 will round up to 3. If the digit to the right of the 2 is 4 or less, the 2 will remain the same. In the number 4.624, the digit to the right of the hundredths place is a 4. This means the 2 will stay the same. 4.624 becomes 4.62. All digits after the hundredths place are eliminated.

32. D: TEKS Standard (5.10)(A)

Sales tax is a small percentage-based tax that is added on to a sale price. This occurs during the transaction of goods or services. The customer pays the tax, and the business collects the tax. Choice A is incorrect because it describes property tax. Joshua did not purchase a good or service from a business, so sales tax is not used in this situation. Choice B is incorrect because Craig is not buying a good or service, so he is not paying sales tax. Choice C is incorrect because Susan is paying income tax. She is not paying taxes in order to buy a good or service, so she is not paying a sales tax.

33. A, D: TEKS Standard (5.3)(E)

Susan purchases 3 pounds of apples that cost \$1.75 each. $3 \times \$1.75 = \$5.25$. She also purchases 4 pounds of oranges that cost \$1.14 each. $4 \times \$1.14 = \$4.56$. Susan spends \$5.25 on apples and \$4.56 on oranges. Susan spends $\$5.25 + \$4.56 = \$9.81$ on produce. She has \$10, so her change is calculated as $\$10.00 - \$9.81 = \$0.19$. Susan's change is 19 cents. 19 cents can be made in a variety of ways. 1 dime, 1 nickel, and 4 pennies: $\$0.10 + \$0.05 + \$0.04 = \$0.19$, so this is a correct amount of change for Susan. 2 nickels and 9 pennies: $\$0.05 + \$0.05 + \$0.09 = \$0.19$, so this is also a correct amount of change. 3 nickels and 4 pennies: $\$0.05 + \$0.05 + \$0.05 + \$0.04 = \$0.19$. 1 dime and 9 nickels: $\$0.10 + \$0.45 = \$0.50$, so it does not equal 19 cents. 2 dimes and 9 pennies: $\$0.10 + \$0.10 + \$0.09 = \$0.29$, it also does not equal 19 cents.

34. 340: TEKS Standard (5.4)(F)

Joey mows 8 lawns and charges \$25 for each lawn. He also rakes 6 lawns and charges \$15 for each lawn. Joey also earned a \$50 tip. The expression

$(8 \times 25) + (6 \times 15) + 50$ can be used to calculate Joey's total profit. The order of operations, or PEMDAS, states that parentheses will be calculated first. Multiply 8 by 25 and 6 by 15. $(8 \times 25) + (6 \times 15) + 50$ becomes $(200) + (90) + 50$, which simplifies to 340. Joey earned \$340 this month.

Practice Test #3

1. Each small cube within the rectangular prism below has a volume of 1 cubic unit. The rectangular prism has a volume of ___ cubic units.

a. 165
b. 160
c. 184
d. 170

2. Mrs. Martin plans to repurpose the box as a toy bin for her niece. She wants to paint the four outer walls of the box shown below. How much area will Mrs. Martin be painting?

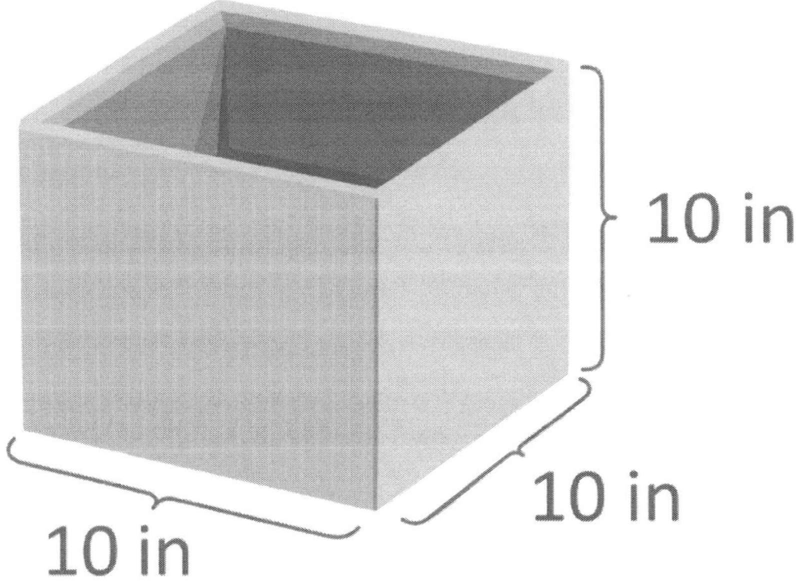

Choose from the options below the blank and write in the options that best complete the expression.

____ _______ inches
100 square
300 cubic
400

3. A baker has 2 pounds of sugar in a large bin. The baker needs to separate the sugar into smaller bins containing 0.25 pounds of sugar each. Each grid contains $\frac{100}{100}$, or one whole. Which model correctly represents the decimal division scenario?

a. 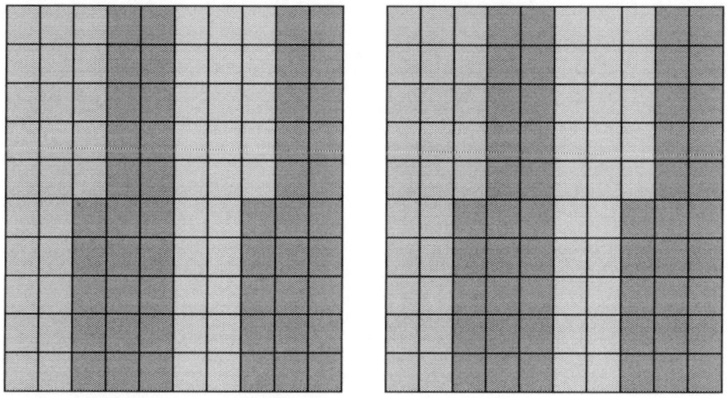

b. 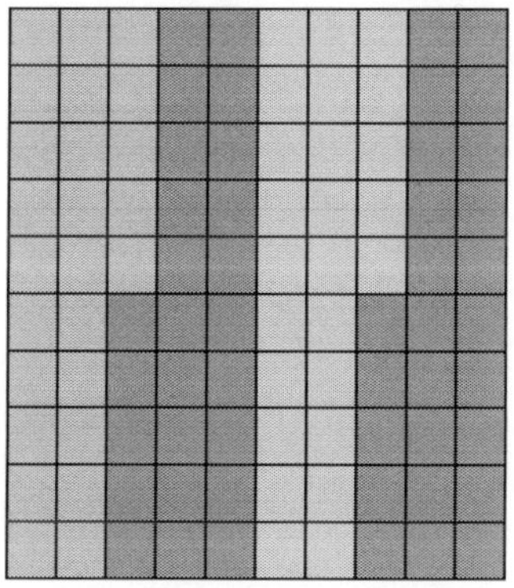

c. 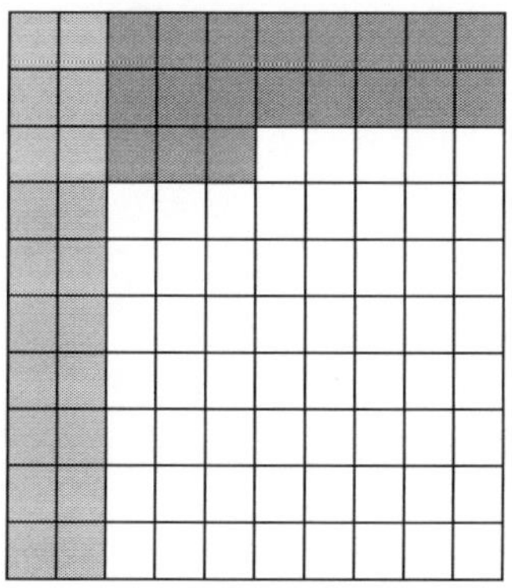

d. 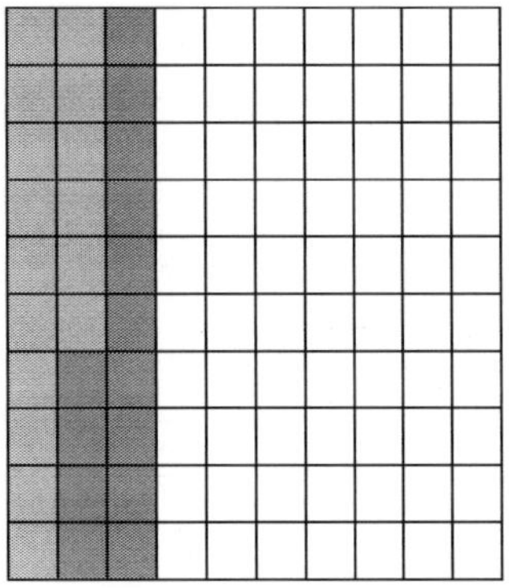

4. Jennifer asks her friends how many pairs of shoes they own. The results are listed below.

Pairs of Shoes: 5, 3, 5, 12, 5, 26, 5, 6, 10, 8, 10, 11, 14

Which stem-and-leaf plot correctly displays the data from the table?

a.

Stem	Leaf
0	3 5 5 5 5 6 8
1	0 0 1 2 4

b.

Stem	Leaf
0	5 3 5 5 5 8 6
1	1 2 4 0 0
2	6

c.

Stem	Leaf
0	3 5 5 5 5 6 8
1	0 0 1 2 4
2	6

d.

Stem	Leaf
3 5 5 5 5 6 8	0
0 0 1 2 4	1
6	2

5. Write the decimal values in the boxes in order from the least to the greatest.

37.618	36.09	37.96	37.16

6. The points on the graph below represent Fredrick's age and Erick's age for a given year. Based on the graph below, which equation can be used to determine the age of Erick?

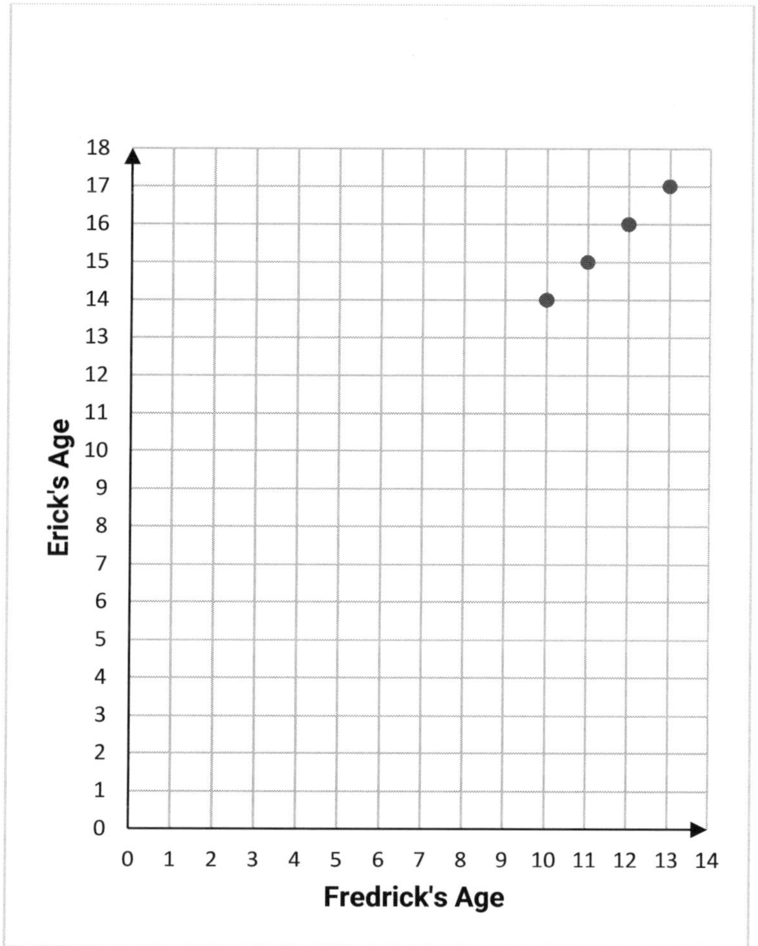

a. $y = 4x$
b. $x = 4y$
c. $y = x - 4$
d. $y = x + 4$

7. Choose from the options below the blank and write in the options that best complete the expression.

On Monday, Erin sold 10 bird houses. She sold 4 bird houses each day for the next 6 days. What is a numerical expression that can be used to determine the number of bird houses Erin sold this week?

____________ = ____________

$4 \times 6 \times 10$	20 bird houses
$(4 + 6) + 10$	100 bird houses
$(4 \times 6) + 10$	240 bird houses
$10(4 + 6)$	34 bird houses

8. Paul's dog just had a litter of three puppies. Each puppy is wearing a different colored collar. The puppy with the orange collar weighs 2.71 pounds, the puppy with the green collar weighs 2.09 pounds, the puppy with the pink collar weighs 1.99 pounds, and the puppy with the blue collar weighs 2.17 pounds. Which puppy is the heaviest?

a. The puppy with the pink collar.
b. The puppy with the green collar.
c. The puppy with the blue collar.
d. The puppy with the orange collar.

9. Use the order of operations to simplify the expression below.

$$45 + (20 - 6 \times 3) \div 2$$

a. 24
b. 43.5
c. 46
d. 88.5

10. Mrs. Derby asks her students to describe the process of plotting the point $(8, 4)$ on a graph. Which student correctly describes the process?

a. Avery: Start at the origin. Move 8 units to the right and then 4 units up. Plot the point (8,4).
b. Bryce: Start at the point (8,4). Move 8 units to the right and then 4 units up. Plot the point (8,4).
c. Carlos: Start at the origin. Move 4 units to the right and then 8 units up. Plot the point (8,4).
d. Damion: Start at the point (0,0). Move 8 units to the left and then 4 units up. Plot the point (8,4).

11. Roger purchased breakfast for his co-workers. He buys coffees for \$4.50 each and 6 bagels for \$2 each. Roger uses the expression $(4.5 \times c) + (2 \times 6)$ to represent his purchase. If Roger bought 4 coffees, what was the total cost of breakfast?

a. \$30
b. \$36
c. \$20
d. \$32

12. What is the value of $\frac{1}{7} \div 3$?

a. 21
b. $\frac{7}{3}$
c. $\frac{1}{24}$
d. $\frac{1}{21}$

13. Heather needs to purchase a new set of tires for her car. The set of tires she is interested in costs $455.40. The auto shop informs Heather that next month this set of tires will be on sale. The price of the tires will be reduced by $99 during the sale. If Heather buys the tires next month, how much will she spend on her new tires? Write your answer in the blank.

14. Grace kept track of the number of points she scored in each of her basketball games this season. The results are displayed in the stem-and-leaf plot.

Stem	Leaf
0	3 3 8 9
1	0 1 3 3 6
2	2

Grace scored ___ points in her highest scoring game.

a. 3
b. 16
c. 19
d. 22

15. Select the prime numbers from the list below.

3	9	11	17	24	37	42

16. The graph below represents the total cost of a hot air balloon ride based on the number of passengers. The total cost depends on the number of passengers. What kind of numerical pattern does the graph illustrate?

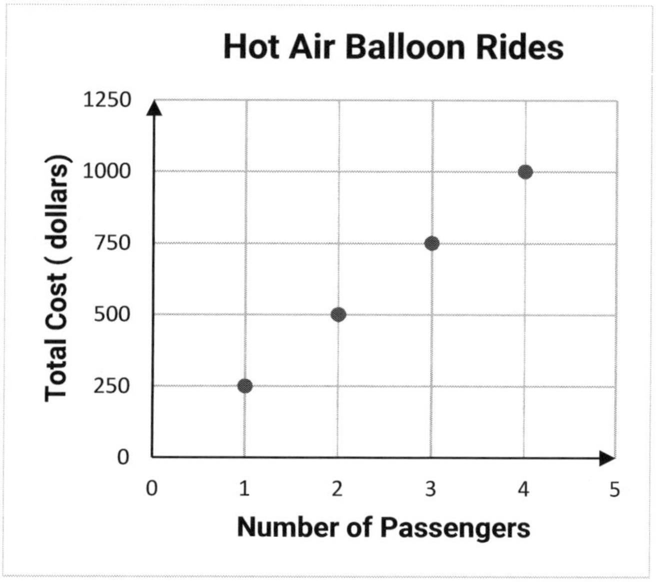

a. Multiplicative
b. Distributive
c. Additive
d. Associative

17. Choose from the options below the blank and write in the option that best complete the statement.

David has two jobs. This year he earned $28,000 from one job, and $47,500 from another job. The total amount of money he earned, before taxes, is $75,500.

$75,000 represents David's ________ income.

net
fiscal
gross
quarterly

18. Cooper earns $3,800 each month. Which choice shows a balanced budget based on Cooper's income?

a.

Expense	Amount (dollars)
Rent	2,400
Health Insurance	466
Internet Bill	98
Savings	880

b.

Expense	Amount (dollars)
Rent	2,400
Health Insurance	466
Internet Bill	98
Savings	836

c.

Expense	Amount (dollars)
Rent	2,400
Health Insurance	466
Internet Bill	140
Savings	836

d.

Expense	Amount (dollars)
Rent	2,800
Health Insurance	466
Internet Bill	98
Savings	836

19. Sam paid a total of $1,860 on electricity bills this year. If Sam paid the same amount each month, what was his monthly electricity bill? Write your answer in the blank.

20. Bethany walked dogs in June, July, and August. Bethany earned the same amount each month and earned a total of $985.65. How much money did Bethany earn from walking dogs in June?

a. $321.44
b. $328.55
c. $354.64
d. $493.90

21. A car is traveling at a consistent speed of 35 miles per hour. The rule $y = 35x$ can be used to describe this relationship where y represents the total distance in miles, x represents the number hours, and 35 represents the distance traveled each hour. All of the statements below are true, except one. Which two statements below are correct? Select all that apply.

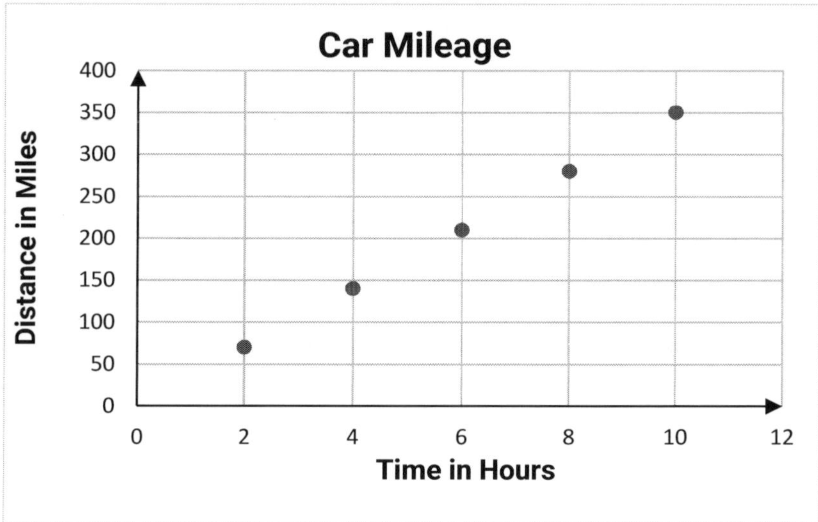

a. The car will travel 350 miles in 10 hours.
b. The number of hours of driving depends on the number of miles traveled.
c. It will take over 4 hours to travel 200 miles.
d. It will take 8 hours to travel 250 miles.
e. The rule tells us it will take 35 minutes to travel 1 mile.

22. Peter earns $4,025 each month. About how much money will Peter earn after 4 years?

a. Approximately $350,000
b. Approximately $300,000
c. Approximately $200,000
d. Approximately $100,000

23. Ryan spent $94 at the thrift store. Ryan purchased 3 sweatshirts that cost $12 each, two pairs of sunglasses that cost $3 each, and $2 on a pair of gloves. The rest of the money was spent on kitchen supplies. Which choice shows an equation that can be used to determine the amount of money Ryan spent on kitchen supplies? Let k represent the amount of money Ryan spent on kitchen supplies.

a. $94 = 3(10) + 2(3) + 2$; Ryan spent $48 on kitchen supplies.
b. $94 = 3(12) + 2(3) + 2 + k$; Ryan spent $50 on kitchen supplies.
c. $94 = 3(12) + 2(3) + k$; Ryan spent $48 on kitchen supplies.
d. $k = 3(12) + 2(3) + 2 + 94$; Ryan spent $52 on kitchen supplies.

24. Andre is framing a 4 inch by 6 inch photo. The photo will fit into a frame without any gaps or overlaps. The frame has a width of 2 inches, all the way around the photo. What is the total area of the photo and frame?

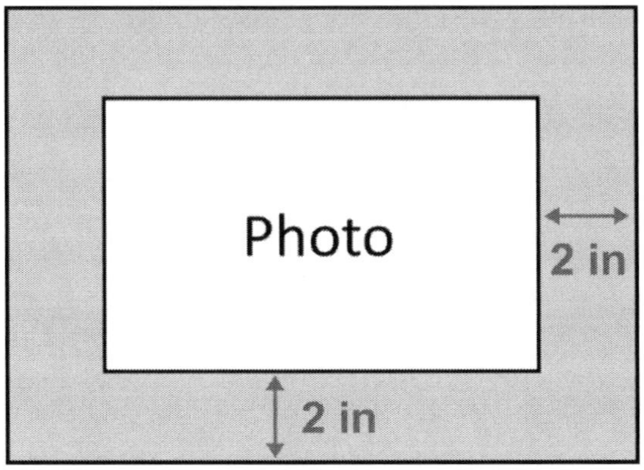

a. 24 square inches
b. 48 square inches
c. 56 square inches
d. 80 square inches

25. Julia is selecting cans of cat food. If Julia selects 10 cans of salmon flavor, 10 cans of tuna flavor, and 20 cans of seafood blend, what will her total bill be?

Cat Food Flavor	Price per can
Salmon	89 cents
Tuna	75 cents
Seafood Blend	90 cents

a. $24.40
b. $34.40
c. $34.90
d. $44.40

26. The dot plot below shows the number of books read by a group of students over the summer. Each dot represents one student.

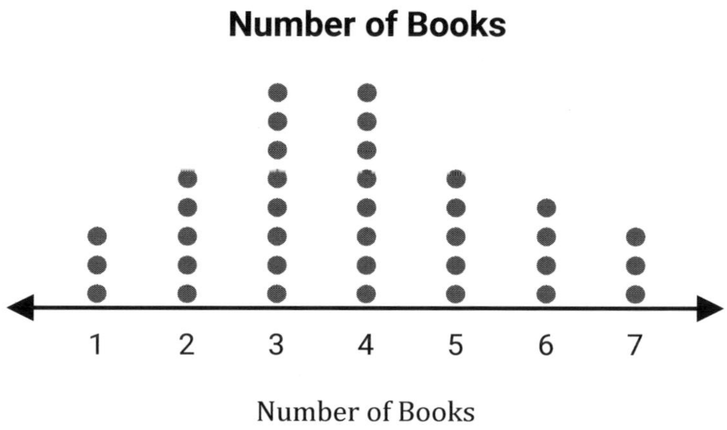

How many more students read 4 books than 1 book?

a. 8

b. 5

c. 2

d. 7

27. Rebecca creates small watercolor paintings and sells them for $5 each. Plot at least three points on the graph to display the relationship between the number of paintings Rebecca sells and the amount of money that she earns.

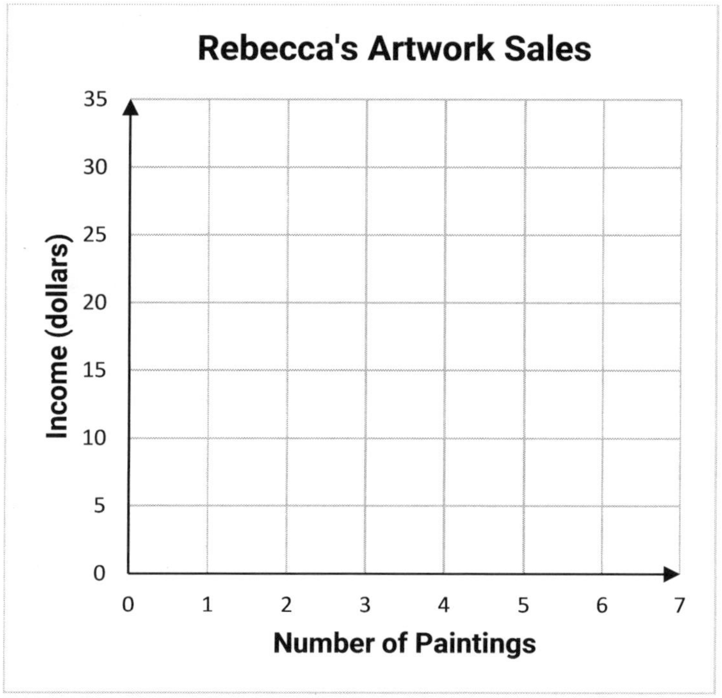

28. Mark is paying the bill for his family's dinner. He estimates the price of each meal as shown below. If Mark orders one more meal that costs \$33.50, what is his total estimation for the entire bill?

Meal	Price	Estimate
Steak Dinner	\$51.90	\$50
Clam Chowder	\$27.50	\$30
Taco Bowl	\$18.70	\$20
Risotto	\$34.20	\$30

Write your answer in the blank.

29. The block below consists of unit cubes. Calculate the volume of the block in cubic units.

a. 14 cubic units
b. 64 cubic units
c. 100 cubic units
d. 125 cubic units

30. It takes John 2 hours to make a small birdhouse and 3 hours to make a large birdhouse. John needs to make 6 small bird houses and 6 large birdhouses. Which equation can be used to find the unknown amount of time?

a. $h = 2(6) + (6)$; it will take John 28 hours to build the birdhouses.
b. $h = 2(6) \times 3(6)$; it will take John 20 hours to build the birdhouses.
c. $h = (2 + 6) + (3 + 6)$; it will take John 32 hours to build the birdhouses.
d. $h = 2(6) + 3(6)$; it will take John 30 hours to build the birdhouses.

31. Marcus drove 175.5 miles and then took a flight that was 2,340.6 miles. How many miles did Marcus travel in all?

a. 2,516.1 miles
b. 2,916.1 miles
c. 2,516 miles
d. 3,516.1 miles

32. Roger rides his stationary exercise bike 1,500 meters each day. How many kilometers does Roger ride in a week? ($1 \text{ km} = 1,000 \text{ m}$)

a. 0.15 km
b. 10.5 km
c. 1,050 km
d. 10,500 km

33. Write the letter for each shape where the shape belongs in the Venn diagram. Labels for shapes that do not belong inside the diagram can be written outside of the diagram.

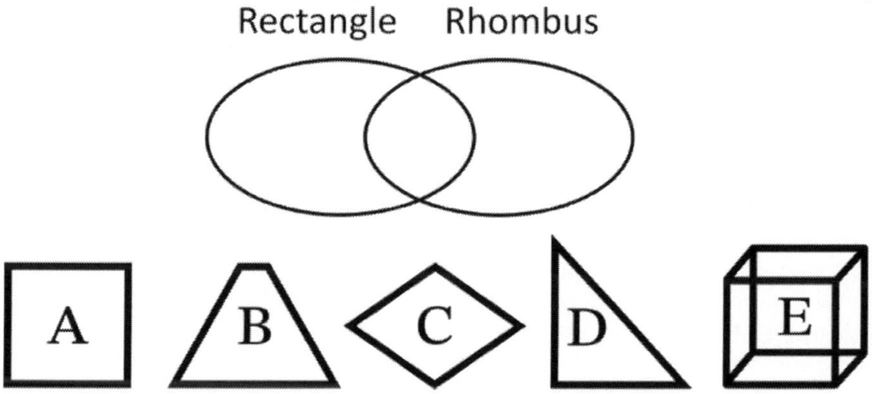

34. Ayla is modeling a multiplication scenario using an area model.

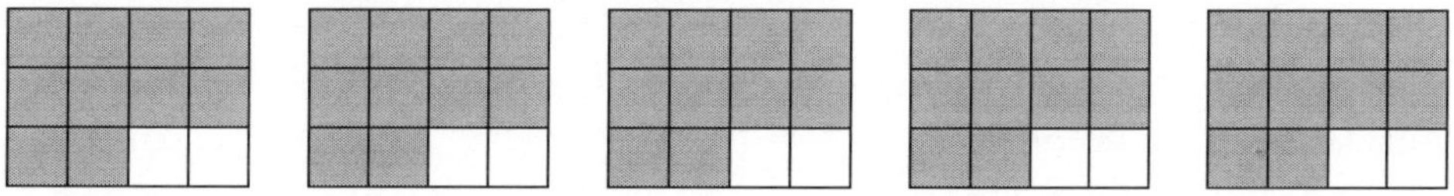

Which two expressions below describe the area model? Select all that apply.

a. $5 \times \frac{10}{12}$
b. 5 groups of $\frac{10}{12}$
c. $\frac{12}{10} \times 5$
d. 10 groups of $\frac{5}{12}$
e. $10 \times \frac{5}{12}$

Answer Key and Explanations for Test #3

1. B: TEKS Standard (5.6)(A)

The volume of a rectangular prism can be calculated as the product of its length, width, and height. The formula $V = l \times w \times h$ can be applied in this scenario. The length of the prism is 4 units. The width of the prism is 8 units. The height of the prism is 5 units.

$V = l \times w \times h$ becomes $V = 4 \times 8 \times 5$, which simplifies to 160 cubic units. The units are *cubic* because three dimensions are multiplied.

2. 400, square: TEKS Standard (5.4)(H)

There are four outer walls on the box. Each wall has a length of 10 inches and a width of 10 inches. The area of each wall is calculated using the formula $A = l \times w$. Each wall has an area of $A = 10 \times 10$ which simplifies to 100 square inches. Mrs. Martin is painting all four walls, so the total area is calculated as $100 \times 4 = 400$ square inches.

3. A: TEKS Standard (5.3)(F)

2 pounds of sugar is being divided into groups of 0.25 pounds.

$2 \div 0.25$ can be solved using a model. Each grid contains $\frac{100}{100}$, or one whole. There are 2 cups of sugar, so there needs to be 2 full grids. Divide the grids into groups of 0.25 which is represented by 25 squares. This is done by shading groups of 25 of 100 squares. There are 8 groups, which means $2 \div 0.25 = 8$. Choice A correctly models the decimal division scenario.

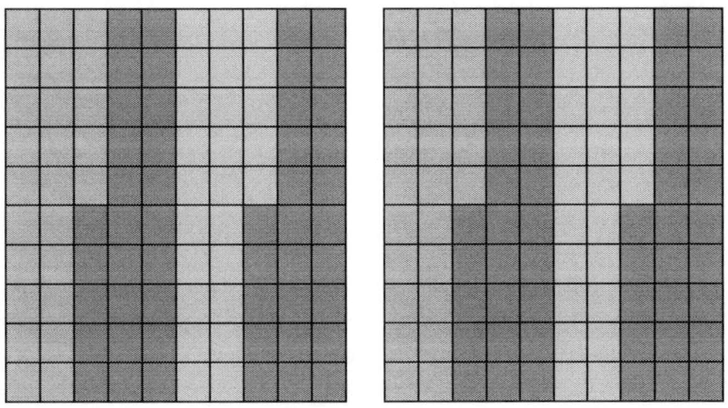

4. C: TEKS Standard (5.9)(A)

Stem-and-Leaf plot C correctly displays the data. The stem values on the left represent the tens digit and the leaf values on the right represent the ones digit. Leaf values are arranged from smallest to largest from left to right.

Choice A is missing the value 26.

Choice B does not have the leaf values in ascending order from left to right.

Choice D has the stem values and leaf values located in the wrong position. Stem values need to be on the left and leaf values need to be on the right.

5. 36.09, 37.16, 37.618, 37.96: TEKS Standard (5.2)(B)

Arrange each decimal value by comparing each digit one at a time from left to right.

All of the values in the list have a 3 in the tens place.

3	7	.	6	1	8
3	6	.	0	9	
3	7	.	9	6	
3	7	.	1	6	

Move right to compare the next digit.

3	7	.	6	1	8
3	6	.	0	9	
3	7	.	9	6	
3	7	.	1	6	

Since 6 is less than 7, or $6 < 7$, the number 36.09 is the smallest number.

Move right to compare the next digit.

3	6	.	0	9	
3	7	.	1	6	
3	7	.	6	1	8
3	7	.	9	6	

Since 1 is less than 6, which is less than 9, or $1 < 6 < 9$, the numbers can be ordered as $37.16 < 37.618 < 37.96$.

The final arrangement from least to greatest is 36.09, 37.16, 37.618, 37.96.

6. D: TEKS Standard (5.4)(C)

The plotted points show that Erick will always be 4 years older than Fredrick. This means that Erick's age can always be described as Fredrick's age plus 4. In other words, Erick = Fredrick + 4. Since Eric's age depends on Frederick's age, Eric's age goes on the y-axis and Frederick's age goes on the x-axis. Using the form $y = a + x$, the rule Erick = Fredrick + 4 becomes $y = x + 4$.

7. $(4 \times 6) + 10 = 34$ bird houses: TEKS Standard (5.4)(F)

Erin sells 10 bird houses on Monday, so express this as $+10$. Erin sells 4 bird houses each day for 6 days, which can be expressed as (4×6). Altogether, the expression is $(4 \times 6) + 10$. To simplify the expression, multiply 4 and 6, and then add 10. The result is 34. Erin sold 34 bird houses this week.

8. D: TEKS Standard (5.2)(B)

List each decimal value, and compare the digits from left to right.

2.71

2.09

1.99

2.17

1.99 has a 1 in the ones place, and all of the other values have a 2 in the ones place. This means 1.99 is the smallest number. Now compare 2.71, 2.09, and 2.17. All values have a 2 in the ones place, so move one digit to the right. The tenths values are 7, 0, and 1. The smallest value is 0, followed by 1, then 7, so $0 < 1 < 7$. Therefore, $2.09 < 2.17 < 2.71$. The heaviest puppy weighs 2.71 pounds. The heaviest puppy has the orange collar.

9. C: TEKS Standard (5.4)(F)

The expression $45 + (20 - 6 \times 3) \div 2$ can be simplified using the order of operations, also known as PEMDAS. P represents parentheses, so simplify inside of the parentheses first. There is subtraction and multiplication inside of the parentheses. According to PEMDAS, multiplication needs to occur before subtraction. This means that $(20 - 6 \times 3)$ becomes $(20 - 18)$ and then 2. Now the expression is $45 + 2 \div 2$. Division occurs before addition, so $45 + 2 \div 2$ becomes $45 + 1$, which simplifies to 46.

10. A: TEKS Standard (5.8)(B)

The point (8,4) indicates that the x-value is 8 and the y-value is 4. Start at the origin (0,0), and make the appropriate movements. The point (8,4) is plotted by moving 8 units to the right and 4 units up. Avery is the only student to correctly describe this process.

11. A: TEKS Standard (5.4)(F)

Roger purchased coffees and bagels. He buys 6 bagels at \$2 each. This is represented as (2×6). He purchases 4 coffees for \$4.50 each, which is represented as (4.5×4). The expression $(4.5 \times 4) + (2 \times 6)$ can be simplified by multiplying inside of the parentheses, and then finding their sum.

$$(4.5 \times 4) + (2 \times 6)$$

$$(18) + (12) = 30$$

The total cost of the breakfast is \$30.

12. D: TEKS Standard (5.3)(L)

The expression $\frac{1}{7} \div 3$ can be modeled by shading in $\frac{1}{7}$ of a whole.

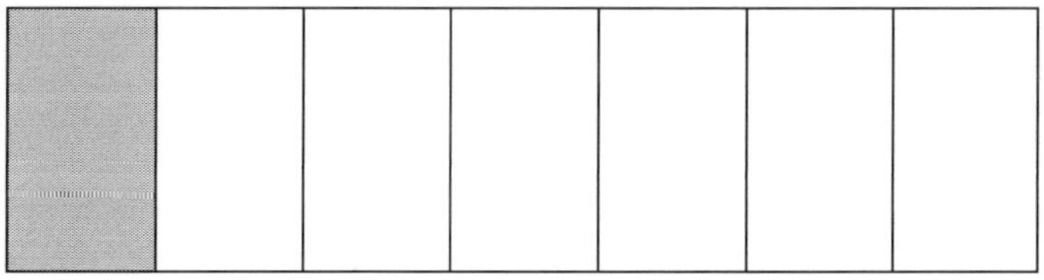

and then dividing this shaded region into 3 equal shares. Each share represents $\frac{1}{21}$ of the whole: $\frac{1}{7} \div 3 = \frac{1}{21}$.

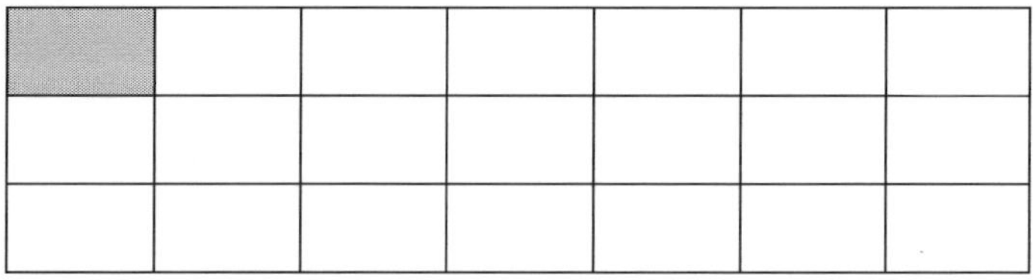

13. 356.40: TEKS Standard (5.3)(K)

The original price of the tires is \$455.40. This price will be reduced by \$99 during the upcoming sale. This means that \$99 can be subtracted from \$455.40. When subtracting 99 from 455.40, line up the decimal points, and subtract each place value from right to left. Regroup when necessary. For example, 9 can't be subtracted from 5 in the ones place. Borrow from the 5 in the tens place, making it a 4, then change the 5 in the ones place to 15. 9 can be subtracted from 15. Continue this process for subtraction. Bring the decimal point straight down into the answer. The result is 356.40. The sale price of the tires is \$356.40.

$$\begin{array}{r} {}^{3\ 14\ 15} \\ \not{4}\not{5}\not{5}.\ 40 \\ -\ \ 99.\ 00 \\ \hline 356.\ 40 \end{array}$$

14. D: TEKS Standard (5.9)(C)

The stem-and-leaf plot lists the tens digit on the left (stem), and the ones digit on the right (leaf). This stem-and-leaf plot displays the following values: 3, 3, 8, 9, 10, 11, 13, 13, 16, 22. Grace scored 22 points in her highest scoring game.

15. 3, 11, 17, 37: TEKS Standard (5.4)(A)

Prime numbers have only two factors, 1 and the number itself. For example, 5 is prime, and its only factors are 1 and 5. Numbers that are not prime are considered composite. 3, 11, 17, 37 are the only prime numbers in the list. The numbers 9, 24, and 42 are not prime. The factors of 9 are 1, 3, and 9. The factors of 24 are 1, 2, 3, 4, 6, 8, 12, and 24. The factors of 42 are 1, 2, 3, 6, 7, 14, 21, and 42.

16. A: TEKS Standard (5.4)(D)

The graph shows that the cost for 1 passenger is \$250, the cost for 2 passengers is \$500, the cost for 3 passengers is \$750, and the cost for 4 passengers is \$1,000. The total cost can be determined by multiplying the number of passengers by \$250. This represents a multiplicative relationship because each y-value is calculated by multiplying the corresponding x-value by 250.

17. gross: TEKS Standard (5.10)(B)

The amount of money a person earns, from all revenue sources, before taxes or deductions, is considered gross income. Net income is the amount of money a person earns before taxes or deductions are taken out. Individuals do not receive fiscal income. Quarterly income is the amount of money a person earns in one quarter of a time period, usually a quarter of a year. The time period in which David earned this money is not mentioned.

18. B: TEKS Standard (5.10)(F)

Cooper earns \$3,800 each month. Cooper has a balanced budget if his expenses do not exceed his income. Check each table by adding the expenses to determine the total amount. The only budget with expenses equal to \$3,800 is table B.

$$\$2{,}400 + \$466 + \$98 + \$836 = \$3{,}800$$

19. 155: TEKS Standard (5.3)(C)

Sam paid a total of \$1,860 over the course of 12 months. Sam paid the same amount each month which means his monthly payment can be calculated as \$1,860 ÷ 12. This can be found using long division.

12 does not fit into 1. However, 12 fits into 18 one time. Write 1 above the 8.

$$\begin{array}{r} 1 \\ 12\overline{)\,1860} \\ -12 \\ \hline 66 \end{array}$$

$1 \times 12 = 12$. Write 12 below 18, and subtract: $18 - 12 = 6$. Write 6 and bring down the next digit which is 6. 6 becomes 66. Repeat the process. 12 fits into 66 five times. Write 5 above 6. $5 \times 12 = 60$. Write 60 below 66, and subtract: $66 - 60 = 6$. Write 6 and bring down the next digit, which is 0. 6 becomes 60. Repeat the process one more time.

$$\begin{array}{r} 15 \\ 12\overline{)\,1860} \\ -12 \\ \hline 66 \\ -60 \\ \hline 60 \end{array}$$

12 fits into 60 five times. Write 5 above 0. $5 \times 12 = 60$. Write 60 below 60, and subtract: $60 - 60 = 0$. This indicates no remainders.

$$\begin{array}{r} 155 \\ 12\overline{)\,1860} \\ -12 \\ \hline 66 \\ -60 \\ \hline \end{array}$$

```
  60
 -60
   0
```

The quotient of 1,860 and 12 is 155. This means that Sam's monthly electricity bill is $155.

20. B: TEKS Standard (5.3)(G)

Bethany earns $985.65 in three months. The amount of money earned in each month is the same, so $985.65 can be divided by 3 in order to determine the amount earned in June. 985.65 can be divided by 3 using long division.

Follow the 4-step process: Divide, Multiply, Subtract, Bring Down.

```
3)985.65
```

Divide: 3 fits into 9 three times. Write 3 on the answer line.

Multiply: 3 times 3 is 9.

Subtract: 9 minus 9 is 0.

Bring Down: Bring down the next digit, which is 8.

```
   3
3)985.65
 -9
  08
```

Repeat the process.

Divide: 3 fits into 8 two times. Write 2 on the answer line.

Multiply: 2 times 3 is 6.

Subtract: 8 minus 6 is 2.

Bring Down: Bring down the next digit, which is 5.

```
   32
3)985.65
 -9
  08
  -6
   25
```

Repeat the process.

Divide: 3 fits into 25 eight times. Write 8 on the answer line.

Multiply: 8 times 3 is 24.

Subtract: 25 minus 24 is 1.

Bring Down: Bring down the next digit, which is 6.

```
   328.
3)985.65
 -9
  08
  -6
   25
  -24
    16
```

Repeat the process.

Divide: 3 fits into 16 five times. Write 5 on the answer line.

Multiply: 5 times 3 is 15.

Subtract: 16 minus 15 is 1.

Bring Down: Bring down the next digit, which is 5.

```
   328.5
3)985.65
 -9
  08
  -6
   25
  -24
    16
   -15
     15
```

Repeat the process.

Divide: 3 fits into 15 three times. Write 3 on the answer line.

Multiply: 5 times 3 is 15.

Subtract: 15 minus 15 is 0.

Bring Down: There are no more digits to bring down.

```
   328.55
3)985.65
 -9
  08
  -6
   25
  -24
    16
   -15
     15
```

$$\begin{array}{r} -\ 15 \\ \hline 0 \end{array}$$

Bethany earned $328.55 in June.

21. A, C: TEKS Standard (5.4)(C)

The relationship between the time and distance the car travels is $y = 35x$, where y is distance and x is time. Consider choice A, $35(10) = 350$, so choice A is correct. Additionally, since $35(4) = 140$, and 140 is less than 200, choice C is also correct. Since x, the independent variable, represents time, and y, the dependent variable, represents distance, the distance traveled depends on the number of hours spent traveling, not the other way around. Choice B is incorrect. According to the graph, 8 hours of travel results in a little under 300 miles traveled, so choice D is incorrect. According to the rule $y = 35x$, 35 miles are traveled each hour, not 35 minutes to travel 1 mile, so choice E is also incorrect.

22. C: TEKS Standard (5.3)(A)

Peter earns $4,025 each month, which is approximately $4,000 each month. There are 12 months in one year, and 48 months in 4 years. 48 months can be rounded to 50 months. This means that Peter earns approximately $4,000 for 50 months. This can be calculated as $4{,}000 \times 50 = 200{,}000$. Peter will earn approximately $200,000 in 4 years.

23. B: TEKS Standard (5.4)(B)

Ryan spent a total of $94. Start by setting up an equation with the total payment, $94, on the left, and all the expenses on the right.

The expenses include:

3 sweatshirts at $12 each: 3(12).

2 sunglasses at $3 each: 2(3).

1 pair of gloves at $2: 1(2) or just 2.

k represents the amount of money spent on kitchen supplies.

The sum of the purchases should equal the total purchase price of $94.

The equation becomes $94 = 3(12) + 2(3) + 2 + k$.

To figure out how much Ryan spent on kitchen supplies, start by finding out how much he spent on everything except kitchen supplies.

$$3(12) + 2(3) + 2 = 36 + 6 + 2 = 44$$

Ryan spent $44 on everything except kitchen supplies. Subtract this amount from the total amount of money he spent.

$$\$94 - \$44 = \$50$$

This means that Ryan spent $50 on kitchen supplies.

24. D: TEKS Standard (5.4)(H)

The photo is 4 inches by 6 inches. The frame is 2 inches wide on all sides of the photo. This means that the total width of the frame is $4 + 2 + 2 = 8$ inches. The total length of the frame is $6 + 2 + 2 = 10$ inches. The total area of the frame and photo is calculated using the dimensions of the frame. $8 \times 10 = 80$ square inches.

25. B: TEKS Standard (5.3)(E)

The salmon cans cost 89 cents each, and Julia purchases 10 cans. 89 cents is \$0.89, so the cost of the Salmon cans is calculated as 10×0.89. Move the decimal point one spot to the right when multiplying by 10. 10×0.89 becomes 8.9, or \$8.90.

The tuna cans cost 75 cents each, and Julia purchased 10 cans. 75 cents is \$0.75, so the cost of the Tuna cans is calculated as 10×0.75. Move the decimal point one spot to the right when multiplying by 10. 10×0.75 becomes 7.5, or \$7.50.

The seafood blend cans cost 90 cents each, and Julia purchased 20 cans. 90 cents is \$0.90, so the cost of the seafood blend cans is calculated as 20×0.90.

20×0.90 is the same thing as $10 \times 0.90 + 10 \times 0.90$. The value of $10 \times 0.90 = 9$, and

$9 + 9 = 18$. This means that Julia spent \$18 on the seafood blend cans.

Julia's total payment is calculated by finding the sum of all the purchased cans.

$\$8.90 + \$7.50 + \$18.00 = \$34.40$. Julia spent \$34.40 on cans of cat food.

26. B: TEKS Standard (5.9)(C)

Each dot represents one student. There are 8 dots above the mark for 4 books. This means 8 students read 4 books over the summer. There are 3 dots above the mark for 1 book. This means 3 students read 1 book over the summer. The difference between 8 books and 3 books is 4: $8 - 3 = 5$. 5 more students read 4 books than 1 book.

27. TEKS Standard (5.8)(C)

Correct points may be any three of the following:

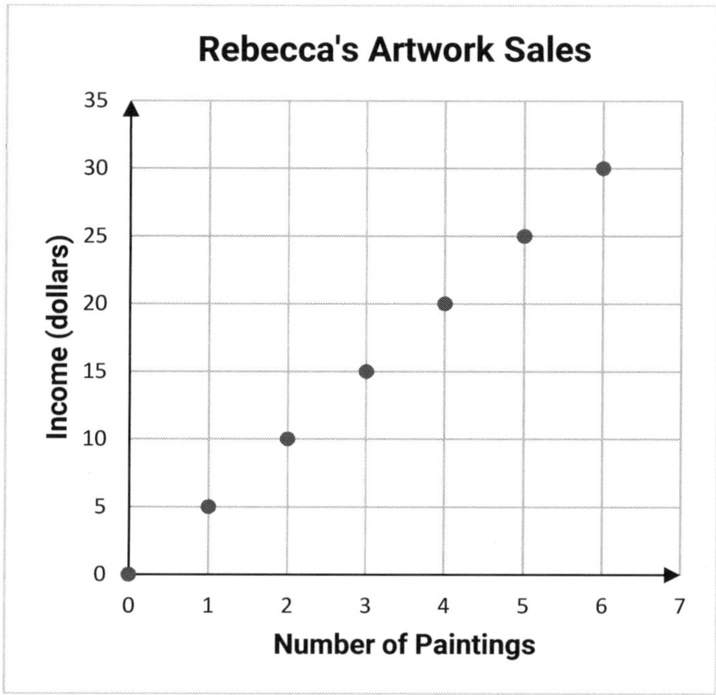

Rebecca earns \$5 for each painting she sells. If Rebecca sells 0 paintings, she earns \$0: (0,0). If Rebecca sells 1 painting, she earns \$5: (1,5). If Rebecca sells 2 paintings, she earns \$10: (2,10). 3 paintings will earn her \$15: (3,15). 4 paintings will earn her \$20: (4,20). 5 paintings will earn her \$25: (5,25). 6 paintings will earn her \$30: (6,30). The points (0,0), (1,5), (2,10), (3,15), (4,20) (5,25), and (6, 30) are correct.

To plot a point, move to the right the value in the x position of the coordinate point, then move up the value in the y position of the coordinate point. For example, to plot the point (2,10), move right to the value 2 and then up to the value 10 and plot a point.

28. 160: TEKS Standard (5.3)(A)

Mark has estimated each meal price by rounding to the nearest ten. When Mark rounds \$33.50 to the nearest ten, it becomes \$30. The total for all meal price estimations becomes $50 + 30 + 20 + 30 + 30 = 160$. Therefore, Mark's total estimation for all the meals is \$160.

29. C: TEKS Standard (5.6)(B)

The block consists of 4 horizontally stacked layers. Each layer has a length of 5 unit cubes and a width of 5 unit cubes. This means that each layer contains $5 \times 5 = 25$ unit cubes. There are 4 layers in the block. The total volume of the block is calculated by multiplying 25 by 4: $25 \times 4 = 100$. The block has a volume of 100 cubic units.

30. D: TEKS Standard (5.4)(B)

Let h represent the unknown total hours it takes John to build the birdhouses. Start the equation as $h =$. It takes John 2 hours to make one small birdhouse. If John makes 6 small birdhouses it will take him 2(6) hours. It takes John 3 hours to make one large birdhouse. If John makes 6 large birdhouses it will take him 3(6) hours. Add the hours spent on each type of birdhouse to find the total number of hours it takes John to make the birdhouses. In equation form, this is $h = 2(6) + 3(6)$, which simplifies to $h = 30$. It will take John 30 hours to complete all 12 bird houses.

31. A: TEKS Standard (5.3)(K)

Marcus drove 175.5 miles and flew 2,340.6 miles. Add these two values to determine the total travel distance. Stack the numbers and line up the decimal points. Add each place value from right to left. Regroup when necessary. Bring the decimal point straight down into the answer line. The result is 2,516.1. Marcus traveled 2,516.1 miles.

$$\begin{array}{r} {}^{1}\;\;{}^{1}\;\;\;\;\;\;\;\; \\ 2340.6 \\ +\;\;175.5 \\ \hline 2516.1 \end{array}$$

32. B: TEKS Standard (5.7)(A)

Roger rides his bike 1,500 meters each day. There are 7 days in a week, which means that Roger rides his bike $7 \times 1{,}500 = 10{,}500$ meters in a week. There are 1,000 meters in 1 kilometer. In order to convert 10,500 meters to kilometers, divide the number of meters by 1,000. $10{,}500 \div 1{,}000$ can be calculated mentally. Move the decimal point in 10,500.0 three places to the left. Each decimal movement to the left represents division by 10. The result is $10{,}500 \div 1{,}000 = 10.5$. Roger rides his stationary exercise bike 10.5 kilometers in a week.

33. TEKS Standard (5.5)(A)

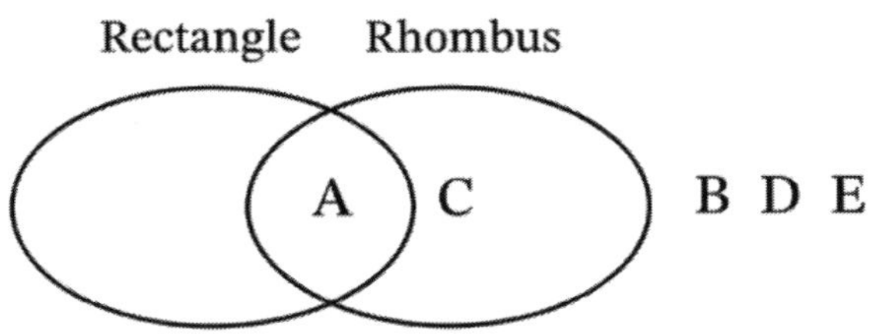

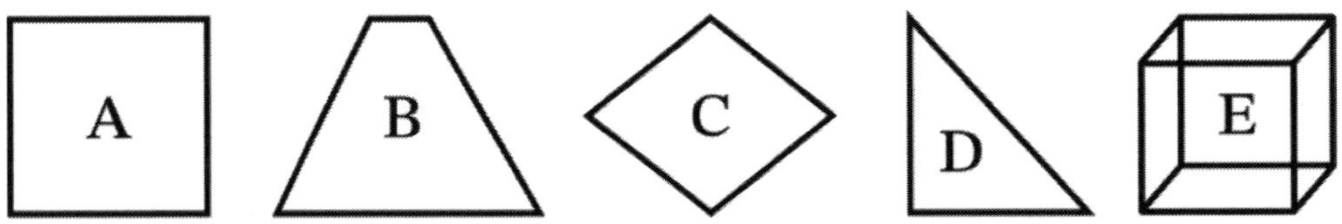

Left Section: Empty, Middle Section: A, Right Section: C, Outside: B, D, and E: A square can be classified as both a rectangle and a rhombus. A square is the only shape in the list that can be placed in the overlapping middle section of the Venn diagram. A rectangle has four right angles and two sets of parallel sides. A rhombus has four congruent side lengths and two sets of parallel sides. A square has four right angles, two sets of parallel sides, and four congruent side lengths. This means that squares fall into the category of both rectangle and rhombus. Shape C is a rhombus, but it does not have right angles, so it belongs in the right section of the diagram. Shape B is a trapezoid, and shape D is a triangle. Neither of these shapes are rectangles or rhombi. Shape E is a cube, and while it is made of squares, it is a three-dimensional figure. Three-dimensional figures do not belong in these categories.

34. A, B: TEKS Standard (5.3)(I)

Each large square has 12 equal shares, with 10 of those shares shaded. Altogether, there are 5 groups of $\frac{10}{12}$. This can be expressed in word form or as a numerical expression using multiplication, so answers A and B both represent the scenario. Answer C is incorrect because the model shows five squares with 12 equal shares, not five squares with 10 equal shares. Answers D and E are incorrect because the model shows 5 squares, or groups, not 10.

How to Overcome Test Anxiety

Just the thought of taking a test is enough to make most people a little nervous. A test is an important event that can have a long-term impact on your future, so it's important to take it seriously and it's natural to feel anxious about performing well. But just because anxiety is normal, that doesn't mean that it's helpful in test taking, or that you should simply accept it as part of your life. Anxiety can have a variety of effects. These effects can be mild, like making you feel slightly nervous, or severe, like blocking your ability to focus or remember even a simple detail.

If you experience test anxiety—whether severe or mild—it's important to know how to beat it. To discover this, first you need to understand what causes test anxiety.

Causes of Test Anxiety

While we often think of anxiety as an uncontrollable emotional state, it can actually be caused by simple, practical things. One of the most common causes of test anxiety is that a person does not feel adequately prepared for their test. This feeling can be the result of many different issues such as poor study habits or lack of organization, but the most common culprit is time management. Starting to study too late, failing to organize your study time to cover all of the material, or being distracted while you study will mean that you're not well prepared for the test. This may lead to cramming the night before, which will cause you to be physically and mentally exhausted for the test. Poor time management also contributes to feelings of stress, fear, and hopelessness as you realize you are not well prepared but don't know what to do about it.

Other times, test anxiety is not related to your preparation for the test but comes from unresolved fear. This may be a past failure on a test, or poor performance on tests in general. It may come from comparing yourself to others who seem to be performing better or from the stress of living up to expectations. Anxiety may be driven by fears of the future—how failure on this test would affect your educational and career goals. These fears are often completely irrational, but they can still negatively impact your test performance.

Elements of Test Anxiety

As mentioned earlier, test anxiety is considered to be an emotional state, but it has physical and mental components as well. Sometimes you may not even realize that you are suffering from test anxiety until you notice the physical symptoms. These can include trembling hands, rapid heartbeat, sweating, nausea, and tense muscles. Extreme anxiety may lead to fainting or vomiting. Obviously, any of these symptoms can have a negative impact on testing. It is important to recognize them as soon as they begin to occur so that you can address the problem before it damages your performance.

The mental components of test anxiety include trouble focusing and inability to remember learned information. During a test, your mind is on high alert, which can help you recall information and stay focused for an extended period of time. However, anxiety interferes with your mind's natural processes, causing you to blank out, even on the questions you know well. The strain of testing during anxiety makes it difficult to stay focused, especially on a test that may take several hours. Extreme anxiety can take a huge mental toll, making it difficult not only to recall test information but even to understand the test questions or pull your thoughts together.

Effects of Test Anxiety

Test anxiety is like a disease—if left untreated, it will get progressively worse. Anxiety leads to poor performance, and this reinforces the feelings of fear and failure, which in turn lead to poor performances on subsequent tests. It can grow from a mild nervousness to a crippling condition. If allowed to progress, test anxiety can have a big impact on your schooling, and consequently on your future.

Test anxiety can spread to other parts of your life. Anxiety on tests can become anxiety in any stressful situation, and blanking on a test can turn into panicking in a job situation. But fortunately, you don't have to let anxiety rule your testing and determine your grades. There are a number of relatively simple steps you can take to move past anxiety and function normally on a test and in the rest of life.

Physical Steps for Beating Test Anxiety

While test anxiety is a serious problem, the good news is that it can be overcome. It doesn't have to control your ability to think and remember information. While it may take time, you can begin taking steps today to beat anxiety.

Just as your first hint that you may be struggling with anxiety comes from the physical symptoms, the first step to treating it is also physical. Rest is crucial for having a clear, strong mind. If you are tired, it is much easier to give in to anxiety. But if you establish good sleep habits, your body and mind will be ready to perform optimally, without the strain of exhaustion. Additionally, sleeping well helps you to retain information better, so you're more likely to recall the answers when you see the test questions.

Getting good sleep means more than going to bed on time. It's important to allow your brain time to relax. Take study breaks from time to time so it doesn't get overworked, and don't study right before bed. Take time to rest your mind before trying to rest your body, or you may find it difficult to fall asleep.

Along with sleep, other aspects of physical health are important in preparing for a test. Good nutrition is vital for good brain function. Sugary foods and drinks may give a burst of energy but this burst is followed by a crash, both physically and emotionally. Instead, fuel your body with protein and vitamin-rich foods.

Also, drink plenty of water. Dehydration can lead to headaches and exhaustion, especially if your brain is already under stress from the rigors of the test. Particularly if your test is a long one, drink water during the breaks. And if possible, take an energy-boosting snack to eat between sections.

Along with sleep and diet, a third important part of physical health is exercise. Maintaining a steady workout schedule is helpful, but even taking 5-minute study breaks to walk can help get your blood pumping faster and clear your head. Exercise also releases endorphins, which contribute to a positive feeling and can help combat test anxiety.

When you nurture your physical health, you are also contributing to your mental health. If your body is healthy, your mind is much more likely to be healthy as well. So take time to rest, nourish your body with healthy food and water, and get moving as much as possible. Taking these physical steps will make you stronger and more able to take the mental steps necessary to overcome test anxiety.

Mental Steps for Beating Test Anxiety

Working on the mental side of test anxiety can be more challenging, but as with the physical side, there are clear steps you can take to overcome it. As mentioned earlier, test anxiety often stems from lack of preparation, so the obvious solution is to prepare for the test. Effective studying may be the most important weapon you have for beating test anxiety, but you can and should employ several other mental tools to combat fear.

First, boost your confidence by reminding yourself of past success—tests or projects that you aced. If you're putting as much effort into preparing for this test as you did for those, there's no reason you should expect to fail here. Work hard to prepare; then trust your preparation.

Second, surround yourself with encouraging people. It can be helpful to find a study group, but be sure that the people you're around will encourage a positive attitude. If you spend time with others who are anxious or cynical, this will only contribute to your own anxiety. Look for others who are motivated to study hard from a desire to succeed, not from a fear of failure.

Third, reward yourself. A test is physically and mentally tiring, even without anxiety, and it can be helpful to have something to look forward to. Plan an activity following the test, regardless of the outcome, such as going to a movie or getting ice cream.

When you are taking the test, if you find yourself beginning to feel anxious, remind yourself that you know the material. Visualize successfully completing the test. Then take a few deep, relaxing breaths and return to it. Work through the questions carefully but with confidence, knowing that you are capable of succeeding.

Developing a healthy mental approach to test taking will also aid in other areas of life. Test anxiety affects more than just the actual test—it can be damaging to your mental health and even contribute to depression. It's important to beat test anxiety before it becomes a problem for more than testing.

Study Strategy

Being prepared for the test is necessary to combat anxiety, but what does being prepared look like? You may study for hours on end and still not feel prepared. What you need is a strategy for test prep. The next few pages outline our recommended steps to help you plan out and conquer the challenge of preparation.

Step 1: Scope Out the Test

Learn everything you can about the format (multiple choice, essay, etc.) and what will be on the test. Gather any study materials, course outlines, or sample exams that may be available. Not only will this help you to prepare, but knowing what to expect can help to alleviate test anxiety.

Step 2: Map Out the Material

Look through the textbook or study guide and make note of how many chapters or sections it has. Then divide these over the time you have. For example, if a book has 15 chapters and you have five days to study, you need to cover three chapters each day. Even better, if you have the time, leave an extra day at the end for overall review after you have gone through the material in depth.

If time is limited, you may need to prioritize the material. Look through it and make note of which sections you think you already have a good grasp on, and which need review. While you are studying, skim quickly through the familiar sections and take more time on the challenging parts.

Write out your plan so you don't get lost as you go. Having a written plan also helps you feel more in control of the study, so anxiety is less likely to arise from feeling overwhelmed at the amount to cover.

Step 3: Gather Your Tools

Decide what study method works best for you. Do you prefer to highlight in the book as you study and then go back over the highlighted portions? Or do you type out notes of the important information? Or is it helpful to make flashcards that you can carry with you? Assemble the pens, index cards, highlighters, post-it notes, and any other materials you may need so you won't be distracted by getting up to find things while you study.

If you're having a hard time retaining the information or organizing your notes, experiment with different methods. For example, try color-coding by subject with colored pens, highlighters, or post-it notes. If you learn better by hearing, try recording yourself reading your notes so you can listen while in the car, working out, or simply sitting at your desk. Ask a friend to quiz you from your flashcards, or try teaching someone the material to solidify it in your mind.

Step 4: Create Your Environment

It's important to avoid distractions while you study. This includes both the obvious distractions like visitors and the subtle distractions like an uncomfortable chair (or a too-comfortable couch that makes you want to fall asleep). Set up the best study environment possible: good lighting and a comfortable work area. If background music helps you focus, you may want to turn it on, but otherwise keep the room quiet. If you are using a computer to take notes, be sure you don't have any other windows open, especially applications like social media, games, or anything else that could distract you. Silence your phone and turn off notifications. Be sure to keep water close by so you stay hydrated while you study (but avoid unhealthy drinks and snacks).

Also, take into account the best time of day to study. Are you freshest first thing in the morning? Try to set aside some time then to work through the material. Is your mind clearer in the afternoon or evening? Schedule your study session then. Another method is to study at the same time of day that you will take the test, so that your brain gets used to working on the material at that time and will be ready to focus at test time.

Step 5: Study!

Once you have done all the study preparation, it's time to settle into the actual studying. Sit down, take a few moments to settle your mind so you can focus, and begin to follow your study plan. Don't give in to distractions or let yourself procrastinate. This is your time to prepare so you'll be ready to fearlessly approach the test. Make the most of the time and stay focused.

Of course, you don't want to burn out. If you study too long you may find that you're not retaining the information very well. Take regular study breaks. For example, taking five minutes out of every hour to walk briskly, breathing deeply and swinging your arms, can help your mind stay fresh.

As you get to the end of each chapter or section, it's a good idea to do a quick review. Remind yourself of what you learned and work on any difficult parts. When you feel that you've mastered the material, move on to the next part. At the end of your study session, briefly skim through your notes again.

But while review is helpful, cramming last minute is NOT. If at all possible, work ahead so that you won't need to fit all your study into the last day. Cramming overloads your brain with more information than it can process and retain, and your tired mind may struggle to recall even previously learned information when it is overwhelmed with last-minute study. Also, the urgent nature of cramming and the stress placed on your brain contribute to anxiety. You'll be more likely to go to the test feeling unprepared and having trouble thinking clearly.

So don't cram, and don't stay up late before the test, even just to review your notes at a leisurely pace. Your brain needs rest more than it needs to go over the information again. In fact, plan to finish your studies by noon or early afternoon the day before the test. Give your brain the rest of the day to relax or focus on other things, and get a good night's sleep. Then you will be fresh for the test and better able to recall what you've studied.

Step 6: Take a Practice Test

Many courses offer sample tests, either online or in the study materials. This is an excellent resource to check whether you have mastered the material, as well as to prepare for the test format and environment.

Check the test format ahead of time: the number of questions, the type (multiple choice, free response, etc.), and the time limit. Then create a plan for working through them. For example, if you have 30 minutes to take a 60-question test, your limit is 30 seconds per question. Spend less time on the questions you know well so that you can take more time on the difficult ones.

If you have time to take several practice tests, take the first one open book, with no time limit. Work through the questions at your own pace and make sure you fully understand them. Gradually work up to taking a test under test conditions: sit at a desk with all study materials put away and set a timer. Pace yourself to make sure you finish the test with time to spare and go back to check your answers if you have time.

After each test, check your answers. On the questions you missed, be sure you understand why you missed them. Did you misread the question (tests can use tricky wording)? Did you forget the information? Or was it something you hadn't learned? Go back and study any shaky areas that the practice tests reveal.

Taking these tests not only helps with your grade, but also aids in combating test anxiety. If you're already used to the test conditions, you're less likely to worry about it, and working through tests until you're scoring well gives you a confidence boost. Go through the practice tests until you feel comfortable, and then you can go into the test knowing that you're ready for it.

Test Tips

On test day, you should be confident, knowing that you've prepared well and are ready to answer the questions. But aside from preparation, there are several test day strategies you can employ to maximize your performance.

First, as stated before, get a good night's sleep the night before the test (and for several nights before that, if possible). Go into the test with a fresh, alert mind rather than staying up late to study.

Try not to change too much about your normal routine on the day of the test. It's important to eat a nutritious breakfast, but if you normally don't eat breakfast at all, consider eating just a protein bar. If you're a coffee drinker, go ahead and have your normal coffee. Just make sure you time it so that the caffeine doesn't wear off right in the middle of your test. Avoid sugary beverages, and drink enough water to stay hydrated but not so much that you need a restroom break 10 minutes into the test. If your test isn't first thing in the morning, consider going for a walk or doing a light workout before the test to get your blood flowing.

Allow yourself enough time to get ready, and leave for the test with plenty of time to spare so you won't have the anxiety of scrambling to arrive in time. Another reason to be early is to select a good seat. It's helpful to sit away from doors and windows, which can be distracting. Find a good seat, get out your supplies, and settle your mind before the test begins.

When the test begins, start by going over the instructions carefully, even if you already know what to expect. Make sure you avoid any careless mistakes by following the directions.

Then begin working through the questions, pacing yourself as you've practiced. If you're not sure on an answer, don't spend too much time on it, and don't let it shake your confidence. Either skip it and come back later, or eliminate as many wrong answers as possible and guess among the remaining ones. Don't dwell on these questions as you continue—put them out of your mind and focus on what lies ahead.

Be sure to read all of the answer choices, even if you're sure the first one is the right answer. Sometimes you'll find a better one if you keep reading. But don't second-guess yourself if you do immediately know the answer. Your gut instinct is usually right. Don't let test anxiety rob you of the information you know.

If you have time at the end of the test (and if the test format allows), go back and review your answers. Be cautious about changing any, since your first instinct tends to be correct, but make sure you didn't misread any of the questions or accidentally mark the wrong answer choice. Look over any you skipped and make an educated guess.

At the end, leave the test feeling confident. You've done your best, so don't waste time worrying about your performance or wishing you could change anything. Instead, celebrate the successful completion of this test. And finally, use this test to learn how to deal with anxiety even better next time.

Review Video: Test Anxiety
Visit mometrix.com/academy and enter code: 100340

Important Qualification

Not all anxiety is created equal. If your test anxiety is causing major issues in your life beyond the classroom or testing center, or if you are experiencing troubling physical symptoms related to your anxiety, it may be a sign of a serious physiological or psychological condition. If this sounds like your situation, we strongly encourage you to seek professional help.

Online Resources

Due to our efforts to try to keep this book to a manageable length, we've created a link that will give you access to all of your online resources:

mometrix.com/resources719/staarg5math

It's Your Moment, Let's Celebrate It!

Share your story @mometrixtestpreparation

Mometrix
TEST PREPARATION

STAAR

Test Prep Guide Grade 7 Reading Language Arts

Introduction

Thank you for purchasing this resource! You have made the choice to prepare yourself for a test that could have a huge impact on your future, and this guide is designed to help you be fully ready for test day. Obviously, it's important to have a solid understanding of the test material, but you also need to be prepared for the unique environment and stressors of the test, so that you can perform to the best of your abilities.

For this purpose, the first section that appears in this guide is the **Success Strategies**. We've devoted countless hours to meticulously researching what works and what doesn't, and we've boiled down our findings to the four most impactful steps you can take to improve your performance on the test. We start at the beginning with study planning and move through the preparation process, all the way to the testing strategies that will help you get the most out of what you know when you're finally sitting in front of the test.

We recommend that you start preparing for your test as far in advance as possible. However, if you've bought this guide as a last-minute study resource and only have a few days before your test, we recommend that you skip over the first two Success Strategies since they address a long-term study plan.

If you struggle with **test anxiety**, we strongly encourage you to check out our recommendations for how you can overcome it. Test anxiety is a formidable foe, but it can be beaten, and we want to make sure you have the tools you need to defeat it.

Strategy #1 – Plan Big, Study Small

There's a lot riding on your performance. If you want to ace this test, you're going to need to keep your skills sharp and the material fresh in your mind. You need a plan that lets you review everything you need to know while still fitting in your schedule. We'll break this strategy down into three categories.

Information Organization

Start with the information you already have: the official test outline. From this, you can make a complete list of all the concepts you need to cover before the test. Organize these concepts into groups that can be studied together, and create a list of any related vocabulary you need to learn so you can brush up on any difficult terms. You'll want to keep this vocabulary list handy once you actually start studying since you may need to add to it along the way.

Time Management

Once you have your set of study concepts, decide how to spread them out over the time you have left before the test. Break your study plan into small, clear goals so you have a manageable task for each day and know exactly what you're doing. Then just focus on one small step at a time. When you manage your time this way, you don't need to spend hours at a time studying. Studying a small block of content for a short period each day helps you retain information better and avoid stressing over how much you have left to do. You can relax knowing that you have a plan to cover everything in time. In order for this strategy to be effective though, you have to start studying early and stick to your schedule. Avoid the exhaustion and futility that comes from last-minute cramming!

Study Environment

The environment you study in has a big impact on your learning. Studying in a coffee shop, while probably more enjoyable, is not likely to be as fruitful as studying in a quiet room. It's important to keep distractions to a minimum. You're only planning to study for a short block of time, so make the most of it. Don't pause to check your phone or get up to find a snack. It's also important to **avoid multitasking**. Research has consistently shown that multitasking will make your studying dramatically less effective. Your study area should also be comfortable and well-lit so you don't have the distraction of straining your eyes or sitting on an uncomfortable chair.

The time of day you study is also important. You want to be rested and alert. Don't wait until just before bedtime. Study when you'll be most likely to comprehend and remember. Even better, if you know what time of day your test will be, set that time aside for study. That way your brain will be used to working on that subject at that specific time and you'll have a better chance of recalling information.

Finally, it can be helpful to team up with others who are studying for the same test. Your actual studying should be done in as isolated an environment as possible, but the work of organizing the information and setting up the study plan can be divided up. In between study sessions, you can discuss with your teammates the concepts that you're all studying and quiz each other on the details. Just be sure that your teammates are as serious about the test as you are. If you find that your study time is being replaced with social time, you might need to find a new team.

Strategy #2 – Make Your Studying Count

You're devoting a lot of time and effort to preparing for this test, so you want to be absolutely certain it will pay off. This means doing more than just reading the content and hoping you can remember it on test day. It's important to make every minute of study count. There are two main areas you can focus on to make your studying count.

Retention

It doesn't matter how much time you study if you can't remember the material. You need to make sure you are retaining the concepts. To check your retention of the information you're learning, try recalling it at later times with minimal prompting. Try carrying around flashcards and glance at one or two from time to time or ask a friend who's also studying for the test to quiz you.

To enhance your retention, look for ways to put the information into practice so that you can apply it rather than simply recalling it. If you're using the information in practical ways, it will be much easier to remember. Similarly, it helps to solidify a concept in your mind if you're not only reading it to yourself but also explaining it to someone else. Ask a friend to let you teach them about a concept you're a little shaky on (or speak aloud to an imaginary audience if necessary). As you try to summarize, define, give examples, and answer your friend's questions, you'll understand the concepts better and they will stay with you longer. Finally, step back for a big picture view and ask yourself how each piece of information fits with the whole subject. When you link the different concepts together and see them working together as a whole, it's easier to remember the individual components.

Finally, practice showing your work on any multi-step problems, even if you're just studying. Writing out each step you take to solve a problem will help solidify the process in your mind, and you'll be more likely to remember it during the test.

Modality

Modality simply refers to the means or method by which you study. Choosing a study modality that fits your own individual learning style is crucial. No two people learn best in exactly the same way, so it's important to know your strengths and use them to your advantage.

For example, if you learn best by visualization, focus on visualizing a concept in your mind and draw an image or a diagram. Try color-coding your notes, illustrating them, or creating symbols that will trigger your mind to recall a learned concept. If you learn best by hearing or discussing information, find a study partner who learns the same way or read aloud to yourself. Think about how to put the information in your own words. Imagine that you are giving a lecture on the topic and record yourself so you can listen to it later.

For any learning style, flashcards can be helpful. Organize the information so you can take advantage of spare moments to review. Underline key words or phrases. Use different colors for different categories. Mnemonic devices (such as creating a short list in which every item starts with the same letter) can also help with retention. Find what works best for you and use it to store the information in your mind most effectively and easily.

Strategy #3 – Practice the Right Way

Your success on test day depends not only on how many hours you put into preparing, but also on whether you prepared the right way. It's good to check along the way to see if your studying is paying off. One of the most effective ways to do this is by taking practice tests to evaluate your progress. Practice tests are useful because they show exactly where you need to improve. Every time you take a practice test, pay special attention to these three groups of questions:

- The questions you got wrong
- The questions you had to guess on, even if you guessed right
- The questions you found difficult or slow to work through

This will show you exactly what your weak areas are, and where you need to devote more study time. Ask yourself why each of these questions gave you trouble. Was it because you didn't understand the material? Was it because you didn't remember the vocabulary? Do you need more repetitions on this type of question to build speed and confidence? Dig into those questions and figure out how you can strengthen your weak areas as you go back to review the material.

Additionally, many practice tests have a section explaining the answer choices. It can be tempting to read the explanation and think that you now have a good understanding of the concept. However, an explanation likely only covers part of the question's broader context. Even if the explanation makes perfect sense, **go back and investigate** every concept related to the question until you're positive you have a thorough understanding.

As you go along, keep in mind that the practice test is just that: practice. Memorizing these questions and answers will not be very helpful on the actual test because it is unlikely to have any of the same exact questions. If you only know the right answers to the sample questions, you won't be prepared for the real thing. **Study the concepts** until you understand them fully, and then you'll be able to answer any question that shows up on the test.

It's important to wait on the practice tests until you're ready. If you take a test on your first day of study, you may be overwhelmed by the amount of material covered and how much you need to learn. Work up to it gradually.

On test day, you'll need to be prepared for answering questions, managing your time, and using the test-taking strategies you've learned. It's a lot to balance, like a mental marathon that will have a big impact on your future. Like training for a marathon, you'll need to start slowly and work your way up. When test day arrives, you'll be ready.

Start with the strategies you've read in the first two Success Strategies—plan your course and study in the way that works best for you. If you have time, consider using multiple study resources to get different approaches to the same concepts. It can be helpful to see difficult concepts from more than one angle. Then find a good source for practice tests. Many times, the test website will suggest potential study resources or provide sample tests.

Test-Taking Strategies

This section contains a list of test-taking strategies that you may find helpful as you work through the test. By taking what you know and applying logical thought, you can maximize your chances of answering any question correctly!

It is very important to realize that every question is different and every person is different: no single strategy will work on every question, and no single strategy will work for every person. That's why we've included all of them here, so you can try them out and determine which ones work best for different types of questions and which ones work best for you.

Question Strategies

✓ Read Carefully

Read the question and the answer choices carefully. Don't miss the question because you misread the terms. You have plenty of time to read each question thoroughly and make sure you understand what is being asked. Yet a happy medium must be attained, so don't waste too much time. You must read carefully and efficiently.

✓ Contextual Clues

Look for contextual clues. If the question includes a word you are not familiar with, look at the immediate context for some indication of what the word might mean. Contextual clues can often give you all the information you need to decipher the meaning of an unfamiliar word. Even if you can't determine the meaning, you may be able to narrow down the possibilities enough to make a solid guess at the answer to the question.

✓ Prefixes

If you're having trouble with a word in the question or answer choices, try dissecting it. Take advantage of every clue that the word might include. Prefixes can be a huge help. Usually, they allow you to determine a basic meaning. *Pre-* means before, *post-* means after, *pro-* is positive, *de-* is negative. From prefixes, you can get an idea of the general meaning of the word and try to put it into context.

✓ Hedge Words

Watch out for critical hedge words, such as *likely, may, can, often, almost, mostly, usually, generally, rarely,* and *sometimes.* Question writers insert these hedge phrases to cover every possibility. Often an answer choice will be wrong simply because it leaves no room for exception. Be on guard for answer choices that have definitive words such as *exactly* and *always.*

✓ Switchback Words

Stay alert for *switchbacks.* These are the words and phrases frequently used to alert you to shifts in thought. The most common switchback words are *but, although,* and *however.* Others include *nevertheless, on the other hand, even though, while, in spite of, despite,* and *regardless of.* Switchback words are important to catch because they can change the direction of the question or an answer choice.

✓ Face Value

When in doubt, use common sense. Accept the situation in the problem at face value. Don't read too much into it. These problems will not require you to make wild assumptions. If you have to go beyond creativity and warp time or space in order to have an answer choice fit the question, then you should move on and consider the other answer choices. These are normal problems rooted in reality. The applicable relationship or explanation may not be readily apparent, but it is there for you to figure out. Use your common sense to interpret anything that isn't clear.

Answer Choice Strategies

✓ Answer Selection

The most thorough way to pick an answer choice is to identify and eliminate wrong answers until only one is left, then confirm it is the correct answer. Sometimes an answer choice may immediately seem right, but be careful. The test writers will usually put more than one reasonable answer choice on each question, so take a second to read all of them and make sure that the other choices are not equally obvious. As long as you have time left, it is better to read every answer choice than to pick the first one that looks right without checking the others.

✓ Answer Choice Families

An answer choice family consists of two (in rare cases, three) answer choices that are very similar in construction and cannot all be true at the same time. If you see two answer choices that are direct opposites or parallels, one of them is usually the correct answer. For instance, if one answer choice says that quantity *x* increases and another either says that quantity *x* decreases (opposite) or says that quantity *y* increases (parallel), then those answer choices would fall into the same family. An answer choice that doesn't match the construction of the answer choice family is more likely to be incorrect. Most questions will not have answer choice families, but when they do appear, you should be prepared to recognize them.

✓ Eliminate Answers

Eliminate answer choices as soon as you realize they are wrong, but make sure you consider all possibilities. If you are eliminating answer choices and realize that the last one you are left with is also wrong, don't panic. Start over and consider each choice again. There may be something you missed the first time that you will realize on the second pass.

✓ Avoid Fact Traps

Don't be distracted by an answer choice that is factually true but doesn't answer the question. You are looking for the choice that answers the question. Stay focused on what the question is asking for so you don't accidentally pick an answer that is true but incorrect. Always go back to the question and make sure the answer choice you've selected actually answers the question and is not merely a true statement.

✓ Extreme Statements

In general, you should avoid answers that put forth extreme actions as standard practice or proclaim controversial ideas as established fact. An answer choice that states the "process should be used in certain situations, if…" is much more likely to be correct than one that states the "process should be discontinued completely." The first is a calm rational statement and doesn't even make a definitive, uncompromising stance, using a hedge word *if* to provide wiggle room, whereas the second choice is far more extreme.

✓ Benchmark

As you read through the answer choices and you come across one that seems to answer the question well, mentally select that answer choice. This is not your final answer, but it's the one that will help you evaluate the other answer choices. The one that you selected is your benchmark or standard for judging each of the other answer choices. Every other answer choice must be compared to your benchmark. That choice is correct until proven otherwise by another answer choice beating it. If you find a better answer, then that one becomes your new benchmark. Once you've decided that no other choice answers the question as well as your benchmark, you have your final answer.

✓ Predict the Answer

Before you even start looking at the answer choices, it is often best to try to predict the answer. When you come up with the answer on your own, it is easier to avoid distractions and traps because you will know exactly what to look for. The right answer choice is unlikely to be word-for-word what you came up with, but it should be a close match. Even if you are confident that you have the right answer, you should still take the time to read each option before moving on.

General Strategies

✓ Tough Questions

If you are stumped on a problem or it appears too hard or too difficult, don't waste time. Move on! Remember though, if you can quickly check for obviously incorrect answer choices, your chances of guessing correctly are greatly improved. Before you completely give up, at least try to knock out a couple of possible answers. Eliminate what you can and then guess at the remaining answer choices before moving on.

✓ Check Your Work

Since you will probably not know every term listed and the answer to every question, it is important that you get credit for the ones that you do know. Don't miss any questions through careless mistakes. If at all possible, try to take a second to look back over your answer selection and make sure you've selected the correct answer choice and haven't made a costly careless mistake (such as marking an answer choice that you didn't mean to mark). This quick double check should more than pay for itself in caught mistakes for the time it costs.

✓ Don't Rush

It is very easy to make errors when you are in a hurry. Maintaining a fast pace in answering questions is pointless if it makes you miss questions that you would have gotten right otherwise. Test writers like to include distracting information and wrong answers that seem right. Taking a little extra time to avoid careless mistakes can make all the difference in your test score. Find a pace that allows you to be confident in the answers that you select.

✓ Keep Moving

Panicking will not help you pass the test, so do your best to stay calm and keep moving. Taking deep breaths and going through the answer elimination steps you practiced can help to break through a stress barrier and keep your pace.

Final Notes

The combination of a solid foundation of content knowledge and the confidence that comes from practicing your plan for applying that knowledge is the key to maximizing your performance on test day. As your foundation of content knowledge is built up and strengthened, you'll find that the strategies included in this chapter become more and more effective in helping you quickly sift through the distractions and traps of the test to isolate the correct answer.

Now that you're preparing to move forward into the test content chapters of this book, be sure to keep your goal in mind. As you read, think about how you will be able to apply this information on the test. If you've already seen sample questions for the test and you have an idea of the question format and style, try to come up with questions of your own that you can answer based on what you're reading. This will give you valuable practice applying your knowledge in the same ways you can expect to on test day.

Good luck and good studying!

Reading

Vocabulary

Dictionary

A print or digital dictionary can be used to find out many things about a word. A dictionary will show the correct pronunciation of a word, provide its meaning, and identify what part of speech the word is. It will also tell how the word was derived—that is, what words it came from originally. A dictionary will have a **pronunciation guide** for each word that shows how to sound it out and where its syllables start and end. It will use symbols to indicate sounds, and will also use sample sounds (the "a" in "bad," for instance). A dictionary lists all of the meanings of a word and the parts of speech the word can be used as.

Example

Philippe used his dictionary to check the various meanings of the word *eliminate*. He found this entry:

eliminate \ i-ˈli-mə-ˌnāt \ verb

1. to put an end to or get rid of
2. to expel from the living body
3. to cause to disappear by combining two or more equations

Identify which definition of *eliminate* is used in the following sentence:

> Harold couldn't wait to *eliminate* the other team from the playoffs by winning the first two games.

The correct answer is meaning 1: "to put an end to or get rid of." If you substitute that definition for the word, the sentence makes sense. Meanings 2 and 3 do not fit with the context of the sentence. When considering which meaning is being used, always check for context clues in the sentence or in the sentences before or after the sentence in which the word is used. Dictionaries also tell you how to pronounce words and often the derivation of the word, although that is not given here.

Thesaurus

A thesaurus is a reference book that gives **synonyms** of words. It is different from a dictionary because a thesaurus does not give definitions. A thesaurus can be helpful in finding the meaning of an unfamiliar word when reading. If the meaning of a synonym is known, then the meaning of the unfamiliar word will be known. Another time in which a thesaurus can be helpful is when writing. Using a thesaurus helps authors to vary their word choice.

Glossary

A glossary is a **list of terms and their definitions** that can be found **at the back** of certain types of books, such as textbooks or reference books. A glossary does not have the definitions of all words, like a dictionary, but instead gives the definitions of the important terms within that particular book which are either uncommon or newly introduced. One may use a glossary when reading a book about economics or a chapter in a science textbook, for example, to define some of the technical terms within the text.

Denotative and Connotative Meanings

The **denotative meaning** of a word is the exact dictionary definition of the word. The **connotative meaning** of a word is the emotion conveyed by the use of the word in context. The word may have associated meaning in addition to its dictionary definition. A good way to remember the difference between denotative and connotative is to think "direct" or "dictionary" in relation to denotative.

An example of a denotative meaning for the adjective *ablaze* would be "burning", as in the logs burning in a fireplace. A connotative meaning for the adjective *ablaze*, based on the context of the word, may indicate a level of comfort while sitting in front of a fireplace. For instance, in the context: "A logs were *ablaze* in the fireplace, radiating heat out into the corners of the snow-enclosed room", the word *ablaze* implies comfort and coziness within the space described. The connotative meaning of a word can often have an emotional association for the reader.

Example

Define the denotative and connotative meaning of the word *palace* in the following sentence:

> The golden *palace* gates opened slowly to reveal an expansive garden that was well-tended by precise gardeners all wearing the king's insignia.

In the example, the denotative meaning of the word is that a *palace* is literally a place where royalty lives. A *palace* implies, or connotes, a place of riches and is usually associated with wealth. The words "golden", "expansive garden", and "king's insignia" all give clues that the *palace* can be viewed as a place of importance, one that is well taken care of.

When looking for the denotative meaning of a word, remember to think "direct", or the literal meaning of the word. The connotative meaning of the word is implied and not directly stated; the connotative meaning is often associated with emotion and feeling about the typical context of the word.

Using Context to Determine the Meanings of Words

Readers of all levels will encounter words that they have either never seen or that they have seen before but still don't know what it means. The best way to define a word in **context** is to look for nearby words that can assist in learning the meaning of the word.

Context Clues

Context clues are hints about the meaning of a word. They are the words or phrases in the sentence or sentences before and after a new or unfamiliar word. Context clues give the reader an idea about what a word means. A context clue may also contain words that help define the new word or an example of what the new word means. A context clue in the form of an example may contain the words including 'such as', a dash, or a colon before stated information.

Using context clues to figure out meaning can be helpful when learning a new set of vocabulary words or reading a difficult text. The dictionary definition of a word can always be looked up to double-check intended meaning.

Review Video: Reading Comprehension: Using Context Clues
Visit mometrix.com/academy and enter code: 613660

Example

Using context clues, determine the meaning of *gregarious* in the following excerpt.

> Beverly is the most *gregarious* person I have ever known. She loves people and spends a lot of her time talking to her friends and arranging get-togethers. She doesn't mind spending hours cooking as long as she knows that her house will be filled with people.

This excerpt says Beverly loves people and spends a lot of her time talking with friends and arranging get-togethers. It also says that she likes her house filled with people. These clues in the sentence help the reader determine that *gregarious* means Beverly is someone who likes to talk with other people, so she is "sociable."

Example

Read the sentence and explain the meaning of *sense of foreboding:*

> All day long Ron kept thinking about Sue. For some unknown reason he was worried about her. He had a strong *sense of foreboding* that something was about to go wrong in Sue's city. Then he heard about the earthquake there. Luckily Sue was not injured.

To figure out the meaning of the phrase *sense of foreboding*, the reader needs to look for context clues in just the same way the reader would do to figure out the meaning of a single word. The excerpt says that Ron was "worried" about Sue for "some unknown reason." It also says that he felt that "something was going to go wrong in Sue's city." Ron also heard about an earthquake taking place in Sue's city. A "sense of foreboding" must mean that Ron had an idea that something bad was going to happen. The context clues help the reader figure out the meaning of the phrase.

Substitution to Find Meaning

One way to find out if you have figured out the correct meaning of a new word is to **substitute** the meaning for the word. Using the example for *basin*, if the reader substituted in "depression in the earth," the sentence would read:

> The "depression in the earth" had filled with water over the summer months, so that the rocky bottom was no longer visible to the casual hiker.

This is a way for the reader to confirm that they have used the context clues in the sentence correctly.

Synonyms and Antonyms

When you understand how words relate to each other, you will discover more in a passage. This is explained by understanding **synonyms**, which are words that mean the same thing, and **antonyms**, which are words that mean the opposite of one another. As an example, *dry* and *arid* are synonyms, and *dry* and *wet* are antonyms.

Review Video: What are Synonyms and Antonyms?
Visit mometrix.com/academy and enter code: 105612

Definition Within a Text

An author may **define** a word in the text. For example, an author may write, "The company did not have sufficient capital, that is, available money, to continue operating." The author defined "capital" as "available money." Authors will use words and phrases, such as "that is," "or," "meaning," and "which is," to let the reader know that they are defining the word.

ANALOGY

Analogies are used to **compare relationships**. For example, the analogy "restaurant is to eating as store is to shopping." A restaurant is a place where you eat, and a store is a place where you shop. The analogy compares locations and the things people do at those locations. **Analogies** can also be used to show the meaning of unfamiliar words. For example, consider the analogy "author is to writing as artisan is to crafting." *Artisan* may be an unfamiliar word to some. However, this analogy begins with "author is to writing." An author writes to create books, articles, and poems. The first part of the analogy pairs a person's job title with the action that their job requires. Based on this, a reader can conclude that an artisan is someone who crafts things.

EXAMPLES THAT CLARIFY MEANING

An author may use a word and then give examples that reveal its meaning. Consider this text: "Those who do not know sign language can communicate with people who are deaf or hard of hearing by using gestures. These may include pointing their fingers to indicate which direction to look or go or holding up a hand to indicate stopping." The author of this text has used the word *gestures* and then followed it with examples. This shows a reader who is unfamiliar with the word that gestures are hand motions. Readers can find examples by looking for signal words like "for example," "for instance," "like," and "such as."

CONTRAST

Readers can use these **contrasting** words and **opposites** as context clues to help them understand unfamiliar words. For example, an author may write, "Our conversation was not cheery. We sat and talked very solemnly about the events." Because the author says the conversation was "not cheery," a reader who is not familiar with the word "solemnly" can see that "solemn" means the opposite of cheery. This shows that *solemn* must mean serious or sad.

CAUSE AND EFFECT

A text that discusses a **cause and effect** can also show the meaning of an unfamiliar word. Consider the following sentence: "The student was mortified after she learned that she accidentally sang the wrong song at the talent show." *Mortified* may be an unfamiliar word. However, this sentence shows that the student became mortified as a result of her mistake. The reader can understand that making a mistake in front of many people is the cause. Usually, this would have the effect of making someone very embarrassed. *Mortified* means "extremely embarrassed," which is supported by the event in the sentence.

MULTIPLE-MEANING WORDS

A multiple-meaning word has different definitions, depending on the contextual use of the word. A multiple-meaning word is also called a **homonym**. A homonym is defined as a word that has more than one meaning, but is spelled and pronounced the same for all of them. For example, look at the word *leaves* in the following two sentences:

1. Michelle *leaves* the building at 5 o'clock every day.
2. The *leaves* fell off the oak tree in September.

In the first sentence, *leaves* means exits. In the second sentence, *leaves* refers to parts of a tree. By looking at the rest of each sentence, the reader can understand which definition of the multiple-meaning word the author is referring to.

Similar Words

Homophones are words that are pronounced the same, but may be spelled differently. An example of two homophones would be *heir* (someone due to inherit an estate) and *air* (the invisible substance people breathe).

Homographs are words that are spelled the same, but may be pronounced differently. An example of a homograph is the word *row*, which is pronounced one way when used to mean a horizontal grouping and is pronounced another way when used to mean an argument.

Root Words and Affixes

A **root word** is a word that can be added onto. An **affix** is a prefix or suffix that is added onto a root word. Often, the affixes in the English language come from Latin or Greek origins. A **prefix** is added to the beginning of a root word and a **suffix** is added to the end of a root word.

For example, the word "inscription" is made up of three sections. The root *script* means "write" or "writing." There are two affixes in the word. The prefix *in-* can mean various things such as "not," but also "on." In this case it means "on." The suffix *-tion* means "action" or "process." So, put together, the word "inscription" means "the act of writing on." Studying roots and affixes is important because it allows you to decode words you might not otherwise understand with relative ease.

Common Greek and Latin Root Words

Root	Meaning	Example
gen	born	genealogy (the study of ancestry)
luc	light	translucent (something light can be seen through)
log/logue	spoken	monologue (a speech performed by one person)
mis/mit	to send	transmit (to send something to another place)
omni	all	omniscient (all knowing)
phil	loving	philanthropist (someone that acts for the good of others)
photo	light	photon (a small particle of light)
scrib/script	to write	transcript (a written copy of spoken words)
sens/sent	to feel	sensory (an experience related to one of the five senses)
vac	empty, void	vacant (the state of being empty)
vid/vis	related to sight	video (a recording that is viewed, or watched)

COMMON PREFIXES

Prefix	Meaning	Example
dis-	not	disagree (not agree)
im-	not	impossible (not possible)
in-	in, into, not	injustice (an action that is not just)
mis-	wrongly	misspell (to spell wrongly)
non-	not	nonpaid (not paid)
pre-	before	preview (to view before)
sub-	under	submerge (to sink below the surface)
super-	over or greater than	superhuman (greater than a regular human)
trans-	across, through, or change	translate (to write or say in a different language)

COMMON SUFFIXES

Suffix	Meaning	Example
-able	can be done	likeable (can be liked)
-er	a person connected with	teacher (a person connected with teaching)
-ful	full of	wonderful (full of wonder)
-it/ity	state of	activity (state of being active)
-ive	cause to, tend to, or doing	creative (a person who tends to make new things or think of new ideas)
-logy	study of	biology (study of life)
-ment	the result	payment (the result of being paid)
-ness	state of being	darkness (being dark)
-y	characterized by	cloudy (characterized by clouds)

EXAMPLE

Use knowledge of affixes to figure out the meaning of the word *mournful* in the following sentence:

> "Well, it being away in the night and stormy, and all so mysterious-like, I felt just the way any other boy would a felt when I see that wreck laying there so *mournful* and lonesome in the middle of the river." (From *The Adventures of Huckleberry Finn* by Mark Twain).

Mourn means to grieve for something, while *-ful* refers to being "full of". Putting the two components together, *mournful* means "full of grief or sadness". This definition makes sense in the context of the sentence. The "wreck" in the sentence is sad looking because it is in the river by itself.

When trying to determine the meaning of a word, always look for a root word and any prefixes or suffixes that have been added on to the root word. If a component of a word is not familiar, decipher what is clear about the word, then look at the word as used in context.

Chapter Quiz

1. A thesaurus can do all of the following, EXCEPT:

a. Give synonyms of words
b. Give word definitions
c. Help find the meaning of an unfamiliar word
d. Help authors vary their word choice when writing

2. Which of the following are words that sound alike, but are spelled differently and have different meanings?

a. Synonyms
b. Antonyms
c. Homophones
d. Homographs

3. What common suffix indicates state of being?

a. -ness
b. -y
c. -ful
d. -er

Chapter Quiz Answer Key

1. B: See section **Thesaurus**

2. C: See section **Similar Words**

3. A: See section **Common Suffixes**

Comprehension Skills

Making Predictions

When you read a story, you should look for clues to make a prediction about what will happen. At the end of the story, you may even think about what will happen next to the main character, and use the clues in the story to make a prediction. You can also use personal experience to help make a prediction.

Suppose there is a story about a boy going swimming, and he swims too far out. Suppose the story says the boy can't get back to shore and starts to yell. Suppose the lifeguard comes and helps him. Suppose the story stops after the boy goes back in the water again. The reader might make the prediction that the boy won't swim as far out this time. This may not be true, but it is the most likely thing to happen.

EXAMPLE

Describe what prediction can be made based on the following sentences:

> When Glen is sick, his mother keeps him home from school. He stays in bed all day and takes medicine. Glen woke up this morning with a sore throat. His head was hot, and he felt achy.

The story says that Glen's mother keeps him home when he is sick and that Glen spends the day in bed when he is sick. The story says that Glen woke up this morning with a sore throat. His head was hot, and he felt achy. The reader can figure out that Glen was sick. Because Glen's mother always keeps him home when he is sick, the reader can predict that Glen will be staying home from school and spending the day in bed.

You can also use text features find information to make predictions and verify conclusions determined about different texts. Using key words as clues, looking for bold print words, looking for sentences that include captions, and words that are written in italics are a few features that can be used to help understand and make predictions about a text.

USING STRUCTURE AND GENRE TO MAKE PREDICTIONS

The structure and genre of a story can also help readers make predictions. Most stories follow the same structure. They have an exposition, rising action, a climax, falling action, and a resolution. Because most stories follow this structure, readers can predict that each of these parts will occur in the story. For example, rising action usually begins after the conflict of the story is introduced. This means that if characters have not faced any conflict, the reader can predict that something will go wrong for the characters. Likewise, stories in the same genre may contain similar events. For example, in a mystery, the characters work to solve a crime or explain a strange event. So, when reading a mystery, the reader can predict that the conflict will be a crime or event that the characters must learn more about.

MAKING CONNECTIONS TO ENHANCE COMPREHENSION

Reading involves thinking. For good comprehension, readers make text-to-self, text-to-text, and text-to-world connections. Making connections helps readers understand text better and predict what might occur next based on what they already know, such as how characters in the story feel or what happened in another text. Readers can make connections before, during, and after reading. Venn diagrams and other graphic organizers can help readers visualize connections.

TEXT-TO-SELF

Reading while looking for connections with the reader's life and experiences makes literature more personally relevant and meaningful to readers. Sentences showing text-to-self connections may begin with these examples

- This is similar to a time when...
- I understand how the character feels because...
- The setting makes me think of...
- I experienced this same thing when...

TEXT-TO-TEXT

Reading while looking for connections to other texts helps the reader learn to identify the way authors use genre, setting, characters, plot elements, literary structure and devices, and themes to create meaning. Sentences showing text-to-text connections may begin with these examples

- The character in this story reminds me of the character in...
- These two stories are alike because...
- The conflict in this story is similar to the conflict in...
- The relationship between the friends in this story is different than the relationship in...

TEXT-TO-WORLD

Reading while looking for connections to the world helps the reader begin to see literature as a reflection of real life and notice patterns in history and current events. Sentences showing text-to-world connections may begin with these examples

- The event in this story sounds like the event in history when...
- The actions of this character sound like...
- This is like what happened in real life when...
- I heard about this on the news when...

MAKING INFERENCES

An **inference** is a **conclusion** or generalization that the reader makes based on the information provided within a text. Certain facts are included to help a reader come to a specific conclusion. It is what the story may hint about, and what a reader can conclude as a result of what the author says in the passage. It is also the best guess that a reader can make based on what happened or was said or in a story. A good inference is based on or supported by details in the passage.

Readers may come to their own conclusion about a topic, or the author may state a conclusion at the end of a story. When readers are in the middle of a story, they can predict what will happen at the end of it based on the events that have occurred so far and the typical characteristics that have been presented by the author up to that point. A reader needs to consider all of the information that an author has presented, including the main point and supporting points, to make logical conclusions and inferences about the story.

For instance, if a passage says that Joan is holding her mouth and moaning, you might conclude, or **infer,** that she has a sore mouth or a toothache. You cannot be sure of this, but it is the best conclusion that you can reach using the information at hand. Inferences are considered **implicit information**. They are not found directly in a passage, but they can be supported by explicit information from the passage.

Review Video: Inference
Visit mometrix.com/academy and enter code: 379203

FINDING EXPLICIT INFORMATION

Explicit information is the term for information that is **directly stated** in a story or passage. It is what **the author tells you**. It is not information that is hinted at or that you have to make a conclusion about. Explicit information can be facts or details about an event, something or someone. There is usually a lot of explicit information in a story and this information is often used to make an inference or draw a conclusion. to answer questions that ask about explicit information, simply reread the story until you find the answer. in fiction, details about characters, events, and setting are often explicit.

EXAMPLE

Read the following excerpt. Tell whether it contains explicit information or not.

> I think the most famous person in the Old West is Annie Oakley. Annie is the best rifle shot who ever lived. She almost never missed. Many men challenged her to contests of speed and accuracy. She won them all.

Most of the information in the excerpt is explicit information. The information tells the reader about Annie Oakley: that she was the best rifle shot who ever lived and that she almost never missed. It also says that many men challenged her to contests and she won them all. This information is found right in the excerpt. It is not suggested or hinted at. Everything that is said is clearly what it means. The first sentence is a personal opinion; it is also explicit because the reader does not have to guess what the author thinks of Annie Oakley.

IMPLICIT INFORMATION

Implicit information is information that is **not directly stated** in a text, but can be inferred from something that the author explicitly states. For instance, the author may say "Seth buys a new TV, laptop, and home theater system every year." from this the reader could infer several things. For instance, Seth probably likes electronics and has a lot of spending money.

EXAMPLE

Draw a conclusion based on the implicit information in the following sentence from the *Adventures of Tom Sawyer* by Mark Twain:

> He had discovered a great law of human action, without knowing it—namely, that in order to make a man or a boy covet a thing, it is only necessary to make the thing difficult to attain.

The reader can clearly see from the sentence that the character did not set out to learn something, but through an action, the character learned that people will want what is hard to attain. Although it's not explicitly stated, the reader can draw the conclusion that the character gained the experience of coveting (or desiring) something that was hard to get.

EXAMPLE

Read the passage and discuss why the conclusion that the Vikings were searching for new farmland is valid.

> The Vikings set out in their boats in summer. The number of people in Scandinavia was growing fast. They needed to grow more food. In the late 900s, Eric the Red sailed across the Atlantic to Greenland. In 985, Viking farmers settled in Greenland.

The passage says that the Viking population was growing and that they needed to be able to grow more food. It is logical to guess that they sailed in search of new farmland. There is really not another possibility. Remember, inferences are assumptions that are hinted at or suggested by the text. They are not like explicit information; they are implicit in the text based on the explicit information that is found there. They are the best guess a reader can make.

EXAMPLE

Read the following sentence and draw a conclusion based upon the information presented:

> "You know the reason Mother proposed not having any presents this Christmas was because it is going to be a hard winter for everyone; and she thinks we ought not to spend money for pleasure, when our men are suffering so in the army." (from *Little Women* by Louisa May Alcott, p. 3)

Based on the information in the sentence, the reader can conclude, or infer, that the men are away at war while the women are still at home. The pronoun 'our' gives a clue to the reader that the character is speaking about men she knows. In addition, the reader can assume that the character is speaking to a brother or sister, since the term Mother is used by the character while speaking to another person. The reader can also come to the conclusion that the characters celebrate Christmas, since it is mentioned in the context of the sentence. In the sentence, the Mother is presented as an unselfish character who is opinionated and thinks about the well-being of other people.

EXAMPLE

Draw a conclusion based on the following sentence from *The Adventures of Tom Sawyer* by Mark Twain:

> He had discovered a great law of human action, without knowing it—namely, that in order to make a man or a boy covet a thing, it is only necessary to make the thing difficult to attain.

The reader can conclude from the sentence that the character did not set out to learn something, but through an action, the character learned that people will want what is hard to attain. The character learned a fact about human nature: that a person will value something more if they have to work hard for it, than if it is simply given to them. The word *covet* means to desire, which the character learns can be manipulated by making an item or an outcome more difficult to grasp. In everyday life, this could apply toward taking a hard test and doing well. If someone studies for a hard test and does well, the person will value their score more than if the test was very easy and he or she did not study for the test.

KEY IDEAS AND SUPPORTING DETAILS

Identifying **key ideas** helps the reader see what a text or story is mostly about. They are the **most important ideas** in a text, and everything else in the text builds around and supports them. Every piece of writing has key ideas. The **supporting details** in a story, such as the characters, events, and settings, will work together to reveal the key ideas. The details are not key ideas, themselves. They make the key ideas clear and show the reader the author's purpose for writing the text.

SYNTHESIZING A TEXT WITH EXISTING KNOWLEDGE

Synthesizing is similar to summarizing but it takes it one step further. Synthesizing involves taking the main points of a text and comparing it with existing knowledge to create a new idea, perspective, or way of thinking.

Another term for knowledge that you already have is **schema**. The plural form of this word is **schemata**. Schemata contain all the ideas you have about something. Synthesizing is all about how schemata change over time with the introduction of new information.

EXAMPLE

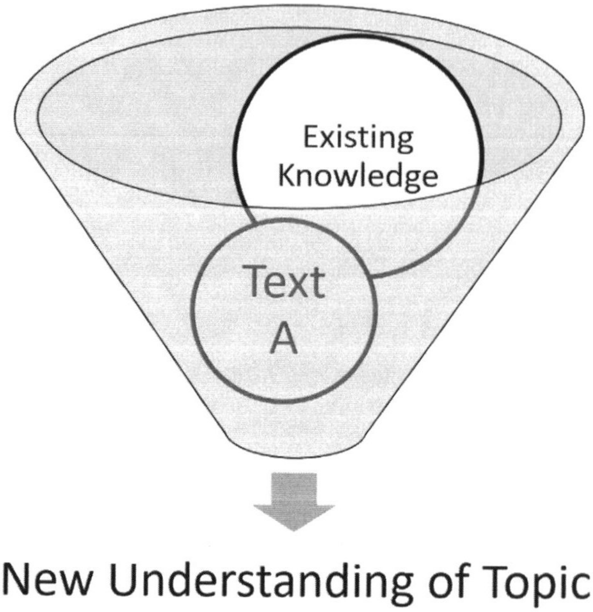

Using self-questioning strategies can help readers synthesize texts with their schemata to increase or change their understanding of topics. These questions include

- What do I already know about this topic?
- Is any of this new information?
- Has my perspective changed now that I've read this?
- What do I understand now that I didn't before?
- What are the main ideas of this text?
- How do the parts of the text fit together to create meaning?
- Are there any text-to-text, text-to-self, or text-to-world connections here?

Synthesizing Texts Without Existing Knowledge

If the reader is completely unfamiliar with the topic, they will have no background knowledge. In this case, instead of using existing knowledge, synthesizing may instead be done by combining the ideas provided in two or three different texts. The reader must make connections between the texts, determine how the ideas fit together, and gather evidence to support the new perspective.

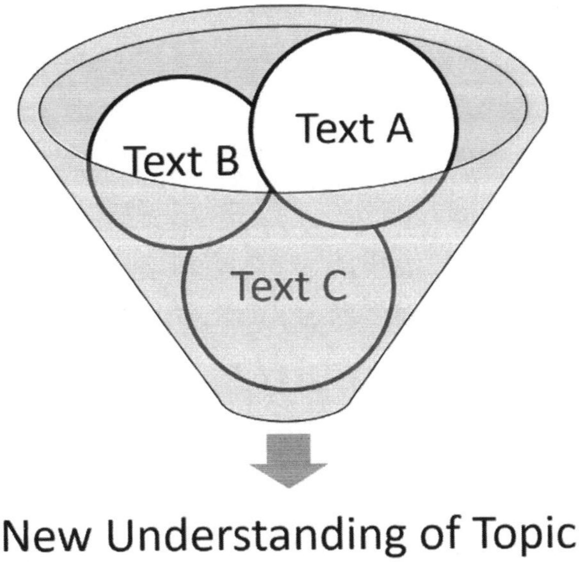

Using self-questioning strategies can help readers synthesize texts to increase their understanding of topics. In this case, readers are creating new schemata as they read. These questions include

- What do these texts have in common?
- What is different between these texts?
- What new information have I learned?
- What do I understand now that I didn't before?
- How do these texts relate to one another?
- If I think of these texts as parts of one whole, what meaning do they create together?
- What predictions can I make about this topic?

Chapter Quiz

1. Which of the following helps the reader learn to identify ways authors use genre, setting, characters, plot elements, literary structure and devices, and themes to create meaning?

a. Reading while looking for connections to the reader's life
b. Reading while looking for connections to other texts
c. Reading while looking for connections to the world
d. Reading while looking for connections to history

2. Which of the following is a conclusion that the reader makes using clues in the text?

a. Thesis
b. Prediction
c. Inference
d. Guess

3. What term refers to knowledge that you already have?

a. Cognition
b. Glossary
c. Schema
d. Explicit information

Chapter Quiz Answer Key

1. B: See section **Making Connections to Enhance Comprehension**

2. C: See section **Making Inferences**

3. C: See section **Synthesizing a Text with Existing Knowledge**

Response Skills

Text Evidence

The term **text evidence** refers to information found in a text that supports a reader's claim about the text. A reader can draw conclusions or inferences based upon information found in a text. Often, the author will deliberately include information that supports the main point of the text to help the reader make conclusions and inferences that align with the author's purpose for writing the text.

Drawing Conclusions Based on Text Evidence

Readers often need to use prior experience and background information to draw an accurate conclusion about the passage they are reading. Sometimes interpreting the information in a sentence can be difficult, especially if the reader is unfamiliar with some of the words used in a sentence. Looking at the words that the reader does understand in the sentence can help. By taking a pen or pencil and underlining important information in a sentence, the reader can better understand what the author is trying to say and draw a clearer conclusion from that.

Example

Draw a conclusion based on the following sentence:

> New Orleans then was a mere huddle of buildings around Jackson Square; but with the purchase of the Louisiana territory from France, and the great influx of American enterprise that characterized the first quarter of the last century, development was working like yeast...

The sentence describes how New Orleans grew after the "purchase of the Louisiana territory" and how "development was working like yeast". Yeast multiplies rapidly, so the reader can conclude that New Orleans was growing rapidly.

Example

Read the following sentence. Draw a conclusion based upon the information presented.

> "A rosy-faced servant-maid opened the door, and smiled as she took the letter which he silently offered."

The reader can conclude, based on the sentence, that the servant-maid is friendly. The words "rosy-faced" and "smiled" lead the reader to this conclusion. People who are friendly are often described as having rosy complexions and smiling as a common sign of pleasantness. The reader can also assume, from the sentence, that the letter does not present any threat or unpleasantness to the servant-maid. The person presenting the letter does not have anything to say upon offering it, so perhaps he is waiting to see how the servant-maid will react.

When interpreting a sentence, always look for key words that describe a character. The author carefully crafts a description of each character, to form a picture in the reader's mind about what the character is like.

PARAPHRASING AND SUMMARIZING

Paraphrasing and summarizing are two ways readers can work to understand what they read. Both involve reading a text and recalling the main points in an accurate way, but they differ in several ways.

How to Paraphrase	How to Summarize
State the message in the text in the reader's own words, while keeping the original meaning of the text Take all of the original ideas and word them in a way that the reader can better understand Put what the reader has read into their own words, rephrasing what the author has written	State main points of the text clearly and to-the-point. Take information and state it simply, in a much shorter form. Put information in a short form that keeps the main points of the whole text. Do not include many details, just the main idea of the text

Paraphrasing is often done for individual ideas, while summarizing is done for an entire block of text or ideas. Often times, a summary can be done in just one sentence, boiling down the author's words into just main idea.

Review Video: Summarizing Text
Visit mometrix.com/academy and enter code: 172903

PARAPHRASING THE MAIN POINT OF A SENTENCE

Paraphrase the main point of the following two sentences:

> Emmanuel went swimming in the lake by his house, where the water reached a depth of twenty feet in the middle. He did not venture out more than six feet into the water, however.

When paraphrasing a couple sentences or an entire paragraph, always include the main point of the text being reviewed, this is what the reader needs to know about the text. in the example, the reader needs to know that Emmanuel went swimming in the lake, but not more than six feet out. A paraphrase of the text may include: Emmanuel went swimming six feet out in the lake by his house. That is the main point that the audience needs to know.

Recall that a paraphrase is stating the author's ideas in the reader's own words. A summary typically involves including the main points of a longer text, such as a novel or full story.

EXAMPLE

Read the following paragraph and then give a one sentence summary statement:

> When choosing a pet, people need to think about what type of home they can offer the animal. For example, a small apartment might not be a good fit for a large dog,

> but could be a comfortable home for a kitten. A house that has a big yard would be great for a puppy, but a rabbit does not need a large yard.

In order to summarize, one has to identify the main idea and any supporting ideas in the author's work. The summary is an overview of the author's paragraph and will tell what it is about without getting into any of the details. The summary needs to be broad enough to cover all of the information in the author's paragraph. Here is a possible summary statement for the above paragraph:

> People need to consider a number of factors, particularly the available space they have, when choosing a pet.

Example

Read the following sentences and then paraphrase the material:

> The government is debating a new health care system for our country. The Senate and the House of Representatives have both passed bills; now they need to resolve these two bills into one bill that a majority can agree on.

When paraphrasing information, one needs to read carefully and pay attention to details, then put the material away and write or tell it in their own words. One does not want to look at the material while paraphrasing to avoid plagiarizing by accident. Here is one example of a way to paraphrase the sentences:

> Our government is trying to adopt a new health care system. The Senate has passed a bill and so has the House of Representatives. Their bills are different so now they have to compromise on one bill that can be passed.

Summarizing Literature to Support Comprehension

When reading literature, especially demanding works, summarizing helps readers identify important information and organize it in their minds. They can also identify themes, problems, and solutions, and can sequence the story. Readers can summarize before, during, and after they read. They should use their own words, as they do when describing a personal event or giving directions. Previewing a text's organization before reading by examining the book cover, table of contents, and illustrations also aids summarizing. So does making notes of key words and ideas in a graphic organizer while reading. Graphic organizers are another useful method; readers skim the text to determine main ideas and then narrow the list with the aid of the organizer. Unimportant details should be omitted in summaries. Summaries can include description, problem-solution, comparison-contrast, sequence, main ideas, and cause-and-effect.

Chapter Quiz

1. If a reader takes an author's original idea and then restates it, putting the idea into their own words, this is an example of:

a. Outlining text
b. Paraphrasing text
c. Summarizing text
d. Abstracting text

2. Which of the following is NOT true of summarizing?

a. A summary can be just one sentence that boils down the author's words into the main idea.
b. Summarizing helps readers work to understand what they have read.
c. A summary typically involves restating the main points of a text in a simpler, shorter fashion.
d. A summary should be subjective and include brief personal opinions on the subject.

Chapter Quiz Answer Key

1. B: See section **Paraphrasing and Summarizing**

2. D: See section **Paraphrasing and Summarizing**

Literary Elements

Theme

The **theme** of a story is a unifying idea that is used throughout the text; it can take the form of a common setting, idea, symbol, design, or recurring event. The theme of a story may vary according to place, time, and characters, but theme is often based on common human experience. A plot line is built around the theme of a story. Most themes are about life, society, or human nature. The theme is often why a passage is written. It helps give a passage unity. The theme is created through the development of the story. The events of a story help shape the kind of theme the passage. A theme is not usually stated explicitly. The reader **infers** the theme from the topic, information, or plot of a passage.

For example, a series of events in a story may be based upon people being willing to trust the actions of others. The story may be centered on why people need to trust others in order to carry out important actions. For example, a character may trust that a bus driver will stay on the road while the bus driver, in turn, trusts that the passengers stay in their seats so that they do not distract him.

The theme of a story is not the same as the topic of a story. The topic is what the story is about, but the theme is what a reader is meant to learn. When readers are discussing theme, they can determine both theme topics as well as theme statements.

Theme topics are broad ideas that apply to the text. Examples include:

- Love changes people
- Man versus man
- Man versus nature
- Man versus himself
- Fate versus free will
- Triumph over adversity
- Coming of age
- The importance of friendship
- Good vs. evil
- The circle of life

Themes may also be complete statements written in sentence form. Examples are:

- Acts of courage can bring positive changes to the world.
- True friendship can withstand the hardest challenges.

Review Video: Themes in Literature
Visit mometrix.com/academy and enter code: 732074

Example

Tell why the theme of the following excerpt should be "Overconfidence can lead to a fall."

> Bella was happy. She auditioned for the starring role in the school play and she felt sure she'd got the part. Afterwards, she told her friends she would be starring in the play. But on Tuesday when the director said they had offered the part to Sara Goodwin, she started crying.

The excerpt tells the story of a girl who has an audition and thinks she got the starring role. She is so confident that she even tells her friends that she has the part. But then she learns that the role was offered to someone else and she starts to cry. She was overly confident about her success and was subsequently devastated when she learned of her failure, and that is the lesson of the story. If you are overly confident you may have a fall. That is the theme of the story. A theme is the lesson that a story teaches. This particular theme is found often in literature. A theme is not stated in a passage: the reader must deduce it from the plot of the story.

Universal Themes

Some themes are fairly common. These themes are called **universal themes** and they suggest things about life, society, and human nature. If a reader is trying to decide whether a theme is universal or not, they must consider whether the theme they have identified can be applied to other works as well. Some examples of universal theme topics are:

Good Versus Evil

- The universal theme of a small number of people invested in doing good works becoming a powerful force against those doing evil works can be seen in multiple texts, including the *Harry Potter* series by J.K. Rowling, *The Hunger Games* by Suzanne Collins, and *Cinder* by Marissa Meyer.

Change Versus Tradition

- *The Giver* by Lois Lowry, the *Divergent* series by Veronica Roth, and *Children of Eden* by Joey Graceffa all reveal the universal theme of the ongoing struggle for societies to welcome change rather than being stuck in tradition.

Man Versus Man

- Learning that people are capable of committing horrifying acts against other people is a universal theme evident in *The Boy in the Striped Pajamas* by John Boyne, *A Long Walk to Water* by Linda Sue Park, and *All the Light We Cannot See* by Anthony Doerr.

Characters

Character Trait

The traits of a character may include how they act and physical characteristics; a character trait is a behavior or physical characteristic that is unique to a specific character. For example, a character may be outgoing, which means he or she likes to talk a lot, or they may have bright red hair. These are both character traits.

An author uses character traits to describe a character in a story and help the reader to learn more about how the character acts and what they look like. By comparing the character traits in a story, the reader can see similarities and differences between characters. The author includes character traits to help the reader understand why a character may act a certain way in the story. For example, a character who is shy may not want to talk with a lot of people in a new classroom, but a character who is outgoing may want to talk with many people.

An author typically provides many details about a character so that the reader can learn more about the character's traits, motivations, relationships, and any conflicts they may have in the story. The traits of a character may include how they act and how they look. Characters are often motivated by things that have already happened in their life or how they feel about a topic. The author will often give the reader enough information about the character so that the reader can figure out why the character responds to a situation in a certain way. The author will also often give details about the relationships between characters and points they may conflict on. For example, a character may be good friends with another character; however, the two characters may disagree on where to play outside if one character likes being near the water and the other character does not.

EXAMPLE

Read the following description of a character and decide, logically, whether the character is likely to go hiking outdoors:

> Jeremy lived in a high-rise in Chicago. He was studious, and not very athletic. Jeremy preferred to stay indoors and read a book, rather than enjoy outdoor weather.

Based on the description of the character's traits, preferences, and personality, he is not likely to go hiking outdoors. The description indicates that the character prefers reading, rather than enjoying outdoor weather. In addition, the character lives in a tall building in the middle of a large city, in order for him to enjoy the outdoors, he would have to travel away from where he lives. The character is not likely to change his preferences. A situation may lead the character to go hiking, but he is not likely to initiate the action on his own. A description of a character that is likely to go hiking outdoors may include a preference for outdoor activity and living near trails.

CHARACTER CHANGES AND RESPONSES

Characters can change in a multitude of ways throughout a story; however, there are main aspects of a character that change. A character's identifying **characteristics**, such as personality or behavior traits, may change as the result of a prominent event in the story, current **motivations**, and conflicts. As **conflicts** change or are resolved, a character may no longer be motivated by striving toward a goal that was previously important to them. Furthermore, a character's development may also lead them to make **different choices**, which can **impact the plot**. As the plot of a story moves along, characters can constantly change in relation to events that occur. Relationships between characters and the points of view of characters may change throughout a story as well.

Each story will have many different types of characters and each of these characters will have a different relationship with other characters. Stories usually have a protagonist, antagonist, and a variety of other characters including round, flat, and stock characters.

Protagonist

The main character in a drama, movie, novel, or other fictional text. The author portrays the protagonist in a way that the audience is most like to identify with themselves. The protagonist is generally undertaking some type of personal challenge throughout the story. The author writes the story so that the reader becomes aware of the protagonist's emotions and is generally able to empathize with the personal challenge.

Antagonist

The character that actively opposes the protagonist by trying to prevent them from succeeding. The antagonist is usually presented in such a way as to make the audience dislike them, and want them to fail at stopping the protagonist. The protagonist and antagonist oppose each other, so their relationship is almost always one of dislike.

Flat Character

Does not have any substantial changes throughout the story. They stay the same despite the conflict, and do not learn any lessons. They are usually minor characters that might interact with the main character in some way.

Round Character

Major characters in the story that will be more fully developed than other minor characters. They will usually encounter some type of conflict that they must overcome, and usually learn a lesson about life or themselves along the way.

Stock Characters

Often get their characteristics and mannerisms from stereotypes of people that are widely recognized. These types of characters are often repeated and well-known. Readers should be aware that stereotypes are rarely accurate in reality, and are generally intended to be humorous or dramatic. Some examples are evil stepmothers, unintelligent blondes, rude athletes, and loyal servants.

Characters' Influence on the Plot

There are many ways in which the action of a story may be driven. Dialogue is one of them. What a character says either to another character or about a situation may propel the action by revealing what a character is thinking or what he may do. Similarly, what a character says will tell the audience what he is like. His manner of speaking, what he says, and how he says it are all clues to his personality. Dialogue can also provoke a decision by showing what the character intends to do in the future. Incidents in a story also propel the action because the plot is made up of events that build on events. Incidents such as a confrontation could reveal aspects of a character or provoke a decision.

Example

Read the excerpt and tell how this incident propels the action of the story and provokes a decision.

> It was a perfect day it seemed, until Sam saw the thunderheads roll in. He knew that it would be dangerous to be in a rowboat in the middle of the lake during a thunder and lightning storm. Suddenly the sky became darker and he heard a clap of thunder.

This incident certainly propels the action of the story. It would appear that Sam is in a rowboat in the middle of the lake having a lovely time when he hears a clap of thunder. He realizes that a lake is a dangerous place to be so this event means that Sam must take action. What that action is would be of interest to the reader because it will help form the plot of the story. The incident also forces Sam to make a decision about what he should do. This will help the reader better understand Sam as a character.

PLOT

The storyline of any text is also called a **plot**. The characters and events in the story determine what the plot will be. Readers may find a **plot line** useful as they try to put the events in the text in order and determine the relationships between events.

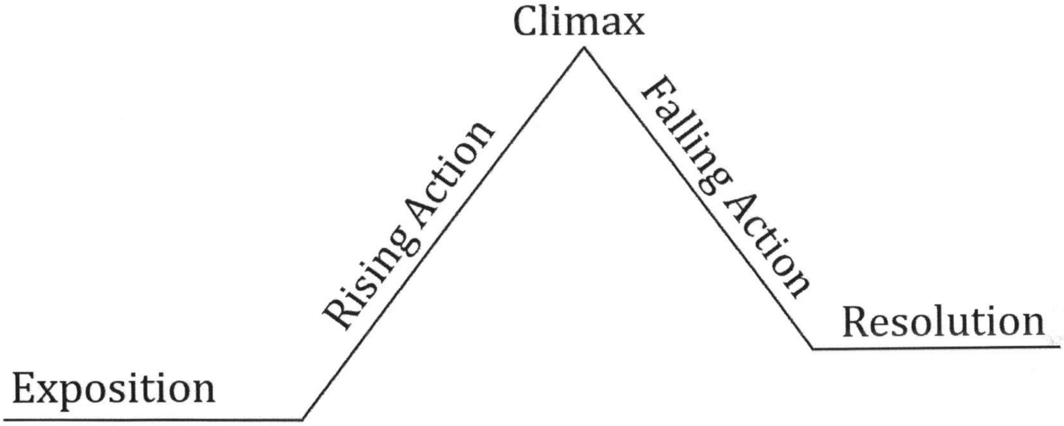

Review Video: Plot Line
Visit mometrix.com/academy and enter code: 944011

Every plot will begin with **exposition**, which introduces the characters and the setting of the story. The plot will continue to develop as new ideas and events centered on the main conflict in the story are revealed, which is called the **rising action**. The action in the story will rise until a **climax** is reached within the conflict. The climax can also be referred to as the turning point in the story, since the climax is where each character makes an important decision. After the climax, the action starts to wind down during the **falling action**. At this point, the characters begin to follow the paths they chose in during climax. The events of the story reach **resolution** in some way by the end of the story. Some conflicts are left open-ended, so that the reader is left to decide what really happened at the end of the story. Keep in mind that not all resolutions are happy or peaceful.

EXAMPLE

Read the following plot and analyze what event is missing from the plot sequence.

> Martin's family decided to go camping at the local park over the weekend. They packed all the camping necessities and drove to the park. Thick sheets of rain poured down all day, so they were stuck in their tent.

Martin and his family forgot to check the weather forecast before they left for their camping trip. to fill in the missing detail, the author may write: "Martin and his family checked the forecast and saw that it was going to rain, but decided to go camping anyway." the flow of the story is broken up by the sudden realization that it is raining, something that could be prevented by adding in the missing detail.

When details are missing from a plot sequence, the audience has trouble following the action in a story. By adding in additional details, the point of each step in a story can be made clearer to the audience.

CONFLICT

An important part of analyzing the plot of a passage is identifying the **main conflict**. There will likely be many smaller conflicts in the story, but there will be one main problem that influences the characters and events. to identify the main conflict, first look at who the main character is. Now ask yourself what they want. They may want to something to happen or not happen, another character to do or not do something, or to confront or avoid a problem, among other things. Once you know what they want, now ask yourself what is standing in the character's way. It may be a person, an event, or something less tangible like the passing of time. Combining what the main character wants and why they do not currently have leaves the reader with a summary of the main conflict.

EXAMPLE

Read the following sentence from the *Call of the Wild* by Jack London and describe the main conflict in the sentence. Explain how the conflict may be resolved.

> The breaking down of discipline likewise affected the dogs in their relations with one another.

Based on the information in the sentence, an event has caused the dogs, the characters in the story, to not follow their regular routine. The sentence indicates that there has been a breaking down of discipline which is affecting how the dogs relate to each other. in order to solve this conflict, discipline needs to be restored. However, in order to return to previous relations between the dogs, any problems that are in the way of conflict resolution need to be taken care of. The word *likewise* means *also*, which tells the reader that other parts of the story are being affected besides the relations between the dogs.

EXAMPLE

Read the following sentence and explain the main conflict between the two characters:

> Joe stared angrily at Jamie's retreating back as Jamie raced away down the field with Joe's soccer ball.

The main conflict in the sentence is that Jamie has Joe's soccer ball. There may be additional conflicts between the two characters, but none are evident from the evidence shown in the sentence. in any story, a conflict may be minor and only affect part of the story, or be the main focus, taking an entire story to solve a conflict between characters. in the context of the sentence, it is not clear whether or not the entire story will revolve around Jamie taking Joe's soccer ball.

RESOLUTION

The term **resolution** usually indicates the result of a conflict in a story. Conflict between characters, within a character, or against an external element is necessary in order to have a plot for a story. without conflict, no events would occur to form the story. A conflict will come to a climax, and then conclude in some way. The resolution of a problem may be open-ended, end tragically, or end in a way that is good for everyone involved. The problem resolution typically occurs near the end of a story, after the climax has happened. A problem may be resolved by the characters involved within the conflict or by an external event; an upcoming resolution may be foreshadowed in the text, or may be completely unexpected by the reader. If the resolution is completely unexpected, it is considered to be a **twist** in the story.

Foreshadowing

Foreshadowing is a technique authors use to give readers **hints** about events that will take place later in a story. Sometimes, foreshadowing is also used to build **suspense**. Foreshadowing most often takes place through a character's dialogue or actions. Sometimes the character will know what is going to happen and will purposefully allude to future events. For example, consider a protagonist who is about to embark on a journey through the woods. Just before the protagonist begins the trip, another character says, "Be careful, you never know what could be out in those woods!" This alerts the reader that the woods may be dangerous and prompts the reader to expect something to attack the protagonist in the woods. This is an example of foreshadowing through warning.

Alternatively, a character may unknowingly foreshadow later events. For example, consider a story where a brother and sister run through their house and knock over a vase and break it. The brother says, "Don't worry, we'll clean it up! Mom will never know!" However, the reader knows that their mother will most likely find out what they have done, so the reader expects the siblings to later get in trouble for running, breaking the vase, and hiding it from their mother.

Non-Linear Plot Development

Some texts contain a **non-linear plot**, which means the plot is not told in chronological order, or is not told from "beginning to end" in one straight line. There are several devices that authors can use to make their plot non-linear, including:

- **Foreshadowing:** the author gives the reader hints early on in a work about something that will become clearer (or more important) later on.
- **Flashback:** the author shows the reader an event that happened in the past to explain something about the present.
- **Subplot:** a side story, usually about a supporting character, is told along with the main story. Sometimes subplots occur within flashbacks.
- **Parallel plot:** two stories are told alongside each other, often narrated by two different characters in alternating chapters. The events in the stories usually end up overlapping or coming together at some point, most often the climax of the text.

Setting

The setting is where a story **takes place**. The setting of a story may stay the same for the entire story, or change as events in the story unfold. For example, an entire story may take place in one room or cross continents as the reader follows the characters along on a trail of events.

The setting of a story is described by the author in terms of what it looks like, how the character feels, and anything else that is happening at that location at the time. For example, a character may be caught on a doorstep on a cold, rainy day. The character may feel frustrated as they shiver in the doorway, waiting for the heavy rain to let up a bit.

Shaping a Character with Setting or Plot

The setting of a story shapes character because it helps to define the situation that a character finds herself in. A character is limited to the setting of a story. For example, if a story takes place in a cold environment filled with snow and ice, this is certain to impact what actions a character can and will take. Frequently, the setting changes the way characters behave based on time. For example, the character of a woman who is a single mother in 1920 would be seen and behave very differently than a single mother in 2020.

EXAMPLE

Read the excerpt and determine how the setting influences the character in this excerpt.

> She had swum too far out. The waves were higher than she thought. She was struggling hard to get to shore. She wondered if she would make it. She thought of her childhood. Had she been right to run away from home, she wondered? Just then, a lifeguard grabbed her and helped her to shore.

The setting of the ocean and the high waves creates a conflict in the character. She is worried. She thinks about her childhood and her parents. She doesn't know if she will make it to shore. This is how the setting affects the character in this excerpt. Without the high waves and the struggle, she would not become so worried and start to think about her past. She probably would not have questioned herself. This is an example of how a setting influences a character. If the waves had not been high, there probably would not have been a struggle or any self-searching of the swimmer's past.

HISTORICAL AND CULTURAL SETTING

Historical context influences literature in a number of ways. The style of the author's writing can be impacted by the historical period during which it was written (e.g., Dickens wrote at a time when authors were paid by the word; this is why his novels are so long). Obviously, the setting of the book includes its historical context. In addition, dialect may be a function of the historical period of the book. When a reader understands the historical context of a particular book, he or she can have a deeper understanding of the novel. Knowing about the time period during which the author wrote, as well as the time period discussed in the novel, helps the reader understand some of the author's choices, including character motivations.

EXAMPLE

Slavery used to be the norm in Southern states. One of the major ways in which the historical context of slavery impacted literature coming out of the South was the birth of the slave narrative. Slaves wanted to have their experiences documented. After the Civil War, former slaves wrote their stories. These slave narratives have given historians valuable firsthand accounts of life in the South. From a literary perspective, slave narratives are one of the most important genres of African-American writing. Slavery influenced literature by delving into themes of power, racial injustice, and equality. Literature from this time period can help the reader better understand the perspectives and experiences of the slaves themselves, as well as the slave holders.

PATTERNS RELATED TO SETTINGS

The setting of a story can allow the reader to draw on personal experience about where the story takes place. If a story takes place on a farm, the reader will likely picture a rural, peaceful setting, which may go along with (or be in contrast to) the actual plot of the story. For example, a reader would not expect a scary story to occur on a farm on a sunny day. Conversely, a reader may view a dark subway as a dangerous place, while the plot of a story set there may be based on a very calm series of events. When an author is crafting a story, they need to consider what the audience may already think about a particular setting in order to properly present the events of a story for greatest impact.

Chapter Quiz

1. What type of character often gets their characteristics and mannerisms from stereotypes of people that are widely recognized?

a. Minor characters
b. Stock characters
c. Flat characters
d. Round characters

2. Every plot will begin with __________, which introduces the characters and the setting of the story.

a. Conflict
b. Rising action
c. Foreshadowing
d. Exposition

3. What plot device that authors can use to make their plot non-linear, is a side story told along with the main story?

a. Anecdote
b. Flashback
c. Subplot
d. Parallel plot

4. Which of the following would most likely convey a peaceful setting to the reader?

a. Sunny farm
b. Damp basement
c. Loud construction site
d. Dark subway

Chapter Quiz Answer Key

1. B: See section **Stock Characters**

2. D: See section **Plot**

3. C: See section **Non-Linear Plot Development**

4. A: See section **Patterns Related to Settings**

Literary Genres

Literary Genres

Literature contains many different **genres**, which are categories that texts can be divided into. Genres are used to group types of writing together for purposes of study, reading, or simple organization. Some common literary genres are

- **Realistic fiction** -A story that could actually happen and reflects life in a realistic way.
- **Adventure stories** -Short, mostly fictional stories that follow characters as they go on an adventure or quest.
- **Historical fiction** -Often strays from historical reality in order to tell a story and make a true historical event more interesting to the reader.
- **Mysteries** -Fiction stories about solving crimes or revealing secrets.

- **Humor** –Stories, mostly fictional, full of fun and excitement meant to entertain readers. Can be seen in stories from all genres.
- **Myth** -A legend or traditional narrative, often based on a historical event. The story reveals something about human behavior or the natural world, and often involves actions of gods.
- **Fantasy** -Fictional stories that contain unusual and other worldly settings and characters. The sense of "realness" in other stories is not present. The fantasy genre is known for including elements like magic and imaginary creatures like fairies, dragons, and elves.
- **Science fiction** -Fiction based on what could happen if actual, imagined, or possible scientific advances occurred. Usually set in the future, a modified past, or on other planets.

Poetry

Poet Versus Speaker

The author of a poem is called a **poet**. Many poems are written in first person, which means the **stanzas** (groups of lines) include words like "I" and "me." However, the poet is not always the **speaker** of the poem. In a novel, the author can create characters with different points of view. The characters can argue or have different roles to play in telling the story. Similarly, a poet may write a poem from a different point of view or even include more than one voice. The speaker is the voice of the poem, and is not always the same person as the poet him or herself. The reader or listener should know that the person telling the story is a character, and not always a real person.

For example, this excerpt from a poem by Dr. Seuss reads:

> When you think things are bad,
> when you feel sour and blue,
> when you start to get mad...
> you should do what I do!
> Just tell yourself, Duckie,
> you're really quite lucky!
> Some people are much more...
> oh, ever so much more...
> oh, muchly much-much more
> unlucky than you!

Even though one line has the word "I" in it, the poem is not from the perspective of Dr. Seuss. He is the author of the poem, but not the speaker. The person saying "I" is a character, just like in a story.

Meter, Rhyme, and Repetition in Poetry

The **meter** of a poem refers to the number of syllables per line as well as the pattern of emphasis on those syllables. The use of meter gives a poem a rhythmic context and contributes to the poem's flow. Certain types of meter can also make a poem more appealing to the reader or represent natural speech rhythms.

Rhymes repeat the ending sound of words: "So very soon/We will fly to the moon." Here the "oo" sound is repeated in the words *soon* and *moon*. Rhymes are frequently used in poetry, mostly older forms of poetry rather than modern poems.

Another type of repetition is **alliteration**. Alliteration repeats beginning sounds, usually consonants: "Rah, rah, rah," the crowd cried, "rah, rah, rah." It is often used in poetry as well as in spoken forms of writing.

Rhyme Scheme

When determining what a poem's rhyme scheme is, readers should look at the last word of each line to see which words rhyme with each other. Words that rhyme are assigned a letter of the alphabet, beginning with "a." The next time words rhyme, if the rhyme is different than the last one, they assigned a new letter, going forward in order of the alphabet until the poem is over or there are no more rhymes. This sounds complicated, but it's easy with practice.

Let's take a look at an excerpt from Dylan Thomas' poem "Do not go gentle into that good night":

> Do not go gentle into that good night,
> Old age should burn and rave at close of day;
> Rage, rage against the dying of the light.
>
> Though wise men at their end know dark is right,
> Because their words had forked no lightning they
> Do not go gentle into that good night.

The words at the end of the lines are *night, day, light, right, they,* and *night.*

We know that the first rhyme is assigned the letter "a," and can clearly see that *night, light,* and *right* all rhyme, so we can mark the poem like this

> Do not go gentle into that good night, **a**
> Old age should burn and rave at close of day;
> Rage, rage against the dying of the light. **a**
>
> Though wise men at their end know dark is right, **a**
> Because their words had forked no lightning they
> Do not go gentle into that good night. **a**

Now, we'll look at the only other rhyme in the poem, which is made up of the words *day* and *they.* This rhyme does not rhyme with the first set of words, so it gets a new letter, "b."

> Do not go gentle into that good night, **a**
> Old age should burn and rave at close of day; **b**
> Rage, rage against the dying of the light. **a**
>
> Though wise men at their end know dark is right, **a**
> Because their words had forked no lightning they **b**
> Do not go gentle into that good night. **a**

After looking at all six lines and determining how they rhyme, we can confidently say that the rhyme scheme for this excerpt is a, b, a, a, b, a.

Rhymes are used at the discretion of the poet and are not always mandatory. Many modern poems—actually, most of them—use a blank verse, where there are no rhyme schemes. However, there are many formal poetic types, such as the sonnet, that have a specific rhyme scheme that poets must follow to achieve that kind of poetic form.

Example

Explain the rhyme scheme of the following excerpt from a poem entitled "Alone" by Edgar Allan Poe.

> From childhood's hour I have not been
> As others were; I have not seen
> As others saw; I could not bring
> My passions from a common spring.
> From the same source I have not taken
> My sorrow; I could not awaken
> My heart to joy at the same tone;
> And all I loved, I loved alone.

The rhyme scheme that Edgar Allan Poe uses in this excerpt from his poem "Alone" is: a, a, b, b, c, c, d, d, e, e. Every two lines rhyme, but the rhyme is not repeated in the other lines. This is a rather unusual rhyme scheme; many others have lines that repeat the rhyme scheme, but not in a consecutive order, such as a, b, a, b or a, b, c a, b, c.

Graphical Elements in Poetry

Graphic elements in a poem such as capitalization, line length, and word position can call special attention to words or phrases. **Capitalization** can signal the beginning of a sentence, or all caps may be used to provide emphasis. **Line length** can be used to help create a shape, like in concrete poems, or to create a bold statement, like a one-word line. A poet can create tension by using line length and punctuation independently of one another. **Word position** can be used to contribute to a feeling, or it can also be used to help create a shape, so poets are often careful where they end lines.

Line Breaks

Line breaks are used to end a line of poetry. Poets use **line breaks** to control the **length** of **each line**. The length of lines in a poem can impact the poem's meaning and the **speed** at which the poem is read. **Long** lines are usually read more **quickly**, while **short** lines cause the reader to briefly pause and look to the next line, so their reading is **slowed**. These effects often contribute to the reader's experience when reading the poem, so poets aim to make the effects match the tone of their message in the poem.

Punctuation

The punctuation in each line of a poem causes the reader to **pause** after certain words. This lets the poet **emphasize** specific **ideas** or **images**. Similar to the effects of line length, punctuation at the end of a line can guide the **speed** at which the reader reads each line. Lines with a punctuation mark at the end cause readers to pause, while lines that do not end with a punctuation mark carry a sentence to the next line. This creates an effect that is like the effect of long lines.

Capitalization

Poets also use capitalization to **highlight** certain words in their poetry. Authors will often capitalize words that are not proper nouns so that the reader pays more attention to them. While this is not grammatically correct, it is used in poetry to create a certain effect and guide the reader as they read and form their understanding of the poem.

Drama

Dramas are texts that are written to be performed by people reading the lines or acting the stories out. They can also be presented as monologues (one character speaks), dialogues (two character speak to each other), or pantomimes (body movements are used instead of spoken words). Dramatic texts are called plays or **scripts**, and they are written differently than other texts.

Text Structure in Drama

Plays are divided into **acts** (large units) and **scenes** (small sections inside acts) instead of chapters. There are also **stage directions**, which are instructions from the playwright about where items go, where actors should move, and what the characters should be doing during the scene. Stage directions are usually in italics to set them apart from other parts of the play. When it is time for a character in a play to speak, there will be **character tag** on the left side of the page which shows the name of the character (all letters of the name are capitalized) followed by a colon.

Here is an example of how a page from a play might look:

Title of Play

Act Number

Scene Number

The setting of the scene is being described here. The reader is being introduced to the characters and the things happening around them. Characters will enter speak to one another during the scene.

CHARACTER 1:

I am speaking. These are words I say. *(stage directions)* I am still speaking.

CHARACTER 2 *enters and does something.*

CHARACTER 2:

Now I am speaking. This is my dialogue.

Dialogue and Stage Directions

Dialogue refers to what the characters say in a play when they are talking to each other, talking to themselves, or even talking to the audience. The type of speech, word choice, and accent a character uses is specific to the role he is playing. For example, a person cast to play a cowboy would have certain words in his vocabulary that a character from a big city in the North would not have.

A playwright also uses stage directions to make the play flow smoothly. Character interaction helps the viewer to understand the mood of the scene. If two characters are confrontational, the viewer is aware that there is some type of conflict occurring. Stage directions create order when all the characters are on stage together.

Informational Text

Controlling Idea

The controlling idea, also called the main idea or thesis, of a passage is usually located in the first paragraph or two of text. Having the controlling idea near the beginning of the passage allows the author to grab the reader's attention and let them know what the rest of the passage will discuss.

To find the controlling idea in a passage, there are questions the reader can ask while reading: What is this passage about? What does the author want the reader to know about the topic? The supporting details will provide evidence that the controlling idea is correct and are found in the body of a passage. The supporting details often provide examples of the controlling idea.

For example, a passage may contain the controlling idea: "Ellis Island was an entry-point to America for many immigrants during the Industrial Revolution." A supporting detail for the controlling idea may be "Immigrants were examined for contagious diseases at Ellis Island before being granted entry to America."

Review Video: Thesis Statements
Visit mometrix.com/academy and enter code: 691033

EXAMPLE

Determine the controlling idea the following sentence tells the reader and indicate what details support the controlling idea:

> Her breath billowed out in clouds of white and disappeared into the quiet air.

The controlling idea is what the author wants the reader to understand about the text. Details help to explain or support that controlling idea. A controlling idea usually states the point of an entire essay, article, or book, but can be simply stated in one sentence. The controlling idea in the sentence above is that a girl is outside in the cold. Details to support this statement include the word 'her,' showing that the character is a girl, and 'clouds of white,' which indicate that the air is cold. in order to conclude that the girl is out in the cold, the reader needs to understand that breath can be seen when the air is cold.

SUPPORTING DETAILS

Authors use supporting details to provide evidence and backing for the main point. All texts contain details, but they are only classified as supporting details when they serve to reinforce some larger point. Supporting details are most commonly found in informative and persuasive texts. in some cases, they will be clearly indicated with words like **for example** or **for instance**, or they will begin with words like **first**, **second**, and **last**. However, these special words are not a requirement. As a reader, it is important to consider whether the author's supporting details really back up his or her main point. Supporting details can be factual and correct but still not relevant to the author's point. Sometimes, supporting details can seem important but they might not support the controlling idea in the story well because they are based on opinion that cannot be proven.

EXAMPLE

Decide whether the following sentence is the main point or a supporting point of a text, and state where the information would be placed in an outline:

> One type of horseback riding, bareback horseback riding, involves sitting on a moving horse without a saddle and grasping the horse's mane.

This sentence is a supporting point, with the main point of the entire text likely about horseback riding in general. As a supporting point, this sentence would go further down in an outline, next to any numeral after numeral I. This sentence can be followed by additional sub-points that further explain the concept of bareback horseback riding. When a supporting point is used to clarify a main point or topic, the supporting point helps to break the topic down into smaller pieces.

STRUCTURAL FEATURES OF INFORMATIONAL TEXT

Texts which intend to inform the reader about a topic are often accompanied by visual aids or graphics. Some common examples are listed below.

- **Forewords** appear before the actual text. Usually, forewords are not written by the author of the text. They are written by a different person who is well-respected in a related field of work or study. The author of the foreword usually provides some information about the texts and explains why they support the text.
- **Prefaces** are written to provide the reader with supporting information that was not included in the text. This information may help the reader better understand the text or may show the reader why the topic of the text is important or interesting to the author.
- **Introductions** usually appear as the first paragraph in a text. An introduction is used to catch the reader's attention and let the audience know what the text is about and how the topic will be covered by the text.
- **Insets and sidebars** show additional information related to the text in boxes or on the sides of the page. Insets can contain pictures or text, and sometimes have different colored backgrounds or font types to make them stand out from the text.
- **Visual aids** include features like diagrams, graphs, and charts. These can help the user think about information in a different way. They do this by visually presenting the relationship between the information in the text.
- **Bullet points** list items separately, making facts and ideas easier to see and understand.
- **Numbers** can also be used to list separate items. Usually, numbers are used to show that the items are part of a sequence. For example, in a list of instructions, each instruction may be numbered to show the reader the order in which each instruction should be completed.
- **References** are the sources of the information the author included in the text. In most works, the references will all be listed after the last page of the main text. These may be included on a page titled "Bibliography," "Works Cited," or, simply, "References." Reviewing the author's sources and reviewing their credibility can show the reader whether the work itself is credible, unbiased, and accurate.
- **Acknowledgements** appear near the end of books, after the main text and any resources that the author has included for the reader. The acknowledgements section is used by authors to thank the people that helped them create the work. People who encouraged the author, assisted the author with writing and editing, or made it possible for the work to be published are usually named in the acknowledgements section.

ORGANIZATIONAL PATTERNS

When writing there are a variety of ways that an author can choose to organize their text. It is important for them to choose the pattern that best presents their information, as not all patterns will work for every piece of writing. Some examples are

ADVANTAGE/DISADVANTAGE

The author chooses a topic or concept and addresses both the advantages and disadvantages (or pros and cons) of the subject. In this type of text the author is not trying to persuade their audience to choose a side, but rather, to inform the reader of all the possible positive and negative effects.

CAUSE AND EFFECT

The author will write about relationship between two events that occur, where the second event occurs as a result of the first.

For example, a text may discuss a school policy stating that when a student is late to school too many times, they receive a detention. Later in the text, we might see a student repeatedly arriving late to school, after which he is given a detention. In this example, the **cause** is the student being late to school, and the **effect** is the student receiving a detention.

Classification

The author chooses a topic and divides it into smaller parts or groups in order to discuss them individually. These types of texts address how parts work within a whole, or what characteristics can be used to classify a given subject or concept.

Chronological Order

The author organizes the progression of events based upon when they occurred and what was included in each step of the story. By organizing the text in this way the author presents all necessary information about the six questions readers can ask to help themselves understand the text: who, what, when, where, why, and how.

Compare and Contrast

The author will show similarities and differences between items or events.

For example, the author may write about cats and dogs. They might start by giving a brief description of the two. Then they will want to point out all of the similarities, such as; they both have tails, and both are kept as pets. Next, they will explain the differences, such as; dogs are canines, while cats are felines. They will try to provide as much detail as possible about both the similarities and the differences.

Definition

Authors introduce a concept or word and then explain or describe it. This type of text often included examples that will help the reader gain understanding of what is presumably a new concept for them.

Inductive / Deductive

Authors organize ideas from general to specific or specific to general. If ideas are organized **inductively**, they are arranged from specific facts to general conclusions. If ideas are organized from general conclusions to specific facts, they are organized **deductively**. A reader can make a logical assumption about a topic based on the facts that are presented in the text.

For example, in these two sentences the ideas are organized deductively, from general to specific.

> Many canoers use the lake in the summer. Jeff learned how to canoe last summer, and is on his way to the lake now.

The idea that "Many canoers use the lake in the summer" is a general idea. The facts that Jeff already knows how to canoe and is headed to the lake are specific to him as a character.

Order of Importance

The author puts the information in the text in order of what is most important. **Order of importance** can be either increasing or decreasing, depending on how the writer wants to structure the work.

Proposition and Support

The author states a proposition that they believe to be true, and then provides support for that proposition in the paper. The topics that use this type of structure are generally things that reader might feel uncertain about or might not already have an opinion about. The support that the author gives for the proposition should include facts, statistics, logic, and reasoning. The more hard evidence an author can give the reader, the better it will help convince them to see things from the author's point of view.

Identifying Organizational Strategies

Example

Explain which organization pattern would be the best choice for this writer and why.

> Sara is writing a report on sea turtles. She has researched the various dangers that they face: their predators, the difficulties they encounter in their life cycle starting with their birth, their migration to the ocean, and the dangers that await them as they mature. She is unsure of how to organize her report.

A cause and effect order would seem to be the best idea for Sara because she would be able to identify the causes and effects of the dangers that sea turtles encounter. She could organize the report so that each paragraph deals with a different threat, using headings to identify what would be in each section. A chart would also be useful because it puts the same information in a clear format so that readers would be able to refer to it. She might also consider using a video showing baby turtles migrating towards the open sea, which would give her audience an even greater understanding of the turtles' plight.

Example

Identify the text structure that is used in the following sentences:

> Madison and her brother Jake used to live on a wind-torn island in the Chesapeake Bay. Last year they moved to Baltimore, a city in Maryland. Next summer they plan to visit the island where they grew up.

Chronological order is used as a text structure in the example sentences, as they are organized according to the passage of time. Note that each sentence refers to a point in time. The first sentence refers to where the siblings lived in the past. The second sentence refers to the siblings' move to Baltimore last year. The final sentence refers to what the siblings plan to do in the future. By referring to a specific place in time, the reader can see what occurred in the story during that time period. An author will often use flashback to indicate what happened in the past, and foreshadowing to give the reader a glimpse of what may occur in the future.

Example

Identify the text structure that is used in the following sentences:

> Three cousins lived in the same small town. One day the cousins decided to journey together to enter a singing contest across the country. The cousins won the contest and made their hometown fans proud.

The information in the story can be organized according to the passage of time, called chronological order. The story will start based in the cousins' hometown, to give some background on where the cousins come from. Subsequent events in the story will occur over time based on the cousins' motivations due to their background. The story will end by referring back to how far the cousins have come from their small-town roots.

EXAMPLE

Read the following thesis statement and discuss the organizational pattern that the author will use:

> Throughout his life, Thomas Edison used his questioning and creative mind to become one of America's greatest inventors.

Based on the thesis statement, the reader can assume that the author is going to use chronological order to organize the information in the rest of the essay. The words "throughout his life" clue the reader in to the chronological organizational structure, which presents information in the order than it occurred. The author will probably discuss Edison's childhood and initial inventions first and then move on to his later queries and inventions. Chronological order is often used as the organizational structure in biographies as a way to logically present the important events in a person's life.

ARGUMENTATIVE TEXTS

IDENTIFYING THE CLAIM

In a persuasive or argumentative text, the author is writing in order to make and support a claim. A claim is similar to the key idea of an informational text. However, a claim can be argued, which means that some readers may not agree with it. The author of the text will need to use the body of the text to support the claim and show readers why they should agree with it. To identify the claim of a text, first identify the topic. Then, read the introduction text to see what the author writes about the topic.

The claim should be clearly stated in the introduction. However, if the claim is still not clear, read the body to see what kind of evidence the author uses to support the claim. The way that the author gives and applies evidence may also show what the claim of the text is.

CALL TO ACTION

Another strategy is to look for a call to action in the text. A call to action is a statement that instructs the reader to do something after reading the text. Often, the call to action will tell the reader to do something that shows that he or she agrees with the author's claim. For example, if an author's claim is that reading is better than watching a movie, the author may include a call to action that says "Turn off the TV and dig in to a new book today!" By including this statement, the author is telling the readers to show their agreement by choosing to read rather than watch a movie.

IDENTIFYING HOW THE AUTHOR SUPPORTS A CLAIM

In a persuasive or argumentative text, the author must use information to support his or her claim. This information is called evidence. Below are common types of evidence an author may use to support a claim:

- **Facts:** Authors may use facts that show that their claim is true. For example, a claim that fish are better pets than dogs can be supported by the fact that fish cannot make a mess inside a house.
- **Personal Anecdotes:** A personal anecdote is a story from a person's own experience. Authors can use personal anecdotes to tell stories that show why their claim is true. For example, an author can support the claim that people should wear elbow pads when riding a bike can be supported by sharing a story about their experience of scraping their elbow after falling off of a bicycle.

- **Statistics:** Statistics are observations that are based on a collection of data. Statistics can show trends or preferences among members of a group. An author can use statistics to support a claim by sharing the statistic says is likely to happen or be true for many people.
- **Examples:** Authors may give examples of events or experiences that suggest that their claim is true. For example, an author may claim that people should exercise because it will make them healthier. The author could give an example of how exercise can improve a person's health in order to support this claim.
- **Quotes:** An author can support a claim by using quotes from other people or texts. If the person or text makes a statement that shows that the author's claim is true, the author can include that quote in his or her text. When authors include quotes in their work, they must always tell the reader where the quote came from.

The author must use enough evidence to support the claim. If the evidence does not fully support the claim in the text, then the author must continue working to find evidence for the claim. The evidence used to support a claim must also be believable and come from a reliable source.

COUNTERARGUMENTS

A counterargument is a claim that seeks to disprove another claim. Sometimes, an author of a persuasive or argumentative text will include a **counterargument** to their own claim in a text. Doing this allows the author to show why someone may disagree with his or her claim and then show why the counterargument is wrong. Authors include counterarguments in order to strengthen their own argument and show the reader why claims that oppose their own are incorrect.

IDENTIFYING THE INTENDED AUDIENCE

Authors of persuasive and argumentative texts want to convince others to agree with a claim or take a certain action. Because of this, they will often write to a specific audience. Often, the target audience will include people who disagree with the author's claim. The author's desire is to give these people information that will lead them to change their minds or actions.

STRATEGIES FOR IDENTIFYING THE INTENDED AUDIENCE

One way to identify the intended audience of a persuasive or argumentative text is to first identify the author's claim. Then, consider who would disagree with the author's claim. This group of people is likely the group that the author wants to persuade.

Another way to identify the audience is to look for clues in the text. Sometimes, authors will clearly state which people are included in the intended audience. For example, imagine that an author includes the statement, "Teachers should reward their students every time they make a good grade on a test." This shows that the text is written to persuade teachers who do not already reward their students for good test grades. Similarly, a call to action may show who the target audience is by instructing the members of the audience to take a certain action.

CHAPTER QUIZ

1. Literature in what genre is often based on historical events, reveals something about human behavior or the natural world, and often involves actions of gods?

a. Historical fiction
b. Myth
c. Fantasy
d. Adventure

2. In dramatic texts (plays or scripts), which of the following are usually in italics to set them apart from other parts of the play?

a. Dialogues
b. Acts and scenes
c. Stage directions
d. Character tags

3. What structural feature is used to list items separately, making facts and ideas easier to see and understand?

a. Boldface
b. Bullet points
c. Sidebars
d. Headings

4. In what organizational pattern does the author choose a topic and then divide it into smaller parts or groups in order to discuss them individually?

a. Deductive
b. Inductive
c. Classification
d. Definition

5. If an author writes about cats and dogs, showing their similarities and differences, this would be an example of what type of organizational pattern?

a. Cause and effect
b. Problem and solution
c. Proposition and support
d. Compare and contrast

6. In an informational text, when is the main idea of a passage often presented?

a. In the first sentence
b. In the first one to two paragraphs
c. In the middle
d. At the end/conclusion

Chapter Quiz Answer Key

1. B: See section **Literary Genres**

2. C: See section **Text Structure in Drama**

3. B: See section **Structural Features of Informational Text**

4. C: See section **Classification**

5. D: See section **Compare and Contrast**

6. B: See section **Controlling Idea**

Author's Purpose and Craft

Author's Purpose

The purpose of a text is the author's main reason for writing the text. As the reader reads a text, they should always try to figure out the author's purpose for writing as this will help them to better understand the message that the author is trying to convey.

Informational Texts

- Inform the reader on a topic that they previously knew nothing about, such as many non-fiction texts.
- The author will usually include sources of information for an informative piece.
- For example, an informative paper on early Native American Indian tribes would detail where Native American Indians lived, what types of foods they ate, how they bartered for goods, and other aspects of their culture.

Persuasive Texts

- Influence the reader to think a certain way about a topic, calling them to action or pointing them toward resources that would help them to learn more about the topic.
- A **proposition and support** paper would be an example of this, where an author gives their opinion and then tries to convince the reader to see something from their point of view.
- An author will often use positive expert testimonials when trying to persuade the reader to accept a given point-of-view.
- For example, an author may try to persuade the reader that technology is negatively affecting social interaction, and that limits should be set on how much people can use their technological devices.

Expressive Texts

- Express the author or speaker's opinion or emotions about a topic. Generally, expressive texts include descriptive words to clearly show the reader how the author or speaker feels.
- For example, the author may think that history is important for all people to study, and express the opinion that education without history class would be incomplete.

Entertaining Texts

- Entertain the reader, such as in most fictional texts.
- For example, Lois Lowry, the author of *The Giver,* entertains his readers with the story of a young boy named Jonas who is learning how to navigate his unexpected life assignment.
- Entertaining texts can be either fiction or non-fiction, but are usually stories such as a fairy tale or fictional piece of writing. Entertaining texts usually follow a chronological order.

Authors usually write to entertain, to inform, or to persuade their readers. The organization structure or pattern they use is related to what the author's purpose is. It is important to choose the pattern that best presents the information, as not all patterns will work for every piece of writing.

Determining the Purpose of a Text

When reading, the reader should always determine the purpose of a text. to do so, ask yourself what effect the writing has on you. Does the text try to explain or persuade you of something? Perhaps the text is making an appeal to your emotions. The signs that a text is attempting to persuade you include an author offering an opinion and explaining why she thinks this way. On the other hand, if a text is simply informative, it will have many facts that will give details about an event, person, or idea without trying to persuade you of anything. Manuals that come with equipment are clearly not persuasive, simply instructive.

Review Video: Understanding the Author's Intent
Visit mometrix.com/academy and enter code: 511819

Print and Graphic Features

An author may show information in a chart, a graph, in paragraph format, or as a list. Information may also be shown in a picture or a diagram. The way an author chooses to show information is often based on the purpose of the text and the audience that the text is meant to reach.

A reader may be asked to answer questions based on the graphic by itself, how the graphic relates to the text, or how the text would best be shown in a graphic form. Some common examples of graphics are cause and effect organizers, circle graphs, bar graphs, illustrations, and diagrams.

Cause and Effect Graphic Organizers

Cause-and-effect graphic organizers are often used to map the **elements of a story**. A reader might read a story about a string of events and then be asked to correctly fill in either the **cause** or **effect** of an event in the story.

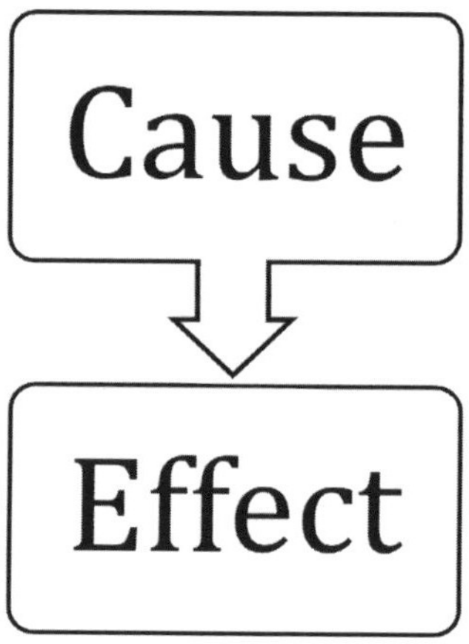

Example

Read the following excerpt from *Ramona Quimby, Age 8* by Beverly Cleary and decide what the cause of the hectic morning at the Quimby house is.

> With all four members of the family leaving at different times in different directions, mornings were flurried in the Quimby household.

A **cause and effect** graphic organizer for this excerpt might look something like this:

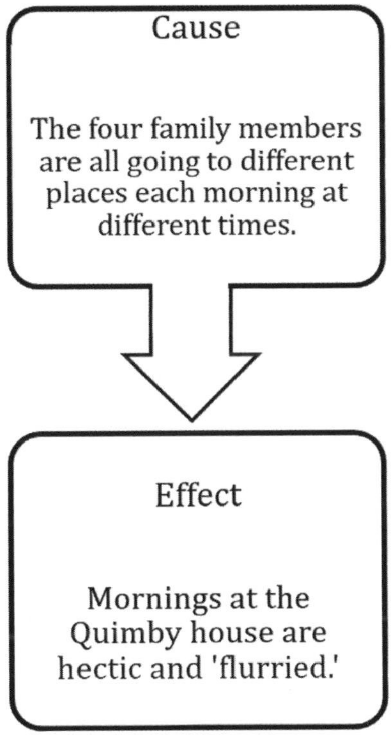

LINE GRAPHS

Line graphs are used for measuring general **trends over time**. For example, this line graph shows an overall upward trend in the amount of candy bars sold for four weeks.

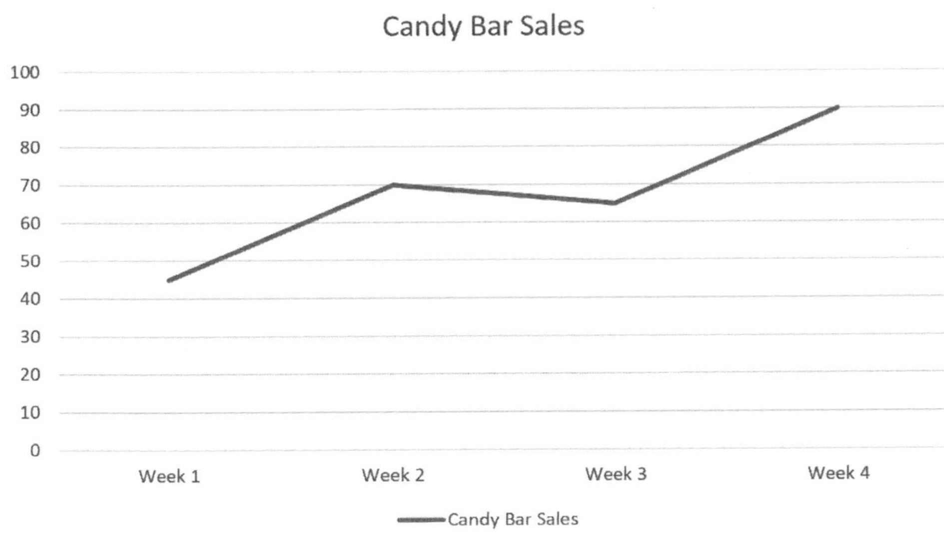

CIRCLE GRAPHS

Circle graphs, also called pie charts, are often used to represent information that can be shown as **parts of a whole**. For example, this graph shows the results of people being asked about their favorite color:

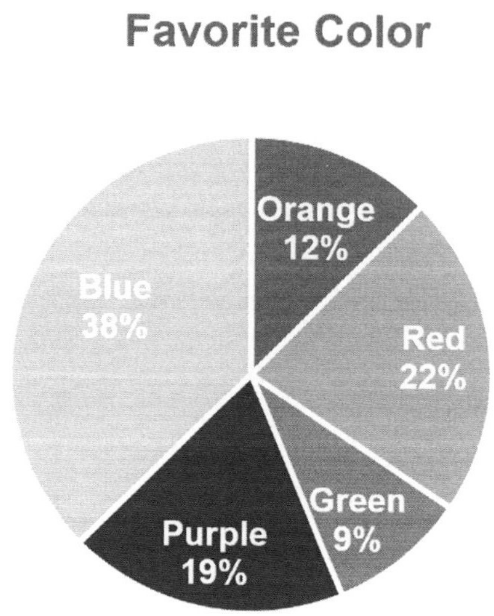

BAR GRAPHS

Bar graphs are used to show information about **numbers**. For example, this graph is a different way of representing the same results as those in the circle graph.

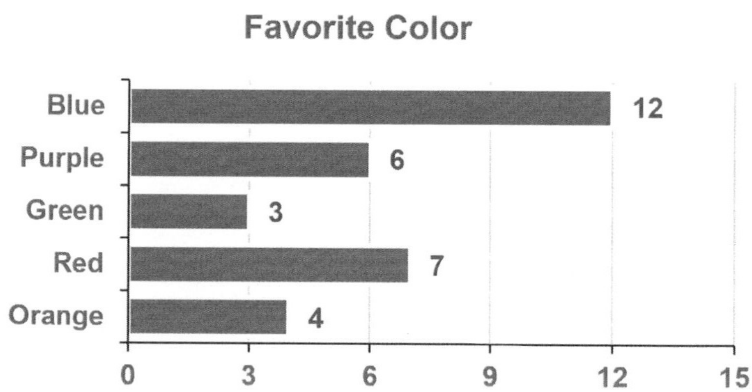

ILLUSTRATIONS AND PHOTOGRAPHS

Authors may choose to include **illustrations** or **photographs** (or both) with their texts. These two image types both show something from the text or give more information about the text.

Illustrations are drawings of an object. They may be based on reality, or they may represent an artist's abstract idea. For example, this is an illustration of a 1903 automobile:

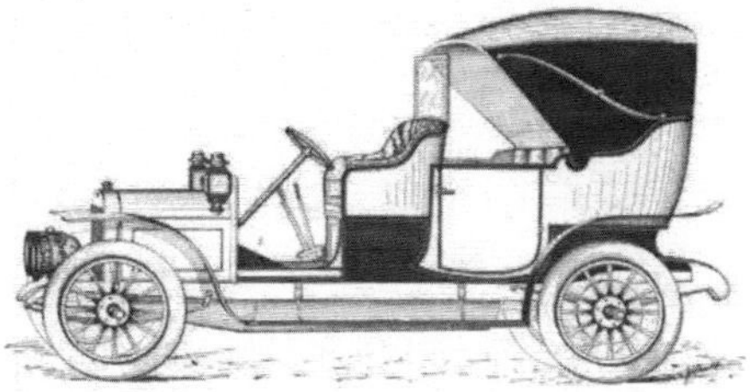

Photographs are pictures of objects. They are generally extremely realistic, and most often show an object as it actually existed at that moment in time. For example, this is a photograph of a 1917 automobile:

Both illustrations and photographs give the reader another way to relate to and understand the text. The reader may be asked how the image relates to the text, what type of caption the image should be given, or why the author chose to include the image with the text.

Diagrams

Diagrams are used to show information in a visual way. There are many different types of diagrams, including:

Diagrams that show the parts of an object, how they work together, or how they should be put together. This is an example of a diagram which shows how gears turn together

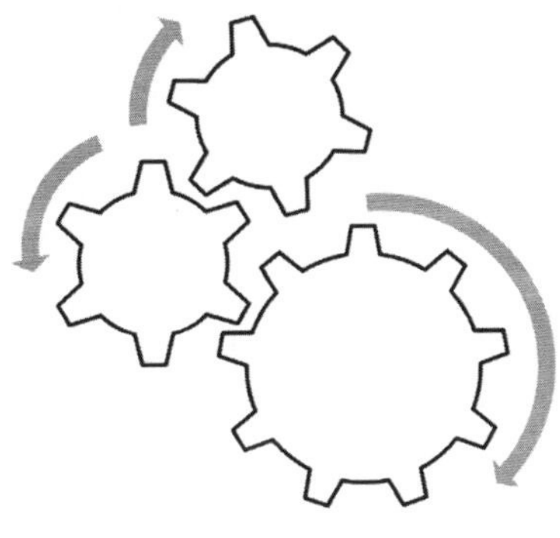

Diagrams that show how information is related are called **Venn Diagrams**. These are ways to visually see the way in which two different ideas overlap. This is an example of a Venn Diagram comparing cats and dogs:

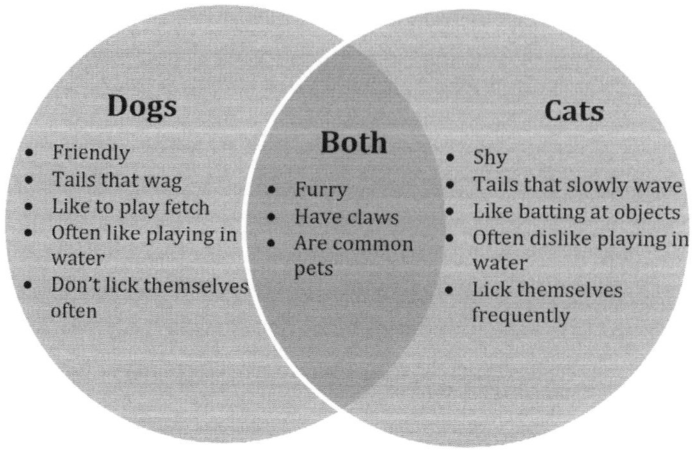

IMAGERY

Imagery is the use of **descriptive language** to add life or feeling to a work of literature. Many authors add literary and sound devices to create vivid pictures in the minds of their readers. Most of the time, imagery is thought to be one of the best ways to help readers fully understand and remember a work.

The most common forms of imagery are those that appeal to the sense of sight and sound. Imagery that appeals to the sense of sight, or **visual imagery**, helps the reader picture an event in their mind, usually by including specific details in the text that are not strictly necessary for the purpose of the story, but allow the reader to more easily "see" the scene. Some common forms of figurative language can help create visual imagery.

Review Video: Sensory Language
Visit mometrix.com/academy and enter code: 177314

LITERAL AND FIGURATIVE LANGUAGE

Many types of text use both **literal language**, which means just what it says, and **figurative language**, which allows the writer to expand the way in which he or she uses language. When an author uses figurative language, she connects things in an exaggerated and non-literal way in order to create a memorable image, which helps to describe a situation in a new way for the reader.

Review Video: Figurative Language
Visit mometrix.com/academy and enter code: 584902

SIMILE

- Shows similarity between two ideas or objects, using the words "**like**" or "**as**"
- For example, an author might write "The princess is as beautiful as a rose" to compare the appearance of a woman to a beautiful flower.

Metaphor

- Puts one idea in place of another to draw a parallel between the two ideas.
- For example, an author might write "Her room was a pigsty," to compare a person's bedroom to a dirty spot where pigs sleep.

Symbolism

- Using one object to stand for something else.
- For example, an author may include a flag flying high throughout a story to show pride in the characters' country and to represent the idea of patriotism.

Hyperbole

- An extreme exaggeration of an idea.
- For example, a character might say "I'm starving to death!" to show that they are really hungry. Most of the time a character who says this is not literally going to die from hunger, they are just ready for a snack.

Irony

- Uses sarcasm or humor (usually with an emphasis on the opposite) to show difference from literal meaning.
- For example, if a character says "Well today must be my lucky day!" after they left their homework on the kitchen table, they are being ironic. The irony used here helps show that it is definitely *not* the character's lucky day.

Personification

- Gives life or human characteristics to an inanimate object
- For example, if an author writes "The trees whispered to each other across the wide blue sky," they are using personification to help the reader imagine the scene. Trees are not human beings, so they do not whisper, but the image created in the reader stands out more than a literal description would.

Example

Based on current knowledge, identify whether metaphor, simile, or hyperbole is used in this sentence:

> The chiming bell was a beacon of hope for the downtrodden villagers.

A **metaphor** is used in this sentence to draw a parallel between "the chiming bell" and "a beacon of hope." The bell is being compared to something else in the sentence, which indicates the use of metaphor or simile, but the reader knows that the sentence does not contain a simile, because the words **like** and **as** are not used to show the comparison. The sentence also does not contain an exaggeration of facts, so the reader can see that hyperbole is not used.

Example

Discuss the kind of figurative language used in the following poem by the Scottish poet Robert Burns.

> O my luve's like a red, red rose
> That's newly sprung in June;
> O my luve's like the melodie
> That's sweetly played in tune.

The poet uses **similes** to create an image in this poem. The two similes here occur when the speaker says that his love is "**like** a red, red rose" and that she is also "**like** the melodie." These are examples of similes because they use the comparing word 'like' to compare two things. They are not metaphors because metaphors do not use the comparing words 'like' or 'as.' The poem paints an image of the speaker's love by comparing her to a red rose that has newly sprung and a melody that is sweetly played.

EXAMPLE

Read the following excerpt from "The Raven" by Edgar Allan Poe, identify the metaphor, and discuss how it impacts the text:

> And the raven, never flitting, still is sitting, still is sitting
> On the pallid bust of Pallas just above my chamber door;
> And his eyes have all the seeming of a demon's that is dreaming

One **metaphor** in the excerpt from "The Raven" by Edgar Allan Poe is: 'And his eyes have all the seeming of a demon's that is dreaming' The metaphor compares the raven's eyes with a demon, which shows that the speaker thinks there is evil in the bird. This helps contribute to the overall tone of the poem and the reader's understanding of how the speaker views the bird.

EXAMPLE

Read the excerpt from a poem by William Blake and describe what form of figurative language it uses.

> The wild winds weep,
> And the night is a-cold;
> Come hither, sleep,
> And my griefs unfold.

This poem contains several examples of **personification**. In the poem, the speaker says "The wild winds weep," thereby giving the winds the human characteristic of weeping. Later it says "Come hither, sleep," which is another use of personification asking that sleep to go somewhere as though it were a person. The poem gives the winds and sleep human characteristics. This is the definition of personification. It is not an example of simile because there is no comparison using the words "as" or "like." It is not a metaphor because there is no comparison between two things sharing a similar quality. And it is not an example of hyperbole because there is no exaggeration. The poem does contain some alliteration, however; the repetition of the letter "w" in "wild winds weep" qualifies as alliteration, which is another literary technique.

POINT OF VIEW

Authors choose which character tells the story they are writing. This is called **point of view**. The point of view affects the story in many ways. There are three general types of point of view:

FIRST PERSON

- Tells a story through the eyes of one character.
- Uses the pronouns 'I,' 'me,' 'we,' and 'my.'
- The reader gets only one side of the story, without any other angles on what may have happened in the text

Second Person

- Tells a story using the pronoun 'you.'
- The least common point of view.

Third Person

- Tells a story about a character or group of characters from an outside viewpoint.
- Uses the words 'her', 'his,' 'they,' or a name to talk about a character or characters.
- A common way to show action in a story which allows the author to easily and realistically tell a story from more than one person's viewpoint.
- Gives readers a more complete view of a story as it is told from many different perspectives.

Different Forms of Third Person

When an author writes in third-person point of view, there are a few options to choose from:

- **Third person omniscient** - There is an all-knowing narrator telling the story as well as interpreting events, and relating thoughts of the characters.
- **Third person limited (or closed)** - The author writes in the third person, but does so from only one character's point of view. There are two different variations of this type of narration: the narrator can either stay with the same character throughout or cycle through different characters over the course of the story.

Subjective and Objective Point of View

The point of view of a character or narrator can either be **subjective** or **objective**. When a character or narrator is describing a person, object, or idea using phrases that are based on opinions or motivated by feelings, their point of view is subjective. When they use phrases based on facts or something that can be proven, their point of view is objective. For example, if a character describes a person walking toward them and they say "Her shirt was a beautiful shade of yellow, which made her blonde hair shine even brighter" they are speaking in subjective point of view. The yellow color they think is beautiful could be someone else's least favorite color. If the same character described the situation objectively, they might say "As she walked by, I noticed her shirt was yellow and her hair was blonde." The narrator doesn't comment on his opinion of the color, just that it is factually yellow.

Style, Voice, Tone, and Mood

Style, tone, and mood all play an important role in the development of a story. The reader's impression of a story can vary based on the style, tone, and mood established by the author.

- **Style** refers to the way an author uses words, phrases, and sentence structure. The style of the text can change depending on whether the author uses short, choppy sentences, long, elaborate sentences, formal language, or informal language.
- **Voice** refers to the characteristics of a text that show the author's personality and distinguish the author from other writers. An author's voice may be recognized through the way they use words or the way they organize and present their thoughts. Voice is specific to each writer, and it can be as specific and unique as personality.
- **Tone** refers to the attitude of the writer toward the subject matter. The tone can change throughout the text or stay the same. There are many ways to describe the tone of the text, such as light, playful, questioning, humorous, serious, solemn, or tense. The reader can identify the tone by paying attention to the author's word choice.

- **Mood** refers to the overall feeling conveyed by a setting. For example, a story may be dark in terms of setting, characters, and events that occur. If a story is presented in a picturesque countryside location where the characters are content and the style of speaking is elaborate, the reader will have a different impression of the story than if the setting is in a rundown house with a pale, unhappy caretaker that rarely speaks.

Review Video: Style, Tone, and Mood
Visit mometrix.com/academy and enter code: 416961

Rhetorical Devices vs Logical Fallacies

Writers of persuasive and argumentative texts will often use strategies that may help them persuade the reader to agree with their claims. These strategies may be used to convince the reader on a logical or emotional level. The writer may also use them to prove his or her own credibility, or reliability. These strategies are called **rhetorical devices**. However, writers make statements that seem like rhetorical devices, but are not actually logical. They may sound persuasive, but they are unreasonable and may leave out part of the truth or try to prove a weak argument. These are called **logical fallacies**.

Common Rhetorical Devices

- **Direct Address**: Direct address is a strategy that authors can use to create a call to action or lead their audience to make a personal connection to the author's claim. When making a direct address, the author will make a statement or claim as if they mean to say it to each audience member, personally.
- **Analogy:** An analogy is a comparison of relationships. For example, saying that a hen is to a chick as a mare is to a colt. Both pairs include a mother animal and a baby animal, and the analogy shows a similarity between hens and mares and a similarity between colts and chicks. Authors may use analogies to explain their claims. Analogies allow authors to show how their claim is similar to a concept that the reader is more familiar with or already approves.
- **Juxtaposition:** Juxtaposition is when two contrasting ideas are presented together. Authors can use juxtaposition to make the differences between the two ideas more obvious to the reader. This may also help the author lead the reader to pay attention or prefer one idea over the other.
- **Rhetorical Question:** A rhetorical question is a question that does not need to be answered. Authors may use rhetorical questions to encourage a reader to think more deeply about an idea or apply it to their own lives. Authors may also use rhetorical questions to influence the way a reader thinks about an idea.

Common Logical Fallacies

- **Bandwagon Appeals:** Bandwagon appeals claim that everybody else agrees with the author's argument, so readers to should conform and agree, also.
- **Circular Reasoning:** When authors use circular reasoning, they use the idea they want to prove as part of their proof for the idea. People using circular arguments are actually "talking in circles." For example, someone argues, "X is illegal. Because it is illegal, one should not do it. Because one shouldn't do it, the government should prevent people from doing it. This is why it is illegal."

- **Sweeping Generalizations:** When an author makes a statement as if it is true for everyone, the author is making a sweeping generalization. For example, the statement, "Everyone loves chocolate," is a sweeping generalization. While most people do enjoy chocolate, the statement is still not true because there are people who do not like chocolate. Authors may use sweeping generalizations as evidence because they will expect the reader to ignore the fact that they are not true. Readers must be careful to consider whether statements that apply to many people are actually true.
- **Loaded Language:** An author uses loaded language when he or she makes claims that include words or phrases that lead the audience to react emotionally. While making an emotional appeal can be an effective strategy, loaded language is often used only to draw on emotions. Authors use loaded language in order to lead the audience to agree based on how the author's words have made them feel, rather than whether or not the author's words are logical and supported by evidence. Loaded language may rely on the sympathy, anger, or fear of the audience.

Chapter Quiz

1. An author's purpose in writing fiction is most often to:

a. Persuade
b. Inform
c. Entertain
d. Express

2. What is the least common point of view, that tells a story using the pronouns "you"?

a. First person
b. Second person
c. Third person
d. Narrator

3. Which of the following refers to the overall feeling conveyed by a setting?

a. Style
b. Pace
c. Tone
d. Mood

4. What type of graphic can be used to visually see the way in which two different ideas overlap?

a. Circle graph
b. Bar graph
c. Venn diagram
d. Cause and effect organizer

5. What common form of figurative language puts one idea in place of another to draw a parallel between the two ideas?

a. Metaphor
b. Simile
c. Hyperbole
d. Irony

6. What type of logical fallacy claims that everybody else agrees with the author's argument, so readers should conform and agree also?

a. Sweeping generalizations
b. Appeal to pity
c. Circular reasoning
d. Bandwagon appeals

7. What rhetorical device presents two contrasting ideas together, and can be used to make the differences between ideas more obvious to the reader?

a. Direct Address
b. Rhetorical Questions
c. Analogy
d. Juxtaposition

Chapter Quiz Answer Key

1. C: See section **Author's Purpose**

2. B: See section **Second Person**

3. D: See section **Style, Voice, Tone, and Mood**

4. C: See section **Diagrams**

5. A: See section **Metaphor**

6. D: See section **Common Logical Fallacies**

7. D: See section **Common Rhetorical Devices**

Writing

Writing Process

Brainstorming

When choosing what to write about, activities like brainstorming can help inspire new ideas or help writers see how their ideas go together. **Brainstorming** means considering a variety of topics or ideas and is mainly used to find a creative approach to a subject or problem. A good first step in brainstorming is simple **free-association** with a topic. One way of doing this is sitting down with paper and pen and writing every thought that comes to mind about the topic in a word or phrase. It does not matter how helpful or good the thought seems at first; the writer should write down everything that comes to mind about the topic. Then, the writer should read the list over a few times. Next, he or she should look for patterns, repetitions, and clusters of ideas. This allows a variety of fresh ideas to come as the writer thinks about the topic.

Free Writing

Free writing is a more organized form of brainstorming. **Free writing** means taking a limited amount of time, like 2 to 3 minutes, to write everything that comes to mind about a topic in complete sentences. When the time is up, the writer should review everything he or she has written down. Many of the sentences may not make sense, but they may contain ideas and details that help the writer organize his or her ideas and prepare to plan the composition. Usually, free writing results in more useful ideas than brainstorming because the writer's thoughts and connections are written in complete sentences. However, both methods can be used together to help the writer prepare to plan and write a composition.

Mapping

One specific way to use graphic organizers is to map an essay. There are many different types of graphic organizers. One easy method to create one is to draw a circle in the middle of the page and write a broad topic in it. Then, draw smaller circles with related topics and ideas, or with topics that fit within the broad topic, written inside and draw line to connect each circle to the main circle. This method can show ideas that fit within the broad topic and will help guide the essay, or it can show which ideas may work better as the main topic of the essay.

Once the main idea and other ideas and details for the essay have been chosen, they can be used to map the essay. Mapping is another word for using a certain type of graphic organizer. These graphic organizers look like a map and organize ideas and details as they will appear in the essay. The essay map can have the main idea at the top or in the center. If the main idea is at the top, the supporting ideas will appear below it in a row, and any additional details will appear under the supporting idea they go with. If the main idea appears in the center, the supporting ideas may appear around it, and the additional details will appear around the supporting ideas they go with.

Planning

Planning is the process of organizing a piece of writing before writing a draft. At the beginning of planning, writers should decide **why they are writing** and **who will read what they write**. The writer must also choose a **genre**, which is the **type** of composition he or she will write. There are fiction genres, such as comedy, folklore, action, and mystery. There are also nonfiction genres, such as essays, reports, poems, and journals. To plan his or her composition, a writer may create an outline or a graphic organizer, such as a Venn diagram, a spider-map, or a flowchart. These methods should help the writer choose their topic, main ideas, and how to organize the composition. If the writer needs to do research for the composition, he or she may also do so as they plan. Planning helps writers organize all of their ideas and decide if they have enough information to begin their first draft. However, writers should remember that the decisions they make during planning may change later, so their plan does not have to be perfect.

DRAFTING

Writers may then use their plan, outline, or graphic organizer to compose their first draft. They may write more drafts after the first one to improve their writing. Writing multiple drafts can help writers think of different ways to state their ideas and correct mistakes that may be hard to fix without rewriting a section of the composition, or the whole composition. There is no "right" number of drafts, so different writers may write a different number of drafts. Writing drafts also makes it easier to write freely because a writer can improve his or her composition with each draft they write.

REVISING, EDITING, AND PROOFREADING

Once a writer completes a draft, he or she can move on to revising, editing, and proofreading to improve the draft. **Revising** is making sure that the composition is right for the audience, is not missing important information, is on topic, and is well organized. The writer should also consider the composition's style when revising and ensure that it is appropriately formal or serious. Revising may happen after the first draft so that errors are not repeated in the next draft. Each draft should be revised before the next one is written so that no mistakes are missed. **Editing** comes next. Editing a composition includes steps like improving transitions between paragraphs and making sure each paragraph is on topic. While editing, the writer must pay attention to the words he or she uses and the way the information in each paragraph is organized. Writers may also fix grammar mistakes in the editing phase, since some errors will require a writer to rewrite large parts of their work. **Proofreading** means fixing misspelled words, errors in grammar, and any other small mistakes in the composition.

During the revising, editing, and proofreading steps, it can be helpful for writers to ask a peer to read their work, since he or she may notice mistakes or problems the writer missed before. A writer may also choose to read his or her own work aloud, or listen to someone else read it. Hearing a composition aloud can help writers find mistakes or opportunities for improvement in their work more easily. This happens because when something is read aloud, the person reading the text must pay closer attention to the words on the page. When a writer or a peer reads the composition, they should point out any sentence that confuses them the first time they read it. Most of these sentences can be revised in a way that makes it easier to read and understand.

ADDING AND REMOVING INFORMATION

While both revising and editing may involve changing the words in a composition, they can also involve adding or taking away words. When a writer has completed a draft and reread it, he or she may notice that something, such as a transition, important details, or an explanatory sentence, is missing. Simply changing the words to make the passage sound better will not solve this problem, so the writer must **add** whatever words and information is needed to make the passage make sense and achieve the writer's purpose.

In other cases, a writer may have words, a sentence, or sometimes an entire paragraph that gives unnecessary information or explains the information in a way that is confusing. When this happens, the extra words and information weaken the composition and must be **removed**. Sometimes, this is difficult for writers to do because it may require them to remove writing they are proud of or a fact they find interesting. Despite this, revising and editing are steps meant to improve and strengthen a composition, so the writer should change, add, or remove parts of his or her writing in a way that makes it better and achieves his or her purpose.

Revising Sentences

Sentence variety is important to consider when writing an essay. A variety of sentence lengths and types can make an essay more engaging, and different types of sentences can sometimes help readers better understand information. For example, a sentence containing a list may make more sense when written with a simple sentence structure, since writing a compound sentence containing a list may give the reader too much information at once. On the other hand, information that is closely related and can be connected with a conjunction should be written in a compound sentence, rather than a simple sentence, since a compound sentence helps the reader see that the information goes together.

Using only simple sentences often makes writing boring and bothersome to read. Writing using only compound sentences makes it difficult for writers to explain information well and difficult for readers to understand, since every sentence will include a coordinating conjunction. To check an essay for sentence variety, it is helpful to look at whether the essay contains different sentence structures and lengths. It is also important to pay attention to the way each sentence starts and avoid beginning with the same words or phrases.

Revising Vocabulary

When writing informational or argumentative texts, it is important to use **precise vocabulary**, or **word choice**, to explain your main idea and supporting details. Generalized vocabulary will not help the audience fully understand the points that you are attempting to make because it will not accurately explain your main idea and supporting details. Precise vocabulary is important to use because it will accurately describe the ideas that are central to your text. When you research a subject, make sure to familiarize yourself with any vocabulary that is involved in its explanation. Use context clues, dictionaries, or, if necessary, a technical dictionary to decode any words that you are not familiar with. Precise vocabulary also impacts the effectiveness of narrative text. Carefully choosing vocabulary to describe sensory details, or imagery, helps writers paint the best possible picture of the events they are describing through their writing.

Chapter Quiz

1. Which of the following means taking a limited amount of time, like 2 to 3 minutes, to write everything that comes to mind about a topic in complete sentences?

a. Brainstorming
b. Drafting
c. Mapping
d. Free writing

2. What is often the first step after a writer completes a draft, and involves making sure that the composition is right for the audience, it is not missing important information, is on topic, and is well organized?

a. Adapting
b. Editing
c. Proofreading
d. Revising

3. When revising sentences in an essay, which of the following is NOT good advice?

a. Avoid beginning sentences with the same words or phrases
b. Include a variety of sentence lengths
c. Improve understanding by only using compound sentences
d. Keep sentences simple when they include lists

4. In what step of the writing process does the writer decide why they are writing, who will read what they write, and what genre they want to write?

a. Brainstorming
b. Drafting
c. Mapping
d. Planning

Chapter Quiz Answer Key

1. D: See section **Free Writing**

2. D: See section **Revising, Editing, and Proofreading**

3. C: See section **Revising Sentences**

4. D: See section **Planning**

Essay Structure and Organization

Controlling Ideas and Supporting Details

In the first paragraph of a composition, writers include a sentence that explains the **controlling idea.** This sentence is also known as the **thesis**. The rest of the paragraph shows the reader why the topic of the essay is interesting and includes details that support the controlling idea. One way to understand the relationship between the controlling idea and supporting information is to think about a table: the tabletop is the controlling idea, and each of the table's legs is a supporting detail or group of details. All of the legs work together to support the tabletop and create a table, just like the supporting details work together to support the controlling idea and create a composition.

Introduction

The introduction is used to capture the reader's attention and announce the essay's controlling idea. Normally, the introduction contains about 3-5 sentences. An introduction can begin with an interesting quote, a question, a strong opinion, or something else that will **interest** the reader's and prompt them to keep reading. If the composition has a prompt, the introduction should **restate** or **summarize** some part of the prompt so that the reader will have an idea of what information will be in the essay. Finally, your introduction should include the **controlling idea**, the primary thing the essay will tell the reader.

Review Video: Introduction
Visit mometrix.com/academy and enter code: 961328

Body

In an essay's introduction, the writer states the controlling idea and prepares the reader for the information in the rest of the composition. In the body of the composition, the writer **explains, demonstrates**, and **gives more information about** the **controlling idea**. This is done using supporting details and examples that are relevant to the controlling idea of the composition. For example, if the composition's controlling idea is a vacation the writer took, the body will include descriptions of where the writer went, what they experienced, and what they thought of the trip. If the composition's controlling idea is the writer's opinion, the body will include examples and facts that show why he or she has formed that opinion. If composition's controlling idea is a topic and the writer wants to instruct the reader, the body will contain facts, explanations, and examples that help teach the reader about the controlling idea. A writer will use supporting details to explain the controlling idea throughout the body.

The body should also contain multiple paragraphs, and the order the writer puts these paragraphs in is important. Each paragraph should include at least one supporting detail, but a paragraph may include more than one if two or more supporting details work together to support the controlling idea. If the controlling idea is to describe something that happened, the paragraphs should match the order in which the events occurred. If the controlling idea is to present an opinion or instruct the reader, the paragraphs should be ordered in the way that would make the most sense to the reader. The order of body paragraphs is important because it can impact how easy a composition is to read.

Review Video: Drafting Body Paragraphs
Visit mometrix.com/academy and enter code: 724590

Paragraphs

After the introduction of a passage, the body paragraphs will explain and elaborate upon the controlling idea. While each paragraph should relate to the controlling idea of the composition, each paragraph should focus on one point or supporting detail. Normally, a paragraph has a good topic sentence that summarizes the paragraph's main point. A topic sentence is a sentence that gives an introduction to the paragraph and its contents. Topic sentences should contain information that is more specific than what is in the introduction and may include a supporting detail, but they should not contain explanations or examples.

Supporting Details

The next sentences in the paragraph should support the topic sentence. These sentences can contain examples, explanations, or other specific information that supports the topic sentence, which supports the controlling idea of the composition. While a paragraph may be structured in any way, as long as it logically provides information that supports the controlling idea, it can be best to use a template or pattern to make sure that each paragraph is complete and well organized. For example, a good template to follow is topic sentence, evidence, explanation, conclusion. This means that after the topic sentence, the next sentence should provide evidence, like a quote or example, that supports the paragraph's main point. Next, the paragraph should include a sentence that explains how that evidence supports the paragraph's main point. If there are multiple examples or quotes, more than one sentence may be used to explain them. Finally, there should be a concluding sentence that helps the reader understand the paragraph and prepares them for the next one.

Choosing Supporting Details and Examples

When writing an informative or argumentative text, writers must choose supporting details carefully. Including details that are irrelevant, inaccurate, or vague does not strengthen the author's writing, while relevant, accurate, provable, and specific details do strengthen the author's writing. These details can make the writer's meaning clearer or give evidence that the author's points are true or logical. Such details may include examples or facts, such as statistics, statements from others who have authority on the subject, and common events or experiences. Choosing appropriate supporting details can also help the author show that they put effort into forming their ideas. This can also make the composition more intriguing and enjoyable to read, since the writer's own interest and insight will be apparent to the reader.

Length of a Paragraph

A paragraph must contain enough information to support its main point and the composition's controlling idea. A paragraph of two or three sentences will most likely not support the main point or controlling idea because it is not likely to contain enough information, explanation, or evidence. When a paragraph does not support the main point or controlling idea, it does not help the writer achieve their purpose or goal for writing the essay. A helpful, informative paragraph will often have somewhere from three to five sentences. Also, it is important that the sentences within the paragraph lead the reader through the information. Each paragraph should flow logically and stay on topic throughout.

Starting a New Paragraph

For most forms of writing, you will need to use multiple paragraphs. This means that deciding when to start a new paragraph is very important. Reasons for starting a new paragraph include:

- To separate the introduction and conclusion from the body paragraphs
- To move from one supporting detail or point to another
- To indicate an important shift in time or place
- To show a comparison, contrast, or cause and effect relationship

Coherent Paragraphs

A smooth flow of sentences and paragraphs without gaps, shifts, or bumps will lead to paragraph **coherence**. The connections between old and new information can be shown using several methods:

- **Clearly linking ideas**, from the topic sentence to the body of the paragraph, is essential for a smooth transition. The topic sentence states the main point, and this should be followed by specific details, examples, and illustrations that support the topic sentence.
- The **repetition of key words** adds coherence to a paragraph. To avoid dull language, synonyms of the key words may be used.
- **Parallel structures** are often used within sentences to highlight the similarity of ideas and connect sentences that give similar information.
- Maintaining a **consistent verb tense** throughout the paragraph helps make paragraphs coherent. Shifting tenses affects the smooth flow of words and can disrupt the coherence of the paragraph.

Review Video: How to Write a Good Paragraph
Visit mometrix.com/academy and enter code: 682127

Transitions

Transitions between sentences and paragraphs guide readers from idea to idea and show relationships between sentences and paragraphs. Writers should use transitions carefully and only when they are truly helpful. They should also be selected to fit the author's purpose. Transitions can show relationships such as time, comparison, an order of events, and cause and effect. Transitions are often used at the beginning of a phrase, sentence, or paragraph, since this helps prepare the reader for the next piece of information.

Review Video: Transitions in Writing
Visit mometrix.com/academy and enter code: 233246

Types of Transitional Words

Time	Afterward, immediately, earlier, meanwhile, recently, lately, now, since, soon, when, then, until, before, etc.
Sequence	too, first, second, further, moreover, also, again, and, next, still, besides, finally
Comparison	similarly, in the same way, likewise, also, again, once more
Contrasting	but, although, despite, however, instead, nevertheless, on the one hand... on the other hand, regardless, yet, in contrast
Cause and Effect	because, consequently, thus, therefore, then, to this end, since, so, as a result, if... then, accordingly
Examples	for example, for instance, such as, to illustrate, indeed, in fact, specifically
Place	near, far, here, there, to the left/right, next to, above, below, beyond, opposite, beside
Repetition, Summary, or Conclusion	as mentioned earlier, as noted, in other words, in short, on the whole, to summarize, therefore, as a result, to conclude, in conclusion
Addition	and, also, furthermore, moreover

Review Video: Transition Words
Visit mometrix.com/academy and enter code: 707563

Conclusion

The conclusion of a composition should summarize the controlling idea and show that it has been explained well. A good conclusion shows the reader why the author's controlling idea is meaningful and important and how the supporting details should help the reader understand the controlling idea. The conclusion should also give the reader something to think about that is related to the controlling idea. For example, in the conclusion, the author can invite readers to think about how they feel or what they think after reading the composition. Some things to avoid when writing conclusions include:

- Introducing a completely new idea
- Apologizing for one's opinions or writing
- Repeating the controlling idea word for word rather than summarizing them
- Using the conclusion to summarize every detail in the composition

Review Video: Drafting Conclusions
Visit mometrix.com/academy and enter code: 209408

Chapter Quiz

1. "Too," "and," "next," "still," "besides," and "finally" are all what type of transitional word?

a. Time
b. Sequence
c. Comparison
d. Contrasting

2. Which of the following should be avoided in an essay conclusion?

a. Reminding the reader of the central idea by repeating it word for word
b. Showing the reader why the author's central idea is meaningful and important
c. Showing that the central idea has been explained well
d. Giving the reader something to think about that is related to the central idea

3. A helpful, informative paragraph will often have how many sentences?

a. One to three sentences
b. Three to five sentences
c. Five to ten sentences
d. Ten to fifteen sentences

4. The body of an essay should do all of the following, EXCEPT:

a. Introduce the central idea
b. Demonstrate the central idea
c. Explain the central idea
d. Give information about the central idea

Chapter Quiz Answer Key

1. B: See section **Types of Transitional Words**

2. A: See section **Conclusion**

3. B: See section **Length of a Paragraph**

4. A: See section **Body**

Grammar

Subjects and Predicates

Subjects

Every sentence needs a subject and a predicate. The **subject** of a sentence names who or what the sentence is about. The subject may be directly stated in a sentence, or the subject may be implied. The **complete subject** includes the simple subject and any **modifiers**, such as adjectives, articles, prepositions, and adverbs, that go with it. To find the complete subject, ask *Who* or *What* before the verb to complete the question. The answer, including any modifiers, is the complete subject. To find the **simple subject**, remove all of the modifiers in the complete subject.

Examples:

simple subject

The small, red car is the one that he wants for Christmas.

complete subject

simple subject

The young artist is coming over for dinner.

complete subject

Review Video: Subjects in English
Visit mometrix.com/academy and enter code: 444771

An imperative sentence is a sentence that gives someone instructions or makes a request to someone. In **imperative** sentences, the verb's subject is understood, but is not actually present in the sentence. For example, this about the sentence *Drive to the store*. This sentence is a command, and the subject is *you*. If the subject were directly stated, the sentence would be *You, drive to the store*. Another fact to consider is that, normally, the subject comes before the verb. However, the subject comes after the verb in sentences that begin with *There are* or *There was.*

Direct:

John knows the way to the park.	Who knows the way to the park?	John
The cookies need ten more minutes.	What needs ten minutes?	The cookies
By five o'clock, Bill will need to leave.	Who needs to leave?	Bill
There are five letters on the table for him.	What is on the table?	Five letters
There were coffee and doughnuts in the house.	What was in the house?	Coffee and doughnuts

Implied:

Go to the post office for me.	Who is going to the post office?	You
Come and sit with me, please?	Who needs to come and sit?	You

PREDICATES

In a sentence, there is always a predicate and a subject. The subject tells what the sentence is about, and the **predicate** explains or describes the subject.

Think about the sentence *He sings*. In this sentence, we have a subject, *He*, and a predicate, *sings*. This is all that is needed for a sentence to be complete. Most sentences contain more information, but if this is all the information that is given in a sentence, then it is a complete sentence.

Now, let's look at another sentence: *John and Jane sing on Tuesday nights at the dance hall.*

subject predicate

John and Jane sing on Tuesday nights at the dance hall.

SUBJECT-VERB AGREEMENT

Verbs **agree** with their subjects in number. In other words, singular subjects need singular verbs. Plural subjects need plural verbs. **Singular** is for **one** person, place, or thing. **Plural** is for **more than one** person, place, or thing. Subjects and verbs must also share the same point of view, as in first, second, or third person.

Review Video: Subject-Verb Agreement
Visit mometrix.com/academy and enter code: 479190

NUMBER AGREEMENT EXAMPLES:

Single Subject and Verb: Dan (singular subject) calls (singular verb) home.

Dan is one person. So, the singular verb *calls* is needed.

Plural Subject and Verb: Dan and Bob (plural subject) call (plural verb) home.

More than one person needs the plural verb *call.*

PERSON AGREEMENT EXAMPLES:

First Person: I *am* walking.

Second Person: You *are* walking.

Third Person: He *is* walking.

COMPLICATIONS WITH SUBJECT-VERB AGREEMENT

WORDS BETWEEN SUBJECT AND VERB

Words that come between the simple subject and the verb do not affect subject-verb agreement.

Examples:

The joy (singular subject) of my life returns (singular verb) home tonight.

The phrase *of my life* does not affect the verb *returns.*

The question (singular subject) that still remains unanswered is (singular verb) "Who are you?"

Don't let the phrase *"that still remains..."* confuse you. The subject *question* goes with the verb *is.*

COMPOUND SUBJECTS

A compound subject is formed when two or more nouns joined by *and, or,* or *nor* act together as the subject of the sentence.

JOINED BY AND

When a compound subject is joined by *and,* it is treated as a plural subject and requires a plural verb.

Examples:

plural subject — plural verb

You and Jon are invited to come to my house.

plural subject — plural verb

The pencil and paper belong to me.

JOINED BY OR/NOR

For a compound subject joined by *or* or *nor*, the verb must agree in number with the part of the subject that is closest to the verb.

Examples:

subject — verb

Today or tomorrow is the day.

subject — verb

Stan or Phil wants to read the book.

subject — verb

Neither the pen nor the book is on the desk.

subject — verb

Either the blanket or pillows arrive this afternoon.

INDEFINITE PRONOUNS AS SUBJECT

An indefinite pronoun is a pronoun that does not refer to a specific noun. Different indefinite pronouns are used as a singular noun, a plural noun, or change depending on how they are used.

ALWAYS SINGULAR

Pronouns such as *each*, *either*, *everybody*, *anybody*, *somebody*, and *nobody* are always singular. This is because these pronouns always stand in for one person, place, or thing.

Examples:

singular subject — singular verb

Each of the runners has a different bib number.

singular verb — singular subject

Is either of you ready for the game?

Note: The words *each* and *either* can also be used as adjectives. For example, *each* person is unique. When one of these adjectives modifies the subject of a sentence, it is always a singular subject.

singular subject — singular verb

Everybody grows a day older every day.

singular subject — singular verb

Anybody is welcome to bring a tent.

ALWAYS PLURAL

Pronouns such as *both*, *several*, and *many* are always plural. This is because these pronouns always stand in for more than one person, place, thing, or idea.

Examples:

> Both [plural subject] of the siblings were [plural verb] too tired to argue.
>
> Many [plural subject] have tried [plural verb], but none have succeeded.

DEPEND ON CONTEXT

Pronouns such as *some*, *any*, *all*, *none*, *more*, and *most* can be either singular or plural depending on what they are representing in the context of the sentence.

Examples:

> All [singular subject] of my dog's food was [singular verb] still there in his bowl.
>
> By the end of the night, all [plural subject] of my guests were [plural verb] already excited about coming to my next party.

OTHER CASES INVOLVING PLURAL OR IRREGULAR FORM

Some nouns are **singular in meaning but plural in form**: news, mathematics, physics, and economics.

> The *news is* coming on now.
>
> *Mathematics is* my favorite class.

Some nouns are plural in form and meaning, and have **no singular equivalent**: scissors and pants.

> Do these *pants come* with a shirt?
>
> The *scissors are* for my project.

Note: Look to your **dictionary** for help when you aren't sure whether a noun with a plural form has a singular or plural meaning.

EXAMPLE

Which word should go in the blank?

> If Kelly if going to the party, Joan and Susan ____ going to the store.

a. Is
b. Are
c. Am
d. Was

Try using each choice in the sentence. Choice A, *is*, forms this sentence: If Kelly is going to the party, Joan and Susan is going to the store. There are two people, Joan and Susan, who are going to the store. This makes the subject of the clause plural. *Is* is a singular verb, meaning it does not agree with the subject and cannot be the answer.

Choice B, *are*, forms this sentence: If Kelly is going to the party, Joan and Susan are going to the store. The subject of the clause is still plural. But *are* is a plural verb! The subject and verb agree, so *are* is the correct answer.

Choice C, *am*, forms this sentence: If Kelly is going to the party, Joan and Susan am going to the store. *Am* is a singular verb, and it is also only used in first person, when the writer or speaker is referring to themself. The subject of the clause is plural, and the sentence is in third person, so *am* is not the correct answer.

Choice D, *was*, forms this sentence: If Kelly is going to the party, Joan and Susan was going to the store. *Was* is a singular verb, so it does not agree with the plural subject in this clause.

Complements

A complement is a noun, pronoun, or adjective that is used to give more information about the subject or verb in the sentence.

Direct Objects

A direct object is a noun or pronoun that takes or receives the **action** of a verb. A complete sentence does not need a direct object, so not all sentences will have them. When you are looking for a direct object, find the verb and ask *who* or *what*.

Examples:

> I took *the blanket*.
>
> Jane read *books*.

Indirect Objects

An indirect object is a word or group of words that show how an action had an **influence** on someone or something. If there is an indirect object in a sentence, then you always have a direct object in the sentence. When you are looking for the indirect object, find the verb and ask *to*, *for*, *whom*, or *what*.

Examples:

> We taught [the old dog]ᵢₙₐᵢᵣₑcₜ

We taught the old dog (indirect object) a new trick (direct object).

I gave them (indirect object) a math lesson (direct object).

Review Video: Direct and Indirect Objects
Visit mometrix.com/academy and enter code: 817385

PRONOUN-ANTECEDENT AGREEMENT

The **antecedent** is the noun that has been replaced by a pronoun. A pronoun and its antecedent **agree** when they have the same number (singular or plural) and gender (male, female, or neutral).

Examples:

Singular agreement: John (antecedent) came into town, and he (pronoun) played for us.

Plural agreement: John and Rick (antecedent) came into town, and they (pronoun) played for us.

To determine which is the correct pronoun to use in a compound subject or object, try each pronoun **alone** in place of the compound in the sentence. Your knowledge of pronouns will tell you which one is correct.

Example:

Bob and (I, me) will be going.

Test: (1) *I will be going* or (2) *Me will be going*. The second choice cannot be correct because *me* cannot be used as the subject of a sentence. Instead, *me* is used as an object.

Answer: Bob and I will be going.

When a pronoun is used with a noun immediately following (as in "we boys"), try the sentence **without the added noun**.

Example:

(We/Us) boys played football last year.

Test: (1) *We played football last ye*ar or (2) *Us played football last year*. Again, the second choice cannot be correct because *us* cannot be used as a subject of a sentence. Instead, *us* is used as an object.

Answer: We boys played football last year.

Review Video: Pronoun Usage
Visit mometrix.com/academy and enter code: 666500

Review Video: Pronoun-Antecedent Agreement
Visit mometrix.com/academy and enter code: 919704

A pronoun should point clearly to the **antecedent**. Here is how a pronoun reference can be unhelpful if it is puzzling or not directly stated.

Unhelpful: Ron and Jim (antecedent) went to the store, and he (pronoun) bought soda.

Who bought soda? Ron or Jim?

antecedent pronoun
Helpful: Jim went to the store, and he bought soda.

The sentence is clear. Jim bought the soda.

Example

Tom printed his ticket to the concert, but he forgot ____ at home.

Which pronoun should go in the blank?

a. It
b. Them
c. Him
d. He

What is the antecedent that the missing pronoun must match? There are only four nouns in the sentence. They are *Tom, ticket, concert,* and *home.* Which one should the missing pronoun refer to? Tom is the one who forgot something, so the pronoun does not refer to Tom. The concert is not at Tom's home, so he cannot forget the concert at home. It is also not logical to say that Tom forgot his home at home The antecedent must be *ticket.*

Choice A says that the missing pronoun is *it.* The pronoun refers to *ticket,* which is a singular noun. A ticket is also a nonliving thing. The missing pronoun is also the object in the second clause. *It* is singular, refers to nonliving nouns, and can be used as the object. Choice A is correct.

Choice B says that the missing pronoun is *them.* The pronoun refers to the singular noun *ticket.* While *them* can be used to refer to nonliving nouns and can be the object of a sentence, it is a plural pronoun. Choice B is incorrect.

Choice C says that the missing pronoun is *him.* The missing pronoun refers to a nonliving thing, not a human or animal. *Him* is an objective personal pronoun and is singular, but it only refers to living nouns. *Him* cannot represent *ticket,* so choice C is incorrect.

Choice D says that the missing pronoun is *he.* The missing pronoun refers to a nonliving noun and is the object of the second sentence. While *he* is a singular pronoun, it can only be used as the subject of a sentence and only refers to living nouns. Choice D is incorrect.

Phrases

A phrase is a group of words that functions as a single part of speech, usually a noun, adjective, or adverb. A **phrase** is not a complete thought, and does not contain a subject, but it adds detail or explanation to a sentence, or renames something within the sentence.

Clauses

A clause is a group of words that contains both a subject and a predicate (verb). There are two types of clauses: independent and dependent. An **independent clause** contains a complete thought, while a **dependent (or subordinate) clause** does not. A dependent clause includes a subject and a verb, and may also contain additional information, but it cannot stand as a complete thought without being joined to an independent clause. Dependent clauses function within sentences as adjectives, adverbs, or nouns.

Example:

independent clause | dependent clause

I am running because I want to stay in shape.

The clause *I am running* is an independent clause: it has a subject and a verb, and it gives a complete thought. The clause *because I want to stay in shape* is a dependent clause: it has a subject and a verb, but it does not express a complete thought. This is due to the fact that it begins with *because*, which shows that there is more information needed to complete the thought. This dependent clause adds detail to the independent clause to which it is attached.

Review Video: Independent and Dependent Clauses
Visit mometrix.com/academy and enter code: 556903

SENTENCE STRUCTURE

Sentence structure is based on the type and number of clauses in the sentence. Two common sentence structures are simple sentences and compound sentences:

SIMPLE

A simple sentence has one independent clause with no dependent clauses. A simple sentence may have a **compound subject** or a **compound verb**, or both.

Examples:

single subject | single verb

Judy watered the lawn.

compound subject | single verb

Judy and Alan watered the lawn.

single subject | compound verb | compound verb

Judy watered the lawn and pulled weeds.

compound subject | compound verb | compound verb

Judy and Alan watered the lawn and pulled weeds.

COMPOUND

A compound sentence has two or more independent clauses with no dependent clauses. Usually, the independent clauses are joined with a comma and a coordinating conjunction or with a semicolon.

Examples:

independent clause | independent clause

The time has come, and we are ready.

independent clause | independent clause

I woke up at dawn; the sun was just coming up.

COMPLEX

A complex sentence has one independent clause and at least one dependent clause.

Examples:

dependent clause: Although he had the flu, | independent clause: Harry went to work.

independent clause: Marcia got married | dependent clause: after she finished college.

Review Video: Sentence Structure
Visit mometrix.com/academy and enter code: 700478

SENTENCE FRAGMENTS

Recall that a group of words must contain at least one **independent clause** in order to be considered a sentence. If it doesn't contain even one independent clause, it is called a **sentence fragment**.

Choosing the best steps for **repairing** a sentence fragment depends on what type of fragment it is. If the fragment is a dependent clause, it can sometimes be fixed by simply removing a subordinating word, such as *when*, *because*, or *if*, from the beginning of the fragment. Alternatively, a dependent clause can be joined to a closely related neighboring sentence. If the fragment is missing some required part, like a subject or a verb, it may be fixed by simply adding the missing part.

Examples:

Fragment: Because he wanted to sail the Mediterranean.

Removed subordinating word: He wanted to sail the Mediterranean.

Combined with another sentence: Because he wanted to sail the Mediterranean, he booked a Greek island cruise.

EXAMPLE

Which of the following changes will NOT correct this sentence fragment?

Although she had found the coin first.

a. Remove *Although*.
b. Add a comma and *she let her brother keep it* after *first*.
c. Add *She let her brother keep the coin* before *although*.
d. Remove *first*.

Choice A suggests removing the word *although* to form the following sentence: She found the coin first. This option removes the subordinating conjunction to make the clause independent. The resulting sentence is complete, so removing *although* is an acceptable way to correct the fragment. Choice A is incorrect.

Choice B forms the following sentence: Although she had found the coin first, she let her brother keep it. A comma and an independent clause have been added to the sentence fragment to form a complex sentence. The resulting sentence is complete and written correctly, so choice B is incorrect.

Choice C forms the following sentence: She let her brother keep the coin although she had found the coin first. An independent clause has been added before the sentence fragment to form a complex sentence. This sentence is correctly written and complete, so choice C is an acceptable way to correct the fragment. Choice C is incorrect.

Choice D removes the word *first*, leaving *Although she had found the coin*. This is still a sentence fragment, since it is a single dependent clause. Choice D does not correct the fragment, so D is correct.

RUN-ON SENTENCES

Run-on sentences consist of multiple independent clauses that have not been joined together properly. Run-on sentences can be corrected in several different ways:

Join clauses properly: This can be done with a comma and coordinating conjunction, with a semicolon, or with a colon or dash if the second clause is explaining something in the first clause.

Example:

> **Incorrect**: I went on the trip, we visited lots of castles.
>
> **Corrected**: I went on the trip, and we visited lots of castles.

Split into separate sentences: This correction is best to use when the independent clauses are very long or when they are not closely related.

Example:

> **Incorrect**: The drive to New York takes ten hours, my uncle lives in Boston.
>
> **Corrected**: The drive to New York takes ten hours. My uncle lives in Boston.

Make one clause dependent: This is the easiest way to make the sentence correct and more interesting at the same time. It's often as simple as adding a subordinating word between the two clauses or before the first clause.

Example:

> **Incorrect**: I finally made it to the store and I bought some eggs.
>
> **Corrected**: When I finally made it to the store, I bought some eggs.

Reduce to one clause with a compound verb: If both clauses have the same subject, remove the subject from the second clause, and you now have just one clause with a compound verb.

Example:

> **Incorrect**: The drive to New York takes ten hours, it makes me very tired.
>
> **Corrected**: The drive to New York takes ten hours and makes me very tired.

Note: While these are the simplest ways to correct a run-on sentence, often the best way is to completely reorganize the thoughts in the sentence and rewrite it.

COMMA SPLICES

A comma splice is a specific error that may appear in a run-on sentence. When a sentence has two independent clauses, but the clauses are joined with only a comma, a **comma splice** is formed. Remember that if two independent clauses are joined with a comma, a coordinating conjunction is also needed. Most of the solutions for fixing run-on sentences can also be used to correct a comma splice.

Review Video: Fragments and Run-on Sentences
Visit mometrix.com/academy and enter code: 541989

EXAMPLE

Rick wants to go see a movie tomorrow he would miss his sister's recital.

Identify the change that would NOT correct this run-on sentence.

a. Add a comma after *tomorrow*.
b. Split it into two sentences between *tomorrow* and *he*.
c. Add a comma and *but* after *tomorrow*.
d. Add a subordinating conjunction to make one of the clauses dependent.

Choice A says to add a comma after *tomorrow*. This forms the following sentence: Rick wants to go see a movie tomorrow, he would miss his sister's recital. A comma has been used to join two independent clauses, but there is no coordinating conjunction. This choice forms a comma splice, so it is not an acceptable correction for this sentence. Choice A is the correct answer.

Choice B says to split the sentence into two sentences. This forms the following two sentences: Rick wants to go see a movie tomorrow. He would miss his sister's recital. Both of these sentences are complete. This is an acceptable way to correct the run-on sentence, so choice B is incorrect.

Choice C says to add a coordinating conjunction after *tomorrow*. This forms the following sentence: Rick wants to go see a movie tomorrow, but he would miss his sister's recital. A comma and a coordinating conjunction have been added between the two independent clauses. This is an acceptable way to correct a run-on sentence. Choice C is incorrect.

Choice D says to add a subordinating conjunction to make one of the sentences dependent. There are many new sentences that could be created by adding a subordinating conjunction. For example, consider the following sentence: Although Rick wants to go see a movie tomorrow, he would miss his sister's recital. Alternatively, the following sentence could also be created: Rick wants to go see a movie tomorrow even though he would miss his sister's recital. Both of these sentences have an independent clause and a dependent clause. These sentences are both complete and written correctly, so choice D is incorrect.

EXAMPLE

Identify the sentence that has a comma splice.

a. Tom stopped at the store to buy supplies and his family met him at the campsite.
b. The ball rolled into the living room quietly, but it still startled the dog.
c. Theresa brought her mom some flowers, her mom did not have a vase.
d. Sweet potatoes, pecans, and brown sugar are all ingredients in my cousin's sweet potato casserole.

Choice A has two independent clauses joined by a coordinating conjunction. This is incorrect because there should be a comma before the coordinating conjunction. While the sentence is written incorrectly, there is no comma, so this sentence does not have a comma splice. Choice A is incorrect.

Choice B has two independent clauses joined by a comma and a coordinating conjunction. This is the correct way to write a compound sentence, so there is no error here. Choice B is incorrect.

Choice C has two independent clauses joined by a comma. This is incorrect because independent clauses should be joined together by a comma and a coordinating conjunction. When the comma is present without a coordinating conjunction between two independent clauses, a comma splice is formed. This means that choice C is correct.

Choice D is a simple sentence that contains one independent clause. The only commas used in this sentence are used to separate items in a list. There are no clauses that need to be joined or errors related to commas, so choice D does not contain a comma splice. Choice D is incorrect.

Parts of Speech

Nouns

When you talk about a person, place, thing, or idea, you are talking about a **noun**. The two main types of nouns are **common** and **proper** nouns.

Common Nouns

Common nouns are generic names for people, places, and things. Common nouns are not usually capitalized.

Examples of common nouns:

People: boy, girl, worker, manager

Places: school, bank, library, home

Things: dog, cat, truck, car

Proper Nouns

Proper nouns name specific people, places, or things. All proper nouns are capitalized.

Examples of proper nouns:

People: Abraham Lincoln, George Washington, Martin Luther King, Jr.

Places: Los Angeles, California; New York; Asia

Things: Statue of Liberty, Earth, Lincoln Memorial

Note: When referring to the planet that we live on, capitalize *Earth*. When referring to the dirt, rocks, or land, lowercase *earth*.

Singular and Plural Nouns

Singular nouns name **one** person, place, thing, or idea. **Plural nouns** name **more than one** person, place, thing, or idea. Most nouns have both a singular and plural form. Many plural nouns are spelled like the singular noun with an *-s* at the end, but this is not true for all plural nouns. Singular nouns that already end in an *s*, *o*, *ch*, *sh*, or *x* usually end in *-es* when they are in the plural form.

Singular nouns that end in a consonant followed by the letter *y* will usually lose the *y* and end in *-ies* in the plural form, and words that end with the letter *f* or *fe* will usually lose the *f* and end in *-ves*.

Some plural nouns have much different spellings than their singular form, and some plural nouns are spelled the same as their singular form. There are more rules for spelling plural nouns, but these are the most common spelling changes.

Examples of singular nouns:

> Typical nouns: dog, pencil, girl, store, hope, stingray
>
> Nouns ending in *s*, *o*, *ch*, *sh*, or *x*: mass, hero, lunch, polish, fox
>
> Nouns ending in a consonant and *y*: puppy, baby, fairy, sky
>
> Nouns ending in *f* or *fe*: self, life, calf, hoof

Examples of plural nouns:

> Typical nouns: dogs, pencils, girls, stores, hopes, stingrays
>
> Nouns ending in *s*, *o*, *ch*, *sh*, or *x*: masses, heroes, lunches, polishes, foxes
>
> Nouns ending in a consonant and *y*: puppies, babies, fairies, skies
>
> Nouns ending in a vowel and *f* or *fe*: selves, lives, calves, hooves

Collective Nouns

Collective nouns are the names for a group of people, places, or things that function like singular nouns. The following are examples of collective nouns: *class, company, dozen, group, herd, team,* and *public.* Collective nouns usually require an article, such as *a*, *an*, and *the*, which shows that the noun is a single unit. For example, a choir is a group of singers. Even though there are many singers in a choir, the word choir describes a single group. If we refer to the members of the group, and not the group itself, it is no longer a collective noun.

> Incorrect: The *choir are* going to compete nationally this year.
>
> Correct: The *choir is* going to compete nationally this year.
>
> Incorrect: The *members* of the choir *is* competing nationally this year.
>
> Correct: The *members* of the choir *are* competing nationally this year.

Pronouns

Pronouns are words that are used to stand in for nouns. There are several different types of pronouns, but the two main types are subjective and objective pronouns. **Subjective** nouns and pronouns that those that are the subject of a sentence. **Objective** nouns and pronouns are those that are an object in a sentence. Another important type of pronoun is the personal pronoun, which refers to people. Personal pronouns can be subjective or objective. **Possessive** nouns and pronouns show possession or ownership. Pronouns can also be singular or plural.

Singular

Subjective	Objective	Possessive
I	Me	My, Mine
You	You	Your, Yours
He	Him	His
She	Her	Her, hers
It	It	Its
Who	Whom	Whose

Plural

Subjective	Objective	Possessive
we	us	our, ours
you	you	your, yours
they	them	their, theirs

Reflexive: Reflexive pronouns are pronouns that function as the object of a sentence and refer to the subject. Examples of reflexive pronouns include *myself, yourself, himself, herself, itself, ourselves, yourselves*, and *themselves*.

Indefinite: Indefinite pronouns are used to refer to multiple nouns or an undefined noun. Examples of indefinite nouns include *all, any, each, everyone, either/neither, one, some*, and *several*.

Relative: Relative pronouns are used to connect relative clauses that specify or describe a noun to the rest of the sentence. Examples of relative pronouns include *which, who, whom*, and *whose*.

Review Video: Nouns and Pronouns
Visit mometrix.com/academy and enter code: 312073

VERBS

If you want to write a sentence, then you need a verb. Without a verb, you have no sentence. The verb of a sentence indicates action or being. In other words, the verb shows something's action or state of being or the action that has been done to something.

ACTION VERBS AND LINKING VERBS

Action verbs show what the subject is doing. In other words, an action verb shows action. **Linking verbs** link the subject of a sentence to a noun or pronoun. They can also link a subject to an adjective, so the linking verb helps create a description. You always need a verb if you want a complete sentence. However, linking verbs on their own cannot be a complete sentence. Any verb that shows a condition and connects to a noun, pronoun, or adjective that describes the subject of a sentence is a linking verb.

Action: He sings. | Run! | Go! | I talk with him every day. | She reads.

Linking:

Incorrect: I am.

Correct: I am John. | The roses smell lovely. | I feel tired.

Review Video: Action Verbs and Linking Verbs
Visit mometrix.com/academy and enter code: 743142

Verb Tenses

A verb **tense** shows the different form of a verb to point to the time of an action. The present and past tense are indicated by the verb's form. An action in the present, *I talk,* can change form for the past: *I talked*. However, for future tense, an auxiliary, or helping, verb is sometimes needed to show the change in form. When writing a composition, it is important to use verb tenses consistently. Choose the best tense for the composition and do not switch to a different tense unless it is necessary or appropriate for a particular sentence or paragraph.

Present: I talk
Past: I talked
Future: I will talk

Present: The action happens at the current time.

Example: He *walks* to the store every morning.

Past: The action happened in the past.

Example: He *walked* to the store an hour ago.

Future: The action is going to happen later.

Example: I *will walk* to the store tomorrow.

Review Video: Verb Tenses
Visit mometrix.com/academy and enter code: 269472

Irregular Verbs

While most verbs gain the suffix -ed when used in the past tense, irregular verbs receive different spelling changes when they are written in the past tense. For example, *walk* is a regular verb, and it becomes *walked* when written in the past tense. However, *run* is an irregular verb because it becomes *ran* when written in the past tense.

Example

My mother _____ me about the big nest of ants near the sandbox. I thanked her for telling me!

Which of the following verbs should go in the blank?

a. Warn
b. Warned
c. Will warn
d. Warns

First, look at the sentences. The first sentence does not have enough information to show which tense it is in. However, the second sentence says that the child thanked the mother. The verb here is *thanked*, which is the past-tense form of *thank*. Because the second sentence is in the past tense, it makes sense to say that the first sentence is also in past tense.

Choice A says that the missing verb is *warn. Warn* is a present-tense verb, but it can be used in the future tense if a helping verb is present. However, this sentence is in past tense, so it needs a past-tense verb. Choice A is wrong.

Choice B says that the missing verb is *warned. Warned* is a past-tense verb, and it logically completes the sentence. Choice B is correct!

Choice C says that the missing verb is *will warn. Will warn* is a future-tense verb, meaning that it describes an action that will occur in the future. However, since the speaker already thanked his or her mother for the warning, it is not logical to use a future-tense verb in the blank. Choice C is incorrect.

Choice D says that the missing verb is *warns. Warn* is usually used with plural subjects, and *warns* used with single subjects. *Warns* can be used in the future or present tense, but it cannot be used in the past tense. Since the sentence is in the past tense, it needs a past-tense verb, so D is incorrect.

ADJECTIVES

An **adjective** is a word that is used to modify a noun or pronoun. An adjective answers a question: *Which one? What kind?* or *How many?* Usually, adjectives come before the words that they modify, but they may also come after a linking verb.

> Which one? The *third* suit is my favorite.
>
> What kind? This suit is *navy blue.*
>
> How many? I am going to buy *four* pairs of socks to match the suit.

Review Video: Descriptive Text
Visit mometrix.com/academy and enter code: 174903

COMPARISON WITH ADJECTIVES

Some adjectives are relative, and other adjectives are absolute. Adjectives that are **relative** can show the comparison between things. **Absolute** adjectives can also show comparison, but they do so in a different way. Let's say that you are reading two books. You think that one book is perfect, and the other book is not exactly perfect. It is not possible for one book to be more perfect than the other. Either you think that the book is perfect, or you think that the book is imperfect. In this case, perfect and imperfect are absolute adjectives.

Relative adjectives will show the different **degrees** of something or someone to something else or someone else. The three degrees of adjectives include positive, comparative, and superlative.

The **positive** degree is the normal form of an adjective.

> Example: This work is *difficult.* | She is *smart.*

The **comparative** degree compares one person or thing to another person or thing.

> Example: This work is *more difficult* than your work. | She is *smarter* than me.

The **superlative** degree compares more than two people or things.

Example: This is the *most difficult* work of my life. | She is the *smartest* lady in school.

Review Video: Adjectives
Visit mometrix.com/academy and enter code: 470154

Adverbs

An **adverb** is a word that is used to **modify,** or describe, a verb, adjective, or another adverb. Usually, adverbs answer one of these questions: *When? Where? How?* and *Why?* The negatives *not* and *never* are considered adverbs. Adverbs that modify adjectives or other adverbs **strengthen** or **weaken** the words that they modify.

Examples:

He walks *quickly* through the crowd.

The water flows *smoothly* on the rocks.

Note: Adverbs are usually indicated by the suffix *-ly*, which has been added to the root word. For instance, *quick* can be made into an adverb by adding *-ly* to construct *quickly*. Some words that end in *-ly* do not follow this rule and can function as other parts of speech. Examples of adjectives ending in *-ly* include: *early, friendly, holy, lonely, silly*, and *ugly*. To know if a word that ends in *-ly* is an adjective or adverb, check your dictionary. Also, while many adverbs end in *-ly*, you need to remember that not all adverbs end in *-ly*.

Examples:

He is *never* angry.

You are *too* irresponsible to travel alone.

Types of Adverbs

Different types of adverbs are used to describe particular aspects of a verb, adjective, or other adverb. The following are examples of common types of adverbs:

Time: Some adverbs show when something was done, such as *yesterday*, *today*, or *in two days*.

Manner: Some adverbs show the way something was done, such as *hurriedly*, *neatly*, *grumpily*, or *loudly*.

Frequency: Some adverbs show how often something was done, such as *seldom*, *often*, *never*, or *often*.

Degree: Some adverbs show how much or to what degree something was done, such as *completely*, *barely*, *highly*, or *halfway*.

Conjunctive: Conjunctive adverbs are used similarly to conjunctions, as they connect different ideas, but they can connect ideas from different clauses or sentences. Some examples of conjunctive adverbs are *however*, *alternatively*, *likewise*, and *then*.

COMPARISON WITH ADVERBS

The rules for comparing adverbs are the same as the rules for adjectives.

The **positive** degree is the standard form of an adverb.

Example: He arrives *soon*. | She speaks *softly* to her friends.

The **comparative** degree compares one person or thing to another person or thing.

Example: He arrives *sooner* than Sarah. | She speaks *more softly* than him.

The **superlative** degree compares more than two people or things.

Example: He arrives *soonest* of the group. | She speaks the *most softly* of any of her friends.

Review Video: Adverbs
Visit mometrix.com/academy and enter code: 713951

EXAMPLE

Identify the conjunctive adverb in the following sentences.

Every night, Savannah's brother loudly gets up to get a glass of water. Consequently, she has started sleeping with earmuffs on so that he does not wake her up at night.

a. Every night
b. Loudly
c. Consequently
d. At night

Choice A says that *every night* is a conjunctive adverb. What does *every night* describe in this sentence? It describes how often Savannah's brother loudly gets a glass of water. This means that *every night* shows the frequency that Savannah's brother does this action. Since *every night* is an adverb that shows frequency, choice A is incorrect.

Choice B says that *loudly* is a conjunctive adverb. In this sentence, what does *loudly* describe? It describes the way that Savannah's brother gets a glass of water each night. This means that *loudly* is an adverb that shows manner. *Loudly* is not a conjunctive adverb, so choice B is incorrect.

Choice C says that *consequently* is a conjunctive adverb. What function does *consequently* have in this sentence? It shows the reason that Savannah started wearing earmuffs while she sleeps. It also shows a connection between the information in the first sentence and the information in the second sentence. Since *consequently* connects the ideas in these sentences, it is a conjunctive adverb. Choice C is correct.

Choice D says that *at night* is a conjunctive adverb. *At* and *night* work together to form an adverbial phrase. Which type of adverb do they form? In this sentence, *at night* shows when Savannah wants to avoid being woken up by her brother. This makes *at night* an adverb that shows time, meaning that *at night* is not a conjunctive adverb and choice D is incorrect.

Prepositions

A **preposition** is a word placed before a noun or pronoun that shows the relationship between an object and another word in the sentence.

Common prepositions:

about	before	during	on	under
after	beneath	for	over	until
against	between	from	past	up
among	beyond	in	through	with
around	by	of	to	within
at	down	off	toward	without

Examples:

> The napkin is *in* the drawer.
>
> The Earth rotates *around* the Sun.
>
> The needle is *beneath* the haystack.
>
> Can you find "me" *among* the words?

Prepositional Phrases

One important thing to know about prepositions is that they form special phrases, called prepositional phrases. A **prepositional phrase** begins with a preposition and ends with a noun or pronoun that is the object of the preposition. Normally, the prepositional phrase functions as an **adjective** or an **adverb** within the sentence.

Examples:

> prepositional phrase
>
> The picnic is on the blanket.
>
> prepositional phrase
>
> I am sick with a fever today.
>
> prepositional phrase
>
> Among the many flowers, John found a four-leaf clover.

Be careful not to mistake the object in a prepositional phrase as the subject of a sentence. The subject of the sentence will not be found in a prepositional phrase because a prepositional phrase is used to describe how an object is related to the subject. Prepositional phrases do not influence subject-verb agreement.

Prepositional phrases do not influence subject-verb agreement. For example, consider the following sentence:

The basket (simple subject) of clothes (prepositional phrase) is (verb) on the floor in the laundry room.

This sentence contains a prepositional phrase between the simple subject and the verb. The simple subject is *basket*, which is a singular noun, and the verb is *is*, which is a singular verb. They are separated by the prepositional phrase "of clothes." Even though the plural noun *clothes* comes right before the singular verb *is*, this verb shows the action of the singular noun *basket*.

> **Review Video: Prepositions**
> Visit mometrix.com/academy and enter code: 946763

EXAMPLE

Which of the following could NOT complete the sentence?

She went ____ the cave.

a. Sadly
b. Into
c. From
d. Through

Choice A says that the missing word is *sadly*. The blank is between *went* and *the cave*, meaning that the missing word will connect these pieces of the sentence. While *sadly* could be used here to show how the girl felt, there would still be missing information. A preposition is needed here to show whether she entered, exited, or stood outside of the cave. *Sadly* is an adverb, so A is the correct answer.

Choice B says that *into* would complete the sentence. Does *into* complete the sentence without leaving missing information? To say *she went into the cave* is a logical, complete sentence. Choice B is incorrect.

Choice C says that the missing word is *from*. This creates the sentence *she went from the cave*. Since she could have left the cave to go somewhere else, this is also a logical, complete sentence. Choice C is incorrect.

Choice D says that *through* would complete the sentence. The sentence would read *she went through the cave*. Since she could have explored the whole cave or found an exit on the other side of it, *through* can logically complete the sentence. Choice D is incorrect.

EXAMPLE

Identify the prepositional phrase in the following sentence.

Mable visited the store to buy some vegetables.

a. To buy
b. Visited the store
c. The store to buy
d. To buy some vegetables

Remember the pieces of a prepositional phrase. Prepositional phrases should begin with a preposition and end with a noun or pronoun. Considering these rules, can any of the answer choices be eliminated? Choice B and choice C can be eliminated because neither choice begins with a preposition!

That leaves choices A and D. Choice A says that the prepositional phrase is *to buy*. This does start with a preposition, and it does give more information about Mable's trip to the store. However, it does not end with a noun or pronoun. Choice D says that the prepositional phrase is *to buy some vegetables*. Choice D begins with a preposition and ends with a noun, and it explains why Mabel went to the store.

Choice D is the only choice that has all of the pieces of a prepositional phrase, so D is correct!

EXAMPLE

Read the sentence below and answer the following question.

> A band with 15 members _____ performing at my restaurant tonight.

Identify the verb that best completes the sentence.

a. Were
b. Is
c. Are
d. Are not

This question is asking which verb should go in the blank. There are a couple of reasons why choosing the correct verb for this sentence may be confusing. First of all, there are two nouns that appear before the verb. Second, one of these nouns is singular and one is plural.

The first step is to determine which noun goes with the verb. The two nouns are *band* and *members*. While *members* is closest to the blank, it is part of a prepositional phrase that describes *band*. The subject of the sentence is *band*, so the verb must agree with *band*.

Is *band* singular or plural? The sentence says that the band has multiple members, but there is only one band. *Band* is a collective noun, meaning that it is a singular noun. This means that the correct verb will also be singular. With this in mind, can any of the answer choices be eliminated?

Choices A, C, and D are all plural verbs. Even though the blank appears after a plural noun, this noun is part of a prepositional phrase. The verb should match the singular subject *band*. The only choice with a singular verb is choice B, so B is the correct answer.

CONJUNCTIONS

Conjunctions join words, phrases, or clauses and they show the connection between the joined pieces. **Coordinating conjunctions** connect equal parts of sentences. Coordinating conjunctions can also be used to create compound subjects and compound predicates, in addition to compound sentences.

Coordinating Conjunctions

The **coordinating conjunctions** include: *and, but, yet, or, nor, for,* and *so*

Compound Subjects:

compound subject
Terry *and* Marissa went to the movies last Saturday.

compund subject
Either pumpkin pie *or* apple pie would be a good dessert to bring to Thanksgiving dinner.

compound subject
Neither the clownfish *nor* the goldfish liked the new fish food very much.

Compound Predicates:

compound predicate
Veronica left school *and* picked up her sister from soccer practice.

compound predicate
The cat did not take a nap *or* play with the dog yesterday.

Compound Sentences:

The rock was small, *but* it was heavy.

She drove in the night, *and* he drove in the day.

Bill dressed nicely today, *for* he must give an important presentation this afternoon.

Correlative Conjunctions

Some examples of **correlative conjunctions** are: *either...or* | *neither...nor* | *not only...but also*. When one correlative conjunction is used, its matching correlative conjunction will be used later in the sentence.

Examples:

Either you are coming *or* you are staying.

He *not only* ran three miles *but also* swam 200 yards.

Review Video: Coordinating and Correlative Conjunctions
Visit mometrix.com/academy and enter code: 390329

Subordinating Conjunctions

Subordinating conjunctions link dependent clauses, clauses with either a subject or a predicate, to independent clauses, clauses with both a subject and a predicate, to form a complex sentence. The subordinating conjunction will always be at the beginning of the dependent clause. When the dependent clause is at the beginning of the sentence, it will end with a comma. When the independent clause is at the beginning of the sentence, no comma is needed.

Common **subordinating conjunctions** include:

after	since	whenever
although	so that	where
because	unless	wherever
before	until	whether
in order that	when	while

Examples:

I am hungry *because* I did not eat breakfast.

He went home *when* everyone left.

While her brother ate dinner, she played his favorite video game.

Review Video: Subordinating Conjunctions
Visit mometrix.com/academy and enter code: 958913

EXAMPLE

Which of the following is a complex sentence?

a. Joseph went grocery shopping and put all of the groceries away at home.
b. Joseph went grocery shopping, and he put all of the groceries away at home.
c. Joseph went grocery shopping and put all of the groceries away when he got home.
d. Joseph went grocery shopping; he put all of the groceries away at home.

Choice A contains one subject and a compound predicate. Because there is only one subject, Joseph, there is only one clause. Since the sentence is made of one independent clause and a prepositional phrase, it is a simple sentence, and choice A is incorrect.

Choice B contains two clauses. The clauses are separated by a comma and a coordinating conjunction, and both are independent clauses. This sentence contains a prepositional phrase and two independent clauses, so it is a compound sentence. Choice B is incorrect.

Choice C contains two clauses. There are two subjects in the sentence, *Joseph* and *he*. Even though one clause is much shorter than the other, these subjects each go with a different clause. The first clause is independent. The second clause is dependent, as it begins with the word *when*. Since the sentence is made of one independent clause and one dependent clause, it is a complex sentence. Choice C is correct.

Choice D contains two clauses. They are both independent clauses, because they both contain a subject and a predicate, and they both form complete thoughts. Since there is no coordinating conjunction, they are linked by a semicolon. Since the sentence is made from two independent clauses, it is a compound sentence. Choice D is incorrect.

EXAMPLE

Identify the sentence that contains correlative conjunctions.

a. She can wait for her friend's letter to arrive, or she can call her now.
b. He must leave now, or he will end up in heavy traffic when he gets on the highway.
c. When your grandfather gets here, you can greet him with a handshake or a hug.
d. I can't decide whether to go to my brother's concert or to study for my test tomorrow.

Read the answer choices carefully. Remember that correlative conjunctions appear in pairs, so there will be at least two conjunctions in the sentence. Additionally, these conjunctions will go together. The information given immediately after the first conjunction will make little sense without the information that comes after the second conjunction.

Choice A contains the conjunction *or*. Though *or* can be a correlative conjunction, in this sentence, it is used by itself to connect two independent clauses. This means it is a coordinating conjunction. There are no correlative conjunctions in this sentence, so choice A is incorrect.

Choice B contains the conjunctions *or* and *when*. Again, *or* can be a correlative conjunction. However, the sentence could end after *traffic*. The information beginning with *when* is not needed to complete the thought, and *or* and *when* do not form a pair of correlative conjunctions. Choice B is incorrect.

Choice C contains the conjunctions *when* and *or*. *When* is used to begin a dependent clause. *Or* is used to form a compound object by linking *handshake* and *hug*. These conjunctions do not work together in this sentence, so they are not correlative conjunctions. Choice C is incorrect.

Choice D contains the conjunctions *whether* and *or*. *Whether* is used to introduce one choice the speaker can make, and *or* is used to introduce an alternative choice. If the sentence ended before *or*, it would be an incomplete thought. The conjunctions *whether* and *or* go together in this sentence, and they are correlative conjunctions. Choice D is correct.

END PUNCTUATION

PERIODS

Use a period to end all sentences except direct questions and exclamations. Periods are also used for abbreviations.

> Examples: 3 p.m. | 2 a.m. | Mr. Jones | Mrs. Stevens | Dr. Smith | Bill, Jr. | Pennsylvania Ave.

Note: An abbreviation is a shortened form of a word or phrase.

QUESTION MARKS

Question marks should be used following a **direct question**. A polite request can be followed by a period instead of a question mark.

> **Direct Question**: What is for lunch today? | How are you? | Why is that the answer?
>
> **Polite Requests**: Can you please send me the item tomorrow. | Will you please walk with me on the track.

Review Video: Question Marks
Visit mometrix.com/academy and enter code: 118471

Exclamation Marks

Exclamation marks are used after a word group or sentence that shows much feeling or has special importance. Exclamation marks should not be overused. They are saved for proper **exclamatory interjections**.

Example: We're going to the finals! | You have a beautiful car! | "That's crazy!" she yelled.

Review Video: Exclamation Points
Visit mometrix.com/academy and enter code: 199367

Commas

The comma is a punctuation mark that can help you understand connections in a sentence. Not every sentence needs a comma. However, if a sentence needs a comma, you need to put it in the right place. A comma in the wrong place or a missing comma will make a sentence's meaning unclear. These are some of the rules for commas:

Use Case	Example
Before a **coordinating conjunction** joining independent clauses in compound sentences	Bob caught three fish, and I caught two fish.
Between **items in a series**	I will bring the turkey, the pie, and the coffee.
After a **dependent clause** that **begins a complex sentence**	Before she left, Ashley turned off all of the lights in her house.
After **transition words**	Consequently, Joel's mother grounded him.
After an **introductory phrase**	After the final out, we went to a restaurant to celebrate.
After a **prepositional phrase** at the **beginning of a sentence**	At 10 in the evening, Georgia finally arrived home from work.
After an **adverbial clause**	Studying the stars, I was awed by the beauty of the sky.
Before and after **nonessential modifiers**	John Frank, who coaches the team, was promoted today.
Before and after **nonessential appositives**	Thomas Edison, an American inventor, was born in Ohio.
Before and after **nonrestrictive phrases** or **clauses**	His favorite movie, which premiered before he was born, is over three hours long.
After **absolute phrases**	Relieved the test was over, Leah dropped her pencil and slouched in her chair.

Commas for Setting Off Nonessential Words, Phrases, and Clauses

Identifying where to place commas for nonessential words, phrases, and clauses is sometimes tricky. If the word, phrase, or clause is necessary for the sentence to be complete or logical, then it is essential, or restrictive. Additionally, if the word, phrase, or clause cannot be removed without changing the meaning of the sentence, then it is essential. Nonessential words, phrases, and clauses are those that give unnecessary information or do not flow smoothly with the rest of the words in the sentence. These words usually can also be logically placed in more than one spot in the sentence. **Appositives** are often nonessential words or phrases. They are most often used to specify which person or thing is being discussed. An appositive is an additional name or description that may be essential or nonessential.

Review Video: When To Use a Comma
Visit mometrix.com/academy and enter code: 786797

Example

Ella's favorite stuffed animal Rory used to be her mother's.

Which word in the sentence is nonessential and should be set off by commas?

a. Be
b. Stuffed
c. Her
d. Rory

Choice A says that *be* should be set off by commas. Since *be* is a verb, it is unlikely that it is a nonessential word. In this sentence, the subject is *stuffed animal*, and *be* is the verb that shows the subject's action. *Be* is essential to the sentence, so choice A is incorrect.

Choice B says that *stuffed* should be set off by commas. *Stuffed* is an adjective, so it may be nonessential. However, it affects the meaning of this sentence. The word *stuffed* shows that the sentence is about a toy, not a live animal. *Stuffed* is essential to the meaning of the sentence, so choice B is incorrect.

Choice C says that *her* should be set off by commas. *Her* is a personal pronoun, so it is unlikely that it is nonessential. This sentence uses the word *her* to identify whose mother previously owned the stuffed animal. *Her* is essential to show who is being discussed. Choice C is incorrect.

Choice D says that *Rory* should be set off by commas. *Rory* is a name, so it could be a nonessential word, or even an appositive. In this sentence, the word tells the reader the name of Ella's favorite stuffed animal. The sentence can only be about one stuffed animal, because Ella can only have one favorite. This means that the stuffed animal's name is extra, or nonessential, information. *Rory* is a nonessential appositive, so choice D is correct.

Example

The singer growing more exhausted with every song decided to stop dancing and stood still while singing.

Identify the nonrestrictive phrase that should be set off by commas in the above sentence.

a. The singer growing more exhausted
b. Decided to stop dancing
c. Growing more exhausted with every song
d. Stop dancing and stood still

Choice A says that *the singer growing more exhausted* is the nonrestrictive phrase. Is the sentence still a complete sentence without this phrase? No, because choice A includes the subject, *the singer*. Choice A is not the nonrestrictive phrase.

Choice B says that *decided to stop dancing* is the nonrestrictive phrase. Does the sentence make sense without this phrase? No, removing this phrase leaves the following sentence: The singer growing more exhausted with every song and stood still while singing. This is not a logical sentence, so choice B is not the nonrestrictive phrase.

Choice C says that *growing more exhausted with every song* is the nonrestrictive phrase. Removing this phrase leaves the following sentence: The singer decided to stop dancing and stood still while singing. This sentence makes sense and has the same meaning as the original sentence. This phrase gives extra information that is not essential to the sentence, so choice C is the nonrestrictive phrase. Choice C is correct.

Choice D says that *stop dancing and stood still* is the nonrestrictive phrase. Removing this phrase leaves the following sentence: The singer growing more exhausted with every song decided to while singing. This sentence is now missing important information. What did the singer decide to do while singing? The remaining sentence is now missing the verb. Removing choice D makes the sentence incomplete, so choice D is not the nonrestrictive phrase.

EXAMPLE

Where should a comma be added in the following sentence?

Though the mountain is very steep he is not afraid to scale it.

a. After *Though*
b. After *mountain*
c. After *steep*
d. After *afraid*

Choice A says there should be a comma after *though*. In this sentence, *though* is a subordinating conjunction that begins a dependent clause. Remember that a comma goes at the end of a dependent clause that appears at the beginning of a sentence. *Though* is at the beginning of the clause, and there is no other need for a comma right after it. Choice A is incorrect.

Choice B says there should be a comma after *mountain*. *Mountain* is the subject of the dependent clause in this sentence. The comma should go at the end of the dependent clause. *Mountain* appears in the middle of the dependent clause, not at the end of it. Choice B is incorrect.

Choice C says there should be a comma after *steep*. *Steep* is the last word in the dependent clause that begins the sentence. Adding a comma here would correctly separate the dependent clause from the following independent clause. This is the correct place for the comma, so choice C is correct.

Choice D says there should be a comma after *afraid*. *Afraid* is the verb in the independent clause, and there is no need to separate it from the rest of the sentence. Choice D is incorrect.

SEMICOLONS

The semicolon is used to connect major sentence pieces of equal value. Some rules for semicolons include:

Use Case	Example
Between closely connected independent clauses **not connected with a coordinating conjunction**	You are right; we should go with your plan.
Between independent clauses **linked with a transitional word**	I think that we can agree on this; however, I am not sure about my friends.
Between items in a **series that has internal punctuation**	I have visited New York, New York; Augusta, Maine; and Baltimore, Maryland.

Review Video: How to Use Semicolons
Visit mometrix.com/academy and enter code: 370605

EXAMPLE

Which of the following sentences is NOT written correctly?

a. My sister burned the lasagna we were going to eat for dinner; we went out to eat instead of cooking something else.
b. The ball rolled into the ditch, therefore, it was muddy and wet when he retrieved it.
c. She has lived in many cities, including Nashville, Tennessee; San Diego, California; and Salt Lake City, Utah.
d. He hung the picture in the wrong spot; now there is a distracting hole in the wall.

Choice A is a compound sentence. The semicolon is used to separate two independent clauses. There is no coordinating conjunction in the sentence. This sentence correctly uses a semicolon, so choice A is incorrect.

Choice B is a compound sentence. In a compound sentence, either a coordinating conjunction or a semicolon can be used to separate the independent clauses. This sentence includes a transitional word, but it uses neither a semicolon nor a coordinating conjunction. To revise this sentence, *therefore* can be replaced by a coordinating conjunction, or the first comma can be replaced with a semicolon This sentence is written incorrectly, so choice B is the correct answer.

Choice C is a sentence that includes a list. Remember that semicolons can be used to separate items in a list when at least one of the items includes a comma. In this sentence, a list of cities is given. Since a comma is required to separate the name of a city from the name of the state it is in, each of the items in the list contain a comma. This means that each full city name must be separated by a semicolon. This sentence is written correctly, so choice C is incorrect.

Choice D is a compound sentence and does not contain a coordinating conjunction. Semicolons can be used to separate independent clauses in a compound sentence instead of a coordinating conjunction. This sentence uses a semicolon correctly, so choice D is incorrect.

QUOTATION MARKS

Use quotation marks to close off **direct quotations** of a person's written or spoken words, which are also called **dialogue**. Do not use quotation marks around indirect quotations. An indirect quotation gives someone's message without using the person's exact words. Use **single quotation marks** to close off a quotation inside a quotation.

> **Direct Quote**: Nancy said, “I am waiting for Henry to arrive.”
>
> **Indirect Quote**: Henry said that he is going to be late to the meeting.
>
> **Quote inside a Quote**: The teacher asked, “Has everyone read Martin Luther King’s ‘I Have a Dream’ speech?”

Quotation marks should be used around the titles of **short works**: newspaper and magazine articles, poems, short stories, songs, television episodes, and radio programs. Titles of **long works** should be italicized when they are part of a typed composition or underlined when they are part of a handwritten composition.

Examples:

"Rip Van Winkle" (short story by Washington Irving)

"O Captain! My Captain!" (poem by Walt Whitman)

Review Video: Quotation Marks
Visit mometrix.com/academy and enter code: 884918

Apostrophes

An apostrophe is used to show **possession** or the **deletion of letters in contractions**. An apostrophe is not needed with the possessive pronouns *his, hers, its, ours, theirs, whose*, and *yours*.

Singular Nouns: David's car | a book's theme | my brother's board game

Plural Nouns that end with -*s*: the scissors' handle | boys' basketball

Plural Nouns that end without -*s*: Men's department | the people's adventure

Review Video: Apostrophes
Visit mometrix.com/academy and enter code: 213068

Review Video: Punctuation Errors in Possessive Pronouns
Visit mometrix.com/academy and enter code: 221438

Apostrophes in Contractions

Contractions are combinations of words. Contractions involve taking two words, removing at least one letter from one of the words, putting an apostrophe in its place, and removing the space. For example, *does not* can be written as the contraction *doesn't*. The *o* is removed from *not* and is replaced with an apostrophe, which represents the removed letter, so it appears as *n't*. The space after does is then removed, turning *does not* into the contraction *doesn't*. Some more examples of contractions are listed below.

First Word	Second Word	Contraction
Can	Not	Can't
Do	Not	Don't
She	Will	She'll
They	Will	They'll
He	Is	He's
It	Is	It's
They	Are	They're
I	Am	I'm

Not all words can be used to form contractions, but many small, commonly used words can.

Capitalization

One important part of using correct grammar is properly capitalizing words. Usually, only nouns will be capitalized, but there are some exceptions. The most important capitalization rule is that the first word of every sentence, no matter what part of speech it is, should be capitalized. Another exception is that the pronoun *I* should always be capitalized.

Proper nouns are always capitalized, but sometimes it can be tricky to decide whether or not a noun is a proper noun. Some words that are usually common nouns may become proper nouns when used with other words or phrases. Also, when words that are not nouns are used with a noun, or when a group of words are used together as one noun, those words may also need to be capitalized.

Titles of Books, Stories, and Essays

Most of the words in titles of things like books, stories, and essays should be capitalized, but some should not. The very first word in a title should always be capitalized. Any other word in a title that is a noun, pronoun, adjective, verb or adverb should be capitalized. Articles, such as *a* or *the*, should not be capitalized. Short conjunctions and prepositions are usually not capitalized.

Abbreviations, Initials, and Acronyms

Abbreviations are shortened versions of other words. When an abbreviation shortens, or abbreviates, a word that should be capitalized, the abbreviation's first letter should also be capitalized. When the shortened word is a noun that is not capitalized, the abbreviation should be in lowercase. Initials are usually written using the first letter from multiple words. For example, John Fitzgerald Kennedy is commonly referred to by his initials, JFK. Acronyms also use the first letter from multiple words, but they are different from initials because they form words on their own. For example, NASA is an acronym for National Aeronautics and Space Administration. Some acronyms, like NASA, omit small words, such as *and*, *of*, and *for*. When initials and acronyms are used for proper nouns, each letter should be capitalized.

The types of words and phrases in the chart below are proper nouns and should always be capitalized:

	Description	**Example**
Historical Periods	A range of time in history that is related to specific events or circumstances	During the Romantic Period, many authors and poets wrote about their emotions.
Historical Events	Names of important events that happened in history	Napoleon Bonaparte led France after the French Revolution.
Historical Documents	Titles of important papers or compositions that are connected to historical events	The Mayflower Compact was written to create rules and expectations for the colony in Plymouth.
Languages	Names of the different languages that people speak	I want to learn to speak Cantonese, Spanish, and German.

	Description	Example
Races and Ethnicities	Words often used to describe a person's heritage or cultural group	Malia taught her granddaughter how to hula so she could share a tradition of her Native Hawaiian heritage with her.
Nationalities	Words that describe which country a person is from	My teacher who moved to Canada last year is Romanian.
Organizations	Titles of official groups formed by people	Fewer than half of the states in America have a team in the National Basketball Association.

Review Video: Capitalization in Grammar
Visit mometrix.com/academy and enter code: 369678

EXAMPLE

Allison and Claire enjoy studying art from the beginning of the renaissance. They started a club so they and other students can learn more about it. Allison and Claire named the club Early Renaissance Art Club, which can be abbreviated to ERA Club. The students that joined elected Claire as the president and Allison as the vice president. The club's first meeting will take place after Christmas vacation.

Which of the following changes should be made in the passage?

a. In the first sentence, *Renaissance* should be capitalized.
b. In the third sentence, *ERA* should be written as *Era*.
c. In the fourth sentence, *president* and *vice president* should be capitalized.
d. In the last sentence, *Christmas* should be in lowercase.

Choice A says that *Renaissance* should be capitalized in the first sentence of the passage. The Renaissance is a historical period, so *Renaissance* is a proper noun that should always be capitalized. Choice A is correct.

Choice B says that *ERA* should be written as *Era*. In the third sentence of the passage, the word *era* is used as an acronym. Remember that all letters in an acronym should be capitalized. The correct capitalization is *ERA*, so choice B is incorrect.

Choice C says that *president* and *vice president* should be capitalized. Titles for people are capitalized when they are used as part of a person's name or in the place of a person's name. In this passage, these titles are not used as part of anyone's name or in place of anyone's name, so they should be in lowercase. Choice C is incorrect.

Choice D says that *Christmas* should be in lowercase. The passage says that the first meeting will be held after Christmas break. Even though *Christmas* is used to describe when the students are getting a vacation from school, it is the name of a holiday. Names of holidays are always capitalized, so choice D is incorrect.

Word Confusion

To, Too, and Two

To can be an adverb or a preposition for showing direction, purpose, and relationship. A dictionary can also be used to see the many other ways to use *to* in a sentence.

Examples: I went to the store. | I want to go with you.

Too is an adverb that means *also, as well, very,* or *in excess.*

Examples: I can walk a mile too. | You have eaten too much.

Two is a number.

Example: You have two minutes left.

There, Their, and They're

There can be an adjective, adverb, or pronoun. Often, *there* is used to show a place or to start a sentence.

Examples: I went there yesterday. | There is something in his pocket.

Their is a pronoun that is used to show ownership.

Examples: He is their father. | This is their fourth apology this week.

They're is a contraction of *they are.*

Example: Did you know that they're in town?

Its and It's

Its is a possessive pronoun that shows ownership.

Example: The guitar is in its case.

It's is a contraction of *it is.*

Example: It's an honor and a privilege to meet you.

Affect and Effect

There are two main reasons that *affect* and *effect* are so often confused: 1) both words can be used as either a noun or a verb, and 2) unlike most homophones, their usage and meanings are closely related to each other. Here is a quick explanation of the four usage options:

Affect (n): feeling, emotion, or mood that is displayed

Example: The patient had a flat *affect.* (i.e., his face showed little or no emotion)

Affect (v): to alter, to change, to influence

Example: The sunshine *affects* the plant's growth.

Effect (n): a result, a consequence

Example: What *effect* will this weather have on our schedule?

Effect (v): to bring about, to cause to be

> Example: These new rules will *effect* order in the office.

EXAMPLE

Choose the correct spelling from each pair of homophones in the following passage.

> I found a unique tree in the forest. (It's/Its) trunk is blue, and it has (two/too) many branches to count. I brought some of my friends to see it, but the tree did not seem to (affect/effect) them. While (their/they're) not fascinated by the strange tree, I am!

The first pair of homophones is *it's* and *its.* Remember that the contraction *it's* is used in place of *it is. Its* is a possessive pronoun that shows a thing's ownership or possession. An easy way to decide whether *it's* or *its* is correct is to see how the sentence sounds with *it is*, instead. *It is trunk is blue* does not make sense. *Its trunk is blue* means that the tree has a blue trunk, so *its* is the correct choice.

The next pair of homophones is *two* and *too. Two* only means the number two. *Too* can mean *also* or *in excess.* Which of these makes the most sense in this sentence? *Two many branches to count* or *too many branches to count*? The correct meaning is that there is an abundance of branches, so *too* is the correct choice for this pair.

The third pair of homophones is *affect* and *effect.* Since both of these words can be used as a noun or verb, identifying the correct part of speech is a helpful first step. The part of speech is a verb, since the correct word will show what *the tree* does to *them. Affect* as a verb means to change or influence. *Effect* as a verb means to lead to or cause something to happen. Replace the homophone with these synonyms. Seeing the tree cannot cause or lead the speaker's friends to exist, but it can change them or influence them. *Affect* is the correct choice for this pair.

The last pair of homophones is *their* and *they're. Their* is a possessive pronoun used to show that multiple people or things own something. *They're* is a contraction used in place of *they are.* Replace the homophone with *they are.* Does the sentence make sense? It does because they, the speaker's friends, are not fascinated by the tree. Saying *their not fascinated* does not make sense. *They're* is the correct choice for this pair.

CHAPTER QUIZ

1. Every sentence always has a subject and a/an:

a. Imperative
b. Preposition
c. Predicate
d. Modifier

2. Which of the following sentences does NOT have an implied subject?

a. Take John on a quick walk.
b. Don't get lost.
c. John knows the way to the park.
d. Bring me back some flowers.

3. Which pronoun can be either singular or plural depending on what it is representing in the context of the sentence?

a. Nobody
b. Either
c. Several
d. All

4. Which of the following is written in third person perspective?

a. I am walking
b. He is walking
c. You are walking
d. We are walking

5. Which of the following best describes the function of an indirect object?

a. Shows how an action had an influence
b. Takes or receives the action of a verb
c. Explains or describes the subject
d. Shows that there is more information needed

6. What sentence has correct pronoun use?

a. Bob and I will be going.
b. Us all love eating ice cream.
c. You and me should go shopping.
d. Us boys played football last year.

7. Which of the following is a group of words that contains both a subject and a verb, and can be either independent or dependent?

a. Antecedent
b. Fragment
c. Phrase
d. Clause

8. Which of the following is an example of a complex sentence (as opposed to a simple or compound sentence)?

a. The time has come, and we are ready.
b. Judy and Alan watered the lawn and pulled weeds.
c. Marcia got married after she finished college.
d. I woke up at dawn; the sun was just coming up.

9. What method of correcting run-on sentences is the easiest way to make the sentence correct and more interesting at the same time?

a. Split into separate sentences
b. Join clauses properly
c. Reduce to one clause with a compound verb
d. Make one clause dependent

10. Which of the following is a word placed before a noun or pronoun that shows the relationship between an object and another word in the sentence?

a. Adjective
b. Adverb
c. Preposition
d. Conjunction

11. What punctuation mark(s) should be added to the following sentence to make it grammatically correct?

Relieved the test was over Leah dropped her pencil and slouched in her chair

a. Relieved the test was over Leah dropped her pencil and slouched in her chair.
b. Relieved the test was over, Leah dropped her pencil and slouched in her chair.
c. Relieved the test was over: Leah dropped her pencil and, slouched in her chair.
d. Relieved, the test was "over" Leah dropped her pencil and slouched in her chair.

12. Which of the following is specifically used to connect major sentence pieces of equal value?

a. Comma
b. Semicolon
c. Colon
d. Hyphen

13. Which of the following should be put in single quotation marks?

a. Quote inside a quote
b. Indirect quote
c. Direct quote
d. All of the above

Chapter Quiz Answer Key

1. C: See section **Predicates**

2. C: See section **Subjects**

3. D: See section **Depend on Context**

4. B: See section **Person Agreement Examples**

5. A: See section **Indirect Objects**

6. A: See section **Pronoun-Antecedent Agreement**

7. D: See section **Clauses**

8. C: See section **Complex**

9. D: See section **Run-on Sentences**

10. C: See section **Prepositions**

11. B: See section **Commas**

12. B: See section **Semicolons**

13. A: See section **Quotation Marks**

Extended Constructed Response

Essays

Essays usually focus on one topic, subject, or goal. There are several types of essays, including informative, persuasive, and narrative. An essay's structure and formality depend on the type of essay and its goal. While narrative essays typically do not include outside sources, other types of essays often require some research and the use of primary and secondary sources.

The basic format of an essay typically has three major parts: the introduction, the body, and the conclusion. The body is further divided into the writer's main points. Most essays will have at least three main points, but essays that go into more depth can have almost any number of main points.

An essay's introduction should answer three questions:

1. What is the **subject** of the essay?

   If an essay is about a book, the answer would include the title and author of the book, as well as any additional information needed, such as the subject or argument of the book.

2. How does the essay **discuss** the subject?

   To answer this, the writer briefly summarizes the main points and the evidence supporting them to let readers know how the essay is organized and what information they can expect to read.

3. What will the essay **prove**?

   This information is in the thesis statement, usually the opening paragraph's last sentence, which clearly states the writer's message.

The body elaborates on all the main points related to the thesis, introducing one main point at a time, and includes supporting evidence with each main point. Each body paragraph should state the point in a topic sentence, which is usually the first sentence in the paragraph. The paragraph should then explain the point's meaning, support it with quotations or other evidence, and then explain how this point and the evidence are related to the thesis. The writer should then repeat this procedure in a new paragraph for each additional main point.

The conclusion restates the content of the introduction, including the thesis, to remind the reader of the essay's main argument or subject. The essay writer may also summarize the highlights of the argument or description contained in the body of the essay, following the same organization originally used in the body. For example, a conclusion might look like: Point 1 + Point 2 + Point 3 = Thesis, or Point 1 → Point 2 → Point 3 → Thesis Proof. Good organization makes essays easier for writers to compose and provides a guide for readers to follow. Well-organized essays hold attention better and are more likely to get readers to believe or agree with the writer.

Using Sources in Essays

Sometimes writers use information from others in their work. This is most common in expository and persuasive writing. For an expository essay, a writer may not know all of the information that he or she needs to finish the composition. The writer may use other people's work to find the missing information and complete the composition. Persuasive writers may do research to find facts or statements from others that support their own beliefs and make their writing more persuasive. In both cases, research helps the writer find information that **supports** his or her **original work**.

Outside information must be relevant, true, and helpful to be appropriate for a composition. Writers must also be careful not to use too much outside information, since this can make the composition unoriginal. If a writer does use outside information, it is extremely important that the writer mention in the composition where the information came from. If the writer forgets or chooses not to say where the information came from, he or she has stolen someone else's work and presented it as their own. Doing this is called **plagiarism**.

Informational Texts

Informational texts, also called instructional or expository texts, are compositions written to inform the reader about a specific topic. An informational essay can inform readers in a variety of ways, such as giving them instructions, telling them facts about the topic, or teaching them why something happens. Informational texts should be logical, meaning that they should present information in an order that the reader can easily understand, and they should include the right amount of information so the writer successfully informs his or her audience of new information.

Informational texts should also focus on a **controlling idea**. In the introduction of an informational text, there may be a sentence or two that clearly state the essay's controlling idea. This sentence, or sentences, is called a **thesis statement**. The controlling idea should be clear throughout the composition. By emphasizing the controlling idea in the introduction, body, and conclusion, the writer can ensure that the controlling idea is clear. One way to make sure that the controlling idea is emphasized is to think about the purpose of each part of the essay. The introduction prepares the reader by telling them what the rest of the essay is about, so the controlling idea should be **introduced** in this section. The body tells the reader the information the writer wants to tell the audience, so this **explains** the controlling idea and facts about it to the reader. The conclusion is used to **remind** the reader of how the information in the body is related and **restates** the controlling idea one final time.

Review Video: Informational Text
Visit mometrix.com/academy and enter code: 924964

Structures or Organizational Patterns in Informational Texts

Informational text can be **descriptive**, meaning that it gives information that can be experienced through the five senses, or it answers the questions what, who, when, where, and why. One common method of organizing informational text is to put it in a certain sequence, or order. **Chronological** texts include events in the order that they occurred, from start to finish. **How-to**, or **instructional**, texts organize information into a series of instructions in the order in which the steps should be followed. **Comparison-contrast** structures of informational text describe different ideas to their readers by pointing out how things or ideas are similar and how they are different. **Cause and effect** structures of informational text describe events that occurred and the causes or reasons for those events. **Problem and solution** structures of informational texts introduce and describe problems and offer one or more solutions for each problem described.

ARGUMENTATIVE WRITING

In argumentative writing, the writer expresses a belief or opinion that he or she wants to lead readers to agree with. When writing an argumentative composition, the writer should first identify the **topic** his or her opinion is about. The topic may be serious or fun, as long as there is one clear topic in the composition. The next step is for the writer to determine his or her opinion on the topic and determine why he or she holds that opinion. In order to persuade others to agree with their opinion, the writer must be able to give readers reasons to support the opinion. If the writer does not know why he or she has an opinion, it will be difficult to convince readers to agree. In addition to having reasons that support their opinion, writers should prepare examples that support each of these reasons in order to strengthen their composition.

Once the writer has determined his or her topic, opinion, and reasons for having the opinion, he or she is ready to begin writing an argumentative essay. In the introduction, the writer should capture the reader's interest, introduce the topic, and reveal his or her opinion about the topic. In the body of the composition, the writer should remind the reader of the opinion and give his or her reasons for holding the opinion. If the writer has any examples, facts, or other information that supports his or her opinion or reasons for believing it, these should also be included in the body. Writers may also use a body paragraph to mention opposing opinions or beliefs and explain why they disagree with them. As in other compositions, the conclusion should remind the reader of the essay's topic and purpose, as well as remind the reader how the opinion has been explained and supported. The conclusion should also invite the reader to continue thinking about the topic and writer's opinion. This can be done through questions or statements that lead readers to consider whether or not they agree with the author's opinion or what their own opinions are.

Review Video: Argumentative Writing
Visit mometrix.com/academy and enter code: 561544

INFORMATIVE VS. PERSUASIVE WRITING

Informative writing, also called explanatory or expository writing, is written to show that something is true or factual, while **persuasive** writing is written to lead the reader to agree with something that may or may not be true or factual. While persuasive text is written to **persuade** readers to agree with the author's position, informative text simply **provides information** to readers. Informative writing **informs** readers about why or how something is as it is. This can include offering new information, explaining how a process works, or describing a concept for readers.

FACTS AND OPINIONS

Writers and readers must always be aware of the difference between fact and opinion. A **fact** can be tested and proven to be true. An **opinion**, on the other hand, is someone's personal thoughts or feelings. Opinions are often not changed by information. If an author writes that a newborn elephant is about five times taller than a newborn giraffe, then he or she is stating a fact. If the author writes that giraffes are more interesting than elephants, then he or she is giving an opinion because this cannot be proven to be true or false. Opinions are often supported by facts. For instance, the author might use a comparison between the way that giraffes eat and the way elephants eat as evidence of how giraffes are more interesting. An opinion supported by facts tends to be more convincing. On the other hand, when authors support their opinions with other opinions, readers should seriously think about and read the argument carefully to see whether it is logical and trustworthy.

Review Video: Distinguishing Fact and Opinion
Visit mometrix.com/academy and enter code: 870899

Responding to a Text

An essay prompt may require writers to write about a text they have read. When writing an essay like this, writers should show that they understand the text they have read. They may mention their own thoughts, ideas, and opinions in the essay. However, the main idea of the essay should be about the text mentioned in the prompt.

When planning the essay, writers should consider what the text is about and how it is written. Writers should identify the purpose, main idea, and structure of the text. For informational and persuasive texts, they should also think about the supporting details the author used in the text. All of these facts about the text will help writers understand the text well and allow the writer to create a response to the text.

Responding to Multiple Texts

Essay prompts may ask writers to write about more than one text. In this case, writers should identify the purpose, main idea, and structure of each text. They should also look at the kinds of supporting details that the author of each text uses. Once writers know these details, they should think about the differences and similarities between the texts. The main ideas of each text may oppose each other, or one may support the other. Writers will need to write about both texts in the essay, so they must understand both texts and the connection between the texts.

Correspondence

Letters are written using a different format than an essay or book. A letter should begin with a greeting that names the person or group that is meant to receive the letter. Consider the following examples of greetings:

- Dear Mr. Johnson,
- To whom it may concern:
- To Bernard,
- Hello Grandma,

The greeting used at the beginning of the letter depends on the writer's purpose for writing the letter. If the letter is being written to a business, an owner or manager of a company, or someone who has a higher rank than the writer, the letter should be **formal**. A formal greeting should begin with "Dear" followed by the name of the recipient. For formal greetings, never address the recipient by their first name only. If the letter is being written to a friend or a family member, it may be **informal**. For informal letters, the greeting may start with a word other than *dear* and may name the recipient by their first name only or by a nickname.

Word Choice and Tone in Letters

The **purpose** of a letter also influences the way the body of the letter is written. For formal letters, the writer should use **formal, professional language**. The purpose of the letter should be clearly stated in the introduction. Whether the letter is written to give a complaint or share an opinion, the writer should keep a formal tone and write in a way that is **respectful** to the recipient. The writer should also be specific and provide any information that the recipient may need to respond appropriately. If a letter is informal, the writer can use **casual, friendly language**. The writer should think about their own relationship with the recipient and use a tone that fits the relationship and purpose for the letter.

Closing Letters

All letters should end with a **closing**, as well. The closing will include a word or phrase that signals that the body of the letter has ended, such as *sincerely*, *best wishes*, *until later*, or *with love*. The word or phrase should be followed by a comma, and the writer's name should be written underneath this on the next line. Formal letters should include closing words like *sincerely* or *thank you*.

Chapter Quiz

1. What type of essay does NOT typically include outside sources?

a. Expository
b. Informative
c. Persuasive
d. Narrative

2. Which of the following is NOT true of informational texts?

a. Informational texts are also called instructional or expository texts
b. Informational texts should be logical
c. Informational texts should focus on a central idea
d. Informational texts can only be structured chronologically

3. In an argumentative essay, which of the following should be included in the body?

a. A reminder of the writer's opinion and his or her reasons for holding the opinion
b. Examples, facts, or other information that supports the writer's opinion
c. Opposing opinions or beliefs and explanations of why the writer disagrees with them
d. All of the above

4. A letter that requires a formal greeting should always start with:

a. Dear
b. To whom it may concern
c. Greetings
d. Hello

5. At the end of a letter the closing is followed by:

a. A period and the writer's name
b. A comma and the writer's name
c. A colon and the writer's name
d. A semicolon and the writer's name

Chapter Quiz Answer Key

1. D: See section **Essays**

2. D: See section **Structures or Organizational Patterns in Informational Texts**

3. D: See section **Argumentative Writing**

4. A: See section **Correspondence**

5. B: See section **Closing Letters**

Informational Text Example

Below is a prompt for an informational text. There is also an example of an essay that addresses the prompt. There are multiple drafts of this essay to show what kinds of changes a writer may make during the writing process to improve his or her work.

PROMPT:

Do you ever dream of going to a new city, state, or even country? Write about one place you want to travel to on vacation. Be sure to share why you would like to visit that place.

Rough Draft

Imagine traveling into the city or the beach and being transported back in time. This is what it must be like to live in Greece. The old buildings, beautiful beaches, and Greek foods are reasons I want to visit Greece.

Several buildings from ancient Greece are still standing, and they can easily be enjoyed by visitors and the people of Greece today. Some of the most famous ones, like the Parthenon, are located throughout the capital. This means that even when you are sitting in an air-conditioned restaurant in Athens, you can still see what is left of history. There are also tours that teach visitors more about these structures and the events that happened at each one. Though seeing these structures is not the only reason I would like to visit Greece, they would be enough of a reason for me to visit.

In addition to the scenery, another reason to visit Greece is to try real Greek and Mediterranean foods. I have tried a few Greek foods, like baklava and pita bread, and I enjoyed them. While these foods are available in America, I think they are probably made a little differently in Greece. I am interested in seeing what the differences are and trying new things. I hope I can visit Greece soon, because I am getting hungry just thinking about the food there!

Greece has a variety of beaches, as some are small with rocky structures and some look like normal beaches. The water is also different from some American waters because Greece is next to the Mediterranean Sea. Also, many historical events and myths took place on some of the beaches. I would love to sit on one of those beaches and try to imagine ships or characters from myths coming to the shore! The beaches in Greece are beautiful, but I think they also sound fun and interesting!

Walking through historical structures, visiting unique beaches, and eating new foods there is my dream. If I only ever have the chance to go on one vacation, I hope it is to Greece!

Revised Draft

Imagine traveling into the city or the beach and being transported back in time. This is what it must be like to live in Greece. The remaining historical sites that are still there allow visitors to see two cultures side by side. The old buildings, beautiful beaches, and Greek foods are reasons I want to visit Greece.

Several buildings from ancient Greece are still standing, and they can easily be enjoyed by visitors and the people of Greece today. Some of the most famous ones, like the Parthenon, are located throughout the capital. This means that even when you are sitting in an air-conditioned restaurant in Athens, you can still see what is left of history. There are also tours that teach visitors more about these structures and the events that happened at each one. Though seeing these structures is not the only reason I would like to visit Greece, they would be enough of a reason for me to visit.

Greece has a variety of beaches, as some are small with rocky structures and some look like normal beaches. The water is also different from some American waters because Greece is next to the Mediterranean Sea. Also, many historical events and myths took place on some of the beaches. I would love to sit on one of those beaches and try to imagine ships or characters from myths coming to the shore! The beaches in Greece are beautiful, but I think they also sound fun and interesting!

In addition to the scenery, a third reason to visit Greece is to try real Greek and Mediterranean foods. I have tried a few Greek foods, like baklava and pita bread, and I enjoyed them. While these foods are available in America, I think they are probably made a little differently in Greece. I am interested in seeing what the differences are and trying new things. I hope I can visit Greece soon, because I am getting hungry just thinking about the food there!

Greece is a special place where the old and the new come together. Walking through historical structures, visiting unique beaches, and eating new foods there is my dream. If I only ever have the chance to go on one vacation, I hope it is to Greece!

Revised Draft Notes

Remember the purpose of the revising stage of the writing process. When revising, it is important to look at the whole composition. Do all of the paragraphs strengthen the composition? Do the introduction and conclusion help the reader understand the controlling idea and main points?

In this revision, nothing has been removed, but there are some additions. Look at the underlined words. In the introduction, a sentence has been added. Why? Previously, the introduction had only a hook and a thesis. The sentences were well written, but the writer did not provide a connection between the hook and the thesis. The new sentence connects the ideas in both sentences and introduces some of the main points the writer will discuss in the essay.

In the conclusion, another sentence has been added. This sentence strengthens the composition by creating a transition from the body to the conclusion. Before, the conclusion began abruptly by listing the three main points from the body of the essay. This sentence makes the essay flow better by giving the reader a transition from the body to the conclusion. This sentence reminds the reader of composition's controlling idea before repeating the writer's main points and sharing his or her hopes.

Finally, the third and fourth paragraphs have been switched. Why is that? Before, the writer discussed ancient buildings, then food, then the beaches. This revised draft discusses buildings, then beaches, then food. This new order puts the more closely related points, the scenery of the buildings and beaches, closer together in the essay. This helps the reader by making the organization of the essay more logical.

Edited Draft

Imagine traveling into the city or the beach and being transported back in time. This is what it must be like to live in Greece, since the remaining historical sites ~~that are still there~~ allow visitors to see two cultures side by side. The ~~old~~ ancient buildings, beautiful beaches, and Greek foods are reasons I want to visit Greece.

Several buildings from ancient Greece are still standing, and they can easily be enjoyed by visitors and the people of Greece today. Some of the most famous ones, like the Parthenon, are located throughout the capital. This means that even when you are sitting in an air-conditioned restaurant in Athens, you can still see ~~what is left~~ glimpses of history. There are also tours that teach visitors more about these structures and the events that happened at each one. ~~Though seeing these structures is not the only reason I would like to visit Greece, they would be enough of a reason for me to visit.~~ Seeing these structures alone is enough of a reason for me to visit Greece!

Another reason I want to travel to Greece is to see the beaches there. There are a variety of beaches, as some are small with rocky structures and some look like ~~normal~~ typical beaches. The water is also different from some American waters because Greece is next to the Mediterranean Sea. Also, many historical events and myths took place on some of the beaches. I would love to sit on one of those beaches and try to imagine ships or characters from myths coming to the shore! The beaches in Greece are beautiful, but I think they also sound fun and interesting!

In addition to the scenery, a third reason to visit Greece is to try ~~real~~ authentic Greek and Mediterranean foods. I have tried a few Greek foods, like baklava and pita bread, and I enjoyed them. While these foods are available in America, I think they are probably made a little differently in Greece, so I am interested in seeing what the differences are and trying new things. I hope I can visit Greece soon, because I am getting hungry just thinking about the food there!

Greece is a special place where the old and the new come together. Walking through historical structures, visiting unique beaches, and eating new foods there is my dream. If I only ever have the chance to go on one vacation, I hope it is to Greece!

EDITED DRAFT NOTES

Since the writer has revised his or her work, the next step is to edit the composition. Remember that editing is very similar to revising, but editing usually includes paying attention to each paragraph, instead of the whole composition. Look at the changes that were made to each paragraph.

There are small changes throughout this draft. First, look at the introduction. Before, the introduction had four sentences that were about the same length. In this draft, the second and third sentences have been combined to make a longer sentence. This creates more sentence variety in the introduction, which makes the composition more entertaining for the writer's audience. A few words have been crossed out, as well. *That are still there* has been replaced with *remaining*. This change makes the writing more concise and formal. Also, *old* has been replaced with *ancient*. This clarifies what kind of buildings the writer is describing by using a word that more specifically describes the age of the buildings.

In the next paragraph, *what is left* has been replaced with *glimpses*. This change makes the writing more concise by using one word instead of three. Furthermore, this change makes the writing more interesting and entertaining by using a better vocabulary word. At the end of the paragraph, the last sentence has been condensed. Most of the sentences in this paragraph are long. Shortening this sentence adds sentence variety to this paragraph and makes the concluding sentence more concise. Overall, these changes make the paragraph easier to read by eliminating unnecessary words and using better vocabulary.

There are a few more changes left in the third and fourth paragraphs. A transition has been added to the beginning of the third paragraph. Now, the writer introduces the next main point before describing the beaches. This makes the essay flow better overall and making it easier for the writer's audience to read. *Normal* has been replaced with *typical*. Since there are so many different beaches in the world, there are not really any normal beaches. *Typical* is a much clearer word. Now, the reader knows that the writer is trying to distinguish the beaches in Greece from the type of beaches that he or she sees most often.

In the next paragraph, *real* has been replaced with *authentic*. The food the writer has tried in America has been real food, not fake food, so this is poor word choice. Now, *authentic* clarifies the writer's meaning that the food will be closer to its original Greek or Mediterranean style. These changes in word choice improve the clarity of the essay by using specific words that better communicate the writer's points. Finally, the third and fourth sentences have been joined together. This increases sentence variety by adding a longer sentence to this paragraph.

FINAL DRAFT

Imagine traveling into the city or the beach and being transported back in time. This is what it must be like to live in Greece, since the remaining historical sites allow visitors to see two cultures side by side. The ancient buildings, beautiful beaches, and Greek foods are reasons I want to visit Greece.

Several buildings from ancient Greece are still standing, and they can easily be enjoyed by visitors and the people of Greece today. Some of the most famous ones, like the Parthenon, are located throughout the capital. This means that even when you are sitting in an air-conditioned restaurant in Athens, you can still see glimpses of history. There are also tours that teach visitors more about these structures and the events that happened at each one. Seeing these structures alone is enough of a reason for me to visit Greece!

Another reason I want to travel to Greece is to see the beaches there. There are a variety of beaches, as some are small with rocky structures and some look like typical beaches. The water is also different from some American waters because Greece is next to the Mediterranean Sea. Also, many historical events and myths took place on some of the beaches. I would love to sit on one of those beaches and try to imagine ships or characters from myths coming to the shore! The beaches in Greece are beautiful, but I think they also sound fun and interesting!

In addition to the scenery, a third reason to visit Greece is to try authentic Greek and Mediterranean foods. I have tried a few Greek foods, like baklava and pita bread, and I enjoyed them. While these foods are available in America, I think they are probably made a little differently in Greece, so I am interested in seeing what the differences are and trying new things. I hope I can visit Greece soon, because I am getting hungry just thinking about the food there!

Greece is a special place where the old and the new come together. Walking through historical structures, visiting unique beaches, and eating new foods there is my dream. If I only ever have the chance to go on one vacation, I hope it is to Greece!

Final Draft Evaluation

The essay answers the prompt and is on topic throughout the composition. The controlling idea is clear and is stated in the introduction, supported in the body, and restated in the conclusion. The thesis statement restates parts of the prompt and gives the reader a preview of the rest of the essay. The body uses well-structured paragraphs to explain the supporting details and examples and connects them to the controlling idea. The conclusion also emphasizes the controlling idea and supporting details and invites the reader to consider what they have read.

The essay is also interesting and written with a variety of sentence types. It uses transitions and good paragraph structure to make the essay easy for the reader to understand. The introduction also uses a hook to get the reader's attention and help him or her relate to the information in the essay. Not only does this essay answer the prompt and have appropriate structure, but it also makes use of good, engaging, and interesting details.

Practice Test #1

Reading

Summer's Heat

(1) I remember the day as if it were yesterday. It was Saturday afternoon and cloudless. The Sun beat down upon my face through the chain-link fenced dugout. It was so hot that I could feel my skin burning, and I was sweating, even though I wasn't on the field. I sat on the bench with a jug of water at my feet and a fistful of sunflower seeds. We were losing, three to one. I looked at our right fielder, Johnny, who was fanning his face with his glove as he was getting ready for the play.

(2) The ball was hit to the third basemen, and he got the last out of the inning at first base. The team ran into a huddle, and our coach told us to keep our eye on the ball. "Concentrate," he said.

(3) Philip hit the ball to the fence and was stopped on second base by the coaches. We were all shouting and very happy with his double. The next batter bunted the ball to the pitcher and moved Philip to third base. Johnny then came to the plate and hit a double. Philip scored, and we were one run away from tying the game.

(4) "Max!" the coach shouted.

(5) I turned my head and was shocked to see that I wasn't imagining things. Coach was pointing right at me.

(6) "You're up," he said.

(7) I threw my sunflower seeds to the ground, stuffed my helmet onto my head, and grabbed my favorite bat. I took two practice swings and was ready for the pitcher.

(8) I hit two foul balls over the side fences. They were hard and flew for a long time before ever hitting the ground. I was going to do it. I was going to get Johnny to home plate. I just needed one good pitch.

(9) The pitcher looked down at his feet and then stared into my eyes. I stared back. It was like there was no one else on the field. It was just us. He started his windup, and I dug my feet into the ground and adjusted my grip on the bat. The ball came in, and I swung as hard as I could.

(10) I was confused. I didn't feel anything.

(11) "Strike three!" the umpire yelled behind me. I was out.

(12) Bradley came up after me and we ended up losing the game, three to two.

(13) The coaches told us we played a good game. They said that it was a team effort and that we should be proud of ourselves. My mom tried to comfort me. "It was no one's fault," she said. "It's just a game."

(14) But it was not just a game to me. I felt like I had let everyone down and disappointed all of my teammates. It was the last game of the season, and we lost.

(15) I decided at that moment to spend my summer vacation training. I was going to do nothing but practice baseball. I spent two weeks outside, with just my baseball bat and a bucket of balls. I hit until it was dark and my mom forced me to come inside and eat dinner. When I asked her if we could install some lights in the backyard so that I could see and practice more, she looked at me with a very stern face and said the most horrible sentence.

(16) "No more baseball for the rest of the summer."

(17) My heart dropped. I felt sick to my stomach and filled with anger.

(18) "How can you do this to me?" I shouted.

(19) "There is more to life than baseball," she said. "I want you to enjoy spending the summer playing with your friends."

(20) She then grounded me for the weekend for shouting at her.

(21) After a few days without baseball, I realized how fun it was to be a regular kid and spend time with my friends, swimming in the pool, fishing in the lake, and climbing trees. Once, someone suggested we play some baseball, and we gathered some of our friends together and played a game in the park. We didn't keep score, and had fun just playing. It was a great summer.

(22) When baseball season came around again, I played center field. My first time up to bat, I smiled. I was having fun. The pitch came and I swung hard. The ball landed on the other side of the fence, and I ran around the bases to cheers after hitting my first homerun.

Refer to the passage "Summer's Heat" to answer questions 1-9.

1. Based on paragraphs 21 and 22, what can the reader predict about the narrator's upcoming baseball season?

a. He will have a better overall batting average this season.
b. He will enjoy the season regardless of his performance.
c. He will play centerfield more often this season.
d. He will be less excited to play this season.

2. What does the first-person point of view used in this passage help the reader understand?

a. The narrator thought the team's loss was his fault.
b. The team felt disappointed when the narrator struck out.
c. The narrator's mother told the narrator that he could not practice anymore.
d. The narrator and his friends decided to play baseball without keeping score.

3. How does paragraph 9 impact the plot?

a. Paragraph 9 foreshadows the fact the narrator's mother will make him stop playing baseball later in the passage.
b. Paragraph 9 creates a plot twist by having the narrator be surprised that he is being called to bat.
c. Paragraph 9 leaves the readers on a cliffhanger by describing an event that is not related to the one in paragraph 8.
d. Paragraph 9 uses suspense to build tension and push the story towards the outcome of an important event.

4. What key idea is supported by paragraph 19?

a. The narrator's mother does not like that her son plays baseball and would rather he spend time with friends.
b. The narrator's mother wants her son to spend more time playing baseball with friends instead of by himself.
c. The narrator's mother is concerned her son is too worried about his baseball skills and is missing out on time with his friends.
d. The narrator's mother believes that her son does not need to practice to become better at baseball.

5. What do paragraphs 4 and 5 help the reader understand about the narrator?

a. He is not often called on to bat when there is someone in a scoring position.
b. He was startled by the coach yelling calling his name, and this caused his confusion.
c. He imagines things while waiting, which is why he thought he imagined his coach talking.
d. He did not want to go up to bat and was hoping that it had been in his head.

6. How does the setting of paragraph 15 contribute to the narrator's character development?

a. It shows the conditions in which the narrator is practicing.
b. It proves that the narrator's mother's reaction was right.
c. It increases the pressure the narrator feels to be successful in batting.
d. It reveals the narrator's dedication to improving his skills.

7. Why did Max think he was imagining things?

a. It was so hot outside.
b. He could not believe his team was losing.
c. The coach was calling his name to come into the game to bat.
d. He was surprised to see that Philip scored.

8. In paragraph 9, what kind of mood does the author create?

a. A tense mood
b. An angry mood
c. A comforting mood
d. A sad mood

9. What does the word *install* mean in paragraph 15? Write your answer in the box below.

The Responsibilities of Bees

(1) While some people see bees as a nuisance or just another insect, they are a crucial part of the global ecosystem and survival. They support human and animal life through their role in food production and help maintain healthy habitats in a variety of ecosystems. Their ability to pollinate plants, provide resources for animals, and support biodiversity are their most important roles.

(2) Bats, birds, and a variety of insects pollinate plants, but bees are responsible for around 80% of global pollination. Pollinators transfer pollen from the male organs of one plant to the female organs of another. Pollination occurs when plants become fertilized and develop seeds. Fruits and vegetables then develop around the seed and grow into the produce that we find at grocery stores and farmer's markets. Bees are one of the most important pollinators. They move from flower to flower transferring pollen while they search for nectar. Without bees, food as we know it would change. Many of the fruits and vegetables we enjoy rely on bees to grow, so without bees the amount of food grown would significantly decrease.

(3) Not only would this impact us by reducing the amount of available food, but it would also hurt farmers economically. If the amount of food a farmer was able to grow decreased because of a decline in the bee population, they would not make enough money to support their farm. Even though there are other animals and insects that help with pollination, they aren't as effective as bees. If there were no more bees, most plants would have to be pollinated by hand to compensate for all of the work they do. The pollen would need to be manually transferred from one plant to another. This would take a lot of time, manpower, and money. The low supply of food would drive up the cost, hurting the consumers as well.

(4) We aren't the only ones who enjoy the fruits and vegetables bees help grow! Many animals eat fruits and vegetables just like us, so they need bees to keep pollinating too. Bees also play a direct role in supporting animal life and habitats. While we need an abundance of bees for our crops to thrive, it is necessary that some are eaten by birds, small mammals, and other insects as part of the food web. If the bee population were to disappear, an important food source for these animals would too. This could cause animals that rely on the bees to begin starving to death or consuming other insects and animals, further disrupting the ecosystem. Changes in food webs are capable of decimating entire species and ecosystems.

(5) Biodiversity is the variety of life found on Earth. This doesn't just include people and animals, but plants, insects, and all living organisms. Bees' role in supporting biodiversity is highlighted in the foods they help produce and the animals they help support, but it also goes beyond that. The seeds produced by the fertilized plants that were mentioned earlier continue to spread and grow new plants, allowing plant life cycles to continue. Sometimes bees help with spreading these seeds in a process known as seed dispersal. The seeds become attached to the bees while they collect nectar and fall off as they fly to another plant. This helps the seeds spread to new places. Not only does this create food for animals, but also habitats. The plants that grow as a result of seed dispersal create grassy, plant-filled homes for animals in a variety of ecosystems like meadows, forests, and grasslands.

(6) Even though bees are not the only pollinators, they're the most important ones. Bees keep our food sources and ecosystems stable! We need to maintain the bee population in order to keep the Earth and its inhabitants safe, healthy, and happy.

Refer to the passage "The Responsibilities of Bees" to answer questions 10-17.

10. Based on the information in the passage, what can the reader infer about bees?

a. The total loss of bees is not preventable.
b. Pollinators can be completely replaced by people.
c. Bees are capable of destroying crops.
d. Protecting bees is beneficial to everyone.

11. Which sentence from the passage best supports the idea that bees support biodiversity?

a. They move from flower to flower transferring pollen while they search for nectar.
b. The plants that grow as a result of seed dispersal create grassy, plant-filled homes for animals in a variety of ecosystems like meadows, forests, and grasslands.
c. Many animals eat fruits and vegetables just like us, so they need bees to keep pollinating too.
d. Many of the fruits and vegetables we enjoy rely on bees to grow, so without bees the amount of food grown would significantly decrease.

12. What is the most likely reason that the author uses a cause-and-effect structure in paragraph 3?

a. To illustrate the financial impact that the loss of bees can have
b. To reveal the importance of bees in many food webs
c. To outline the process for manual pollination
d. To suggest solutions for increasing the bee population

13. What is the most likely reason the author wrote "The Responsibilities of Bees"?

a. To highlight the ways that bees are harmful
b. To describe the importance of bee movement
c. To highlight the worldwide impact of bees
d. To show why so many people appreciate bees

14. What is the controlling idea of this passage?

a. Pollination by bees is required for crops to grow on their own.
b. How diverse a habitat is depends on how many bees are present.
c. Bees support the survival of plants and animals worldwide.
d. Bees are the most efficient pollinators in most ecosystems.

15. Which detail from the selection supports the key idea that bees are an essential part of Earth's global ecosystem?

a. If the amount of food a farmer was able to grow decreased because of a decline in the bee population, they would not make enough money to support their farm.
b. Bats, birds, and a variety of insects pollinate plants, but bees are responsible for around 80% of global pollination.
c. Bees' role in supporting biodiversity is highlighted in the foods they help produce and the animals they help support, but it also goes beyond that.
d. Sometimes bees help with spreading these seeds in a process known as seed dispersal.

16. What is the best summary of this passage?

a. Bees are the most important pollinator. They pollinate the majority of the Earth's plant life. Without them, the cost of producing food would increase. This would harm the economy.
b. Bees are an important part of the global ecosystem. They support animal and human life and maintain a balance in a variety of habitats. Without them, the world as we know it would be very different.
c. Bees help seeds from plants spread across large areas. They then grow and develop into habitats that support biodiversity. Without bees, many organisms would not have homes or food.
d. Bees are a part of the food web in several different habitats. This means that animals and other insects eat them as a source of energy. If bees went extinct, the food web would not be complete.

17. Why did the author most likely use a cause-and-effect structure in this passage?

a. To show the connections between humans and animals
b. To highlight the possible effect of a decline in the bee population
c. To present bees as solutions to pollination problems
d. To demonstrate how animals and humans rely on bees differently

The Road Not Taken

by Robert Frost

Two roads diverged in a yellow wood,
And sorry I could not travel both
And be one traveler, long I stood
And looked down one as far as I could
To where it bent in the undergrowth;
Then took the other, as just as fair,
And having perhaps the better claim,
Because it was grassy and wanted wear;
Though as for that the passing there
Had worn them really about the same,
And both that morning equally lay
In leaves no step had trodden black.
Oh, I kept the first for another day!
Yet knowing how way leads on to way,
I doubted if I should ever come back.
I shall be telling this with a sigh
Somewhere ages and ages hence:
Two roads diverged in a wood, and I—
I took the one less travelled by,
And that has made all the difference.

The Right Thing to Do

Cast of Characters

Cast of Characters

- Jessica: A sixth-grade girl, Amy's friend
- Amy: A sixth-grade girl, Jessica's friend
- Sales Clerk: a clerk in the store Amy and Jessica visit

Scene 1

(1) [JESSICA *stands with a group of friends on the school steps. The group is chatting and laughing.* AMY *approaches from stage right.]*

(2) AMY: Jessica! Jessica!

(3) JESSICA: [*turning away from her friends and taking a step toward* AMY] Hi, Amy. What's up?

(4) AMY: I'm headed to the mall, and I thought you might want to come.

(5) JESSICA: Why me? I thought we weren't friends anymore.

(6) AMY: [*waving her hand and shaking her head*] That old fight? Ancient history. So... do you want to come or not?

(7) JESSICA: [*glancing back at her friends*] Sure. I'll come. Just give me a minute.

(8)[JESSICA *runs back and talks with her friends for a moment, then rejoins* AMY. AMY *and* JESSICA *exit stage right.*]

Scene 2

(9) [*Amy and Jessica are looking at a shelf full of lipstick in a cosmetics store in the mall.*]

(10) AMY: [*picking up a lipstick tube*] Look at this one, Jess. Don't you just love this color?

(11) JESSICA: [*picking up a different lipstick tube*] It's nice, but I like this one better.

(12) A sales clerk enters from stage left.

(13) SALES CLERK: [*stopping by the girls*] Can I help you ladies find something?

(14) AMY: Oh, no. We're just looking.

(15) JESSICA: Thank you, though.

(16) SALES CLERK: Okay. Well, let me know if you need anything.

(17) [SALES CLERK exits stage right.]

(18) AMY: So, which one are you going to get?

(19) JESSICA: [*shaking her head*] I'm not getting one. They're a little pricy for me. Besides, I'm saving up for something special.

(20) AMY: [laughing] Who said anything about money? I didn't ask you which one you were going to buy. I asked which one you were going to get. So, which one will it be?

(21) JESSICA: But—but—that's stealing!

(22) AMY: Look at all these tubes of lipstick. They'll never miss a couple.

(23) JESSICA: [*looking around nervously*] What if that sales clerk comes back and catches us?

(24) AMY: [*Picking up two tubes of lipstick*] You worry too much. Now, was this the one you liked? Or was it this one? Never mind. We'll take them both.

(25) [AMY *slips both tubes into her pocket.*]

(26) JESSICA: Amy! This is wrong. We shouldn't be doing this.

(27) AMY: [*glaring at* JESSICA] Do you even want to be my friend again? It sure doesn't sound like it.

(28) JESSICA: Of course I want to be your friend. It's just—

(29) AMY: Then come on. Let's go. [AMY *starts to walk away, and then turns and looks back.*] Are you coming?

(30) JESSICA: Fine. [*She follows* AMY.] But what if the alarm goes off?

(31) AMY: For a couple of tubes of lipstick? Not gonna happen. Now, follow me. And for heaven's sake, don't look so nervous.

(32) The girls exit stage right.

Scene 3

(33) [JESSICA *reenters the cosmetics store from stage right. She stops at the shelf of lipsticks and looks around.* SALES CLERK *enters from stage left.*]

(34) JESSICA: Excuse me ...

(35) SALES CLERK: [*stopping*] Did you need help with something?

(36) JESSICA: Yes. [*She looks at the floor.*] My friend who was just with me, um, she took—well, actually, she stole two tubes of lipstick. I'm not okay with that. So, um, I wanted to pay for them.

(37) SALES CLERK: That's impressive. I've never seen that happen before. And kids take stuff from this store all the time. What made you come back?

(38) JESSICA: [*shrugging]* I don't know. I guess it was just the right thing to do.

Refer to the passage "The Road Not Taken" to answer questions 18-20.

18. Read lines 18-20 from the poem.

Two roads diverged in a wood, and I—
I took the one less travelled by,
And that has made all the difference.

What can the reader infer from these sentences?

a. The speaker wants to follow the crowd and be the same as others.
b. The decision the speaker made had a large impact on his life.
c. The roads would have both led the speaker to the same outcome.
d. The speaker likes to make travel plans as he goes, not beforehand.

19. Read line 8 from the poem.

Because it was grassy and wanted wear;

Why is figurative language used in this description of the path?

a. To support the speaker's decision to take the more worn path
b. To describe the unique qualities of the grassier path
c. To emphasize that the path was not commonly taken by others
d. To describe the physical qualities of the woods being traveled

20. Which of the following themes is clearly present in this poem?

a. Deciding which road to take while on a hike is difficult.
b. A person can make different choices than the majority of others.
c. It is challenging to make the best of a bad decision.
d. Wondering about the choices that others have made is tempting.

Refer to the passage "The Right Thing to Do" to answer questions 21-24.

21. Which word from the passage best helps the reader understand the meaning of the term *cosmetics*, which is used in line 9?

a. Mall
b. Stealing
c. Lipstick
d. Color

22. How do Jessica's character traits impact the outcome of the play?

a. Her optimism allows her to see past her friend's mistakes and forgive her.
b. Her integrity allows her to return the lipstick and make things right.
c. Her carefree personality allows her to fit in with her friends.
d. Her stubbornness allows her to confront her friend.

23. Which two characteristics of this passage show that it is realistic fiction? Select all that apply.

a. The play takes place in a location that could be real.
b. The dialogue sounds normal and natural.
c. The play includes several stage directions.
d. The events in the story are possible.

e. The play includes more than one character.

24. What does the conversation in lines 20 through 28 reveal about Amy?

a. Amy disagrees with the decision being made by the clerk.
b. Amy has a strong moral compass and makes good choices.
c. Amy wants to be liked by her peers regardless of the consequences.
d. Amy is manipulative and pressures others into doing what she wants.

Refer to the passages "The Road Not Taken" and "The Right Thing to Do" to answer questions 25-27.

25. What theme is found in both "The Road Not Taken" and "The Right Thing to Do"?

a. Doing the right thing is always beneficial.
b. Sometimes we must do what others do not.
c. There is conflict between good and bad.
d. Appearances can be deceiving.

26. Compare scene 3 of "The Right Thing to Do" with lines 14 and 15 of "The Road Not Taken." How are the actions of the characters different?

a. Jessica is able to make up for something that has been done, while the speaker in the poem wants to but cannot.
b. The speaker in the poem does not return to the start of the woods to change his decision, while Jessica returns to do what she had decided is right.
c. Jessica is able to explain why she made the choice she did, while the speaker of the poem is not able to do so.
d. The speaker in the poem cannot control his own actions, while Jessica cannot control the actions of her friend.

27. Which idea is suggested by the writer of "The Road Not Taken" and the author of "The Right Thing to Do"?

a. Doing as others do is usually the best choice.
b. It is sometimes better not to conform.
c. Rules do not apply evenly to all people.
d. Decisions should be simple to make.

Extended Response

Your STAAR test will include the following instructions for your extended response question. The response prompts used here are similar to the prompts you will see on the STAAR test.

28. Read the passages "The Road Not Taken" and "The Right Thing to Do." Based on the information in the passages, write a response to the following:

Argue whether or not it is best to make the same choices as the people around you.

Write a well-organized argumentative composition that uses specific evidence from the passages to support your answer.

Remember to —

- clearly state your thesis
- organize your writing
- develop your ideas in detail
- use evidence from the selection in your response
- use correct spelling, capitalization, punctuation, and grammar

Manage your time carefully so that you can —

- review the selection
- plan your response
- write your response
- revise and edit your response

Revising

Savannah wrote the following paper about a local Greek Festival. Read the following paper and note the revisions that Savannah should make. Once you have read her paper, answer the questions that follow it.

The Greek Festival

(1) Every October my family attends the Greek Festival at the Greek Orthodox Church close to our house. (2) We were first invited four years ago by one of my friends, Amelia. (3) Her family attends the Greek Orthodox Church and works several booths at the festival each year. (4) They told us that everyone was welcome and encouraged us to attend.

(5) When we first arrived at the festival, we could hear it from the parking lot. (6) It was music that I had never heard before, and some of it was in another language. (7) Amelia told me later that it was traditional Greek music. (8) We also noticed the smells that seemed to come from all over the festival grounds.

(9) All around us, there were signs for meat, pastry, coffee drinks, and other side dishes. (10) My mom's favorite was the grape leaves, and my dad loved the baklava, though my mom preferred the grape leaves. (11) It is a dessert that is made of baked thin sheets of pastry dough covered in a sweet sauce that tastes like honey. (12) Amelia suggested that we eat it with ice cream and chocolate sauce. (13) As much as I liked the baklava, my favorite was the gyro pita. (14) Gyro is lamb meat in a warm pita with tomato, lettuce, onion, and a Greek sauce. (15) I ate two pitas, and they were delicious!

(16) After we had eaten, everyone gathered around the dance floor and watched as people from all different age groups danced traditional Greek dances. (17) The dancers were dressed in special clothing and black dress shoes. (18) The dances were different from any I had seen before, but I still thought they were beautiful and fun to watch. (19) I wish we had gotten to learn them while we were there. (20) As we watched the dancers, Amelia's mom told us the purpose of the dances in Greek culture.

(21) Amelia danced in the second group of dancers, and her mom tossed money toward her. (22) Soon, the dance floor was covered in dollar bills from all of the dancers' families. (23) The food was great, the music was fun, and the dancing was even better. (24) As fun as the festival was, we had to go home right after the dancing ended.

29. Which of the following phrases should be used in place of *it* in sentence 5?

a. the people making food
b. the music
c. the dancing
d. the Greek Orthodox Church

30. Sentence 10 is repetitive. On the lines below, rewrite sentence 10 in a way that is clear and not repetitive.

____

____

____

31. Which of the following sentences should be removed from paragraph 4?

a. Sentence 17
b. Sentence 18
c. Sentence 19
d. Sentence 20

32. Sentence 24 is not the best concluding sentence for this paper. Which of the following sentences should be used to replace sentence 24?

a. By the time we got home, I was exhausted from all of the fun that we had.
b. We complimented Amelia's dancing and said goodbye to her family, and then we left.
c. I asked Amelia when the next festival would be, but she has to wait to find out.
d. We had a great time at the Greek Festival, and now I look forward to it every year!

Darien wrote the following paper about his experience as a volunteer. Read the following paper and note the revisions that Darien should make. Once you have read his paper, answer the questions that follow it.

Volunteer Fisherman

(1) As a new volunteer at the youth center, I was expected to help out with activities, like the upcoming fishing field trip. (2) When the director asked me to come along, I accepted right away. (3) I had never been fishing, but it looked easy enough on TV. (4) You just tossed a line into the water and waited for a fish to bite. (5) How hard could that be? (6) It ended up being hard. (7) It was much harder than I expected.

(8) Upon arrival at the Turner Family Trout Farm, I was assigned three rambunctious kindergartners as my responsibility for the day. (9) Keeping them together while herding them toward the equipment shed took every ounce of my focus and every shred of my patience. (10) Finally, we found ourselves in line for poles and bait.

(11) Once we had collected our poles and bait, we marched our way to an empty spot on the rocky banks of a green-black pond. (12) I ordered the boys to line up so that I could bait their hooks. (13) When the first one thrust his red plastic cup full of soil and writhing nightcrawlers into my face, I almost gagged. (14) I looked away and plunged my fingers into the dirt, closing them on the first worm I could find. (15) I pulled him from the dirt and held him up triumphantly. (16) The boys clapped and cheered. (17) Success!

(18) I soon learned that pulling the worm from the plastic cup was one of the easiest parts of fishing. (19) When I finally got hold of the worm, I found that the hook would not penetrate its tough skin. (20) Baiting the hook posed a whole new set of challenges. (21) The worm curled its slimy ridges eagerly around my dirty fingers so I could not keep hold of it. (22) I poked my finger three times before I finally got the worm onto the hook. (23) I breathed a sigh of relief before I realized that I had two more hooks to bait.

(24) With all of the hooks baited, I tried casting the first rod. (25) The hook plopped into the water about two feet out—not the 30-foot cast I had envisioned—and to my horror, the worm floated away. (26) I baited the hook again in discouraged disgust and finally got all the lines cast about five feet out. (27) My fishing wouldn't win any awards, but the kindergarteners were happy, and that was good enough for me.

(28) After nearly an hour of our fishing adventure had passed, we had three trout awkwardly dangling from our lines. (29) The boys were thrilled, and I was exhausted. (30) Between baiting hooks, reeling in catches, and keeping the boys from falling into the pond, my energy was spent. (31) But when the whistle blew to load the bus for the trip home, I felt strangely saddened. (32) Despite the headaches and harrowing challenges, I was proud of all I had accomplished that day. (33) And I knew that the next time they needed a volunteer fisherman, I would be the first to sign up!

33. Which of the following shows the best way to combine sentences 6 and 7?

a. It ended up being hard; it was much harder than I expected.
b. It ended up being hard, so it was much harder than I expected.
c. It ended up being much harder than I expected.
d. It ended up being very hard, much harder than I expected.

34. Which of the following would be the best supporting detail to add after sentence 8?

a. They were tense with excited energy and frequently ran off in various directions.
b. Everyone had to help at least two students out, no matter how old the students were.
c. They were all boys, and only one of them had been fishing before.
d. I introduced myself to them and learned each of their names before we started fishing.

35. Where should sentence 19 be placed to improve the organization of this essay?

a. It should not be moved
b. Before sentence 18
c. After sentence 21
d. After sentence 23

36. Which of the following transition words should be added at the beginning of sentence 24?

a. *Lastly*
b. *However*
c. *Interestingly*
d. *Finally*

Editing

Nia is writing an essay about growing tomatoes. Read the following paragraphs from the body of Nia's essay and look for errors that she needs to correct. Once you have read the paragraphs, answer the questions that follow them.

Cultivating Tomatoes

(1) Tomato plants should be started in window boxes or greenhouses in late march. (2) This allows them to be ready for the garden after the last frost. (3) Gardeners should start tomato plants in a soil of equal parts of sand, peat moss, and manure. (4) They should also planted the seeds about a quarter of an inch deep. (5) After covering the plants, gardeners should water it through a cloth to protect the soil, then cover the box with a pane of glass. (6) The box should be kept in a warm place for a few days, then placed in a sunny window. (7) After the second leaf makes its appearance on the seedling gardeners should move the plant to another box. (8) The seedlings should be placed two inches apart in the new box.

37. Which change would correct the mistake in sentence 1?

a. Change *be* to *have been.*
b. Add a comma after *boxes.*
c. Change *greenhouses* to *green houses.*
d. Change *march* to *March.*

38. Which change would correct the mistake in sentence 4?

a. Change *They* to *He.*
b. Change *planted* to *plant.*
c. Add a comma after *seeds.*
d. Change *of* to *to.*

39. Which change would correct the mistake in sentence 5?

a. Change *covering* to *covered.*
b. Remove the comma after *plants.*
c. Change *it* to *them.*
d. Change *then* to *than.*

40. Which change would correct the mistake in sentence 7?

a. Change *its* to *it's.*
b. Change *appearance* to *apearance.*
c. Add a comma after *seedling.*
d. Change *move* to *moved.*

41. Which change is needed in sentence 8?

a. Change *seedlings* to *seedling.*
b. Add a comma after *placed.*
c. Change *in* to *on.*
d. No change is needed in sentence 8.

Luke is writing an essay about his favorite season. Read the first two paragraphs of Luke's essay and look for errors that he needs to correct. Once you have read the paragraphs, answer the questions that follow them.

The Best Season of the Year

(1) Ice cream cones shrink and drip in the stifling heat. (2) Cool pools shimmer like a welcoming oasis. (3) The blazing sun hangs lazily for hours in the breathtakingly blue sky. (4) It's summer and the whole world seems more content. (5) Summer is the very best season for three main reasons.

(6) First, summer is the best season because school is out, and the days of summer is long and lazy. (7) Without structure and schedule, the nights are late and the afternoons roll on forever. (8) There is no homework, and there is also neither pressure or deadlines. (9) Their is no blaring alarm clock, just the endless cadence of birds and sprinklers and kids playing in the streets. (10) Everything feels simpler and more relaxed.

42. Which change would correct the mistake in sentence 4?

a. Change *It's* to *its.*
b. Add a comma after *summer.*
c. Change *whole* to *hole.*
d. Change *more* to *most.*

43. Which change would correct the mistake in sentence 6?

a. Remove the comma after *First.*
b. Change *school* to *School.*
c. Change *days* to *day's.*
d. Change *is long* to *are long.*

44. Which change would correct the mistake in sentence 8?

a. Change *There* to *Their.*
b. Remove the comma after *homework.*
c. Change *there is also* to *there are also.*
d. Change *or* to *nor.*

45. Select the correct word to use in sentence 9.

_________ is no blaring alarm clock, just the endless cadence of birds and sprinklers and kids playing in the streets.

There
Their
They're
There's

Answer Key and Explanations for Test #1

Reading

1. B: TEKS Standard (7.5)(C)

Based on paragraphs 21 and 22, the reader can predict that the main character will enjoy this season regardless of the outcome. In paragraph 21, the narrator expresses his joy while playing baseball during the summer in a casual setting. In paragraph 22, he writes that he was smiling and having fun. This shows that choice B is correct. Although the narrator hit his "first homerun" in paragraph 22, there is no suggestion in paragraphs 21 and 22 that this will continue throughout the season. This shows that choice A is incorrect. Paragraphs 21 and 22 do not discuss the narrator's performance in centerfield, so no prediction about this can be made and choice C is incorrect. Paragraphs 21 and 22 show that the narrator is excited and happy. Choice D suggests the opposite, so it is incorrect.

2. A: TEKS Standard (7.9)(E)

The narrator thinks that the team's loss was his fault. This is shown when he says "I felt like I had let everyone down and disappointed all of my teammates." Because he felt like this, he became overly committed to practicing. Choice B is incorrect because the passage does not tell the reader the thoughts or feelings of the other teammates. It only shows how the narrator thinks they feel. Choice C is incorrect because first-person point of view allows readers to understand the narrator's inner thoughts and feelings. The fact that the narrator's mother told her son to stop practicing could be told to the reader using any point of view. Choice D is incorrect for the same reason. The fact that they played baseball without keeping score could be known by the reader no matter which point of view was used to tell the story.

3. D: TEKS Standard (7.7)(C)

Paragraph 9 builds suspense by giving details about what occurred right before an important event in the story. In this case, the event is the result of the narrator's swing. This leads up to the moment that he realizes he missed the ball and struck out. Choice D is correct. This paragraph does not mention the narrator's mother or foreshadow that she will make him stop playing baseball. This means that choice A is incorrect. Choice B is incorrect because that narrator is called to bat in paragraph 6. Choice C is incorrect because paragraph 8 describes the narrator's first two swings. These events lead up to the event in paragraph 9, so they are not unrelated and they do not create a cliffhanger.

4. C: TEKS Standard (7.5)(G)

The narrator's mother explains that "there is more to life than baseball," which shows that she thinks her son is investing too much of his time in practicing baseball. She also explains that she would prefer that he spend "the summer playing with friends." This shows that she wants him to socialize with his friends. Choice C is correct. While the narrator's mother wants the narrator to spend more time with his friends, the passage does not show that she does not want him to play baseball. Choice A is incorrect. While the narrator's mother does want her son to spend more time with his friends, she does not want him to be focused on baseball, so choice B is incorrect. The passage does not show that the narrator's mother wants her son to stop practicing because she thinks he is already great at baseball. This makes choice D incorrect.

5. A: TEKS Standard (7.5)(H)

In paragraph 5, the narrator is shocked to have heard his coach call him up to bat. Since he is surprised by this, the reader can infer that this does not usually happen, so choice A is correct. Paragraphs 4 and 5 do not say that he was startled by the coach calling his name. They also do not say that the narrator was confused, so choice B is incorrect. Paragraphs 4 and 5 do not show that the narrator often imagines things, so choice C is incorrect. While the narrator thought he might have imagined the coach calling his name, these paragraphs do not show that he did not want to bat. They also do not show that he was hoping he had imagined the coach calling to him, so choice D is incorrect.

6. D: TEKS Standard (7.7)(D)

The fact that the narrator was playing until it was dark out and late enough for dinner shows that he was extremely dedicated to getting better at batting. This shows that choice D is correct. The paragraph does explain the conditions the narrator is practicing in. However, the conditions do not show the narrator's character development on their own, so choice A is incorrect. Choice B is incorrect because the setting does not prove that the mother's reaction was the right one to have. The setting is at the narrator's home, where his mother tells him to stop practicing. This does not increase the pressure on the narrator, so choice C is incorrect.

7. C: TEKS Standard (7.5)(F)

In paragraph 5, the narrator was shocked to see that he was not imagining the coach calling him up to bat. In the preceding paragraphs, the narrator shows the reader that there is tension at the baseball game. The next batter could help the team by scoring and making them more likely to win. However, the next batter could also hurt the team by striking out and making them more likely to lose. The next batter's success was very important. The reader can conclude that Max was surprised that the coach was calling him up to bat at such an important moment, so choice C is correct. Choice A is incorrect because the narrator does not suggest that the heat was so severe that it would cause confusion for the people outside. Choice B is incorrect because the narrator's reaction comes after the coach calls on him, not when he sees that his team is losing. Choice D is incorrect because the narrator does not give information that suggests that he did not expect Philip to score.

8. A: TEKS Standard (7.9)(F)

Max and the pitcher are both under pressure. Max wants to hit the ball and help his team, and the pitcher wants to help his own team by not letting Max hit the ball. The mood is tense because the author has created a situation that causes tension and pressure for the characters. Choices B and D are incorrect because none of the details in the passage suggest that the characters are angry or sad. Their emotions are not shown. Instead, they appear to be focused on the game. Choice C is incorrect because paragraph 9 describes a situation that is uncomfortable for the narrator and the pitcher, since they are under pressure.

9. TEKS Standard (7.2)(B)

In paragraph 15, the narrator asks his mother if they can install lights in the backyard to help him see better at night. This shows that the narrator is asking his mother if they can add something that was not there before. The word *install* has a similar meaning to "put in," "add," or "establish." These definitions match the meaning suggested in paragraph 15. The correct answer should be similar to these examples and make sense based on the usage of the word in the passage.

10. D: TEKS Standard (7.5)(H)

This passage describes the roles that bees play and explains how they benefit the Earth's inhabitants. The passage shows that bees keep the systems that provide people with food stable, and that bees help flowers and animals get the things they need. Therefore, the reader can infer that protecting bees benefits everyone, so choice D is correct. Choice A is incorrect because the statements in the passage do not suggest that losing all bees is unpreventable. Choice B is also incorrect. The passage mentions that plants would have to be hand pollinated by humans if bees went extinct. However, the passage describes other roles that pollinators play, so it cannot be assumed that they can be replaced by people. Bees support crops by pollinating the plants and assisting in reproduction. The passage does not suggest that their behavior can destroy or harm crops, so choice C is incorrect.

11. B: TEKS Standard (7.6)(C)

The passage defines biodiversity as "the variety of life found on Earth" and explains that this refers to all living organisms. Bees' ability to help create supportive homes for a variety of living organisms through seed dispersal best demonstrates their role in supporting biodiversity. This makes choice B correct. Choice A defines the process of pollination. It does not show that bees support a wide variety of organisms, so it is incorrect. Choices C and D are incorrect as they only focus on bees' role in food production. These statements do not show that bees make it possible for a wide variety of organisms to live as clearly as choice B does, so choices C and D are incorrect.

12. A: TEKS Standard (7.8)(Diii)

The third paragraph uses a cause-and-effect structure to explain what would happen to farmers and the economy if the bee population declined. The loss of bees would cause fewer plants to grow, causing food prices to rise. It would also require farms to pay for plants to be manually pollinated. Choice B is incorrect. The importance of bees in food webs is explained in paragraph 4. Choice C is incorrect. While manual pollination is mentioned in paragraph 3, the structure of the paragraph does not outline the process. Paragraph 3 does not contain solutions for increasing the bee population, making choice D incorrect.

13. C: TEKS Standard (7.9)(A)

The author most likely wrote this passage to highlight the worldwide impact of bees. The passage explains how bees can support all forms of life, so choice C is correct. Choice A is incorrect. This passage does not explain any harmful, or otherwise negative, effects of bees. The movement of bees is discussed and explained as important in both pollinating and seed dispersal. However, this is not the main message of the passage. This makes choice B incorrect. The author does not discuss people's appreciation of bees in the passage. In fact, the author suggests that some people find them to be a nuisance, making choice D incorrect.

14. C: TEKS Standard (7.8)(Di)

The passage explains why plants and animals are dependent on bees for survival. The introduction also states that bees support animal and plant life, so C is the best answer. Choice A comes from the third paragraph and does not show the purpose of the entire passage. Choice B refers to the biodiversity explained in paragraph five, which is also a detail and not the point of the whole passage. Choice D is incorrect. The efficiency of bees is referenced in the passage, but it is not what the passage is about.

15. B: TEKS Standard (7.5)(G)

The idea that bees are an essential part of the ecosystem is supported by the statement that bees are responsible for 80% of global pollination. This shows the widespread need for bees. Choice A shows that the loss of bees could have a financial impact on farmers, not the ecosystem. This makes choice A incorrect. Choice C shows that bees can support biodiversity, but it does not show that biodiversity and bees' role in it are essential to preserving the ecosystem. Choice C is incorrect. Choice D describes another important role bees play, but it is incorrect because it does not explain the global impact of seed dispersal.

16. B: TEKS Standard (7.6)(D)

Choice B best summarizes the passage. It covers the main ideas from the passage, including the fact that bees support human life, animal life, and habitats. It also explains that the world would be different without bees. Choice A is incorrect because it only focuses on the economic issues associated with the loss of bees. Choice C is incorrect because it is only focused on how bees support biodiversity. Choice D discusses the food web and the roles bees play, but doesn't mention any other ways bees support the environment, so it is incorrect. Choices A, C, and D only discuss one idea from the passage, while choice B summarizes all of these ideas.

17. B: TEKS Standard (7.9)(B)

The cause-and-effect structure shows the reader what effects a decline in the bee population may have. This allows the reader to understand what the world would be like without bees, so choice B is correct. While the passage describes connections between humans and animals, this is not the purpose of the passage. It is also not made clear by the cause-and-effect structure, so choice A is incorrect. Choice C is incorrect because the passage does not present bees as a solution to pollination problems. Instead, it describes changes in bee populations as the problem. Though the passage explains why bees are important to both humans and animals, this is not explained through causes and effects, so choice D incorrect.

18. B: TEKS Standard (7.5)(F)

The poem uses roads and traveling as metaphors for making decisions in life. The speaker had to choose between two life paths. In line 20, he states that the path he chose "made all the difference." This demonstrates that the path he chose impacted his life in a large way and that the outcome would likely have been different if he had chosen the other path. Line 19 states that the speaker "took the road less travelled by," meaning fewer people had taken that path than the other one. This shows that choice A is incorrect, since the speaker did not follow the crowd or want to be the same as others. Because the road he picked "made all the difference," choice C is incorrect. Choosing the other road would have had a different outcome. Choice D is incorrect because the traveling mentioned in the poem is not literal.

19. C: TEKS Standard (7.9)(D)

The poet uses personification to describe the grassy path by saying it "wanted wear." The fact that it is both grassy and "wanting wear" shows that the path was not commonly walked by others, so choice C is correct. Choice A is incorrect. Later in the poem, the speaker decides to take the path less traveled, not the more worn path as indicated in the answer choice. Choice B is incorrect. While the statement does describe the physical qualities of the path, the poet's intent was to demonstrate that the path had not been heavily traveled. Similarly, the line is not intended to describe the woods being traveled, making choice D incorrect.

20. B: TEKS Standard (7.7)(A)

This poem describes a speaker choosing to walk down a path that has not been walked by many others. This means that the speaker has chosen an option that is not often chosen by other people. This supports the theme in choice B, so it is correct. Choice A is incorrect because the speaker does not have a difficult time choosing a path, though he thinks about each one for a while. The statement in choice A is also not a theme, since it is very specific and is not true for most people. Choice C is incorrect because the poem does not suggest that the speaker's decision was a bad one. Choice D is incorrect because the speaker does not give much thought to the choices others have made. He observes that most people have chosen the first path. However, he does not wonder about the choices they have made, and he is not tempted to do so.

21. C: TEKS Standard (7.2)(B)

In line 9, the girls enter a cosmetics store where they look at a shelf of lipstick. This helps the reader understand that lipstick is a type of cosmetic. From this, the reader may be able to tell that cosmetics are makeup or beauty products. Choice A is incorrect because a mall contains many different stores with different types of products, so the word *mall* does not tell the reader what cosmetics are. Choice B is incorrect because the fact that Amy steals something does not show the reader what cosmetics are. Choice D is incorrect because many different products have a color or come in different colors, so the word *color* does not show what cosmetics are.

22. B: TEKS Standard (7.7)(B)

In scene 3, Jessica returns to the store to pay for the lipstick her friend stole. This demonstrates her strong integrity, which means she does the right thing no matter what the consequences may be. Jessica is not portrayed as optimistic, and she does not overlook her friend's poor choices. This makes choice A incorrect. Choice C is incorrect. Jessica chooses not to conform to what her friend is doing when she returns to pay for the stolen lipstick. It is also clear that Amy's choice to steal the lipstick has upset her. This demonstrates that she is not carefree. Though Jessica confronted her friend about stealing, it was because she wanted to do what was right, not because she is stubborn. Therefore, choice D is incorrect.

23. A, D: TEKS Standard (7.8)(A)

Realistic fiction takes place in settings that can exist in real life. This play takes place at a mall, which is a commonly appearing location in real life, so choice A is correct. Stories in the genre of realistic fiction include events that could really happen to the average person. The events should be things that can occur in an everyday setting to believable characters. This makes choice D correct. While the passage and other realistic fiction works contain normal and natural dialogue, this is not only seen in realistic fiction. Normal-sounding dialogue can be found in many types of fiction writing, so choice B is incorrect. Stage directions are found in scripts for plays. They tell the person acting as the character what to do. Choice E is incorrect because stories in any genre may include more than one character.

24. D: TEKS Standard (7.8)(C)

In the conversation that takes place in lines 20 through 28, Amy is pressuring Jessica into stealing. She implies that they cannot be friends if Jessica stops her from stealing the lipstick. This shows that Amy is manipulative, as she tries to control others to get what she wants. No decisions made by the clerk are discussed in lines 20-28, which makes choice A incorrect. Because Amy is stealing and pressuring her friend to steal as well, she does not have strong morals or make good choices. This makes choice B incorrect. Choice C is incorrect. While it is clear that Amy is not worried about the consequences of stealing, it is not clear that she is stealing so that she will be liked by her peers.

25. B: TEKS Standard (7.5)(E)

In both passages, the main character decides to make a choice that others have not. The speaker in "The Road Not Taken" chooses to take the path that others do not. In "The Right Thing to Do," Jessica chooses not to steal, unlike Amy. She also returns to the store to make amends. This makes B the correct answer. In "The Road Not Taken," there is not a "right thing" to do like there is in the play. This makes choice A incorrect. Similarly, choosing either path is not morally good or bad in "The Road Not Taken," making choice C incorrect. Neither passage show things that are not as they appear, so choice D is incorrect.

26. B: TEKS Standard (7.5)(E)

In lines 14 and 15 of "The Road Not Taken," the speaker expresses that he will not return to the beginning of the path to walk the other one. In scene 3 of "The Right Thing to Do," Jessica returns to the store to do the right thing. These events show that choice B is correct. The speaker of the poem does not mention a desire to make up for something, so choice A is incorrect. Choice C is incorrect. Jessica is not able to explain exactly why she made the choice she did, while the speaker in the poem explains why he chose the less-travelled path. In the poem, the speaker can control his own actions, making choice D incorrect.

27. B: TEKS Standard (7.5)(E)

In both passages, a main character chooses to do something that is different from what others have often chosen. The speaker in "The Road Not Taken" decides to take a path that others do not. Jessica in "The Right Thing to Do" decides not to steal with her friend and reports the theft while offering to pay. The sales clerk also points out that Jessica's behavior is different from the behavior of other kids who visit the store. Both passages show a character who chooses not to conform, change their behaviors or choices to fit in, or do what others do or expect, so choice B is correct. This leads to the speaker in the poem making a major life decision and Jessica in the play being praised for her choices. Choice A is incorrect as it is contrary to what the speaker of the poem and Jessica chose. Neither character did as others had. Choice C is incorrect because neither passage mentions rules and how they apply to people. The decisions that had to be made were not simple to those making them, so choice D is incorrect.

Extended Response

28. TEKS Standard (7.11)(C)

Please use the rubric below to make sure your response meets these criteria. Try to have a friend or family member grade your response for you or take a break after writing your response and return to grade it yourself with fresh eyes.

Below is an excerpt of the STAAR Grades 6-EII Argumentative/Opinion Writing Rubric.

Score Point	Development and Organization of Ideas
3	• **Argument/opinion is clear and fully developed** The argument/opinion is clearly identifiable. The focus is consistent throughout, creating a response that is unified and easy to follow. • **Organization is effective** A purposeful structure that includes an effective introduction and conclusion is evident. The organizational structure is appropriate and effectively supports the development of the argument/opinion. The sentences, paragraphs, or ideas are logically connected in purposeful and highly effective ways. • **Evidence is specific, well chosen, and relevant** The response includes relevant text-based evidence that is clearly explained and consistently supports and develops the argument/opinion. For pairs in grades 6 through EII, evidence is drawn from both texts. The response reflects a thorough understanding of the writing purpose. • **Expression of ideas is clear and effective** The writer's word choice is specific, purposeful, and enhances the response. Almost all sentences and phrases are effectively crafted to convey the writer's ideas and contribute to the overall quality of the response and the clarity of the message.

Score Point	Conventions
2	Student writing demonstrates **consistent command** of grade-level-appropriate conventions, including correct: • sentence construction • punctuation • capitalization • grammar • spelling The response has few errors, but those errors do not impact the clarity of the writing.

Revising

29. B: TEKS Standard (7.10)(C)

Sentence 5 says that, as the author and her family arrived at the festival, they could hear something. Sentences 6 and 7 describe the music at the festival. These two sentences show that the author and her family could hear the music from the parking lot, so choice B is correct. Choice A is incorrect because the paragraph describes the sound of the music and the smell of the food. The passage does not suggest that the people making food were loud enough to be heard from the parking lot. Choice C is incorrect because the dancing did not take place until after the author and her family had been at the festival for some time. Choice D is incorrect because the church is not something that makes noise.

30. TEKS Standard (7.10)(C)

In sentence 10, the author says that her mother's favorite food at the festival was the grape leaves and that her father loved the baklava. However, the sentence then says that the author's mother preferred the grape leaves to the baklava. This information does not need to be repeated. A revised version of the sentence will be similar to the following example: "My mom's favorite was the grape leaves, and my dad loved the baklava." The sentence should include the fact that the author's mother's favorite food was the grape leaves and that her father loved the baklava. The sentence should also be complete, clear, grammatically correct, and avoid repeating information.

31. C: TEKS Standard (7.10)(Bii)

Paragraph 4 describes the dancing that happens at the festival. All of the sentences, except for sentence 19, give information about the dancers, the dances, or the reasons that the author enjoyed the dances. Sentence 19 states that the author wanted to learn some of the dances. This sentence does not support the other sentences in the paragraph. It is also unnecessary, so it should be removed. Choice A is incorrect because sentence 17 describes the dancers' clothes. Choice B is incorrect because sentence 18 explains that the dances were new to the author and that they were enjoyable. Choice D is incorrect because it shows that the dances are important in Greek culture. The details in sentences 17, 18, and 20 all help the reader understand the dances and the festival, so they are needed in paragraph 4.

32. D: TEKS Standard (7.10)(Bi)

Choice D is the best concluding sentence for this paper because it summarizes the author's thoughts about the festival and clearly concludes the paper. It includes the details that the author enjoyed the Greek Festival and likes to go every year. These details are related to the rest of the paper and help the reader understand the author's final thoughts on the topic. Choice A is incorrect because it does not clearly conclude the paper. It also introduces a new idea that has not been discussed in the paper. Choice B is incorrect because it does not summarize the ideas in the essay or show that the essay is at its conclusion. Choice C is incorrect because it introduces a new idea and does not conclude the paper effectively.

33. C: TEKS Standard (7.10)(C)

Choice C is correct because it is a complete sentence, is grammatically correct, and does not repeat information. It includes the information from sentence 6 and sentence 7 and is clear. Choice A is incorrect because it is repetitive. Choice A correctly uses a semicolon, but it says that the task was hard twice. Choice B is incorrect because it misuses a coordinating conjunction and is repetitive. The coordinating conjunction *so* is used to show that one idea caused another idea. The fact that the task was hard did not cause it to be harder than the author expected. Choice D is incorrect because it is repetitive. The sentence states that the task was hard two times when this information should only be stated once.

34. A: TEKS Standard (7.10)(Bii)

Choice A describes the three kindergarteners' behavior, which helps the reader understand how they were rambunctious. Choice A and shows what the kindergarteners were doing that caused the author to struggle to keep them together in sentence 9. Choice A is the best choice because it helps the reader understand the events and it connects the events in sentences 8 and 9. Choices B, C, and D are incorrect because they do not help the reader understand the events in the story. All three of these sentences include a detail that is unneeded for the story to make sense and be clear.

35. C: TEKS Standard (7.10)(Bi)

Sentence 19 is found in paragraph 4, which describes the author's experience with putting the worms on the fishing hooks. Sentence 18 introduces the paragraph, and Sentence 19 says that the fishing hook would not go through the worm's skin. However, sentence 20 says that baiting the hook came with many challenges. In a well-organized paragraph, the sentences describing the challenges would follow this sentence. The fact that it was difficult to put the worm on the hook is one of those challenges. Sentence 21 describes a challenge that the speaker experienced before the challenge described in sentence 19. The best place for sentence 19 is after sentence 21, since sentence 19 describes a challenge and events that happened after the events in sentence 21, so choice C is correct. Sentence 19 should not go after sentence 23 because the event in sentence 23 happens after the event in sentence 19, so choice D is incorrect.

36. D: TEKS Standard (7.10)(Bi)

The word *finally* is the best word to add at the beginning of sentence 24. Paragraph 4 shows that it took the author a long time to bait just one hook. In sentence 24, the author has baited all three hooks, so the reader can conclude that much time has passed before the event in this sentence. *Finally* is a word that is used to show that something has happened after a long time of waiting for it to happen, so choice D is correct. Choice A is incorrect because *lastly* is used to show that what is being described is the last part, step, or event. The author faces more challenges and completes more tasks after sentence 24, so *lastly* is not the best choice. Choice B is incorrect because the word *however* is used to show contrast between two ideas or events. The events in sentence 23 lead to the events in sentence 24, they do not oppose or contrast them. Choice C is incorrect because it does not show the connection between sentences 23 and 24, so it is not an effective transition here.

Editing

37. D: TEKS Standard (7.10)(Dvii)

Months are proper nouns, so their names must be capitalized. This makes choice D correct, since *march* should be changed to *March*. Choice A is incorrect because the phrase *have been* refers to the past. Sentence 1 is written in present tense, so the verb *be* is used correctly. Choice B is incorrect because a comma is not needed after the word *boxes*. Sentence 1 contains two options for places to start plants: window boxes and greenhouses. Since there are only two items in the list of options, the item before *or* does not need to be followed by a comma. Choice C is incorrect because *greenhouse* is a compound word, and *greenhouses* is the plural form of *greenhouse*. The word *greenhouses* does not need to be split into two words.

38. B: TEKS Standard (7.10)(Dii)

Sentence 4 is written in present tense, as it is describing what gardeners should do in order to grow tomato plants. *Planted* is a past tense verb, and *plant* is a present tense verb. Since the sentence is in present tense, the verb *plant* is the best choice for this sentence. Choice A is incorrect because the word *they* refers to multiple gardeners. *He* is a singular pronoun used in place of the name of a boy or man. *They* can be used to represent a plural noun, so it is the correct pronoun to use in this sentence. Choice C is incorrect because there is no need for a comma after *seeds*. There is a prepositional phrase after the word *seeds*, but commas are usually placed after prepositional phrases, not before. Choice D is incorrect because changing the word *of* to *to* would change the meaning of the sentence. The phrase "a quarter of an inch" means one fourth of the length of one inch. The phrase "a quarter to an inch" would describe a distance that is between a quarter and an inch. This change would make the meaning of the sentence incorrect and unclear.

39. C: TEKS Standard (7.10)(Dv)

The word *it* is a pronoun that can be used in the place of a singular noun. The word *them* is a pronoun that is usually used in place of a plural noun. Since the sentence is describing how the gardeners should water multiple plants, the word *them* should be used, so choice C is correct. Choice A is incorrect because the sentence tells the gardeners to complete an action. The verb *covered* would show that the gardeners have already completed the action, but this is not true. Choice B is incorrect because the comma after *plants* is needed. Usually, a comma is placed after a prepositional phrase that appears at the beginning of the sentence. The word *plants* is the last word in the prepositional phrase that started the sentence. Choice D is incorrect because changing *then* to *than* would change the meaning of the sentence. *Then* is used to show that an event occurs after another one. *Than* is used to show a comparison. The sentence is not comparing the act of protecting the soil to the act of covering the box, so *than* would not make sense in this sentence.

40. C: TEKS Standard (7.10)(Di)

Sentence 7 begins with a dependent clause: "After the second leaf makes its appearance on the seedling." When a sentence begins with a dependent clause, the clause must be followed by a comma. Since the last word of the clause is *seedling*, the comma must be placed after *seedling*. Choice A is incorrect because *it's* means "it is." This change would change the meaning of the sentence and make it unclear. Choice B is incorrect because *appearance* is spelled with two *p*s, not one. Choice D is incorrect because *moved* is a past tense verb. The sentence instructs gardeners to move the plants, so the gardeners have not moved the plants in the past.

41. D: TEKS Standard (7.10)(D)

Sentence 8 does not contain any spelling errors or grammatical mistakes, so choice D is correct. Sentence 8 is about multiple seedlings, so changing *seedlings* to the singular noun *seedling* is not the right choice, and choice A is incorrect. Choice B is incorrect because there is no need for a comma after *placed*. *Placed* is the last word of an independent clause. Since sentence 8 is not a compound sentence, the independent clause can be written without a comma at the end. Choice C is incorrect because the plants are being placed inside of the box, not on top of the box. Changing *in* to *on* in sentence 8 would make the meaning of the sentence incorrect.

42. B: TEKS Standard (7.10)(Dviii)

Sentence 4 is a compound sentence. Compound sentences are made of two independent clauses, which must be linked using either a semicolon or a comma and a coordinating conjunction. Sentence 4 currently includes two independent clauses and a coordinating conjunction, *and*. The sentence does not contain a comma, so one should be placed between the words *summer* and *and*. Choice B is correct. Choice A is incorrect because *it's* is a contraction for "it is" and *its* is a possessive pronoun that shows that an object has or owns something. The word *it's* is used correctly in this sentence, since the sentence is stating that it is summer. Choice C is incorrect because *hole* means a gap or a puncture in some material, while *whole* describes the full amount of something. Sentence 4 is describing the entire world, so *whole* is the correct word to use. Choice D is incorrect because *more* is used to compare two things while *most* is used to compare more than two things. In sentence 4, summer is being compared to the rest of the year. Summer and the rest of the year are only two things, so *more* is the best word to use in this sentence.

43. D: TEKS Standard (7.10)(Div)

Is is a singular verb, so it must be used with a singular noun. *Are* is a plural verb, so it must be used with a plural noun. The verb *is* comes after the phrase "the days of summer." Even though the words *is long* appear right after *summer*, a singular noun, they are describing *days*, a plural noun. *Is long* should be changed to *are long*, so choice D is correct. Choice A is incorrect because *first* is used as an introductory word in sentence 6, so it should be followed by a comma. Choice B is incorrect because *school* is a common noun. Sentence 6 is not talking about a specific school, so *school* is not a proper noun and should not be capitalized. Choice C is incorrect because the sentence is describing multiple days, not something that a day has or possesses.

44. D: TEKS Standard (7.10)(Dvi)

The word *neither* is used to show that two things will not happen or that two options cannot be chosen. The word *or* is used to show that one option can happen or be chosen, while the other cannot. The word *nor* shows that two options cannot happen or be chosen. Because *or* contradicts the meaning of *neither*, these words do not work well together. In sentence 8, *or* should be changed to *nor*, so choice D is correct. Choice A is incorrect because *their* is a pronoun that is used to show ownership. *Their* does not make sense in sentence 8, since no ownership is being shown. *Homework* is the last word of an independent clause. Sentence 8 is a compound sentence, and the clause "There is no homework" is the first clause in the sentence and is followed by a coordinating conjunction. In a compound sentence, a comma must be used between the first independent clause and the conjunction, so choice B is incorrect. Choice C is incorrect because *there* is used as a singular pronoun in sentence 8, and *is* is a singular verb.

45. There: TEKS Standard (7.10)(Dix)

The word *there* is used to either replace the name of a location or to show the state or position of a noun. Since the sentence is saying that a blaring alarm clock is not present. The clause "there is no blaring alarm clock" has the same meaning, so *there* is the correct answer. *Their* is a possessive pronoun that shows ownership. Sentence 9 does not show ownership, so *their* is incorrect. *They're* is a contraction of *they* and *are*. The phrase "they are is no" does not make sense and is not grammatically correct, so *they're* is not the correct answer. *There's* is a contraction of *there* and *is*. Since the word after the blank is *is*, *there's* would create a grammatical error, so it is not the correct answer.

Practice Test #2

Reading

"The Ettrick Shepherd"

by James Baldwin

(1) In Scotland there once lived a poor shepherd whose name was James Hogg. His father and grandfather and great-grandfather had all been shepherds.

(2) It was his business to take care of the sheep which belonged to a rich landholder by the Ettrick Water. Sometimes he had several hundreds of lambs to look after. He drove these to the pastures on the hills and watched them day after day while they fed on the short green grass.

(3) He had a dog which he called Sirrah. This dog helped him watch the sheep. He would drive them from place to place as his master wished. Sometimes he would take care of the whole flock while the shepherd was resting or eating his dinner.

(4) One dark night James Hogg was on the hilltop with a flock of seven hundred lambs. Sirrah was with him. Suddenly a storm came up. There was thunder and lightning; the wind blew hard; the rain poured.

(5) The poor lambs were frightened. The shepherd and his dog could not keep them together. Some of them ran towards the east, some towards the west, and some towards the south.

(6) The shepherd soon lost sight of them in the darkness. With his lighted lantern in his hand, he went up and down the rough hills calling for his lambs.

(7) Two or three other shepherds joined him in the search. All night long they sought for the lambs.

(8) Morning came and still they sought. They looked, as they thought, in every place where the lambs might have taken shelter.

(9) At last James Hogg said, "It's of no use; all we can do is to go home and tell the master that we have lost his whole flock."

(10) They had walked a mile or two towards home, when they came to the edge of a narrow and deep ravine. They looked down, and at the bottom they saw some lambs huddled together among the rocks. And there was Sirrah standing guard over them and looking all around for help. "These must be the lambs that rushed off towards the south," said James Hogg.

(11) The men hurried down and soon saw that the flock was a large one.

(12) "I really believe they are all here," said one.

(13) They counted them and were surprised to find that not one lamb of the great flock of seven hundred was missing.

(14) How had Sirrah managed to get the three scattered divisions together? How had he managed to drive all the frightened little animals into this place of safety?

(15) Nobody could answer these questions. But there was no shepherd in Scotland that could have done better than Sirrah did that night.

(16) Long afterward James Hogg said, "I never felt so grateful to any creature below the sun as I did to Sirrah that morning."

Refer to the passage "'The Ettrick Shepherd'" to answer questions 1-8.

1. How does the setting of this passage affect the plot?

a. The country this passage takes place in is the only one in which sheep and lambs are found.
b. The lack of technology at the time caused the shepherds to rely on Sirrah while searching for the lambs.
c. The farm where the passage takes place is isolated and causes James to work alone.
d. The terrain surrounding the farm included several places where the shepherds had to look for the sheep.

2. Read this section of the passage.

He had a dog which he called Sirrah. This dog helped him watch the sheep. He would drive them from place to place as his master wished. Sometimes he would take care of the whole flock while the shepherd was resting or eating his dinner.

What do these sentences help the reader understand about Sirrah?

a. His habits kept him from eating with his owner.
b. His behavior was inconsistent throughout.
c. His commitment to his owner was unchanging.
d. His energy prevented him from resting with his owner.

3. Which line from the passage best helps the reader understand that the other shepherds care for James?

a. Morning came and still they sought. They looked, as they thought, in every place where the lambs might have taken shelter.
b. Nobody could answer these questions. But there was no shepherd in Scotland that could have done better than Sirrah did that night.
c. The shepherd soon lost sight of them in the darkness. With his lighted lantern in his hand, he went up and down the rough hills calling for his lambs.
d. At last James Hogg said, "It's of no use; all we can do is to go home and tell the master that we have lost his whole flock."

4. What is the best summary of this passage?

a. James Hogg was a poor man left alone to care for the sheep of a rich man. He was to attend to them all day and night with no breaks. One night, the flock of lambs vanished. Hogg searched for them for hours before finding they had been herded by his dog, Sirrah.
b. James Hogg and his dog, Sirrah, were responsible for caring for a rich man's sheep. One stormy night, a frightened flock of lambs scattered from a hilltop in different directions. Hogg and a group of other shepherds were unable to locate the lambs after several hours of searching and were giving up. However, they soon found that the dog had located and safely herded all the lambs.
c. James Hogg was a shepherd in Scotland. He liked to work alone to care for his flock, so he did not appreciate the appearance of a dog on his farm. A storm startled a flock of lambs and caused them to run in several different directions. Hogg searched for them and eventually discovered they had been safely rescued by the dog, leading him to appreciate the dog.
d. Sirrah was a typical dog who lived and worked on a sheep farm. He helped his owner keep the flock safe from harm. During a storm, a flock of 700 lambs managed to escape the farm. Sirrah was able to track them all down and keep them safe until his owner arrived. Ever since that night, Sirrah has been regarded as the best sheepdog in Scotland.

5. What is the most likely reason James Baldwin wrote "The Ettrick Shepherd"?

a. To give an autobiographical account of a stormy night in Scotland.
b. To describe how shepherds support one another in times of need.
c. To suggest that trained dogs can replace human farmers.
d. To share a narrative of the bond between a shepherd and his dog.

6. How does the language in paragraphs 8 and 9 affect the mood of the passage?

a. It conveys a sense of frustration.
b. It expresses a feeling of hopelessness.
c. It creates a spirit of teamwork.
d. It portrays the goal as achievable.

7. Based on paragraph 16, what can the reader predict would have happened if the lambs had not been found?

a. Their owner would have replaced the herd with new lambs.
b. The shepherd would likely have been in trouble with the owner.
c. The shepherds that helped Hogg would have been held responsible.
d. The lambs would have been found and kept by other farmers.

8. Which detail from the passage supports the key idea that loyal dogs are valuable companions?

a. They looked down, and at the bottom they saw some lambs huddled together among the rocks.
b. With his lighted lantern in his hand, he went up and down the rough hills calling for his lambs.
c. But there was no shepherd in Scotland that could have done better than Sirrah did that night.
d. He drove these to the pastures on the hills and watched them day after day while they fed on the short green grass.

The Inventions of Technology

(1) Stories have been a part of the world since the beginning of recorded time. For centuries before the invention of the printing press, stories were passed down to generations through oral tradition. With the invention of the printing press, which made written material available to a wider audience, books were mass-produced and introduced into greater society.

(2) For the last several centuries, books have been at the forefront of education and entertainment. With the invention of the internet, the reliance on books for information quickly faded. Suddenly, almost everything that anyone needed to know could be accessed through the internet. Large, printed volumes of encyclopedias became unnecessary, as all of the information was easily available on the internet.

(3) Despite the progression of the internet, printed media is still very popular in the forms of both fiction and non-fiction books. While waiting for an appointment, enduring a several-hour flight, or relaxing before sleep, books have been a reliable and convenient source of entertainment that society has not been willing to give up.

(4) With the progression and extreme convenience of technology, printed books are going to soon become a thing of the past. Inventions such as the iPad and the Kindle have made the need for any kind of printed media unnecessary. With a rechargeable battery, a large screen, and the ability to have several books saved on file, electronic options will soon take over and society will no longer see printed books.

(5) Although some people may say that the act of reading is not complete without turning a page, sliding a finger across the screen or pressing a button to go to the next page is just as satisfying to the reader. The iPad and Kindle are devices that have qualities similar to a computer and can be used for so much more than just reading. These devices are therefore better than books because they have multiple uses.

(6) Due to a longstanding tradition in world culture, stories will always be an important way to communicate ideas and provide information and entertainment. Centuries ago, stories could only be passed down through speech. Printed media changed the way the world communicated and was connected, and now, as we move forward with technology, it is only a matter of time before we must say goodbye to the printed past and welcome the digital and electronic future.

The Power of Print

(1) There are many ways to engage with a book. You can listen to it on audio. You can swipe through the pages on an electronic device. You can watch a video of the author reading it aloud online. However, none of these methods will ever compare to the experience of reading a physical book.

(2) The feel of printed books is one of their primary draws. Readers like to feel the weight of the book, turn the pages, and see how much they have read at a glance. There is a sense of satisfaction gained when a reader closes a book for the final time and places it on the shelf among their collection of loved titles. Even more satisfying is the feeling of gifting a treasured book to a friend who is sure to enjoy it. While a reader can see what percentage of a book they have read and loan books for limited periods through a digital library on an electronic reader, the inability to physically see or do these things makes them unfulfilling and impersonal.

(3) On the other hand, electronic reading devices function too similarly to a phone or computer. This can give reading the feeling of being a work-related task as opposed to an enriching hobby. There are also situations in which these devices are inconvenient. Electronics should be avoided around water, meaning they should not be used for poolside or beach-day reading. They can also be difficult to see in full sun. Electronic readers require access to electricity to charge, meaning there will be times when they need power and are unusable. Books are always charged and ready to read anytime, anywhere.

(4) Opinions aside, it has been scientifically proven over several studies that reading physical materials is best for learning new information. Readers retain more information when reading a printed book than they do when reading from a screen. The act of turning a page causes the brain to map information in a way that makes it easier to remember. Similarly, it has been proven that readers recall more information when they read an article as opposed to listening to the same article in a podcast format.

(5) Overall, physical books are far superior to other methods of reading. Their physicality fulfills many needs for readers. They are always available to be pulled from a shelf and enjoyed immediately with no wait times or loading screens. Printed books are better for learning than other formats. This all goes to prove that there is nothing better than a physical book!

Refer to the passage "The Inventions of Technology" to answer questions 9-12.

9. In the selection "The Inventions of Technology," what does the chronological structure help readers understand?

a. The changes to reading technology will eventually be undone and society will return to paper copies of books.
b. The invention of e-readers was a necessary part in the evolution of education in society.
c. The changes in technology over time have influenced the way stories are passed on and read.
d. The development of electronic books is more historically significant than the printing press.

10. This question has two parts. After you answer Part A, answer Part B:

Part A: What is the main argument of this essay?

a. iPad and Kindles are easier to read than books.
b. The printing press was a great invention.
c. The internet is how people receive information.
d. Digital text will soon replace printed text.

Part B: Which sentence from the passage most clearly supports the answer to Part A?

a. Stories have been a part of the world since the beginning of recorded time.
b. Despite the progression of the internet, printed media is still very popular in the forms of both fiction and non-fiction books.
c. With the progression and extreme convenience of technology, printed books are going to soon become a thing of the past.
d. These devices are therefore better than books because they have multiple uses.

11. How does the author's reference to examples like the iPad and the Kindle support the main idea of the passage?

a. By explaining that the internet can quickly make printed books obsolete
b. By showing how technology can change how people read over time
c. By describing how stories used to be shared
d. By creating a sense of nostalgia for the time period before electronic readers

12. How does the author's organization of this essay impact his or her purpose for writing?

a. The author compares the advantages and disadvantages of using an iPad.
b. The author tells of the events that led from reading stories to oral tradition.
c. The author lists examples of technology that remove the need for books.
d. The author gives the history of storytelling in society and shows how it has changed.

Refer to the passage "The Power of Print" to answer questions 13-16.

13. What primary claim does the author make in this selection?

a. Readers should use whatever format of book appeals to them.
b. Paper copies of books are overall the best format for all reading.
c. Electronic devices can make reading more difficult.
d. Books should be read and then shared so others can enjoy them.

14. What is the most likely reason the author cites studies in the fourth paragraph?

a. To provide scientific evidence to support his or her argument
b. To highlight the beliefs of individuals who only read physical books
c. To provide factual information on the benefits of reading
d. To eliminate any counterarguments to his or her point

15. Who is the intended audience of this essay?

a. Reading teachers
b. Authors and illustrators
c. Librarians
d. Readers

16. Read this excerpt from paragraph one.

> But none of these methods will ever compare to the experience of reading a physical book.

What is the most likely reason the author uses hyperbole in this sentence?

a. To help readers better understand the point of view
b. To provide readers with a statement of factual evidence
c. To further emphasize his or her stance on physical books
d. To appeal to the reader's sense of curiosity

Refer to the passages "The Inventions of Technology" and "The Power of Print" to answer questions 17-19.

17. In what way is the author of "The Inventions of Technology" UNLIKE the author of "The Power of Print"?

a. He or she would likely think any reading is better than no reading.
b. He or she would be more open to accepting new reading formats over time.
c. He or she would probably support increasing library funding for physical books.
d. He or she would prefer to read nonfiction articles instead of fiction novels.

18. Which topic is present in both "The Inventions of Technology" and "The Power of Print"?

a. The pitfalls of electronic readers
b. The struggle of choosing a type of book
c. The debate surrounding the best format of books
d. The impact of changes in reading on education

19. The author of "The Inventions of Technology" and the author of "The Power of Print" would both most likely agree with which statement?

a. Reading as a hobby should continue through generations.
b. Reading on devices makes it easier to read anywhere you go.
c. Reading physical books is the most rewarding hobby.
d. Reading is a pastime that should not change over time.

Ten American Girls from History: Clara Barton

by Kate Dickinson Sweetser

(1) [Clara has begun her work of ministering to soldiers on the front lines of the civil war. Her tireless efforts and care have taken her to some of the most horrific battles of the war]

(2) Clara Barton!—Only the men who lay wounded or dying on the battle-field knew the thrill and the comfort that the name carried. Again and again her life was in danger—once at Antietam, when stooping to give a drink of water to an injured boy, a bullet whizzed between them. It ended the life of the poor lad, but only tore a hole in Clara Barton's sleeve. And so, again and again, it seemed as if a special Providence protected her from death or injury. At Fredericksburg, when the dead, starving and wounded lay frozen on the ground, and there was no effective organization for proper relief, with swift, silent efficiency Clara Barton moved among them, having the snow cleared away and under the banks finding famished, frozen figures which were once men. She rushed to have an old chimney torn down and built fire-blocks, over which she soon had kettles full of coffee and gruel steaming.

(3) As she was bending over a wounded rebel, he whispered to her: "Lady, you have been kind to me ... every street of the city is covered by our cannon. When your entire army has reached the other side of the Rappahannock, they will find Fredericksburg only a slaughter-pen. Not a regiment will escape. Do not go over, for you will go to certain death."

(4) She thanked him for the kindly warning and later told of the call that came to her to go across the river, and what happened. She says:

(5) "At ten o'clock of the battle day when the rebel fire was hottest, the shells rolling down every street, and the bridge under the heavy cannonade, a courier dashed over, and, rushing up the steps of the house where I was, placed in my hand a crumpled, bloody piece of paper, a request from the lion-hearted old surgeon on the opposite shore, establishing his hospitals in the very jaws of death:

(6) "'Come to me,' he wrote. 'Your place is here.'

(7) "The faces of the rough men working at my side, which eight weeks before had flushed with indignation at the thought of being controlled by a woman, grew ashy white as they guessed the nature of the summons, ... and they begged me to send them, but save myself. I could only allow them to go with me if they chose, and in twenty minutes we were rocking across the swaying bridge, the water hissing with shot on either side.

(8) "Over into that city of death, its roofs riddled by shell, its every church a crowded hospital, every street a battle-line, every hill a rampart, every rock a fortress, and every stone wall a blazing line of forts.

(9) "Oh, what a day's work was that! How those long lines of blue, rank on rank, charged over the open acres, up to the very mouths of those blazing guns, and how like grain before the sickle they fell and melted away.

(10) "An officer stepped to my side to assist me over the débris at the end of the bridge. While our hands were raised in the act of stepping down, a piece of an exploding shell hissed through between us, just below our arms, carrying away a portion of both the skirts of his coat and my dress, rolling along the ground a few rods from us like a harmless pebble in the water. The next instant a solid shot thundered over our heads, a noble steed bounded in the air and with his gallant rider rolled in the dirt not thirty feet in the rear. Leaving the kind-hearted officer, I passed on alone to the hospital. In less than a half-hour he was brought to me—dead."

(11) She was passing along a street in the heart of the city when she had to step aside to let a regiment of infantry march by. At that moment General Patrick saw her, and, thinking she was a frightened resident of the city who had been left behind in the general exodus, leaned from his saddle and said, reassuringly:

(12) "You are alone and in great danger, madam. Do you want protection?"

(13) With a rare smile, Miss Barton said, as she looked at the ranks of soldiers, "Thank you, but I think I am the best-protected woman in the United States."

Refer to the passage "Ten American Girls from History: Clara Barton" to answer questions 20-28.

20. Which two sentences suggest that Clara Barton seems to be under the care of some form of divine guidance? Select all that apply.

a. Only the men who lay wounded or dying on the battle-field knew the thrill and the comfort that the name carried.
b. And so, again and again, it seemed as if a special Providence protected her from death or injury.
c. She thanked him for the kindly warning and later told of the call that came to her to go across the river, and what happened.
d. The faces of the rough men working at my side, which eight weeks before had flushed with indignation at the thought of being controlled by a woman, grew ashy white as they guessed the nature of the summons, ... and they begged me to send them, but save myself.
e. With a rare smile, Miss Barton said, as she looked at the ranks of soldiers, "Thank you, but I think I am the best-protected woman in the United States."

21. Read the dictionary entry (from Merriam-Webster).

Charge \ chärj \v
1. to fix or ask as fee or payment
2. to place the guilt or blame for
3. to rush against
4. to command, instruct, or exhort with authority

Which definition matches the way *charged* is used in paragraph 9?

a. Definition 1
b. Definition 2
c. Definition 3
d. Definition 4

22. Read paragraph 3.

> As she was bending over a wounded rebel, he whispered to her: "Lady, you have been kind to me ... every street of the city is covered by our cannon. When your entire army has reached the other side of the Rappahannock, they will find Fredericksburg only a slaughter-pen. Not a regiment will escape. Do not go over, for you will go to certain death."

What key idea is supported by this paragraph?

a. Clara was not always trusted by the soldiers, so her life was in danger each time she went to a new location.
b. Clara relied on the soldiers to help her understand the danger in a location so she could prepare herself.
c. Clara helped wounded soldiers in dangerous locations, which put her life in jeopardy.
d. Clara did not help every soldier that she came across when she was traveling between assignments.

23. How does the character of the officer in paragraph 10 impact the conflict in Clara's story?

a. His resourcefulness prevents Clara from getting hurt while trying to cross the bridge.
b. His dedication and sad fate emphasize the danger Clara is in and the intensity of the violence around her.
c. His rank in the army allows him to be in the same location as Clara and save her from the exploding shell.
d. The kindness and unexpected passing of the officer made Clara realize life was too precious to spend it in battle.

24. Read this information about the roots of the word Providence.

> From Latin *providentia* meaning "guidance or wisdom from a higher, spiritual force"
> *pro,* meaning "ahead or before" + *videre* meaning "to see"

Based on this meaning, what does Providence mean in paragraph 2?

a. Fragile shield of armor over one's body
b. Divine protection from an all-knowing source
c. Worldly guidance from colleagues
d. Unreliable shelter from harm during battle

25. What does the third-person point of view used in this passage help the reader understand?

a. Clara's courage and dedication to a dangerous career
b. Clara's overall opinion on the war and its purpose
c. Clara's inability to care for patients who were too hurt
d. Clara's internal motivation for continuing when warned otherwise

26. In paragraph 10, what tone does the author create?

a. A resentful tone
b. A tense tone
c. A content tone
d. A passionate tone

27. What can be inferred from the fact that the men's faces turned "white" in the following sentence?

> "The faces of the rough men working at my side, which eight weeks before had flushed with indignation at the thought of being controlled by a woman, grew ashy white as they guessed the nature of the summons, ... and they begged me to send them, but save myself."

a. The men were afraid that Clara would be seriously hurt or killed by going to help.
b. The men were glad for Clara to leave so she could no longer order them around.
c. The men were terrified of the coming war and wanted Clara to escape with them.
d. The men did not want to be moved to the hospital on the other side of the bridge.

28. What could be one reason the author wrote about Clara Barton?

a. She wanted people to understand what life on the battlefield was like during the Civil War.
b. She wanted readers to get a feeling of the conditions faced by doctors and nurses practicing medicine during the Civil War.
c. She hoped to show how great a sacrifice Clara made by becoming a nurse during the war.
d. She knew that future readers would most likely not know who had fought in the war or how Clara tended to the victims.

Extended Response

Your STAAR test will include the following instructions for your extended response question. The response prompts used here are similar to the prompts you will see on the STAAR test.

29. Read the passage "Ten American Girls from History: Clara Barton." Based on the passage, write a response to the following:

Explain how Clara Barton showed selflessness as she worked as a nurse during the Civil War.

Write a well-organized informational composition that uses specific evidence from the article to support your answer.

Remember to —

- clearly state your thesis
- organize your writing
- develop your ideas in detail
- use evidence from the selection in your response
- use correct spelling, capitalization, punctuation, and grammar

Manage your time carefully so that you can —

- review the selection
- plan your response
- write your response
- revise and edit your response

Revising

Martha wrote the following paper about her experience at a dog show. Read the following paper and note the revisions that Martha should make. Once you have read her paper, answer the questions that follow it.

Dogs in the Park

(1) On Saturday, my mom took me to a dog show at the park by our house. (2) The sun was out, and it was a very warm day. (3) I ride my bike to the park almost every day in the summer. (4) The dogs were all lying in the grass when we arrived, and they looked warm in the sun. (5) One of my mom's friends, Mary, is a dog trainer, and she invited us to watch the dog show after my mom told her how much I love dogs.

(6) There were all kinds of dogs at the show. (7) Some were really little, some were big, and some had really long hair. (8) My favorite dogs were the ones in the toy and sporting categories. (9) The dogs that were waiting to be shown were with their trainers at different areas of the park getting ready. (10) Some trainers brushed their dog's hair, and some gave their dog treats.

(11) We sat on the grass and watched the show. (12) The trainers were all dressed up. (13) The men wore dress pants and jackets, and the women wore dress skirts, stockings, and blazers. (14) All of the dogs were lined up and stood still while the judges walked down and looked closely at them. (15) The judges looked at the dogs' hair, paws, and teeth. (16) Then it was time for each dog to show off. (17) Each trainer ran with their dog and held the leash high in the air. (18) The judges watched as the dogs ran, and they judged how well they turned corners and listened to their trainers.

(19) At the end of the show, the judges awarded prizes. (20) The dogs and their trainers gathered in a line, and the judges presented the winners with large ribbons. (21) Mary's dog won first place, and she was given a purple ribbon that was bigger than most of the small dogs in the toy category. (22) We left the park, and I told my mom that I wanted to attend another dog show soon.

30. Which sentence should be removed from paragraph 1?

a. Sentence 1
b. Sentence 3
c. Sentence 4
d. Sentence 5

31. On the lines below, rewrite sentence 9 so that it is clear and grammatically correct.

____

____

____

32. Which of the following sentences should be added after sentence 18 to conclude the third paragraph?

a. Our dog never listens to our commands, so she would not have done well.
b. I wondered how much time it had taken to train each dog.
c. One of the judges was very kind and smiled as each dog completed its run.
d. I was amazed by how well the dogs listened to their trainers.

33. Which of the following transition words would be best to add at the beginning of sentence 22?

a. However
b. Later
c. Otherwise
d. Consequentially

Colt wrote the following paper about his success at a baseball game. Read the following paper and note the revisions that Colt should make. Once you have read his paper, answer the questions that follow it.

Strike Three

(1) As I stared down at the hitter in the batter's box, I remembered what my dad had said to me. (2) "Shut everything else out." (3) I focused on the glove in front of me. (4) I looked into the deep, blackened pocket and saw my target. (5) The batter tapped his bat against the sides of his cleats and rested the bat on his shoulders. (6) With hard eyes, he stared back at me.

(7) I kicked the front of my cleat into the bright white rubber on the pitching mound and took a deep breath. (8) "Shut everything else out," my dad had said. (9) Slowly, the noises disappeared. (10) I could no longer hear the shouts from the parents in the stands. (11) In my head, I silenced the cheers from both dugouts. (12) The umpire did not exist. (13) There were no players, no coaches, not even a catcher. (14) There was just me, the ball, and the glove. (15) I had shut everything else out.

(16) I took a deep breath and brought my hands together at my chest. (17) I looked over at first base, but there was no runner. (18) In one motion, my feet left the rubber and connected with the ground. (19) Dirt flew in the air as my arm rotated forward and released it in front of me. (20) I watched as the ball spun and landed in the glove with a hard crack. (21) The umpire shot up from his crouched position, pointed his finger to the right, and yelled, "Strike Three!"

(22) The noises came back. (23) The crowd cheered in the stands, and I could hear their stomping feet as they cheered. (24) My teammate clapped his hand to his glove and ran toward me. (25) My coach raised a fist into the air in celebration. (26) I was surrounded by my teammates, and they were patting me on the back. (27) My dad was sitting on a bleacher behind home plate. (28) He raised his thumb to me and smiled as I ran off the field with my teammates.

34. Which sentence should be added before sentence 1 to improve the introduction?

a. It was the last inning of the game, we were only one run ahead, and the bases were loaded with players from the other team.
b. The Sun was beating down and blinding me as I prepared to throw the next pitch of the game.
c. I will always remember the time I threw the final pitch of the championship game during my eighth baseball season.
d. All of the long afternoons practicing pitching in my backyard became worth it when I stood on the pitcher's mound that day.

35. Which sentence in the second paragraph repeats details and should be removed?

a. Sentence 8
b. Sentence 11
c. Sentence 13
d. Sentence 15

36. The word *it* in sentence 19 is unclear. Which phrase should be used to replace *it* to make the sentence clearer?

a. The batter
b. The dirt
c. The ball
d. The glove

37. Sentence 23 is repetitive. Rewrite sentence 23 below so that it is clear, complete, and not repetitive.

___

___

___

Editing

Kate is writing a narrative about a boy named Gibson. Read the following paragraphs from the body of Kate's essay and look for errors that she needs to correct. Once you have read the paragraphs, answer the questions that follow them.

Musically Inclined

(1) Gibson could not remember a time when he did not know how too play music. (2) His mother was a singer when she was younger, and his father played the lead guitar in a band. (3) Growing up, he learned to read music at the same time he learned to read words. (4) Music felt as natural to him as walking it was a big part of his life.

(5) There were many instruments in Gibson's house, and over the years, he had learned how to play most of them. (6) Started with a piano when he was very young, then he moved to the harmonica and drums when he was a bit older. (7) He had just begun learning how to play the violin as well. (8) But Gibson's favorite instrument of all were the one he had been playing the longest: his father's Gibson Les Paul guitar.

38. Which change would correct the mistake in sentence 1?

a. Add a comma after *time.*
b. Change *when* to *once.*
c. Change *did* to *does.*
d. Change *to* to *too.*

39. Which change would correct the mistake in sentence 4?

a. Change *him* to *he.*
b. Add a semicolon after *walking.*
c. Change *it* to *It.*
d. Change *of* to *in.*

40. Which change would correct the mistake in sentence 6?

a. Change *Started* to *He started.*
b. Change *with* to *for.*
c. Change *moved* to *moves.*
d. Add a comma after *drums.*

41. Which change would correct the mistake in sentence 8?

a. Change *Gibson's* to *Gibsons'.*
b. Change *were* to *was.*
c. Change *longest* to *longer.*
d. Change *Gibson Les Paul* to *Gibson Les paul.*

Gabriel is writing an essay about Paul Revere. Read the following paragraphs from the body of Gabriel's essay and look for errors that he needs to correct. Once you have read the paragraphs, answer the questions that follow them.

Paul Revere

(1) In the early 1760s, Paul Revere ran a busy metalworking shop. (2) People from all over Boston came to buy the silver and gold cups, medals, and cutlery he made. (3) However, everything changed in 1765 when many colonists ran low on money and stopped shopping at Paul's shop.

(4) Things got worse when the british passed the Stamp Act. (5) The Stamp Act was a tax that cost the colonists money, which goes to the British. (6) Colonists like Paul Revere hated the Stamp Act because they made things more expensive.

(7) Under the Stamp Act, colonists needed to pay a tax to England on everything that was printed, such as newspapers, magazines, and business contracts. (8) Actually, colonists were forced to purchase stamped paper made in London for printing. (9) The Stamp Act made it very expensive for Paul to run his business.

42. Which change would correct the mistake in sentence 4?

a. Change *got* to *get*.
b. Add a comma after *worse*.
c. Change *british* to *British*.
d. Change *passed* to *past*.

43. Which change would correct the mistake in sentence 5?

a. Change *was* to *were*.
b. Remove the comma after *money*.
c. Change *goes* to *went*.
d. Change *British* to *british*.

44. Select the correct pronoun to use in sentence 6.

Colonists like Paul Revere hated the Stamp Act because ______ made things more expensive.

they
he
it
them

45. Which change would correct the mistake in sentence 8?

a. Change *Actually* to *Additionally*.
b. Change *stamped* to *Stamped*.
c. Add a comma before and after *made in London*.
d. Change *for* to *to*.

Answer Key and Explanations for Test #2

Reading

1. D: TEKS Standard (7.7)(D)

The terrain surrounding the farm has hills and ravines, creating several places the shepherds must check while looking for the sheep. This causes them to search for a long time in many places without finding the sheep, which is a key event in the passages' plot. Therefore, choice D is correct. Choice A is incorrect because sheep are found in many countries, not just Scotland. The time period of the story is unclear, but no matter the time period, the lack of technology did not cause the shepherds' reliance on Sirrah. Sirrah was able to find the flock because he is a dog and has different instincts than humans. Technology would not have necessarily helped the shepherds find the flock, so choice B is incorrect. Choice C is incorrect because James was able to work with others to look for his missing flock. This shows that the farm is not isolated.

2. C: TEKS Standard (7.5)(H)

The shepherd was able to rely on Sirrah to care for the herd even when he was away. The fact that Sirrah did what the owner desired without direct supervision shows his unwavering commitment to the shepherd. Sirrah was loyal to his owner regardless of the situation, so choice C is correct. Choice A is incorrect. While the passage mentions that Sirrah cared for the flock while his owner ate dinner, caring for the flock was not just a habit of Sirrah's. It was a way he helped his owner. Choice B is incorrect because Sirrah was consistently loyal throughout the passage. Choice D is incorrect because, though Sirrah did not rest with his owner, the passage does not describe Sirrah's energy levels.

3. A: TEKS Standard (7.6)(C)

The shepherds band together and look for the missing flock throughout the night and into the morning. The author shows this by writing "morning came and still they sought," which means that they were still searching for the flock in the morning hours. This line also shows that the shepherds are going to great efforts to help James since it states that the shepherds looked in every place they could think to check. The shepherds' efforts show that they care for each other, including James, so choice A is correct. Choice B says that the shepherds could not explain or achieve what Sirrah had done. This does not show that the shepherds care for James, so choice B is incorrect. Choice C shows James's dedication to finding his own flock, not the dedication or care of others, so it is incorrect. Choice D shows that James is ready to quit the search. This does not show that the other shepherds care for James, so choice D is incorrect.

4. B: TEKS Standard (7.6)(D)

Choice B provides an accurate summary of the main events that took place in the passage. It presents the ideas in an order that makes sense and matches the order of events in the story. Choice A incorrectly states that James was not permitted to take breaks. In the passage, James was able to take breaks to eat and rest while Sirrah watched over the flock. Additionally, this summary does not include enough information about the night that the flock went missing. Choice C describes James having a change of heart toward Sirrah, but this is not shown in the passage. The passage also does not say that James likes to work alone, so choice C is incorrect. Choice D is incorrect because it includes unnecessary details. For example, the summary does not need to state that Sirrah lived and worked on a sheep farm or that he was regarded as the best sheepdog in Scotland.

5. D: TEKS Standard (7.9)(A)

The author's purpose for writing this passage was most likely to entertain readers with a story of a shepherd and his dog, so choice D is correct. Choice A is incorrect because this story is not told from James Hogg's point of view. It is also not only about the night that the flock went missing. Choice B is incorrect because, while the passage describes the support from the other shepherds, this is only a detail in the passage. Choice C is incorrect because the passage does not suggest that trained dogs can replace human farmers. Instead, it demonstrates that they can work together to support a farm.

6. B: TEKS Standard (7.9)(F)

Paragraphs 8 and 9 show that James Hogg and the other shepherds have looked everywhere for the flock. At this point, James says there is nothing more they can do other than return and tell the owner that the flock is gone. Put simply, he is giving up. Since the shepherds' efforts were not successful and James wants to quit the search, these paragraphs create a sense of hopelessness, so choice B is correct. Choice A is incorrect. Paragraphs 8 and 9 do not suggest that any of the characters are frustrated. While James says, "It's of no use," this statement could show disappointment or fear. It does not specifically show that he is frustrated. These lines do not create a spirit of teamwork, so choice C is also correct. Though the shepherds do work together, they do not succeed, and James is preparing to face the consequences of his failure. James and the other shepherds have given up hope that they will find the flock, so choice D is incorrect.

7. B: TEKS Standard (7.5)(C)

Paragraph 16 states "Long afterward James Hogg said, "I never felt so grateful to any creature below the sun as I did to Sirrah that morning." Hogg's gratitude for Sirrah's actions shows that Sirrah likely prevented a troublesome outcome for him, so choice B is correct. There is no indication that the owner would have replaced the lambs if they had not been found, so choice A is incorrect. Choice C is also incorrect. Since the shepherds who helped in the search did not work for the same farm owner, it is not likely that they would have been held responsible. The passage does not suggest that the lambs would have been kept by other farmers, so choice D is incorrect.

8. C: TEKS Standard (7.5)(G)

Sirrah's loyal behavior led him to herd the entire flock of lambs for his owner during an emergency. This feat was very difficult for the shepherds to do as a group, and it would have been even harder for them to do so individually. Failing to find the herd would likely have had negative impacts for Sirrah's owner, James. By explaining that Sirrah had done what no shepherd could do by gathering all the lambs, the author supports the key idea that loyal dogs are valuable companions. Therefore, choice C is correct. Choice A explains the setting in which the lambs were found but does not discuss the actions of the dog, so it is incorrect. Choice B is incorrect because it shows James Hogg's dedication to finding the herd, not Sirrah's. Similarly, choice D describes the responsibilities of the shepherd, not the dog.

9. C: TEKS Standard (7.8)(Diii)

The author of this passage uses a chronological structure to explain that the way readers consume stories has changed over time. Society has evolved from remembering and retelling stories verbally to writing and reading them in print, and now many people use electronic devices to access them.

This idea is best described in choice C. The passage does not suggest that society will eventually go back to using only printed media, making choice A incorrect. It also does not state that the invention of electronic readers was necessary for education to advance, making choice B incorrect. The printing press has had a much larger impact on society and history than the invention of electronic books, so choice D is incorrect.

10. TEKS Standard (7.8)(Di)

Part A: D: The author argues that digital technology will replace printed text, so choice D is correct. Choice A is incorrect because the author does not mention the ease of reading digital or printed text. The author only mentions that digital text can be more convenient than physical books and just as enjoyable to use. Choice B is incorrect because the essay is about the evolution of technology and texts. The invention of the printing press is only a detail mentioned in the essay. Similarly, the introduction of the internet is a detail mentioned in the essay, but it is not the main topic of the essay, so choice C is incorrect.

Part B: C: The sentence in choice C states that printed books will eventually no longer be used as a result of technological advancements, so choice C is correct. Choice A is incorrect because it only states that stories have stood the test of time. It does not show that the main argument of the essay is about the way that people read stories. Choice B is incorrect because it gives an example of printed materials being used despite new technology, which contradicts the main argument of the essay. Choice D is incorrect because it is only a supporting detail. It does not clearly show what the main argument of the essay is.

11. B: TEKS Standard (7.8)(Dii)

The main idea of the passage is that technology is continually changing the way people access information. The author suggests that the need for physical books may soon be eliminated and that readers should welcome this change. Referencing the invention of the iPad and Kindle demonstrates that technology can continually change the way people do the same activity, such as reading, so choice B is correct. The internet was referenced in the passage to give an example of how technology changes culture. The iPad and Kindle were invented long after the internet and digital text came into use, so choice A is incorrect. Choice C is incorrect because iPads and Kindles are used in modern times, so referencing them does not show how stories used to be shared. Choice D is incorrect. Because the author supports the use of electronic readers, he or she does not give the reader a reason to reflect on the time before these devices were used.

12. D: TEKS Standard (7.9)(B)

In the beginning of the essay, the author explains how stories were passed down through oral tradition. The author then states that this was changed by the printing press, which is becoming less important due to the invention of technologies like the internet, the iPad, and the Kindle. This makes choice D correct. Choice A is incorrect because the author only explains the advantages of using devices like an iPad. Choice B is incorrect because oral tradition was common before reading stories was common. Choice C is incorrect because the essay was written in a chronological structure. It does not simply list examples, and the examples of technology are supporting details, not the topic of the passage.

13. B: TEKS Standard (7.8)(Ei)

The author's primary claim is that paper copies of books are the best format for reading. This is supported by the author's explanation of the positive effects of reading physical books. The author also explains why other methods, like using electronic readers, are not as beneficial as reading physical books. Therefore, choice B is correct. Choice A is incorrect. The author mentions other formats of books but does not state that readers should read the format of their choice. The author wants to persuade readers to choose physical books. Choice C is also incorrect. The author mentioned the difficulties that come with using electronic readers in the third paragraph, but this is not the focus of the whole essay. Similarly, the author says that books in physical or digital formats can be shared with others, but sharing books is not the focus of the essay. This is only supporting information, so choice D is incorrect.

14. A: TEKS Standard (7.8)(Eii)

The author mentions scientific studies that support the argument that physical books are superior to other formats, so choice A is correct. Choice B is incorrect because the paragraph mentions and uses data that has been proven, not just beliefs. Choice C is incorrect because the passage is not focused on the benefits of reading. It focuses on the benefits of reading physical copies of books. Finally, the fourth paragraph does not include any counterarguments to the author's claim, so choice D is incorrect.

15. D: TEKS Standard (7.9)(Eiii)

This essay is meant to persuade readers to use physical copies of books when they read. It is most likely written for people who enjoy reading and do so regularly, so choice D is correct. Choice A is incorrect because the essay does not address using reading in classroom instruction. Choice B is also incorrect. The essay does not address how writing or illustrating books is different for books of different formats. This essay is not targeted at librarians, so choice C is incorrect. The essay does not include information about choosing, lending, or caring for books.

16. C: TEKS Standard (7.9)(G)

This sentence states the author's stance on physical books. It makes it clear that the author strongly believes that physical books are the best format for reading, so choice C is correct. Choice A is incorrect. This sentence does not help the reader determine the point of view of the essay, as it contains no pronouns. Choice B is incorrect because, while the sentence is a statement, it is not factual. It is the author's opinion. Choice D is incorrect. The statement is not meant to make readers curious since it lacks qualities that would make someone wonder about the topic.

17. B: TEKS Standard (7.5)(E)

The author of "The Inventions of Technology" seems more willing to use changing and advancing technology than the author of "The Power of Print," so choice B is correct. It is likely that both authors would agree that any type of reading is better than no reading at all since both seem to believe reading is a good thing, so choice A is incorrect. The author of "The Inventions of Technology" supports the use of electronic books and would be more likely to support increased funding for them, not physical books. The author of "The Power of Print" would be more likely to support funding for physical books. This makes choice C incorrect. The preferred genre or content each author likes to read is not addressed. While the author of "The Inventions of Technology" references a significant amount of historical information, this is not enough evidence for the reader to assume the author would prefer to read nonfiction articles. Therefore, choice D is incorrect.

18. C: TEKS Standard (7.5)(E)

Each essay focuses on its author's preferred format of books and why that format is superior, so choice C is correct. Only "The Power of Print" discusses the downsides of electronic readers, making choice A incorrect. Neither essay suggests that choosing a book format may be difficult. The authors of these essays only explain why their respective preference is best, so choice B is incorrect. The author of "The Inventions of Technology" mentions that changes in technology have impacted education. However, the author of "The Power of Print" does not, so choice D is incorrect.

19. A: TEKS Standard (7.5)(E)

Both essays focus on the best format for readers to use. This shows that, regardless of their different opinions on the format, both authors think reading as a pastime should continue, so choice A is correct. Choice B is incorrect because the author of "The Power of Print" would not agree with this statement. This author included reasons that electronic readers are inconvenient. The author of "The Inventions of Technology" would not agree with choice C. This author feels that reading on a device is just as satisfying as reading a physical book. This author would also disagree with choice D, as "The Inventions of Technology" suggests that reading should change as technology does.

20. B, E: TEKS Standard (7.6)(C)

Clara seems to be protected by some divine form of guidance that has kept her safe during many near misses and brushes with death. The sentence "And so, again and again, it seemed as if a special Providence protected her from death or injury" clearly states this. This idea is also demonstrated in the statement "Thank you, but I think I am the best-protected woman in the United States." Choice A explains how important Clara was to injured soldiers, but it does not describe Clara's own safety. Choice C explains that Clara appreciated the soldier's warning of the dangers she would face in Fredericksburg and that she later recalled the experience of receiving a request to go across the river. Choice D describes the feelings many males in Clara's position felt towards her, but it does not reveal any information about Clara's fate.

21. C: TEKS Standard (7.2)(A)

In paragraph 9, the author uses "charged" to describe the actions of the lines of soldiers advancing across the field toward the enemy. This most closely matches "to rush against," as it is used to refer to their movement. This meaning is shown by the use of the word *over* after *charged*. If something goes over something else, it has to move. Definition 3 is the only definition that involves movement. Definition 1 would be used to refer to money or payment owed in exchange for something. Definition 2 would be used if someone had committed a crime and was being formally blamed. Definition 4 would be used if an individual of higher authority were telling a lower-ranking individual what to do.

22. C: TEKS Standard (7.5)(G)

By describing Fredericksburg as a "slaughter-pen," stating that no "regiment will escape," and telling Clara that she will "go to certain death," the soldier is warning Clara that she will surely die if she attempts to go into the town. This supports the key idea that Clara Barton risked her own life by providing care for soldiers in dangerous locations, so choice C is correct. The soldier does not imply that he or other soldiers will harm Clara. In fact, he expresses his gratitude for her care and tries to warn her to protect her, so choice A is incorrect. Choice B is incorrect because the rest of the passage suggests that Clara Barton knows that each place she visits will be dangerous and horrific. She does not need the soldiers to tell her what she will see and encounter. Choice D is incorrect because this is not a key idea of the passage. Additionally, this paragraph does not suggest that Clara did not help the soldier. In fact, he states that she has been kind to him, which suggests that she helped him in some way.

23. B: TEKS Standard (7.7)(B)

Clara and the officer interacted shortly before he died and was brought to her. This demonstrated how common death was in this situation and how close Clara had been to danger, making choice B the correct answer. There is not enough information to support the idea that Clara would have died crossing the bridge without assistance. The officer only helped her to step over debris. This makes choices A and C incorrect. Additionally, the officer does not show resourcefulness in this paragraph, and there is not enough information to see that his rank influenced where he was at that time. Choice D is also incorrect. The death of the officer made Clara feel lucky, but it did not deter her from working on the battlefields. It made her feel safer doing so, as she thought it meant that she was protected from harm in some divine way.

24. B: TEKS Standard (7.2)(C)

In paragraph 2, a bullet narrowly misses Clara Barton but kills a soldier. This is followed by the statement "and so, again and again, it seemed as if a special Providence protected her from death or injury." Using both the information provided in the question and context clues in the passage, it can be determined that it seems as if Clara is being protected by some heavenly source that knows what is going to happen. As such, the best meaning for Providence is "divine protection from an all-knowing source." Therefore, choice B is correct. There is no suggestion that Clara's protection is fragile or unreliable since she is continually kept safe. This makes choices A and D incorrect. Because this protection comes from something that can "see ahead," it is not from colleagues, or the people that work with her. This makes choice C incorrect.

25. A: TEKS Standard (7.9)(E)

The passage highlights Clara's dedication to aiding the wounded during the Civil War. It makes it clear that doing so is dangerous and shows that Clara decided to continue her work anyway. This makes choice A correct. Clara's opinion of the war is not made clear in the passage, so choice B is incorrect. Choice C is incorrect because the passage does not discuss patients who were too hurt to be saved. Choice D is incorrect since the reason Clara was motivated to help is not discussed in the passage.

26. B: TEKS Standard (7.9)(F)

The author uses statements like "exploding shell hissed through between us," " a solid shot thundered over our heads," and "a noble steed bounded in the air and with his gallant rider rolled in the dirt not thirty feet in the rear" to show the danger Clara is facing. Though the author does not directly state that Clara is in danger, she creates a sense of tension for the reader. The tension continues to build until it is revealed that the officer who helped her in this paragraph has died. Therefore, choice B is correct. Choice A is incorrect because no character's feelings toward another are described, and there is no sense of resentment. Paragraph 10 does not suggest that Clara is happy or pleased with what is occurring, so choice C is incorrect. While Clara is clearly passionate about helping injured soldiers, the language in this paragraph is not used to demonstrate this, making choice D incorrect.

27. B: TEKS Standard (7.5)(F)

This sentence shows that the men had a change of heart toward Clara and that the likelihood that she would be harmed or killed deeply upset and scared them. The men understood that "the nature of the summons" was that Clara was being asked to go to a dangerous place, so choice A is correct. The men clearly cared for Clara because they were eager to take her place on a dangerous assignment to keep her safe. They were not glad to see her leave, so choice B is incorrect. Choice C is incorrect because the war had already begun and the men were willing to face danger to protect Clara. Choice D is incorrect because the men were not being asked to move to the hospital, Clara was. They were willing to go to the other hospital with Clara.

28. C: TEKS Standard (7.9)(A)

A key idea of this passage is that Clara Barton risked her life to help soldiers during the American Civil War. This is a sacrifice that she made, and it is clearly shown by the passage, so choice C is correct. Choice A is incorrect because the passage does not describe what life on the battlefield looked like. It only shows a few events and tells what Clara Barton saw and faced. This is not a picture of what life was like for soldiers or others in battle. Choice B is incorrect because this passage describes the conditions that one nurse faced during a war. It does not show what medical practices were like during the Civil War. Choice D is incorrect because it does not include many details about how Clara Barton tended to victims. It focuses on the danger that she put herself in and the fact that she was able to survive this danger.

Extended Response

29. TEKS Standard (7.6)(B)

Please use the rubric below to make sure your response meets these criteria. Try to have a friend or family member grade your response for you or take a break after writing your response and return to grade it yourself with fresh eyes.

Below is an excerpt of the STAAR Grades 6-EII Informational Writing Rubric.

Score Point	Organization and Development of Ideas
3	• **Controlling idea/Thesis is clear and fully developed** The controlling idea/thesis is clearly identifiable. The focus is consistent throughout, creating a response that is unified and easy to follow. • **Organization is effective** A purposeful structure that includes an effective introduction and conclusion is evident. The organizational structure is appropriate and effectively supports the development of the controlling idea/thesis. The sentences, paragraphs, or ideas are logically connected in purposeful and highly effective ways. • **Evidence is specific, well chosen, and relevant** The response includes relevant text-based evidence that is clearly explained and consistently supports and develops the controlling idea/thesis. For pairs in grades 6 through EII, evidence is drawn from both texts. The response reflects a thorough understanding of the writing purpose. • **Expression of ideas is clear and effective** The writer's word choice is specific, purposeful, and enhances the response. Almost all sentences and phrases are effectively crafted to convey the writer's ideas and contribute to the overall quality of the response and the clarity of the message.
Score Point	**Conventions**
2	Student writing demonstrates **consistent command** of grade-level-appropriate conventions, including correct: • sentence construction • punctuation • capitalization • grammar • spelling The response has few errors, but those errors do not impact the clarity of the writing.

Revising

30. B: TEKS Standard (7.10)(Bii)

Sentence 3 gives a detail that is not related to the main idea of the paper. This detail is distracting and does not help the reader understand the rest of the information in the paragraph, so choice B is correct. Choice A is incorrect because sentence 1 tells the reader the setting of the story, which is important information. Choice C is incorrect because sentence 4 gives a detail that helps the reader imagine the setting and situation. This helps the reader understand the story better. Choice D is incorrect because sentence 5 gives the reader more information about the characters, why they are at the dog show, and what might happen later in the story.

31. TEKS Standard (7.10)(C)

Sentence 9 is currently difficult to read and contains too many words. A better way to write sentence 9 is: "The dogs that were waiting to be shown were getting ready with their trainers in different areas of the park." The revised sentence should be clear, easy to read, complete, and grammatically correct. It should also not repeat any information, and it must include the same information as the original sentence.

32. D: TEKS Standard (7.10)(Bi)

The third paragraph describes the parts of the dog show. In sentence 18, the author tells the reader that the dogs were expected to listen to their trainers and complete the course well. A concluding sentence should be connected to the ideas in sentence 18, let the reader know that the paragraph is ending, and prepare the reader for the next paragraph. Choice D achieves these goals. It shares the author's thoughts about what she observed in sentence 18. It also closes the paragraph by making a statement about all of the dogs and prepares the reader for the next paragraph, which tells the results of the dogs' performance. Choice A is incorrect because it does not support the flow of ideas in the passage. Choice B is incorrect because it introduces a new idea that does not help connect the ideas that are already present. Choice C is incorrect because it also introduces a new idea and does not signal to the reader that the paragraph is ending.

33. B: TEKS Standard (7.10)(Bi)

Time has passed between the event in sentence 21 and the event in sentence 22. An appropriate transition word would show that time has passed. *Later* shows that there is time between two events, so choice B is correct. Choice A is incorrect because *however* shows contrast. Sentence 22 is not contrasting sentence 21. Choice C is incorrect because *otherwise* is used to introduce an alternate result, which is not the purpose of sentence 22. Choice D is incorrect because *consequentially* is used to show that one thing caused another. Mary's success and her award did not cause Martha and her mother to leave the dog show.

34. A: TEKS Standard (7.10)(Bi)

Choice A lets readers know why this pitch is so important earlier in the story. This sentence gives the reader a better explanation of the situation that the author is facing, so choice A is correct. Choice B is incorrect because it does not match the rest of the story. The Sun does not bother the pitcher again during the story, so this sentence is misleading. Choice C is incorrect because it does not give readers any information that helps them understand the story better. It also does not grab the reader's attention because it gives away the ending at the beginning of the story. Choice D is incorrect because it adds details that are irrelevant and do not support the reader's understanding of the story.

35. D: TEKS Standard (7.10)(Bii)

Sentence 15 is not needed, so it can be removed. Sentence 8 tells the reader that the pitcher is trying to shut all of the distractions out, and sentences 9 through 14 show that he has successfully done so. Sentence 15 unnecessarily confirms that the pitcher shut the distractions out, so choice D is correct. Choice A is incorrect because sentence 8 is needed to tell the reader that the pitcher is remembering and following his dad's advice. This detail is important because it helps the reader understand the characters' actions. Choice B is incorrect because sentences 11 and 13 are details that help the reader understand how many distractions the pitcher is trying to ignore and show the reader how well the pitcher is able to focus on his pitching.

36. C: TEKS Standard (7.10)(C)

Before sentence 18, the pitcher was preparing to throw a baseball, and sentence 19 describes what happened when he threw it. This means that "the ball" is the best replacement for *it* in sentence 19. Therefore, choice C is correct. Choice A is incorrect because the batter is several feet away from the pitcher. Choice B is incorrect because the dirt is coming from the pitcher's foot hitting the ground. He was not holding dirt and his hand did not hit the dirt, so it does not make sense that dirt would be released from his throwing motion. Choice D is incorrect because the glove is on the pitcher's hand. The glove is not supposed to come off of his hand when he throws the ball. Since the previous sentence shows the pitcher preparing to throw a ball, the reader can conclude that the pitcher's glove is not the object that is released as a result of his throw.

37. TEKS Standard (7.10)(C)

Sentence 23 tells the reader twice that the crowd cheered. One example of a correct revision of this sentence is "The crowd cheered in the stands, and I could hear their stomping feet." A correct revision of this sentence should be complete and contain no grammatical or spelling errors. It should also include the facts that the crowd was cheering, the crowd was in the stands, and the narrator could hear their feet stomping.

Editing

38. D: TEKS Standard (7.10)(Dix)

The word *too* means the same thing as *also*. This meaning does not make sense in sentence 1. The word *to* would show that playing music is the thing that Gibson knows how to do, so it should be used instead, and choice D is correct. Choice A is incorrect because a comma is only needed to separate clauses in a complex sentence when the dependent clause comes first. The subordinating conjunction *when* comes after the independent clause, which shows that the dependent clause comes second. Changing *when* to *once* would change the meaning of the sentence. This change would cause the sentence to say that at the point Gibson did not know how to play music, he could not remember a time. This does not make sense, so choice B is incorrect. Choice C is incorrect because *did* is a past tense verb and *does* is a present tense verb. Sentence 1 is in the past tense, so *did* is the correct verb to use.

39. B: TEKS Standard (7.10)(Dviii)

Sentence 4 contains two independent clauses: "Music felt as natural to him as walking" and "it was a big part of his life." When joining two independent clauses to create a compound sentence, the clauses must be linked by a coordinating conjunction with a comma or by a semicolon. Since there is no coordinating conjunction in sentence 4, a semicolon is needed after *walking*. This makes choice B correct. *Him* is an objective pronoun, and *he* is a subjective pronoun. The subject of the sentence is *music*, so the pronoun that is used in place for *Gibson* must be an objective pronoun. *Him* is the right choice, so choice A is incorrect. Choice C is incorrect because, even though "it was a big part of his life" could be a complete sentence, *it* is not the first word in a sentence. This means that it should not be capitalized. Choice D is incorrect because changing *of* to *in* in sentence 4 would change the meaning of the sentence and make it inaccurate.

40. A: TEKS Standard (7.10)(Di)

Sentence 6 is an incomplete sentence. The first clause in the sentence does not have a subject. Adding the word *he* before *started* would correct this error, so choice A is correct. Choice B is incorrect because changing *with* to *for* would change the meaning of the sentence. Writing that he started with a piano means that a piano was the first instrument he learned to play. Writing that he started for a piano means that a piano was the reason he learned to play, which is not the correct meaning. Choice C is incorrect because this sentence is in the past tense, and *moves* is a present tense verb. *Moved* is a past tense verb, so it is the right choice for this sentence. Choice D is incorrect because a comma is not needed before a dependent clause when it is the last clause in the sentence.

41. B: TEKS Standard (7.10)(Div)

Were is a plural verb, so it must be used with a plural noun. Similarly, *was* is a singular verb that must be used with a singular noun. The verb in sentence 8 is describing the action of Gibson's favorite instrument, which is a singular noun. This means that *were* should be changed to *was*, and choice B is correct. Choice A is incorrect because an apostrophe is placed after an *s* to show that something belongs to two owners. Gibson is only one owner, so *Gibson's* is written correctly. Choice C is incorrect because *longest* is a superlative adjective, but *longer* is a comparative adjective. Superlative adjectives are used when comparing more than two things, and comparative adjectives are used when comparing two things. In sentence 8, the instruments Gibson knows how to play are being compared. Since Gibson knows how to play more than two instruments, *longest* is correct. Choice D is incorrect because *Gibson Les Paul* is a proper noun that does not contain any articles or prepositions, so all of the words in it should be capitalized.

42. C: TEKS Standard (7.10)(Dvii)

Nationalities should always be capitalized. The word *British* is used to show that someone is from Britain, so it is a nationality. This means that choice C is correct. Choice A is incorrect because *get*, by itself, is a present tense verb, but sentence 4 is in the past tense. *Got* is a past tense verb, so it is used correctly in sentence 4. Choice B is incorrect because, although sentence 4 is a complex sentence, the independent clause comes before the dependent clause. When the dependent clause appears at the end of a sentence, a comma is not usually used before it. Choice D is incorrect because *past* refers to things that have already happened. *Passed* can be used to say that a law or act was approved and put into effect, which is the meaning that is intended in sentence 4.

43. C: TEKS Standard (7.10)(Dii)

Sentence 5 is in the past tense, but *goes* is not a past tense verb. However, *went* is a past tense verb. *Goes* should be changed to *went* in sentence 5, so choice C is correct. Choice A is incorrect because *was* is a singular verb, but *were* is a plural verb. In sentence 5, the action of the Stamp Act is being described. Since the Stamp Act is a singular noun, it should be used with a singular verb, like *was*. Choice B is incorrect because "which goes to the British" is a nonessential clause. Commas are used to separate nonessential clauses from the rest of a sentence because they are not needed for the sentence to make sense. Choice D is incorrect because nationalities are always capitalized, and *British* is a nationality.

44. it: TEKS Standard (7.10)(Dv)

The Stamp Act is a singular noun, and it is not a living thing. When used to represent nonliving things, *they* and *them* are plural pronouns, so neither can be used in place of the Stamp Act. *He* is a singular pronoun, but it cannot be used in place of the name of a document. Since the Stamp Act is a document, *he* is incorrect. *It* is the correct pronoun because it can be used in place of the name of a singular, nonliving noun.

45. A: TEKS Standard (7.10)(Diii)

The word *actually* is not a good transition word to use at the beginning of sentence 8. *Actually* is used to show a contrast or contradiction, but that is not the purpose of sentence 8. *Additionally* is used to show that more information is being given or that something is being emphasized, which is the purpose of sentence 8. This means that choice A is correct. Choice B is incorrect because *stamped paper* is not a proper noun, so neither of these words should be capitalized. Choice C is incorrect because "made in London" is information that is needed in order for the sentence to give the reader the correct information. Since the phrase is necessary, it should not be separated from the rest of the sentence by commas. Choice D is incorrect because changing *for* to *to* would make sentence 8 unclear.

Practice Test #3

To take this additional STAAR practice test, visit our online resources page:
mometrix.com/resources719/staarg7rla

How to Overcome Test Anxiety

Just the thought of taking a test is enough to make most people a little nervous. A test is an important event that can have a long-term impact on your future, so it's important to take it seriously and it's natural to feel anxious about performing well. But just because anxiety is normal, that doesn't mean that it's helpful in test taking, or that you should simply accept it as part of your life. Anxiety can have a variety of effects. These effects can be mild, like making you feel slightly nervous, or severe, like blocking your ability to focus or remember even a simple detail.

If you experience test anxiety—whether severe or mild—it's important to know how to beat it. To discover this, first you need to understand what causes test anxiety.

Causes of Test Anxiety

While we often think of anxiety as an uncontrollable emotional state, it can actually be caused by simple, practical things. One of the most common causes of test anxiety is that a person does not feel adequately prepared for their test. This feeling can be the result of many different issues such as poor study habits or lack of organization, but the most common culprit is time management. Starting to study too late, failing to organize your study time to cover all of the material, or being distracted while you study will mean that you're not well prepared for the test. This may lead to cramming the night before, which will cause you to be physically and mentally exhausted for the test. Poor time management also contributes to feelings of stress, fear, and hopelessness as you realize you are not well prepared but don't know what to do about it.

Other times, test anxiety is not related to your preparation for the test but comes from unresolved fear. This may be a past failure on a test, or poor performance on tests in general. It may come from comparing yourself to others who seem to be performing better or from the stress of living up to expectations. Anxiety may be driven by fears of the future—how failure on this test would affect your educational and career goals. These fears are often completely irrational, but they can still negatively impact your test performance.

Elements of Test Anxiety

As mentioned earlier, test anxiety is considered to be an emotional state, but it has physical and mental components as well. Sometimes you may not even realize that you are suffering from test anxiety until you notice the physical symptoms. These can include trembling hands, rapid heartbeat, sweating, nausea, and tense muscles. Extreme anxiety may lead to fainting or vomiting. Obviously, any of these symptoms can have a negative impact on testing. It is important to recognize them as soon as they begin to occur so that you can address the problem before it damages your performance.

The mental components of test anxiety include trouble focusing and inability to remember learned information. During a test, your mind is on high alert, which can help you recall information and stay focused for an extended period of time. However, anxiety interferes with your mind's natural processes, causing you to blank out, even on the questions you know well. The strain of testing during anxiety makes it difficult to stay focused, especially on a test that may take several hours. Extreme anxiety can take a huge mental toll, making it difficult not only to recall test information but even to understand the test questions or pull your thoughts together.

Effects of Test Anxiety

Test anxiety is like a disease—if left untreated, it will get progressively worse. Anxiety leads to poor performance, and this reinforces the feelings of fear and failure, which in turn lead to poor performances on subsequent tests. It can grow from a mild nervousness to a crippling condition. If allowed to progress, test anxiety can have a big impact on your schooling, and consequently on your future.

Test anxiety can spread to other parts of your life. Anxiety on tests can become anxiety in any stressful situation, and blanking on a test can turn into panicking in a job situation. But fortunately, you don't have to let anxiety rule your testing and determine your grades. There are a number of relatively simple steps you can take to move past anxiety and function normally on a test and in the rest of life.

Physical Steps for Beating Test Anxiety

While test anxiety is a serious problem, the good news is that it can be overcome. It doesn't have to control your ability to think and remember information. While it may take time, you can begin taking steps today to beat anxiety.

Just as your first hint that you may be struggling with anxiety comes from the physical symptoms, the first step to treating it is also physical. Rest is crucial for having a clear, strong mind. If you are tired, it is much easier to give in to anxiety. But if you establish good sleep habits, your body and mind will be ready to perform optimally, without the strain of exhaustion. Additionally, sleeping well helps you to retain information better, so you're more likely to recall the answers when you see the test questions.

Getting good sleep means more than going to bed on time. It's important to allow your brain time to relax. Take study breaks from time to time so it doesn't get overworked, and don't study right before bed. Take time to rest your mind before trying to rest your body, or you may find it difficult to fall asleep.

Along with sleep, other aspects of physical health are important in preparing for a test. Good nutrition is vital for good brain function. Sugary foods and drinks may give a burst of energy but this burst is followed by a crash, both physically and emotionally. Instead, fuel your body with protein and vitamin-rich foods.

Also, drink plenty of water. Dehydration can lead to headaches and exhaustion, especially if your brain is already under stress from the rigors of the test. Particularly if your test is a long one, drink water during the breaks. And if possible, take an energy-boosting snack to eat between sections.

Along with sleep and diet, a third important part of physical health is exercise. Maintaining a steady workout schedule is helpful, but even taking 5-minute study breaks to walk can help get your blood pumping faster and clear your head. Exercise also releases endorphins, which contribute to a positive feeling and can help combat test anxiety.

When you nurture your physical health, you are also contributing to your mental health. If your body is healthy, your mind is much more likely to be healthy as well. So take time to rest, nourish your body with healthy food and water, and get moving as much as possible. Taking these physical steps will make you stronger and more able to take the mental steps necessary to overcome test anxiety.

Mental Steps for Beating Test Anxiety

Working on the mental side of test anxiety can be more challenging, but as with the physical side, there are clear steps you can take to overcome it. As mentioned earlier, test anxiety often stems from lack of preparation, so the obvious solution is to prepare for the test. Effective studying may be the most important weapon you have for beating test anxiety, but you can and should employ several other mental tools to combat fear.

First, boost your confidence by reminding yourself of past success—tests or projects that you aced. If you're putting as much effort into preparing for this test as you did for those, there's no reason you should expect to fail here. Work hard to prepare; then trust your preparation.

Second, surround yourself with encouraging people. It can be helpful to find a study group, but be sure that the people you're around will encourage a positive attitude. If you spend time with others who are anxious or cynical, this will only contribute to your own anxiety. Look for others who are motivated to study hard from a desire to succeed, not from a fear of failure.

Third, reward yourself. A test is physically and mentally tiring, even without anxiety, and it can be helpful to have something to look forward to. Plan an activity following the test, regardless of the outcome, such as going to a movie or getting ice cream.

When you are taking the test, if you find yourself beginning to feel anxious, remind yourself that you know the material. Visualize successfully completing the test. Then take a few deep, relaxing breaths and return to it. Work through the questions carefully but with confidence, knowing that you are capable of succeeding.

Developing a healthy mental approach to test taking will also aid in other areas of life. Test anxiety affects more than just the actual test—it can be damaging to your mental health and even contribute to depression. It's important to beat test anxiety before it becomes a problem for more than testing.

Study Strategy

Being prepared for the test is necessary to combat anxiety, but what does being prepared look like? You may study for hours on end and still not feel prepared. What you need is a strategy for test prep. The next few pages outline our recommended steps to help you plan out and conquer the challenge of preparation.

Step 1: Scope Out the Test

Learn everything you can about the format (multiple choice, essay, etc.) and what will be on the test. Gather any study materials, course outlines, or sample exams that may be available. Not only will this help you to prepare, but knowing what to expect can help to alleviate test anxiety.

Step 2: Map Out the Material

Look through the textbook or study guide and make note of how many chapters or sections it has. Then divide these over the time you have. For example, if a book has 15 chapters and you have five days to study, you need to cover three chapters each day. Even better, if you have the time, leave an extra day at the end for overall review after you have gone through the material in depth.

If time is limited, you may need to prioritize the material. Look through it and make note of which sections you think you already have a good grasp on, and which need review. While you are studying, skim quickly through the familiar sections and take more time on the challenging parts.

Write out your plan so you don't get lost as you go. Having a written plan also helps you feel more in control of the study, so anxiety is less likely to arise from feeling overwhelmed at the amount to cover.

Step 3: Gather Your Tools

Decide what study method works best for you. Do you prefer to highlight in the book as you study and then go back over the highlighted portions? Or do you type out notes of the important information? Or is it helpful to make flashcards that you can carry with you? Assemble the pens, index cards, highlighters, post-it notes, and any other materials you may need so you won't be distracted by getting up to find things while you study.

If you're having a hard time retaining the information or organizing your notes, experiment with different methods. For example, try color-coding by subject with colored pens, highlighters, or post-it notes. If you learn better by hearing, try recording yourself reading your notes so you can listen while in the car, working out, or simply sitting at your desk. Ask a friend to quiz you from your flashcards, or try teaching someone the material to solidify it in your mind.

Step 4: Create Your Environment

It's important to avoid distractions while you study. This includes both the obvious distractions like visitors and the subtle distractions like an uncomfortable chair (or a too-comfortable couch that makes you want to fall asleep). Set up the best study environment possible: good lighting and a comfortable work area. If background music helps you focus, you may want to turn it on, but otherwise keep the room quiet. If you are using a computer to take notes, be sure you don't have any other windows open, especially applications like social media, games, or anything else that could distract you. Silence your phone and turn off notifications. Be sure to keep water close by so you stay hydrated while you study (but avoid unhealthy drinks and snacks).

Also, take into account the best time of day to study. Are you freshest first thing in the morning? Try to set aside some time then to work through the material. Is your mind clearer in the afternoon or evening? Schedule your study session then. Another method is to study at the same time of day that you will take the test, so that your brain gets used to working on the material at that time and will be ready to focus at test time.

Step 5: Study!

Once you have done all the study preparation, it's time to settle into the actual studying. Sit down, take a few moments to settle your mind so you can focus, and begin to follow your study plan. Don't give in to distractions or let yourself procrastinate. This is your time to prepare so you'll be ready to fearlessly approach the test. Make the most of the time and stay focused.

Of course, you don't want to burn out. If you study too long you may find that you're not retaining the information very well. Take regular study breaks. For example, taking five minutes out of every hour to walk briskly, breathing deeply and swinging your arms, can help your mind stay fresh.

As you get to the end of each chapter or section, it's a good idea to do a quick review. Remind yourself of what you learned and work on any difficult parts. When you feel that you've mastered the material, move on to the next part. At the end of your study session, briefly skim through your notes again.

But while review is helpful, cramming last minute is NOT. If at all possible, work ahead so that you won't need to fit all your study into the last day. Cramming overloads your brain with more information than it can process and retain, and your tired mind may struggle to recall even previously learned information when it is overwhelmed with last-minute study. Also, the urgent nature of cramming and the stress placed on your brain contribute to anxiety. You'll be more likely to go to the test feeling unprepared and having trouble thinking clearly.

So don't cram, and don't stay up late before the test, even just to review your notes at a leisurely pace. Your brain needs rest more than it needs to go over the information again. In fact, plan to finish your studies by noon or early afternoon the day before the test. Give your brain the rest of the day to relax or focus on other things, and get a good night's sleep. Then you will be fresh for the test and better able to recall what you've studied.

Step 6: Take a Practice Test

Many courses offer sample tests, either online or in the study materials. This is an excellent resource to check whether you have mastered the material, as well as to prepare for the test format and environment.

Check the test format ahead of time: the number of questions, the type (multiple choice, free response, etc.), and the time limit. Then create a plan for working through them. For example, if you have 30 minutes to take a 60-question test, your limit is 30 seconds per question. Spend less time on the questions you know well so that you can take more time on the difficult ones.

If you have time to take several practice tests, take the first one open book, with no time limit. Work through the questions at your own pace and make sure you fully understand them. Gradually work up to taking a test under test conditions: sit at a desk with all study materials put away and set a timer. Pace yourself to make sure you finish the test with time to spare and go back to check your answers if you have time.

After each test, check your answers. On the questions you missed, be sure you understand why you missed them. Did you misread the question (tests can use tricky wording)? Did you forget the information? Or was it something you hadn't learned? Go back and study any shaky areas that the practice tests reveal.

Taking these tests not only helps with your grade, but also aids in combating test anxiety. If you're already used to the test conditions, you're less likely to worry about it, and working through tests until you're scoring well gives you a confidence boost. Go through the practice tests until you feel comfortable, and then you can go into the test knowing that you're ready for it.

Test Tips

On test day, you should be confident, knowing that you've prepared well and are ready to answer the questions. But aside from preparation, there are several test day strategies you can employ to maximize your performance.

First, as stated before, get a good night's sleep the night before the test (and for several nights before that, if possible). Go into the test with a fresh, alert mind rather than staying up late to study.

Try not to change too much about your normal routine on the day of the test. It's important to eat a nutritious breakfast, but if you normally don't eat breakfast at all, consider eating just a protein bar. If you're a coffee drinker, go ahead and have your normal coffee. Just make sure you time it so that the caffeine doesn't wear off right in the middle of your test. Avoid sugary beverages, and drink enough water to stay hydrated but not so much that you need a restroom break 10 minutes into the test. If your test isn't first thing in the morning, consider going for a walk or doing a light workout before the test to get your blood flowing.

Allow yourself enough time to get ready, and leave for the test with plenty of time to spare so you won't have the anxiety of scrambling to arrive in time. Another reason to be early is to select a good seat. It's helpful to sit away from doors and windows, which can be distracting. Find a good seat, get out your supplies, and settle your mind before the test begins.

When the test begins, start by going over the instructions carefully, even if you already know what to expect. Make sure you avoid any careless mistakes by following the directions.

Then begin working through the questions, pacing yourself as you've practiced. If you're not sure on an answer, don't spend too much time on it, and don't let it shake your confidence. Either skip it and come back later, or eliminate as many wrong answers as possible and guess among the remaining ones. Don't dwell on these questions as you continue—put them out of your mind and focus on what lies ahead.

Be sure to read all of the answer choices, even if you're sure the first one is the right answer. Sometimes you'll find a better one if you keep reading. But don't second-guess yourself if you do immediately know the answer. Your gut instinct is usually right. Don't let test anxiety rob you of the information you know.

If you have time at the end of the test (and if the test format allows), go back and review your answers. Be cautious about changing any, since your first instinct tends to be correct, but make sure you didn't misread any of the questions or accidentally mark the wrong answer choice. Look over any you skipped and make an educated guess.

At the end, leave the test feeling confident. You've done your best, so don't waste time worrying about your performance or wishing you could change anything. Instead, celebrate the successful completion of this test. And finally, use this test to learn how to deal with anxiety even better next time.

Review Video: Test Anxiety
Visit mometrix.com/academy and enter code: 100340

Important Qualification

Not all anxiety is created equal. If your test anxiety is causing major issues in your life beyond the classroom or testing center, or if you are experiencing troubling physical symptoms related to your anxiety, it may be a sign of a serious physiological or psychological condition. If this sounds like your situation, we strongly encourage you to seek professional help.

Online Resources

Due to our efforts to try to keep this book to a manageable length, we've created a link that will give you access to all of your online resources:

mometrix.com/resources719/staarg7rla

It's Your Moment, Let's Celebrate It!

Share your story @mometrixtestpreparation